Robert Laird Stewart

TheLand of Israel

A Text Book on the Physical and Historical Geography of the Holy Land Embodying

the Results of Recent Research

Robert Laird Stewart

TheLand of Israel
A Text Book on the Physical and Historical Geography of the Holy Land Embodying the Results of Recent Research

ISBN/EAN: 9783337090944

Printed in Europe, USA, Canada, Australia, Japan

Cover: Foto ©Lupo / pixelio.de

More available books at **www.hansebooks.com**

A Text Book on the Physical
and Historical Geography of
the Holy Land embodying the
Results of Recent Research

BY

Robert Laird Stewart, D. D.

Professor of Pastoral Theology and Biblical Archæology in the Theological Seminary of Lincoln University, Pa.

WITH SEVENTEEN MAPS AND NUMEROUS ILLUSTRATIONS

NEW YORK   CHICAGO   TORONTO

Fleming H. Revell Company
Publishers of Evangelical Literature

Copyright, 1899
by
FLEMING H. REVELL COMPANY

TO
THE REV. F. H. ROBARTS AND WIFE
OF
GLASGOW, SCOTLAND
ERST-WHILE COMPANIONS AND FELLOW-TRAVELLERS
IN THE
LANDS OF THE EAST

List of Illustrations

1.	Ascent of Pass of Nahr el Kelb, From North, with one of the Tablets	*Facing page*	44
2.	Capture of Lachish by Sennacherib	" "	95
3.	Tell es Safi (Gath?)	*Page*	102
4.	*Tell Zakariya	*Facing page*	103
5.	General view of Nazareth	" "	116
6.	Nablus and Vale of Shechem	" "	146
7.	Curb of Jacob's Well	*Page*	149
8.	Ruined Crypt, and section of Jacob's Well	"	151
9.	*Wady Suweinet	*Facing page*	161
10.	General view of Jerusalem (Church of St. Anne in foreground)	" "	174
11.	Damascus Gate	" "	176
12.	The southeast angle of Haram Wall	" "	189
13.	Robinson's Arch	" "	192
14.	The probable site of Calvary	" "	200
15.	Bethany	" "	203
16.	The Bridge over the Kedron	" "	205
17.	The Wilderness of Judea	" "	225
18.	Bethlehem of Judah	" "	228
19.	*Abraham's Well, Beersheba	*Page*	239
20.	Kadesh Barnea	"	244
21.	*The new Jordan Bridge at mouth of Wady Shaib	*Facing page*	283

*Reproduced, by permission, from the publications of the Palestine Exploration Fund.

List of Maps

Canaan—Tribal Boundaries in Colors . . . . *Frontispiece*
Palestine in the time of Christ and the Apostles . . . . *Facing page* 41

SECTIONAL MAPS

1. The Maritime Plain north of Mt. Carmel . . . . *Facing page* 65
2. The Maritime Plain south of Mt. Carmel . . . . " " 79
3. The Shephelah . . . . " " 97
4. The Mountains of Galilee . . . . " " 106
5. The Plain of Esdraelon . . . . " " 120
6. The Mountains of Ephraim . . . . " " 134
7. The Mountains of Benjamin . . . . " " 158
    Plan of Ancient Jerusalem . . . . " " 170
    Plan of Modern Jerusalem . . . . " " 173
8. The Mountains of Judah . . . . " " 224
9. The Negeb or South Country . . . . " " 237
10. The Valley of the Jordan . . . . " " 254
11. The Sea of Galilee . . . . *Page* 263
12. The Land of Bashan . . . . *Facing page* 303
13. Gilead and Moab . . . . " " 317

Preface

IN the light of recent research the Geography of the Holy Land has become a study of absorbing interest. It has furnished a clue to the explanation of many historical difficulties; filled old words with new meanings; revealed correspondence with the Bible hitherto unseen; corroborated minute circumstances of position, time and distance, incidentally given by the sacred writers; and, in a word, has restored the *real historic setting* of a series of *real historic narratives*.

The work of exploration on a strictly scientific basis, commenced by Dr. Robinson some sixty years ago, has been carried on to the present time by a worthy corps of successors, who amid many discomforts and perils have given years of patient study and investigation to the identification of places, the translation of ancient records, the excavation of buried cities and the survey of the land as a whole. To these devoted men—the pioneers of Palestine Geography—and to the Societies which supported them in their work, the Christian world is deeply indebted. While this task has been necessarily limited to a small number of specialists, it is given to a larger number to glean after them in the same field of labor, and utilize the results. Herein is the saying true, "Other men have labored, and we are entered into their labors."

A desideratum, in view of the growing importance of this study, is a Text-Book or Manual, abreast of the latest explorations, in which the student may find a summary of the characteristic features and historical associations of every place of importance mentioned in the Scripture whose site has been definitely located.

The present volume, while doubtless imperfect in many respects, is a contribution toward this end. It is the development of the outlines of a course of instruction which has been tested during a period of eight years by several successive classes of theological students; and is now given to the public in the hope that it may supply a want which has been felt in other institutions of learning; and that it may be helpful also as a Handbook to ministers of the Gospel, Sabbath-school teachers and students of the Bible in general. If its author shall receive but a tithe of the favor and encouragement in this wider field, which he has received from his own pupils, he will be amply repaid for the time and labor he has devoted to its preparation.

The chief value of a work of this character must of necessity depend upon the careful selection and orderly presentation of well authenticated facts, gathered from sources not readily accessible to the ordinary student. These are contained in costly memoirs of exploration parties, monographs on places or sections of the country, narratives of travel, quarterlies and other official publications of the Palestine Exploration Fund: and in such standard works as Robinson's Physical Geography and Researches, Ritter's Comparative Geography of Palestine, Stanley's Sinai and Palestine, Thomson's Land and the Book, Tristram's Topography of the Holy Land, and the Historical Geographies of Drs. Henderson and Smith.

While the author has gathered, and adapted to his purpose, the latest and most interesting information attainable from these and other authoritative sources within his reach, he has also availed himself of the impressions which can only come from personal observation. A carefully-planned journey from the borders of the South country to the heart of the Lebanon gave opportunity for studying the Geography of the Land day by day on the spot. In utilizing these impressions the writer has sought to impart something of the life and coloring imprinted on his own mind and memory through the "seeing eye." Quotations from recognized authorities have been freely introduced into the body of the work to give additional value to descriptions or to throw light upon the topography or antiquity of disputed sites.

In the footnotes credit has been given for all citations, and, as far as possible, the sources of direct information have been indicated.

In the first part of the book a *general* description of the Land is given, including its position among the nations, its boundaries and prominent physical features, its present condition and the salient points in its history.

In the second part the *special* features and noteworthy places are grouped together in separate sections for study at close range. These sectional divisions correspond to the natural divisions of the country; and, with scarcely an exception, have familiar Old Testament names descriptive of their physical aspects and relations.

An obvious advantage of this arrangement is the opportunity it affords for studying the characteristic features, and historical associations of each Biblical site in connection with its *natural environment*. In the historical records of the country the several incidents which make up the story of its sacred localities are often widely scattered, but in a Handbook of Sacred Geography they should be brought together.

As Dean Stanley puts it: "A work of this kind in which the local description is severed from the history must necessarily bear an incoherent and fragmentary aspect. It is the framework without the picture—the skeleton without the flesh —the stage without the drama. The materials of a knowledge of the East are worthily turned to their highest and most fitting use only when employed for a complete representation of the Sacred History as drawn out in its full proportions from the condensed and scattered records of the Scriptures."

There are some excellent works on the Geography of Palestine which follow the historical order of the Biblical records. These have their place and value as adjuncts to the study of the Bible, but they are objectionable as *text-books* because this method of arrangement imposes upon the student the task of searching through widely separated epochs for the materials, which make up the story, of each sacred locality.

The necessity for the frequent repetition of places—as in the case of Shechem, which is mentioned in connection with every prominent period of Hebrew history from Abraham to Christ—precludes a full or satisfactory description at any point.

A more serious difficulty, however, is the perplexity which arises from the study in turn of a Palestine of the Patriarchs; of the Conquest; of the Judges; of the Kings; and of the New Testament period. These or similar divisions may properly represent important periods in the history of the Holy Land, but there seems to be no good reason for making them serve as divisions of its geography. On the contrary their use in this connection is bewildering to the student, if not positively misleading.

The land given to Israel by Divine allotment, as a possession among the nations, was not a domain of uncertain area, whose metes and bounds were determined by political changes or revolutions, but a distinct portion of the earth's surface, with well defined boundaries and unique physical features. Within these limits we are concerned with everything which belongs to its configuration, topography, history, antiquity and associations.

To be available for ready reference a work of this character must give an account of every Biblical site, which has been more or less satisfactorily identified. It does not follow, however, that the student should be required to master this formidable list of places in wearisome detail. They can be studied to best advantage as the Astronomer studies the stars in a given section of the heavens; first by resolving them into groups, and second by concentrating attention upon the most conspicuous representatives of these groups.

A synopsis of each chapter will be found in the Table of Contents. This has been made as complete as possible to aid the student in review.

Preface xiii

A series of sectional maps—thirteen in number—illustrate the topographical feature of each subdivision of the country. These have been prepared with great care under the author's personal supervision, and for the most part from reductions of the English Survey Maps. They indicate the exact localities and the special features described in the text. Unimportant and unidentified localities have been left out.

Railroads projected, or in operation, new carriage roads, and the points recently selected for excavation in the Shephelah have been indicated.

I desire to acknowledge my obligations to Mr. R. M. Camden, Jr., of Philadelphia, for careful and accurate detail work on the sectional maps; to Professor Theodore F. Wright, of Cambridge, Honorable Secretary of the Palestine Exploration Fund for the United States, for privileges accorded in connection with the use and reproduction of maps and illustrations published by the Fund; to my associates Drs. I. N. Rendall and J. Aspinwall Hodge for valuable help and suggestions, and especially to Professor George B. Carr, D. D., for assistance in revision of the work in manuscript form.

R. L. S.

Lincoln University, Pa.
April 20th, 1899.

Contents

INTRODUCTION

GENERAL VIEW OF THE LANDS OF THE BIBLE

The Lands of the Bible extend over the contiguous portions of three continents.—Syria preëminent among the lands of Sacred Story.—Its position and boundaries.—Modern Syria. —Syria Proper.—Palestine.—The Land of Israel.—Data for the study of Sacred Geography.—Work of Exploration Societies.—Survey of Palestine.—Maps.—Plan of Study . . 1-4

The Land of Israel
Part I
GENERAL VIEW OF THE LAND

CHAPTER I
PHYSICAL FEATURES

Extent and Boundaries.—" Dan to Beersheba."—" Entering of Hamath to River of Egypt."—Significance of Scriptural definitions.—The *Dominion* promised to Israel (defined in general terms).—The *Inheritance* promised to Israel (defined in specific terms).—Territory *east* of the Jordan.—Territory *west* of the Jordan.—The Domesday Book of the Conquest.—The boundary line on the north (Mount Hor.— Entering in of Hamath, Ziphron, Zedad).—The boundary line on the south (River of Egypt—Kadesh Barnea).— Dimensions of this Greater Palestine.—All of its territory included in the Divine allotment.—Stress to be laid upon authorized possession rather than upon permanent occupation.—Israel reproved for failure to occupy the whole land at once.—Descriptive lists given of the unoccupied portions.—Conquests of David prepared the way for the occupation of the *whole* land.—The promised heritage becomes the actual possession during the Golden Age of the Hebrew nation.—Scriptural statements concerning the recognized boundaries during this period.—The land, as thus described, a *unity* with respect to its physical features.

Position among the Nations.—Its Isolation.—Its Central Location.—Its relation to the chief centres of civilization of three Continents.—The "High Bridge" between the basins of the Nile and Euphrates.

Configuration and Natural Divisions.—Preëminently "a land of hills and valleys; of fountains and depths that spring out of valleys and hills."—Divides naturally into four longitudinal sections: Two parallel mountain ranges; and two corresponding depressions.

1. **The Lebanon and Anti-Lebanon Sections.**—Run continuously side by side throughout the land, except the distinct break made by Plain of Esdraelon.—General features of the Lebanon range.—Prominent Elevations (Dhar el Khodib, 10,052, Jebel Mukhmal, 10,016, Jebel Sunnin, 8,500).—Range corrugated by wadies running east and west.—General features of the Anti-Lebanon range.—Broader surface.—No distinct break—slopes gradually to desert on eastern side.—Culminates in heights of Hermon, 9,383 feet.

2. **The Lowland Sections.**—(1) The Maritime Plain.—Coast line remarkable for its straight, unbroken sweep.—Only one natural harbor.—Continuity broken by Mount Carmel.—Upper portion a narrow strip, 140 miles in length.—The lower portion a broad undulating plain, widening toward the south.—(2) The Valley or Cleft between the mountains.—This a phenomenon unequalled on the earth's surface.—Upper portion known as the Lebanon valley, or Cœle Syria.—Its two Rivers, the Litany and Orontes: lower portion known as the Valley of the Jordan.—Its lowest level 2,600 feet below the surface of the Sea.—Summary of most striking features of the land, viewed as a whole.

Geological Structure.—Limestone the predominating element.
—Basalt the most conspicuous surface formation next to
limestone.—Granite and gneiss in Negeb.—Red sandstone
outcrops from sides of Lebanon.—Rich alluvial deposits in
valleys and on plains 5–21

CHAPTER II
NATURAL HISTORY

(1) **Climate and Productions.**—Summer and Winter.—Wet
and dry seasons.—Former and latter rains.—The harvest
periods.—Remarkable range of levels and corresponding
variation in climate.

(2) **Flora and Fauna.**—Four distinct zones represented.—
Species range from those indigenous to Alpine heights, to
those having affinities in Nubia or Equatorial Africa.—
Species recently described and catalogued in Dr. Post's
Flora number 3,416.—Trees mentioned in the Scriptures.—
Wild animals remaining, and extinct 22–27

CHAPTER III
EARLY INHABITANTS OF THE LAND

1. **Canaanites.**—(1) Philistines.—(2) Phœnicians.—Language of Canaan.—Canaan and Gilead.—Canaanites of the Jordan valley.
2. **Hittites.**—Concentrated principally in Northern Syria.—Land of the Hittites.—Carchemish and Kadesh.—Hittite settlements as far south as Hebron.
3. **Amorites.**—Preceded Hittites in occupation of Canaan.—Occupied greater part of mountain region on both sides of the Jordan.—Land of the Hittites.—Og and Sihon.—Lachish.
4. **Hivites.**—Occupied district north of Jerusalem.—The Hivite Confederacy.
5. **Perrizites.**—Possibly peasantry of the time.—Lower Galilee and foothills of Ephraim.
6. **Jebusites.**—Appear only in connection with Jerusalem and environs.

Aboriginal tribes mentioned in Scripture.—Avim, Horites, Rephaim, Anakim 28–35

CHAPTER IV

TRIBAL AND POLITICAL DIVISIONS

1. **The Division of the Tribes.**—Recovery of old lines of division.—Boundaries conform to natural features of the country.—Evidences of careful survey and apportionment. **Limits of the Several Tribes.**—Judah, Simeon, Benjamin, Ephraim, Dan, Manasseh, Issachar, Zebulon, Ashur, Naphtali. — Limits of the two and one half tribes beyond Jordan, Manasseh, Gad, Reuben.—The Cities of Refuge.
2. Limits of the Kingdoms of Israel and Judah after the death of Solomon.
3. **Political Divisions in the time of Christ.**—Galilee, Samaria, Judea, Idumea.—Divisions of the Trans-Jordanic territory.—Gaulanitis, Auranitis, Iturea, Trachonitis, Batanæa, Perea and Decapolis 36-43

CHAPTER V

HIGHWAYS AND CARAVAN ROUTES

Main routes connecting the Land of Israel with the outside world.—The coast road the oldest and most notable of four main lines of travel.—Egyptian and Assyrian tablets on this route at Dog River.
Main routes of local character within the limits of the land.—Public roadways mentioned in Scripture.—Roman roads.—Chariots.—Khans . . , ... 44-46

CHAPTER VI

PRESENT CONDITION OF THE LAND

A land *in* ruins as well as a land of ruins.— Heights denuded of trees.—Terraces broken down.—Soil washed away.—Ruined cities and towns without inhabitants.—The rugged framework of the land with all its characteristic features yet remain.—Marked changes for the better within the past decade.—Carriage roads.—Railroads.—Hotels, etc.—Signs of Providential oversight and the dawning of a better day . . . 47-49

CHAPTER VII

HISTORY AND ASSOCIATIONS

Relation between the History and the Geography of the Holy Land.—Three periods of national or provincial occupation, viz: The Canaanite, Israelite and Gentile.

1. **The Canaanite Period.**—Comes into view about 2000 B. C.—Monumental Evidences.
   (1) Canaan as a Babylonian Province.—Designated in cuneiform records as the land of the Amorites.—Records of Sargon, Naram-sin, and Gudea establish the fact of the dependence of Canaan before the birth of Abram.—Near the close of this period (c. 1600 B. C.) evidences multiply of a larger population and a higher grade of civilization.
   (2) Canaan as an Egyptian Province.—Dates from battle of Megiddo.—Period of Egyptian domination nearly three centuries.—Testimony of Tell Amarna tablets.—Names of principal cities appear in annals of Egyptian kings.
2. **The Hebrew Period.**—Covers a stretch of nearly fifteen centuries.—Territory of Israel cut short after death of Solomon.—Kingdom of Syria arises and menaces the safety of the northern kingdom.—Conquests of the Assyrians and ultimate fall of the kingdom of Israel.—Ten tribes carried away B. C. 721. Kingdom of Judah suffers reverses and becomes a province of Babylon B. C. 606.—Jerusalem destroyed B. C. 587. After the return from the Captivity the Jews dwelt securely under the protectorate of Persian empire for 200 years.—Following this are periods of Macedonian, Egyptian, Maccabean and Roman rule.
3. **The Gentile Period.**—Dates from destruction of Jerusalem.—Jews banished from Palestine by order of Hadrian.—Roman supremacy ends A. D. 614.—A brief period of Persian rule followed by supremacy of Arabs and Turks.—Period of the Crusades the only interruption to Moslem rule for more than a thousand years.—Impress of Crusaders all over western Palestine.—A deeper and more abiding impression left upon the land by the centuries of Greek and Roman occupation.—Monumental remains of Græco-Roman civilization.—Roman roads.—Christian emblems and inscriptions, etc.—Sacred Associations of the Land. Stands apart from all as the "Holy Land.". 50–58

CHAPTER VIII

THE TESTIMONY OF THE LAND TO THE BOOK

Importance of the study of the Land as a supplemental evidence to the historical accuracy of the Scriptures.—Topographical details fit in with the Biblical narratives.—One answers to the other as the die to its impress.—Both fit together into one unique and grandly comprehensive plan.—Testimony of modern explorers:—Robinson, Thomson, Renan, Stanley, Conder, Besant 59–63

Part II

SECTIONAL VIEW OF THE LAND

The First Longitudinal Section

CHAPTER IX

THE MARITIME PLAIN NORTH OF MOUNT CARMEL

Separated by the Ladder of Tyre into two portions, known as Plains of Phœnicia and Acre.—Description of Ladder of Tyre.

1. **The Phœnician Plain.**—Length and breadth.—Coast line.—Palm belt.—Low hills.—Noted streams which cross the plain:—Eleutherus, Adonis, Lycus, Bostrenus, Litany.—Local subdivisions of plain:—Tripoli, Berytus, Sidon, Tyre.

Cities and Towns.—Tripolis, Tell Arka, Gebal, Beirut, Sidon, Zarephath, Tyre.

2. **The Plain of Acre.**—Extent and boundaries.—Crescent shaped shore line.—Harbor.—Rivers.—Belus and Kishon.—Cities and Towns:—Acre (Ptolemais), Haifa, Achzib, Harosheth, Cabul, Abdon, Beth-emek.—The pass of the Kishon the place of the disastrous defeat of the army of Sisera 65–78

Contents

CHAPTER X

THE MARITIME PLAIN SOUTH OF MOUNT CARMEL

Divisions of the plain:—Athlit, Sharon, Philistia.
1. **The Plain of Athlit.**—Coast ridge.—Ancient road.—Towns of Athlit and Dor.
2. **The Plain of Sharon.**—Boundaries.—Characteristic features.—Crossed by several perennial streams:—The Zerka, Mufjir, Iskanderuneh, Aujeh.—The Nahr Rubin divides Sharon from Philistia.—Cities and Towns:—Cæsarea, Jaffa, Harbor of Jaffa, Lydda, Ono, Hadid, Neballat, Ramleh, Antipatris, Gilgal.—Roadways.—Railroad and Carriage road to Jerusalem.
3. **The Philistine Plain.**—Extent and General Features.—South of Gaza a pastoral region.—Kingdom of Gerar.—Plain north of Gaza a vast grain-field.—Soil porous.—Streams find their way underground to the sea.—Water supply easily obtained by boring or sinking wells.—Orchards and gardens in vicinity of towns and villages.—Chief cities and noteworthy sites of ancient Philistia—Ekron, Ashdod, Gath, Askelon, Gaza, Jabneel, Libnah, Makkedah, Migdol, Lachish.—Results of excavations at Lachish (Tell el Hesy) Eglon.—Gerar.—Evidences that the whole of the Philistine Plain was a thickly populated region in the past 79–96

CHAPTER XI

THE SHEPHELAH

Usage of term by latest authorities.—Valleys of the Shephelah.—Ajalon, Sorek, Elah, Zephathah, Wady el Hesy, Wady esh Sheriah.
Towns of the Shephelah.—Ajalon, Gimzo, Beit Nuba, Emmaus, Gezer, Jabneel, Zorah, Eshtaol, Beth Shemesh, Timnath, Camp of Dan, Shocoh, Adullum, Tell es Safi, Azeka, Tell Zakariya, Beit Jibrin, Mareshah.—Ruined sites of unknown towns and villages all over this region.—The theatre of many notable events in human history.—Its possessors held all the gateways of approach to the Holy City from the west 97–105

Contents

The Second Longitudinal Section

CHAPTER XII
THE MOUNTAINS OF LEBANON AND GALILEE

1. **Lebanon.**—Term applied to the high mountains of the Lebanon range.—Characteristics of Lebanon.—Its beauty, sublimity, and wonderful variety of scenery and production.—Cedars of Lebanon.—Principal rivers.—Deeply cleft chasms.—Gorges of the Kadisha and Litany.—Natural bridges.—Twelve hundred modern villages.—Zahleh.—Carriage road over Lebanon.
2. **The Mountains of Galilee.**—Boundaries and characteristic features.—Mount Naphtali.—Jebel Jermuk (3,934) the dominant peak.—Interspersed Plains.—El Buttauf.—Turan.—Ramah.—Mountain of the Beatitudes.—Wady Hamam.—Storied caves.

Noteworthy Places.—Kedesh, Hazor, Edrei, Safed, Janoah, Migdal El, Heleph, Horem, Beth Anath, Iron, Beth Shemesh, Ramah, En Hazor, Hukkok, Zebulun, Gischala, Nazareth.—Fountain of Mary.—Outlook from hill above Nazareth.—Sepphoris, Cana of Galilee, Khurbet Kana, Gath-hepher, Bethlehem, Japhia 106–119

CHAPTER XIII
THE PLAIN OF ESDRAELON

Opens up a natural passage-way from the Mediterranean to the Jordan Valley.—Divisions of the Plain.—Ancient and modern names.

Esdraelon Proper.—Triangular in outline.—Gateways of Esdraelon.—Fertility.—Present condition.—The Kishon river.—Ancient Sites:—Tell el Kasis, Jokneam, Megiddo, Battle-fields in front of Megiddo, Taanach, Hadad Rimmon, En gannim, Jezreel, Shunem, Chisloth Tabor.

Eastern Extension of the Plain.—Divides into three branches.—Wady Bireh.—Valley of Jezreel.—Fountain of Jezreel.—Hill of Moreh.—Beth Shittah.—Bethshan.

Mountains of Esdraelon: (1) Gilboa.—Characteristics and history.—Jelbon.—Mezar.—(2) Little Hermon.—Characteristic features.—Hill of Moreh.—Nain.—Endor.—(3) Mount

Contents   xxiii

Tabor.—Symmetrical from base to crown.—Range of vision from summit of Tabor.
Stirring events connected with Esdraelon and its outgoings . . 120–133

CHAPTER XIV
THE MOUNTAINS OF EPHRAIM

Characteristic features.—Mount Carmel.—The Excellency of Carmel.—Place of the conflict been Elijah and the priests of Baal.—The Hill of Samaria.—Location and surroundings.—The City of Samaria :—Its glorious beauty.—Its history as the Capital of the ten tribes.—Its magnificence in the time of Christ.
The mountains of Ebal and Gerizim.—Topography of site of the ratification of the book of the Law.—Panoramic view from Mount Ebal.—Baal Hazor.—Highest peak of Mount Ephraim.—Landmark on border line between Ephraim and Benjamin.
Interspersed Plains.—Dothan (Caravan route) Tell Dothan, Mukhna, Vale of Shechem.
Wadies.—Farah, Aujeh, Arah, Selhab, Abu Nar, Shair, Kanah, Deir Balut, Ishar, Nimr.
Towns and Sacred Sites:—Shechem, Jacob's Well, Sychar, Belata, Joseph's Tomb, Salim, Ænon, Tulluza, Tirzah, Thebez Bezek, Samaria, Dothan, Bethulia, Awertah, Tombs of Eleazar and Phinehas, Taanath Shiloh, Arumah, Janoah, Timnath Serah, Neby Nun, Tiphsah, Shiloh, Lebonah, Gilgal 134–157

CHAPTER XV
THE MOUNTAINS OF BENJAMIN

Boundaries and characteristic features.—A mountain fastness.—Isolated knolls.—Terraced slopes and alluvial basins.—A land *in* ruins as well as a land of ruins.—Neby Samwil the probable site of Mizpeh.—" Mountjoye " of the Crusaders.
Wadies and Ravines.—Wadies: Nuweimeh, Kelt, Suweinet, el Hod.
Towns and Sacred Sites of Benjamin.—Gophna, Bethel, Berj Beitin, Beth-aven, Ai, Et Tell, Rock Rimmon, Michmash, Geba, Beeroth, Ramah, Gibeah of Saul, Tell el Ful, Anathoth,

The Beth-horons, Gibeon, Pool of Gibeon, Place of the Tabernacle and Altar, Nob.
Places of minor importance :—Archi, Sechu, Baal Tamar, Gederah, Ananiah, Hazor, Gibeath, Kirjath, Mozah, Chesalon, Parah, Alemeth, Debir, Eleph 158–169

CHAPTER XVI
JERUSALEM AND ITS ENVIRONS

Elevation and Environment.—Kedron Valley.—Hinnon Valley.—Wady en Nar.—Accumulations of rubbish.—Direction and sweep of ancient walls.—**The Mountains around.**—**Internal divisions.**—Ridge on western side.—Ridge on eastern side.—Tyropœon valley.—Lateral valleys.—Acra and Zion.—Bezetha, Moriah and Ophel.—Rubbish and wreckage of not less than eight cities below the present city.—Rock levels and general contour lines obtained by repeated excavations.—**Appearance of modern city.**—Walls and Gates.—(Quarters :—1 The Armenian Quarter : Citadel.—Tower of Hippicus.—Tower of David.—Palace of Herod.—The Armenian Convent.—English Church.—Church of St. James.

2. **The Christian Quarter:**—The Muristan.—Pool of Hezekiah.—Church of the Holy Sepulchre.

3. **The Moslem Quarter :**—Largest division of the city.—Governor's Palace.—Barracks.—Consulates.—Church of St. Anne.—Pool of Bethesda.—Via Dolorosa.—Birket Israil.—Cotton Grotto.—Jeremiah's Grotto.—Geological formation of Jerusalem plateau.

4. **The Jewish Quarters :**—Synagogues.—Dilapidated tenements.—The Wailing Place.—Huge blocks of stone in lower course of wall.

5. **The Temple Area :**—Summit of Moriah.—Quadrangle, thirty-five acres in area.—The Dome of the Rock.—The Sakhra.—Its relation to the Holy House.—Cave under the rock.—Threshing floor of Ornan.—The water supply of the Temple Area.—The Great Sea.—Thirty underground reservoirs.—Walls of the Temple Area.—Fortress of Antonia and connecting wall.—Height of wall at northwest corner.—Phœnician characters 100 feet below the surface.—The Golden Gate.—The Southeast Corner.—Warren's excava-

tions.—Character of masonry.—Solomon's Stables.—The
Single, Triple and Double Gates of the South wall.—Huldah Gate identified with the Double Gate.—Vaulted passage
and vestibule.—Robinson's Arch.—Remains of two ancient
bridges connecting Zion with Moriah.—Wilson's Arch.—
Barclay's Gate.—Sir Charles Warren's conclusions respecting the walls and the several buildings which they enclosed.
—General plan of first and second Temples.—The Court
of the Gentiles and its Cloisters.—The Terraced Mountain,
viewed as a whole.—Its hallowed memories.

Outside the Walls.—1. Catacombs and Tombs.—Tombs of the
Kings and Judges.—Tomb west of the probable site of
Golgotha.—Tombs of Jehoshaphat, Zachariah, Absalom and
St. James.—Reputed tomb of David.—Aceldama.—The
Place of the Crucifixion.—The Mount of Olives.—Three
distinctly marked summits.—Church of the Ascension.—
View from Olivet.—Bethany.—The place where Jesus
wept over Jerusalem.—The place of the Ascension.—The
Garden of Gethsemane.—The King's Dale.—King's Garden.—Gehenna.—Plain of Rephaim.

Pools and Sources of Water Supply.—Fountain of the Virgin
or En Rogel.—Stone of Zoheleth.—Village of Siloam.—
Rock hewn tunnel.—Pool of Siloam.—Siloam Inscription.
—Recent excavations.—Restored pool.—Ancient stairway
leading up to city.—Byzantine Church.—Lower Pool.—Bir
Eyub.—Mamilla Pool.—Sultan's Pool.—Low-level Aqueduct.—High-level Aqueduct.—Inverted syphon two miles
in length.—The **Jaffa Suburb.**—Colonies and charitable
institutions.—Population of Jerusalem.

Southern Wall of Ancient Jerusalem.—Wall recovered by
Warren on eastern brow of Ophel.—Summary of discoveries made by Dr. Bliss along the line of the southern wall.
—The pools of Siloam and all the available portions of the
slopes of Zion and Ophel included in the circuit of the ancient walls.—History and influence of the Holy City . . . 170–223

CHAPTER XVII
THE MOUNTAINS OF JUDAH

Characteristic features.—Land of the olive and vine.—A pastoral land.—Wilderness of Judah.—A land not inhabited.—

xxvi   Contents

Place of John's seclusion.— Place of the temptation of Jesus.
Wadies.—En Nar, El Ghar, Surar, Es Sunt, Afranj.—The desolate heaps of Judah.
Sites which have been identified.—Kirjath Jearim.—Emmaus.—Bethlehem.—Church of the Nativity.—Mar Saba.—Etham.—Tekoa.—Hebron.—Vale of Hebron.—Vineyards of Hebron.—Cave of Machpelah.—Pools of Hebron.—Ziph.—Carmel.—Maon.—Engedi.—Cliff of Ziz.—Valley of Berachah.—Masada.—Hereth.—Keilah.—Places of minor importance: Bethzur, Gedor, Beth Tappuach, Adoraim, Arab, Juttah, Socoh, Jattir, Debir 224–236

CHAPTER XVIII

THE NEGEB OR SOUTH COUNTRY

Limits north and south. Subdivisions.—Characteristics.—Present condition.
Sites of Special Interest.—Beersheba.—Ancient wells. - Associations with the Patriarchs.—Arad.—Sheba.—Aroer.—Rehoboth.—Zephath (Hormah).—Plain Es Seer.—Mount Halak.—Wady Feqreh.—Mount Seir.—Kadesh Barnea.—Recovery, description and history of this long-lost site.—Mount Hor (Jebel Madurah).—The traditional Mount Hor.—Wady Madurah.—Eschol.—Hagar's Well.—Probable direction of the southern border line of the Land of Israel . 237–249

The Third Longitudinal Section

CHAPTER XIX

THE VALLEY OF LEBANON

Length and breadth.—Secondary ridge on eastern side.—Watershed near Baalbek.—Characteristic features.—Baalbek.—Its majestic structures and massive ruins the wonder of the world.—The three immense stones in western wall.—Connection with Baal Gad.—Plain of Aven.—Riblah . . . 250–253

CHAPTER XX

THE VALLEY OF THE JORDAN

Wady et Teim.—Merj Ayun.—Derdarah branch of the Jordan.
—Ijon (Tell Dibbin).—Abel-beth Maachah.—The Jordan Valley Proper.—The three Lakes.—Subdivisions of the valley.

1. **The Upper Basin.**—Plain of the Huleh.—Perennial sources of the Jordan:—(1) The Fountain of the Hasbany near village of Hasbeiya.—Most remote source.—Elevation 1,700 feet.—Descent in 115 miles 3,000 feet.—(2) The Fountain of the Leddan.—Chief source.—Elevation 500 feet.—Tell el Kady.—Oak at Dan.—Rank vegetation.—(3) The Fountain of Banias.—Springs from southern base of Hermon.—Prominent features of the place.—Elevation 1,080.—Cave and shrine of the god Pan.—This "a very sanctuary of waters."—Castle of Shubeiah.—Lake Huleh.—Marsh of Huleh.—Papyrus jungles.—John Macgregor's explorations in the Rob Roy.—Elevation of Lake Huleh.—Semi-tropical climate and luxuriant vegetation of the Huleh.

2. **The Descent between the Lakes.**—Bridge of Jacob's Daughters.—Below it a succession of rapids to level of lower basin.—Hills of Naphtali.

3. **The Galilean Basin.**—Lake deep down in this secluded basin (-682 feet).—Different characteristics of mountains on eastern and western sides.—Plain of Gennesaret.—Wonderful fertility of the plain.—Hallowed memories of the Lake and the region around it.—Towns on the Coasts of Galilee:
—Tiberias, Magdala, Capernaum, Tell Hum, Bethsaida of Galilee, Bethsaida Julias, Chorazin, Gergesa, Wady Fik, Gamala, Semakh, Tarichæa.

4. **The Ghor.**—Length and breadth.—Contractions and expansions.—Plain of Jordan.—Ghor-es Seisaban.—Ciccar.—Climate and Products.—Tributaries of the Jordan.
Places of Special Interest:—Abel Meholah.—Kurn Sartaba.
—Adam.—Zaretan.—Succoth.—Jericho.—Ain es Sultan.—
Tell es Sultan.—Tropical luxuriance of the plain.—The three Jerichos.—Gilgal.—Beth Hogla.—The Cities of the Plain.—Plain of Abel Shittim (Plain of Moab).—The last camping place of Israel east of Jordan.—Beth-nimrah.—
Abel Shittim.—Beth-haran.—Zoar.—Beth-jeshimoth.—Prog-

xxviii   Contents

    ress of Jordan through the Ghor. – The Zor or high level channel.—The "swellings of Jordan."—Fords of the Jordan.—Bethabara.—Bridges and ferries.—Unique features of the Jordan.—History of the Jordan.

5. **The Dead Sea Basin.**—Extent and characteristic features.—Jebel Usdum.—Ghor es-Safieh.—El Lisan.—The Dead Sea.—Unique features. 254–288

The Fourth Longitudinal Section

CHAPTER XXI

THE ANTI-LEBANON MOUNTAINS

Anti-Lebanon Proper (The East Mountain).—Distinguishing features.—The Abana river.—Ain el Fijeh.—Abila.—Zebedany Plain.—Zedad.—Hazar-enan.—Zephron.—Hamath.—Damascus.—Plain of Damascus.—The Merj.—The Pharpar river.—Damascus the Paradise of the Arab world.—365 canals.—30,000 gardens.—Its antiquity and marvellous history.—The great Mosque.—Helbon.—**Mount Hermon:**—The Hermons.—Panoramic view from summit of Hermon.—Circuit of the waters.—True source of the Jordan.—The Place of the Transfiguration.—Hermon within the borders of Israel's possession 289–301

CHAPTER XXII

THE TRANS-JORDANIC HIGHLANDS

Extent of Eastern Palestine.—General characteristics.—Old Testament divisions:

1. **Bashan :**—Boundaries. - District of Jedur.—Jaulan.—Golan.—Oak forests.—Tell Ashtereh.—Aphek.—The Hauran.—En Nukra.—Hajj road.—Damascus.—Hauran railroad.—Natural wealth of Hauran.—Harvests.—Threshing floors.—The Lejah.—An uplifted mass of congealed lava.—Its cavernous depths and winding paths.—Towns of the Lejah.—The stronghold of Og, king of Bashan.—Edrei-Kenath.—Jebel Hauran.—Batanæa.—Salcah.—Kerioth.—Bosrah.—Ruined cities of the Hauran.—Giant cities.—Greek and Roman types of architecture.—Monumental evidences of ex-

istence of active Christian communities.—Records of the days of persecution and martyrdom.—Divergent views with respect to antiquity of Hauran architecture.—Job's country.

2. **Gilead** :—Boundaries and general characteristics.—The Yarmuk river.—The Jabbok.—Jebel Ajlun.—The Belka.— Land of the children of Ammon.—Wood of Ephraim.—Continuous forests.—Jebel Osha.—Outlook from Jebel Osha.— Jacob's route from the East.—Noteworthy Places :—Gadara.—El Hamma.—Land of Tob.—Abila.—Capitolias.— Arbela.—Ramoth.—Mizpeh.—Kulat er Rubab.—Outlook from Kulat er Rubad.—Mahanaim.—Jabesh Gilead.—Pella. —Peniel.—Gerasa (Jerash).—Ramoth Gilead.—Suf.— Debir.—Beth Gamul.—Rabbath Ammon.—Jogbehah.— Kulat Zerka.—Jazer.—Castle of Hyrcanus.

3. **Moab.**—The Mishor.—The Abarim.—The Callirhoe.— Castle of Machærus.—Valley of the Arnon.—Aroer.—Jebel Attarus.—Bamath Baal.—Mount Pisgah.—Jebel Siaghah.— View from Pisgah.—Baal peor.—High places of Moab.— Menhirs, dolmons, etc.—Heshbon, Elalah, Sibmah, Medeba. —Mosaic map of Palestine.—Mashetta.—Mystery of the desert.—Baal Meon.—Dibon.—Moabite Stone.—Aroer.—Kir of Moab (Kerak).—The brook Zered. Limit of the wilderness journeyings 302-338

Equivalents of Arabic Words 339

Index 340-352

INTRODUCTION

GENERAL VIEW OF THE LANDS OF THE BIBLE

THE Lands of the Bible extend over the contiguous sections of three great Continents—Asia, Africa and Europe.

They lie between north latitude 28° and 45°; and east longitude 12° and 50°. This area includes the cradle of the race, the holy cities, and the chief centres of civilization and empire of the ancient world.

The principal events of Old Testament history are included between the four Seas of Western Asia, viz:—the Mediterranean, the Black, the Caspian and the Persian Gulf.

Syria.—Preëminent among all the lands of Sacred Story is the narrow strip, inland of the Mediterranean, which for a period antedating the Christian era, has been covered by the general name Syria.

The Roman Province of Syria extended southward from Mount Amanus, a spur of the Taurus range, to the desert which borders the land of Egypt. Its eastern boundary was the upper Euphrates and the Desert of Arabia. This rugged and singularly-diversified tract was nearly 400 miles in length. In breadth it varied from sixty-five to 150 miles.

Modern Syria, with but slight divergence in outline, covers nearly the same extent of territory.

Syria Proper.—In its ordinary acceptation the name is restricted to the portion of territory which lies north of the southern slopes of Hermon and Lebanon.

Palestine is the familiar designation of that section of Southern Syria which was permanently occupied by the tribes of Israel. The name, as originally used in the Bible and in ancient history was limited to the land of the Philistines.

There are some writers of note who confine the name, at the present time, to the territory of Israel west of the Jordan, but the best authorities, including the Palestine Exploration Society, have given to the name a definite signification, which includes the permanent possession of the twelve tribes on both sides of the river.

The length of Palestine, as usually reckoned, from Dan to Beersheba is only 144 miles. The entire area is less than 11,000 square miles.

The Land of Israel.—As outlined and described by the sacred writers the possession of Israel extended northward to the "Entering in of Hamath," and southward to the "River of Egypt" (Wady el Arish). This includes an area about twice as large as the territory usually covered by the term Palestine. As a matter of fact the characteristic features, and historic events ascribed to the land of Israel cannot be compressed within the limited area between Dan and Beersheba.

Data.—Reliable data for the accurate study of the Geography and Antiquities of this country, which for long ages has borne the exclusive title of "The Holy Land," have been accumulated within the last twenty years; and we are no longer left to the uncertainty of traditional lore or the hasty generalizations of travellers to the East. As a result of patient labors, skillfully-conducted excavations, and accurate surveys, the prominent places and events, which come successively into view in connection with the unfolding of the purpose of Redemption, have been definitely located and accurately described.

Prominent among the agencies to which we are indebted for this important work are: "The Palestine Exploration Fund," "The American Society for Palestine Exploration," and "The German Palestine Society." Very efficient service has been rendered by M. Ganneau, Renan, and other noted French scholars and explorers.

In Palestine very little remains to be done, above ground, in the way of geographical exploration and survey, except in a limited portion of the country east of the Jordan. A triangulation survey of Western Palestine was commenced by the Palestine Exploration Fund in the autumn of 1872, and was completed, so far as the field work was concerned, in 1877. A list of 10,000 names was collected during the progress of this survey, and 172 Biblical sites were discovered. At the present time 434 out of the 622 Biblical names west of the Jordan have been identified with a reasonable degree of certainty.

Maps.—The "Great Map of Western Palestine" embodies the results of this monumental work of exploration, and is recognized as the standard of authority in this department of scientific research. On this map the natural features of the country have been laid down in exact detail, on the scale of one inch to the mile, as beautifully and accurately as on the Ordnance map of England. It has been fittingly described as

A magnificent map with every road and ruin marked, and every conspicuous object filled in; with the hills and mountains correctly delineated and shaded, with the rivers and brooks all running in the right directions; with every vineyard, every spring of water and almost every clump of trees set down in its place, and with thousands of names that never appeared on a Palestine map before.[1]

The survey of Eastern Palestine, commenced by the American Exploration Society under the direction of Dr. Selah Merrill, has been completed, under the auspices of the Palestine Exploration Fund, for a portion of the country only. Enough has been done, however, to secure a reliable map. This has been published in connection with a reduced map of Western Palestine (three-eighths of an inch to the mile) under the title: "Old and New Testament Map of Palestine."

A Raised Map constructed on the same scale by Mr. George Armstrong, Assistant Secretary of the Fund, is the crowning work of all the surveys and explorations of the past. It shows at a glance the relative heights and depressions of this

[1] St. Clair's *Bible Countries*, p. 123.

remarkably diversified land from Baalbec on the north to Kadesh Barnea on the south.

The fully-colored relief map, which is recommended as the most desirable for classroom study has "the seas, lakes, marshes and perennial streams colored blue, the Old and New Testament sites are marked in red, the principal ones having a number to correspond with a reference list of names, the plains in green, the rising ground, hills and mountains in various tints, the olive groves and wooded parts of the country stippled in green, and the main roads are shown in the thin black line."[1]

Arrangements have been made by the London Society to have this map reproduced by Mr. E. E. Howell, of Washington, D. C. Its cost at the present time is $55.

Plan of Study.—In the description of the various sections and sites which come within the range of this study, special emphasis will be given to *three* leading points; viz, Location, Characteristics, and Associations. The entire work is constructed on this threefold arrangement, with a view to clearness of statement, and the more ready retention of the important facts in memory.

The value of a uniform, natural and logical order in description and recitation in connection with this study, can hardly be overestimated. It is this which distinguishes a "Text-book" from an ordinary treatise on this or any other subject.

[1] Quarterly Statement, P. E. F. 1894, p. 93.

THE LAND OF ISRAEL

Part I
General View of the Land

CHAPTER I

PHYSICAL FEATURES

EXTENT and Boundaries.—In the introductory chapter the geographical position of the Holy Land was described in connection with Syria. All authorities are agreed that its location is in the southern part of Syria, but there is a wide divergence of statement in reference to its bounding lines on the north and south.

While many accept the familiar expression "from Dan to Beersheba," as a sufficiently exact geographical definition, it is a notable fact that they invariably go beyond it when giving a complete description of Biblical places and events.

A geography of the Holy Land can hardly be considered as complete, which omits the southern border-lands of Judah and Simeon, associated with events inwoven with Israel's story from the days of the Patriarchs; the coasts of Tyre and Sidon, which marked the northern limit of our Lord's beneficent journeys; the Holy Mount, so conspicuous from every quarter of the land, upon which once shone a flood of light from the excellent glory such as "never was on sea or land"; or that "goodly mountain, even Lebanon,"—mentioned in the Scriptures not less than sixty-eight times,—which Moses so longed to behold. It seems reasonable, also, that if we are to study a Sacred Geography, confessedly based upon a Sacred Book, we should give to the statements of that book the *first* place in authority and importance.

In comparing these statements we find they relate to *two widely extended areas*, one of which was included within the other.

1. In the larger area the borders are defined in *general terms*, in the promise given to Abraham and his descendants—

Gen. xv. 18, "Unto thy seed have I given this land, from the river of Egypt unto the great river, the river Euphrates." Ex. xxiii. 31, "I will set thy bounds from the Red Sea unto the sea of the Philistines and from the desert unto the river." (V. also Josh. i. 4; Ps. lxxii. 8.)

In the closing years of David's reign, and throughout the period of Solomon's rule, this promise was realized, not in a virtual possession, but in a dominion or empire, vast in extent and remarkable in its influence over the nations.

In the exact language of Scripture-corresponding with the original promise —

"Solomon *reigned over all the Kings* from the river even unto the land of the Philistines and to the border of Egypt" (2 Chron. ix. 26). As elsewhere expressed, "Solomon reigned over *all the kingdoms* from the river unto the land of the Philistines, and unto the border of Egypt, they brought presents and served Solomon all the days of his life. For he had *dominion* over all the *region* on this side of the river, from Tiphsah even to Azzah (Gaza), over all the Kings on this side of the river; and he had peace on all sides round about him" (1 Kings iv. 21 and 24).

2. In the smaller area the boundaries are defined in *specific terms*, with a view to its occupation and possession by the Hebrew nation as *its peculiar heritage* among the nations. With respect to this territory the references are numerous and the various descriptions, geographical, poetical, and historical

General View of the Land 7

converge, with wonderful unanimity within the same boundary lines.

In the book of Joshua (xii. 1) the possession of the two and one-half tribes is briefly described as "the land on the other side Jordan toward the rising of the sun from the river Arnon unto Mount Hermon and all the plain to the east." In another reference, (Josh. xiii. 11), "all Mount Hermon, and all Bashan unto Salcah," are included in "the inheritance which Moses gave to these tribes beyond Jordan eastward."

In a passage relating to the later history it is recorded that the children of the half tribe of Manasseh, who dwelt in this portion of the land, " increased from Bashan unto Baal-Hermon and Senir, and unto Mount Hermon" (1. Chron. v. 23). Baal-Hermon has been associated with one of the three peaks of Mount Hermon (Henderson's Palestine, p. 31); and Senir, according to Dr. Robinson, is identified with the ridge of Anti-Lebanon north of Damascus. (Physical Geography, p. 347.)

On the westward side of the Jordan the boundary lines are defined with remarkable accuracy and distinctness. "There is one document in the Hebrew Scriptures—says Dean Stanley—to which probably no parallel exists in the topographical records of any other nation. In the book of Joshua we have what may be termed, without offence the Domesday Book of conquest of Canaan. Ten chapters of that book are devoted to a description of the country, in which not only are its general features and boundaries carefully laid down, but the names and situations of its towns and villages are enumerated, with a precision of geographical terms, which invites and almost compels a minute investigation" (Sinai and Pal., p. 14).

In the apportionment to the nine and one-half tribes, and in several instances in the subsequent history of the nation, the northern limit is defined as "The Entering of Hamath" (Num. xxxiv. 8; Judg. iii. 3; Josh. xiii. 5; 1 Kings viii. 65; 2 Kings xiv. 28; 2 Chron. vii. 8; Ezek. xlvii. 16, etc.).

The record of the original allotment is as follows:

"And this shall be your *north* border; from the great sea ye shall point out for you Mount Hor. From Mount Hor ye shall point out your border unto the entrance of Hamath; and the goings forth of the border shall be Zedad. And the border shall go on to Ziphron, and the goings out of it shall be at Hazar-enan; this shall be your *north border*" (Num. xxxiv. 8, 9).

The exact location of Mount Hor, the first station on this line is not known, but it was probably a conspicuous peak at the northern extremity of the Lebanon mountains.

Dr. Robinson locates the entrance of Hamath at the northern extremity of Lebanon.[1] "All the Scripture notices concerning it show clearly that the entrance of Hamath was at the northern extremity of Lebanon: and that when the children of Israel took possession of the Promised Land this became the geographical name for the great interval or depression between the northern end of Lebanon and the Nusairiyeh mountains.

Mount Hor was obviously between the seashore and the Buka'a (Coele-Syria Plain).

"'The entering in of Hamath' may then refer either generally to the whole of the great depression affording as it does an easy passage from the coast to the plain of the Orontes; or specifically to the pass through the ridge under El-Husn and the low watershed south of the Buka'a. . . . In either application the phrase is intelligible and sufficiently definite."[2]

This view has been confirmed by recent explorations, and is generally accepted by the best modern authorities. Not only does this break or valley furnish a natural passage way from the

---

[1] Some authorities have associated the entrance of Hamath with the low water shed of the Litany and Orontes near Baalbec in the Coeles Syria valley, but this does not seem to fit in with any of the descriptions of the northern boundary. Its position in a long valley running north and south might be available for the description of an eastern boundary, but it seems impossible to make it a point on the northern frontier.

[2] Robinson's Researches, Vol. 3, p. 568.

seacoast to Kadesh and Hamath, but it is found to be the only boundary line of natural formation south of Antioch, which extends from the Mediterranean to the desert eastward.[1]

Zedad, now Sudad, seventy miles northeast of Damascus, is the only one of the three towns on the north border line which has been satisfactorily identified. It lies out on the edge of the desert and must have been near Hazar-Enan, the northeast limit of the land.

It is probable that the border line extended in a *northeasterly direction* from the "entrance of Hamath"—following the base of the Nusairiyeh range—to Ziphron, on the Orontes plain; and thence *southeast* to Zedad and Hazar-Enan.

It should be noted that this is the northern border of the ten and one-half tribes. On the other side of the Jordan the northern limit seems to have been Aram of Damascus.

From Hazar-Enan the east border ran to Shepham (location is not known), and thence to Riblah at the upper end of the Coele-Syria valley. From Riblah the border descended unto the Sea of Chinnereth (Galilee) eastward. (Num. xxxiv. 11.)

With respect to the southern boundary it is definitely stated that the limit was *Kadesh Barnea*, now identified with Ain Gadis, on the edge of the desert. This was the noted resting place of the Israelites before the invasion of Canaan: and it is afterward designated as the lowest town belonging to the inheritance of Simeon.

From this point the line extended westward to the Wady el-Arish, or river of Egypt which it followed to the Mediterranean Sea. (Num. xxxiv. 3-5; Josh. xv. 1-4.)

This, says Canon Tristram, is the boundary drawn from nature, on the north of which is cultivation, on the south desert.

[1] It should be noted here that the reference is to the *Kingdom* or land of Hamath, rather than to the city which gave the name to this kingdom. It meant, in other words, the entrance from the sea to the broad *Valley of the Orontes* extending from Antioch as far southward as Riblah (2 Kings xxv. 21).

Briefly stated the boundaries of the whole land, as described by the Sacred writers, were as follows, viz :

On the *west* the Mediterranean Sea; on the *north* the valley leading from the coast,—in a northeast direction—to Hamath or into the land of Hamath, and then passing by way of Zedad to Hazar-Enan on the border of the eastern desert; on the *east*, except the country east of Anti-Lebanon, the border line of the desert; on the *south* a line on or near the latitude of the lower part of the Dead Sea, passing in a southwesterly direction, to Kadesh Barnea and thence by way of the Wady el-Arish to the Mediterranean Sea.

The territory thus described comes within the limits of $30°30'$ and $35°$ north latitude. The dimensions of this *Greater Palestine* are about 290 miles from north to south: and from west to east an average of about 100 or 120 miles. The area is an uncertain quantity because of the difficulty in fixing a definite limit to the border line east of the Jordan. It is safe to say, however, that it was about 25,000 square miles, or more than double the area ordinarily assigned to Palestine.

The principal objection advanced by modern authorities to the acceptance of these Biblically-defined boundaries, is the fact that only a portion of this territory was actually occupied by the people of Israel as a *permanent* possession.

If this be a valid objection it applies with equal force to a considerable portion of the recognized limits also between Dan and Beersheba. If we lay the stress upon *authorized possession* rather than upon *permanent occupation* the difficulty vanishes. In the closing period of the life of Joshua a descriptive list of the unoccupied portions of Israel's inheritance is given as a reproof of the tardiness of the people in advancing to its conquest. In this list we find the mention, alongside of the land of the Philistines, of "the land of the Giblites, and all Lebanon toward the sun rising from Baal Gad under Mount Hermon unto the entering into Hamath." (Josh. xiii. 5.)

Physical Features

About four hundred years after the conquest of Joshua the kingdom of David was enlarged and established within the limits described, in accordance with the long deferred promise. As the first step in this greater conquest, Jerusalem was taken from the Jebusites and made the central Sanctuary, and world-renowned Capital of Israel. The defeat and subjection of the Philistines gave to David the frontier fortress of Gaza, and the undisputed possession of the southland border to the river of Egypt. The conquest and subjection, in rapid succession, of the territories of Moab, Edom, Amalek, and Ammon secured to its farthest limit the eastern frontier.

Then, by the defeat and overthrow of two powerful Syrian kingdoms, which withstood David, the northeast border was established to the great river Euphrates. In connection with this Syrian campaign it is said (2 Sam. viii. 3) "David smote also Hadadezer the son of Rehob, king of Zobah, *as he went to recover his border at the river Euphrates.*" An alliance with Toi, king of Hamath, and with Hiram, king of Tyre, completed the subjugation of the land.

In this history, as has been already intimated—the twofold promise to Abraham and his descendants was fulfilled. The *dominion* of Israel was extended over all the lands west of the Euphrates: and *the hitherto unoccupied territory of "the Land of Israel"* throughout the limits so carefully defined by Moses and Joshua, was appropriated and held. Thus for a period of about sixty years—the golden age of the Hebrew nation—the promised heritage became the *actual possession.*

As an evidence of the recognized limit of its extent during this period the statement is made that Solomon, at the time of the dedication of the house of the Lord, made a feast and all Israel with him, a great congregation, "from the entering in of Hamath unto the river of Egypt." (1 Kings viii. 65.) At a subsequent period, also, it was recorded that Jeroboam II. restored the coast of Israel from the entering of Hamath unto the sea of the plain or Dead Sea: and again it is said of him that he recovered Damascus and Hamath, which belonged to Judah, for Israel. (2 Kings xiv. 25, 28.)

Still later we find a carefully drawn sketch of the same territory exactly defined along all its borders, in Ezekiel xlvii. 15–20. Whatever meaning we may attach to this passage in its relation to the future of the land, it certainly conveys to us the same conception of its boundaries and extent.

In harmony with these statements is the fact that the land, as thus described, is a *unity* in its physical confirmation. It has the same characteristic features, throughout its extent, from north to south. Beyond these limits they are not found.

While therefore we regard the expression "from Dan to Beersheba" as a convenient, though not strictly accurate, definition of the boundaries of a more permanent possession, we give our adherence to the limits so carefully described by the sacred writers in studying the Land *as a whole*. This is the Land which corresponds with the Book through all the periods of Jewish history. To it in its entirety, belong the glowing descriptions, poetic allusions, and characteristic features, which for long ages have made it preëminent, as the Holy Land among the nations of the earth.

Position among the Nations.—The Land of Israel occupies a unique position among the nations of the ancient world.

Its Isolation.—It was separated from the west by the Mediterranean sea: from the land of Egypt on the south by the great and terrible wilderness of Israel's journeyings: from the east by the desert of Arabia, and from the north by a rugged wall of mountains, which could only be entered through narrow valleys, or passage-ways, easily defended against an invading army.

Its Central Location.—While isolated in this remarkable manner from the nations, the Holy Land shared in common with the rest of Syria, the distinction of being at the centre of the civilization and influence of the ancient world.

To the inhabitants of Babylonia and Elam it was the *West-land*, toward which a restless tide of immigration and adventure had been tending long before the days of Abraham. To the Egyptians on the south it was the *Midland* region on the way to commerce or conquest amid the rich valleys of the Euphrates and Tigris.

To the legions which followed Alexander, and the great generals of Rome, it was the "high bridge," as Ritter terms it, on which they ascended and descended respectively into the basin of the Nile or of the Euphrates. Dr. Geo. Adam Smith has fittingly described it "as a land lying between two Continents,—Asia and Africa; between two primeval homes of men, —the valleys of the Euphrates and the Nile; between two great centres of empire—Western Asia and Egypt; between all these, representing the Eastern and ancient world, and the Mediterranean, which is the gateway to the Western and modern world." (Hist. Geog., p. 6.) While the mountain strongholds of Israel, especially in the centre of the land, were seldom disturbed by invading hosts, this highway on its western border was the favorite route for centuries between the three great Continents,—Asia, Africa and Europe.

This double relation of exclusion and ready intercommunication, paradoxical as it may appear, was a necessary feature in the heritage of a people, who were at one period of their history to *dwell apart* from the nations: and at another to carry the message of life and salvation *to all the people of the earth*.

It was fitting also that the Book, which contained this message, should be given in a land which touched all lands.

Configuration and Natural Divisions.—The mountains of the Holy Land, as a glance at the map will show, extend over the greater part of its area. In the language of Scripture it is "a land of hills and valleys, drinking water of the rain of heaven" . . . "a land of brooks of water, of fountains and depths that spring out of valleys and hills." (Deut.

xi. 11, viii. 7.)[1] The surface of the country is naturally divided into *four* longitudinal tracts or sections; viz: The coast plain, the twin mountain ranges, known as Lebanon and Anti-Lebanon, and the deeply-cleft valley which lies between them. In briefest outline the prominent physical features are:

TWO PARALLEL MOUNTAIN RANGES and TWO CORRESPONDING DEPRESSIONS,—all running north and south throughout the extent of the land. Each of these sections contributes an indispensable part to the peculiar formation of the country, giving to it a universal character which no other country possesses within such limited compass on the face of the earth. Their general characteristics may be seen to best advantage by examining them in pairs, as indicated above.

1. **The Mountains of Lebanon and Anti-Lebanon.**— The double aspect of the broad mountain range, which extends southward from Mount Amanus,—a spur of the Taurus range —is not clearly defined until it reaches the northern border of Israel's inheritance. From this point onward, however, the two ranges run almost continuously side by side to the level of the desert. In the Lebanon section there is only one break in the continuity of the range. This is caused by the deflection of the mountains westward, affording a natural passage-way from the Mediterranean to the valley of the Jordan. The deflected portion of the main ridge is known as Mount Carmel. The broad valley which lies between it and the northern continuation of the range was called, in ancient times, the valley of Megiddo. Its modern designation is the Plain of Esdraelon. The high mountains of this series are in the portion which lies north of the latitude of Dan. This elevated region bears the distinctive name of *Lebanon*. The word is used in this sense throughout the Scriptures, but in modern times it is also applied as a general name to the range itself. The average height

---

[1] In one sheet alone of the twenty-six which make up the great Map of Western Palestine there are 200 fountains.
See Thirty Years' Work, P. E. F., p. 130.

Physical Features

of this rugged block of towering mountains is 7,000 feet. Its extent north and south is about ninety miles. The highest peak, which dominates all the lofty elevations of the land, is the *Dhar el Khodib*. It is in the northern portion of the Lebanon district and rises to the height of 10,052 feet above the sea. Next to it in elevation is Jebel Mukhmal, overhanging the famous grove of Cedars, (10,016 feet).

Mount Sannin (Jebel Sŭnnin) northeast of Beirut, is the most conspicuous summit of this range, as seen from the south. Its elevation is 8,500 feet, and it is generally snow-clad throughout the year.

Near the head waters of the Jordan the general elevation diminishes rapidly, flattening and broadening out into the highlands of Galilee, which have an average height of only 2,800 feet. The lower portion of this district slopes gradually toward the plain of Esdraelon. The division of the central range which lies to the south of this plain is a continuous, closely-compacted, block of rugged mountain territory. It extends to the vicinity of Beersheba, a distance of ninety miles, and fills up most of the space between the Mediterranean and the Jordan. It is almost encircled by a lowland belt, so that it is possible to pass around from the head of the Dead Sea by way of the Jordan valley, the Esdraelon and Coast plains and the lower levels of the South country to Engedi—a short distance from the starting-point—without crossing an elevated ridge or climbing a high hill. This long watershed has been appropriately likened to a capsized flat-bottomed boat of corrugated iron, lying between the Sea and the Jordan; one end of which descends to the Plain of Esdraelon and the other to the Negeb beyond Hebron. Its corrugated sides are the wadies that cut deep toward the plains on either side.[1]

Throughout its extent this Hill country is an immense rock-buttressed stronghold, whose gateways to the plains on either

[1] Good Words, May, 1865, p. 392.

hand are long defiles, or narrow passes, easily defended by a small force against the hosts of an invading army.

The road which traverses the ridge from end to end was the great highway of Israel, over which Patriarchs, Prophets, Kings and Pilgrim bands travelled on their way to and from Jerusalem, and the regions to the south. It was also the route made sacred by the footsteps of Jesus when He journeyed from Judea to Galilee by way of Samaria. (John iv. 3, 4.)

Prominent Elevations.—The highest point in this series is Er Ramah just north of Hebron. It is 3,546 feet above the sea. Next to it is the summit of Baal Hazor (Tell Azur), 3,318 feet. This is a conspicuous landmark north of Bethel on the border line between Ephraim and Benjamin. (2 Sam. xiii. 23.)

Above this dividing line the range was known collectively as Mount Ephraim or the Mountains of Ephraim: below it as the Mountains of Judah. A later designation of the former was the Mountains of Samaria; and of the latter the Mountains of Judea.

The Ras Sherifeh, south of Bethlehem (3,260); Mount Ebal, near Shechem (3,076); and Neby Samwil, northwest of Jerusalem (2,935) are next to Baal Hazor in order of elevation.

The general average of the plateau on which Jerusalem stands is 2,500 feet above the sea. From Hebron there is a gradual descent by steps or terraced slopes to the Negeb. The mountains of Sinai, 250 miles south of Beersheba, are regarded as the outliers of the Lebanon range. They rise abruptly in a closely compacted group from the desert level to a height corresponding very closely to the average elevation of the Lebanon district (7,000 feet). The highest peak in the group is over 9,000 feet, or about the elevation of Mount Hermon.

The general direction of the numerous ravines, or wadies, as they are generally termed, which diversify, and in some sections deeply corrugate, this range, is from east to west. On the eastern side they are short, direct, and deeply cleft: on the western they are comparatively long and shallow, and reach the plain by circuitous routes.

The **Eastern or Anti-Lebanon** range culminates in the snow-covered heights of Mount Hermon, 9,383 feet above the sea. The range as a whole presents a broader surface on its summit. It is not a backbone ridge, like the western section, but slopes gradually to the eastern desert, except in the region of its highest elevation north of Hermon. South of the Lebanon district its summit expands into an elevated plateau noted for its rich pasturage, and surpassingly beautiful stretches of fertile territory. The upper portion is the country of Bashan; the middle, of Gilead, and the southern of Moab. The general elevation of Bashan and Gilead is 2,000 feet. The plateau of Moab is something more than 3,000 feet above the level of the Mediterranean.

In this range there is no distinct break, or passage-way from east to west, as in the Lebanon section. As seen from the intervening depression, it is an unbroken wall, except where the numerous wadies and an occasional tributary of the Jordan, have cut their way down its face. The southern extremity of the Anti-Lebanon range is the traditional Mount Hor, an isolated cone-shaped peak near Petra in the land of Edom. It is about 250 miles from the base of Mount Hermon.

2. **The Lowland Sections.**—The longitudinal sections on either side of the Lebanon mountains are alike only in length and general direction. The one is a coast plain, the other a deep fissure, or mountain valley, which descends to a level far below the surface of the sea.

(1) **The Maritime Plain.**—The coast line, which bounds the Maritime plain on the west, is remarkable for its straight, almost unbroken sweep. It has no deep estuaries or gulfs and there is but one strongly marked indentation along its entire length. This is at Haifa, where the rocky promontory of Carmel juts out into the sea. Aside from this, at best a shallow and unsatisfactory roadstead, there are no natural har-

bors along the line of this coast. At times artificial harbors or extensions have been made at Askalon, Jaffa, Cæsarea and Beirut; but strictly speaking, it is with the single exception mentioned, a harborless coast. Because of this the sea which for centuries has surged against it, has been a barrier rather than a highway.

The promontory of Mount Carmel breaks the continuity of the Maritime plain, separating it into two parts very nearly equal in extent. The upper portion is a narrow strip about 140 miles long, varying from two to twelve miles in breadth. It is a well-watered region remarkable for its fertility; and in former times was cultivated with great care. It is broken into two parts by the "ladder of Tyre," a rocky ridge which projects into the sea about twenty-five miles beyond Mount Carmel. The section below the ladder of Tyre is usually designated as the Plain of Acre. The long strip above it is the famous Phœnician plain. The portion south of the Litany is sometimes designated as the Phœnician plain, but the appellation properly belongs to the lowland which borders the whole extent of the Lebanon district, or, in other words, from Tripoli to the ladder of Tyre.

Below Mount Carmel the plain contracts into narrow limits for a distance of eighteen miles. Beyond this point to the Wady el-Arish, or river of Egypt, the coast line inclines slightly toward the west, leaving a broad, undulating stretch of lowland, famous for its beauty and fertility, between the mountains and the sea.

The northern portion is known as the Plain of Sharon; the southern as the Plain of Philistia. The range of low hills, which lie between the plain of Philistia and the mountains is properly termed the Shephelah. It should be noted, however, that in Scripture the name is sometimes used in a wider sense, to include the whole of the southern portion of the plain. (Josh. xv. 33–40; also x. 40–41.)

(2) **The Depressed Region Between the Mountains.**—

The valley between the two great mountain ridges has been fitly characterized as a phenomenon unique on the earth's surface. Nowhere on its wrinkled face do we find a furrow so deep, or so remarkable for its length, directness and rapid descent. In length it stretches from Antioch to the Red Sea, a distance of 350 miles. Its general course is almost due south. Between the Lebanons it is a deep basin, eighty miles long and four to nine wide, rimmed in by mountain walls 5,000 or 6,000 feet high. This is the famous Cœle-Syria (Hollow Syria) region of ancient history. In the southern portion the valley sinks from sea level to a depression 1,300 feet below, in a distance of less than 100 miles. If we add to this the lower level of the Dead Sea basin the depression is 2,600 feet, or nearly one-half of a mile toward the centre of the earth.

Putting it in another form, "a man who stands at the margin of the Dead Sea is almost as far below the Ocean surface as the miner in the lowest depth of any mine."

In describing the lower portion of this great cleft, Dr. Smith says:

"There may be something on the surface of another planet to match the Jordan valley: there is nothing on this. No other part of our earth, uncovered by water, sinks to 300 feet below the level of the ocean. . . . In this trench there are the Jordan, a river nearly 100 miles long; two great lakes, respectively twelve and fifty-three miles in length; large tracts of arable country, especially about Gennesaret, Bethshan, and Jericho, regions which were once very populous, like the coasts of the lake of Galilee; and the sites of some famous towns—Tiberias, Jericho, and the cities of the Plain. Is it not true that on the earth there is nothing else like this deep, this colossal ditch?"[1]

Three of the great rivers of Syria flow through this longitudinal cleft in different sections of its course. The first, and most noted is the *Jordan*, which traverses its lower level to the Dead Sea. The second is the *Litany*, or Kasimiyeh. This river drains the southern portion of the Coele-Syria basin. It

[1] Smith Hist. Geog., p. 468.

rises near Baalbek and flows southward to a point near the headwaters of the Jordan, where it turns sharply to the west and passes through a deep gorge into the Mediterranean Sea.

The third is the *Orontes*, the largest and longest river of Syria. It rises on a watershed, near the source of the Litany, and flows due north through the great plain within and beyond the Lebanons, for a distance of about 130 miles. Then, like the Litany, it turns sharply to the west and pours its flood of waters into the sea.

These are some of the most striking features of the land, viewed as a whole. Within its limits it is scarcely possible to conceive of any variation, or peculiarity of land formation, that is not represented. Here may be found in close juxtaposition, sea and desert; alpine heights and phenomenal depths; fertile plains and barren wilderness; rolling downs and upland pastures; terraced slopes and deeply-scarred lava beds; park-like stretches and bleakest moorlands; valleys of Edenic beauty and dark cañons suggestive of the shadow of death; rivers and lakes; snow-clad heights and depths of tropical heat and luxuriance; ice-bound streams and steaming fountains; shady glens and interminable wadies; open glades and impenetrable jungles of cane and papyrus—in short every feature of nature's diversified handiwork, which is suggestive of the beautiful, the picturesque or the sublime.

Geological Structure.—The predominating element in the structure of the country throughout its length and breadth is *limestone*. In some sections of the mountain system it appears as a very hard, flinty formation: in others it is soft, porous, chalky, and lends itself easily to the agencies, both natural and artificial, which have made it preëminently a land of grottoes and caverns. This is especially true of the region of the Shephelah and the hill country of Judea.

In the lower strata of the mountains there are occasional outcroppings of an underlying bed of red sandstone, especially on the western side of the ridge of Lebanon.

Physical Features

Next to the limestone the most conspicuous surface formation is volcanic. It is found in dark colossal masses of corrugated lava or hard basaltic and greenstone rock, on the plateau of Bashan and Moab, and in some portions of the Jordan valley.

In the Negeb, and on the desert beyond, the primitive rocks (granite and gneiss) make their appearance in places. Farther south these form the basis of the Sinaitic group.

The alluvial deposits in the valleys and plains are notably rich in the elements which contribute to fertility of soil. Some of them have been cultivated continuously for centuries without any addition of fertilizers except such as nature has supplied.

CHAPTER II

NATURAL HISTORY

1. **CLIMATE and Productions.**—In Scripture allusions the climatic changes of the year are grouped under two divisions only,—summer and winter. The one is usually designated as the "dry season," the other as the "season of rain." The period of rainfall begins near the close of October, and usually ends in March and April. In the intervening months the sky is cloudless and there is no rainfall in any portion of the land.

As Dr. Robinson puts it, the winter period "is marked by *much* rain: the summer by *none at all.*" We must guard against the impression, however, which some have received from the terms used, that the wet season is a period of *continuous* rain.

On the contrary the intervals of sunshine are actually longer in this period than the days of rain. The rainy days usually come in groups, especially at the beginning and end of the season. In these intervals of "clear shining" the husbandmen have ample time to sow the seed and cultivate the growing crops. The plentiful showers which come at the beginning of the season prepare the hard, dry soil for the plowman and the sower. This is the time of the "former rain." "The latter rain," coming at the close of the winter period, is essential to the inbringing of the springtime and the ultimate maturing of the harvests. If either are withheld in their season the supply of food for man and beast is cut short. . . . The rapid transformation of the land, in connection with, and immediately following the latter rains is marvellous. Freshness and verdure take the place of desert-like fields and hillsides; innumerable flowers open out their delicately tinted petals to the warm sunlight; the fig tree putteth forth her green leaves and the vines with the tender grape give a pleasant smell. Then come the days of which the Sacred poets sing when the little hills rejoice on every side; "the pastures are clothed with flocks: the valleys also are covered over with corn; they shout for joy, they also sing." (Ps. lxv. 13.)

In this climate all the cereal and leguminous plants, commonly used for food, whether native or imported, grow readily and yield bountiful harvests. Dr. Post of Beirut claims that no other country in the world yields so large a number of food products as Palestine.

The harvest period varies greatly in the different localities of the land. In the depressed sections the barley ripens in April and the wheat in the latter part of May. In the elevated region the wheat is harvested in the month of June.

Between the time of the wheat harvest in the valley of the Jordan and on the plateau of Jerusalem is an interval of about four weeks, and yet the points are hardly twenty miles apart. The olive, the fig, and the vine yield a later harvest, and appear to be equally at home in all portions of the land.

In former times all the hills were terraced and the rich soil from the valleys was carried up to nourish the vineyards and olive yards, which were planted on these sunny slopes.

The Variations in Climate of the several sections of the country correspond with the variations, already noted, in its physical features.

The sea, the desert, and the extraordinary range of levels are the most potent influences in effecting these variations, which range from alpine cold to torrid heat. From the summits of Lebanon to the lower levels of the Jordan valley, all the zones and climes of the earth, with the forms and varieties of plant and animal life peculiar to each, are represented. As the Arabs have happily expressed it, "Lebanon bears winter on its head, spring on its shoulders, and autumn in its lap, while summer lies at its feet." In a single day's ride Canon

Tristram passed through *four* different zones from the region of the Scotch fir on the top of Mount Gilead to the region of the date palm in the plains of the Jordan. From the snow fields of Hermon to this lower level is less than 100 miles; and yet in the one perpetual winter abides: in the other there is never a trace of snow or hoar frost the year round.

"All the intermediate steps between these extremes," says Dr. Smith, "the eye can see at one sweep from Carmel—the sands and palms of the coast—the wheat fields of Esdraelon; the oaks and sycamores of Galilee; the pines, the peaks, the snows of Anti-Lebanon. How closely these differences lie to each other! Take a section of the country across Judea. With its palms and shadoofs the Philistine plain might be a part of the Egyptian Delta; but on the hills of the Shephelah which overlook it, you are in the scenery of Southern Europe: the Judean moors which overlook them are like the barer uplands of Central Germany; the shepherds wear sheepskin cloaks and live under stone roofs—sometimes the snow lies deep; a few miles further east and you are down in the desert among the Bedouin, with their tents of hair and their cotton clothing; a few miles farther still and you drop down to torrid heat in the Jordan valley; a few miles beyond that and you rise to the plateau of the Belka, where the Arabs say the cold is always at home. Yet from Philistia to the Belka is scarcely seventy miles."[1]

(2) **Flora and Fauna.**—Canon Tristram, whose name stands first among the recognized authorities on the Natural History of Palestine, describes the flora and fauna of four distinct zones in which affinities are traced with many genera and species of *world-wide* distribution. "There are the fauna and flora, first of all on the coast and highlands, that are the most familiar and the most recent. Then there is the flora and fauna of the desert, taking southern Judea and the east side of the Jordan; then there is the flora and fauna of the Jordan valley; and fourthly just a remnant left of the Alpine flora and fauna on the top of Hermon and Lebanon." In the same connection he states the fact that out of a collection of 160 plants, taken from a little valley on the southwest corner of the Dead

[1] Historical Geography, p. 56.

Natural History

Sea basin, 135 were exclusively African. For the most part their kind are only to be found in Nubia or equatorial Africa. In Egypt the Papyrus has long been extinct; but at Lake Huleh, on the upper Jordan valley, a dense mass of it seven miles in extent may still be seen. Affinities as clearly marked have been traced between the fish of the sea of Galilee and the fish found in the Zambezi, and in the Lakes Nyanza and Tanganyika at the head waters of the Nile: also between the birds and wild animals of the Lebanon and kindred species, found on the Appenines, the Alps and the Himalayas.

The Flora of Solomon, which included in its range all the plants of his day, from the Cedar of Lebanon even to the hyssop that springeth out of the wall, has been studied anew in the light of modern attainments; and within the limits of this restricted Syrian territory, with that of Sinai, 126 Orders, 850 Genera and 3,416 Species have been catalogued and described.

The Trees mentioned in the Scriptures, with scarce an exception, are still to be found in some portion of the country. Among these may be named the lofty Cedars of Lebanon, the Oaks of Bashan and Gilead—with other Oaks of different species and localities—the Fir, Cypress, Terebinth, Olive, Fig, Almond, Mulberry, Myrtle, Citron, Acacia (Shittim wood), Pomegranate, Prickly pear, Tamarisk, Oleander, Apricot, Orange, Lime and Palm.

Most noteworthy among the wild animals that still remain, are the Roebuck or Gazelle (several species), Fallow Deer, wild Goat, wild Cat, Fox, Jackal, Wolf, Hyena, Lynx, Leopard, Otter, Badger, Coney, Hare, Buffalo, brown Bear, and wild Boar. Some of the above are rare, but have occasionally been seen. The Auroch, translated Unicorn, in our version, and the Lion have become extinct; but their bones have been found in the caves of Lebanon and in the valley of the Jordan. The feat of Benaiah, who went down and slew a lion in the midst of a pit, or cistern, in the time of snow is referred to by

Dr. Smith as an illustration of the remarkable variation of climate within distances but a few miles apart. To this he adds the statement, "The beast had strayed up the Judean hills from Jordan and had been caught in a sudden snow-storm. Where else than in Palestine could *lions and snow* thus come together?"[1]

With respect to the Auroch or Bison (Unicorn) it is interesting to know that the equivalent of the original word Re'em has been found on Assyrian sculpture written over a wild Ox. This settles the question as to the dual number of its horns in a very summary manner.

"This animal," says Tristram, "is alluded to in the earlier books of the Bible, but *not after the time of David.* Except in one poetical passage the word Re'em never occurs again. Coincidentally with this, in the tablets in Nineveh describing the hunting feats of the kings of the earlier dynasty, the grand game that the king hunted was the Aurochs, the Re'em, but in the later Assyrian Empire, from just about the time of David, from about 1000 B. C., we do not find in any Assyrian or Babylonian tablet or sculpture a single trace of the Re'em, or wild Ox. Population had increased and it had become extinct."[2]

These with other interesting facts may be found in fuller statement in Tristram's Flora and Fauna of Palestine, published by the Exploration Fund, Tristram's Natural History of the Bible, Conder's Hand Book to the Bible, and the Appendices to recent issues of the Oxford and Teachers' Bibles.

A complete Flora of the Holy Land and Sinai excepting the lower forms of cryptogams has recently been issued by the Mission Press at Beirut, Syria. The author, the Rev. G. E. Post, M. D., D. D., has long been a resident of Syria, and aside from his eminent qualifications, has enjoyed exceptional opportunities for the prosecution of this study. It is a standard work of its class and is recommended as an invaluable aid to those who wish to study the plant life of the Holy Land.

For fuller information on the "Geology of Palestine" the student is re-

[1] The City and the Land, p. 64.
[2] The City and the Land, p. 75., P. E. F.

Natural History

ferred to Professor Hull's recent work, published by the Exploration Fund; also to Dr. Robinson's Physical Geography, pages 311 and 372. A very satisfactory article on the "Climate" may be found in the same volume, page 288. Fuller and later information is given in the Quarterly Statements of the Palestine Exploration Fund.

CHAPTER III

EARLY INHABITANTS OF THE LAND

IN the Old Testament the mixed population, which occupied the country before the period of the conquest, is generally classified under six or seven distinct tribal names. In three passages (Deut. vii. 1; Josh. xxiv. 11, and iii. 10) seven tribes or nations are mentioned by name. In nine passages a list of six of the names, on the above mentioned list are given. These are the Canaanites, Hittites, Amorites, Hivites, Perizzites, and Jebusites. (Ex. iii. 8, 17, xxxiii. 2, xxxiv. 11; Deut. xx. 17; Josh. ix. 1, xi. 3, xii. 8; Judges iii. 5.) In these lists the Gergashite tribe is uniformly omitted. Of its location and characteristics we have no definite information.

Recent research has thrown some additional light upon the history of the six nations—mentioned in all the lists—and their position in general has been definitely located.

1. **The Canaanites.**—The name when used in its narrower sense was descriptive of the people who dwelt by the sea and by the coast of Jordan. (Gen. x. 19; Num. xiii. 29; Josh. xi. 3.)

(1) THE PHILISTINES, who occupied the southern part of the lowland region of Palestine came originally from Caphtor, or greater Phœnicia, in lower Egypt. Professor Sayce makes the assertion, based upon careful study of the Egyptian monuments, that some of them were planted on the southern frontier of Palestine by the Egyptians after their conquest of Canaan, in order to garrison the newly acquired territory. In the book of Deuteronomy (ii. 23) we are told that they conquered the Avims and dwelt in their land. In the time of the Patriarchs they appear as a pastoral people occupying the country west of

Early Inhabitants of the Land

Beersheba and Kadesh, known as the kingdom of Gerar. At a later period they held possession of the coastland from the Wady el-Arish to the border of the plain of Sharon and had acquired a high reputation as a powerful and warlike nation. For centuries they were the most formidable and aggressive foes of the Hebrew nation. Their chief cities were Gath, Ashkelon, Ashdod, Gaza and Ekron, on the Philistine plain. The name Palestine, which was originally the Greek equivalent for the land of the Philistines, was afterward used by Greek and Roman writers to cover the whole country of Israel on both sides of the Jordan. In this sense also we use the word at the present time.

(2) THE PHŒNICIANS, who occupied the lowland region north of Mount Carmel, were the original Canaanite population of the country. The exact date of their arrival on the shores of the Mediterranean is not known, but as early as the period of Hyksos rule in Egypt they had established a flourishing colony at the mouth of the Nile, and were then known as the traders, or middle-men of the commercial world. Their oldest city Sidon still bears the name of the firstborn of Canaan. In the Scriptures they are sometimes designated as Zidonians. There is a variety of evidence from reliable sources in confirmation of their own assertion, that they came originally from the lower valley of the Euphrates. "The greater number of modern critics," says Renan, "admit as demonstrated that the primitive abode of the Phœnicians must be placed on the lower Euphrates, in the centre of the great commercial and maritime establishments of the Persian Gulf, conformably to the unanimous witness of antiquity." Throughout the Bible it is assumed that the language of the Canaanites was identical with the language of the Hebrews, and this may readily be accounted for on the ground that originally the progenitors of both nationalities came from the same location on the Persian Gulf. While the Canaanites were the descendants of Ham they had, through early and close associations with the Semites

of this region, many of their characteristics and spoke a language which was practically the same. "The numerous inscriptions on tombs, tablets, etc., amounting in all to several hundreds established the fact that this language (the Phœnician) is almost as closely allied to the Hebrew as German to Dutch or Portuguese to Spanish."[1] It was in Egypt but not in the land of Canaan that "Israel heard a language which he understood not."[2] The name Canaan was originally applied only to the land of Phœnicia, but afterward it was given to the whole of Western Palestine. In this respect its history was similar to that of the term Palestine. It is one of the oldest Biblical appellations of the Promised Land, and is found on Phœnician coins, and on the monuments of Egypt and Assyria, as well as in the Bible.

"There was no wider designation, says Prof. McCurdy, for the whole country than Canaan: and after the Hebrews occupied it the name Israel took its place, though not to the exclusion of the old appellation." The common designation of the country east of the Jordan in early times was "Gilead" or the "Land of Gilead."

The Phœnicians were the traders of the commercial world for almost a thousand years. Before the days of Homer they had become famous for their skill in artistic and ornamental handiwork, and with good reason were chosen by Solomon to execute the difficult and painstaking designs which David had planned under Divine guidance for the erection and ornamenta-

[1] Rawlinson.

[2] "'The language of Canaan' as Isaiah (xix. 18) calls it, was what we term Hebrew. The fact was first made clear by the Phœnician inscriptions; the cuneiform tablets found at Tell el-Amarna in Upper Egypt have carried back the history of the language to *Pre-Mosaic* days. A large part of the tablets consists of letters in the Babylonian language from the Egyptian governors and vassal kings of Canaan, and in some of them the *Canaanitish Equivalents* are given of Babylonian words. In all such cases we might substitute Hebrew for Canaanitish." (Professor Sayce in Homiletical Review, March, 1897, p. 202.)

tion of the Temple. In shipbuilding and navigation, also, they excelled all the nations of antiquity. The crowning honor attributed to the Phœnicians was the invention of the alphabet. Recent research has shorn this tradition of a part of its significance, and points to an earlier system from which the Phœnician alphabet was derived, but it is safe to say that the system which they introduced is the mother of our modern alphabets. "Phœnicia," says Sir Henry Rawlinson, "is rather to be praised for curtailing the excessive redundance of the primitive methods of expressing speech in a written form than for any actual invention or discovery." From whatever source derived it is now certain that a uniform alphabetical system, with slight modifications was used by the Phœnicians, the Jews, the Samaritans, and the Moabites at an early date. In its degenerate form the Phœnician religion was the most sensual, debasing and cruel in character and worship, of all the religions of the East. Baal and Ashtaroth, the synonyms for long ages of cruelty and impurity, were the principal deities, and the influence of their worship was degrading and demoralizing in the extreme.

With respect to location the Phœnicians were sometimes separately designated as Zidonians, Giblites, Arkites and Hamathites.

THE CANAANITES OF THE JORDAN VALLEY dwelt in five cities of "the plain" or "circle" of the Jordan. This, in connection with other descriptions, makes it certain that the district in which these cities were located was at the northern end of the Dead Sea. It was noted for its tropical luxuriance, suggestive of the land of Egypt or the primeval garden of the Lord; but its inhabitants were so grossly immoral and depraved that they were destroyed in the midst of their possessions, by a swift judgment of the Almighty, during the period of Abraham's sojourn in the land.

2. **The Hittites.**—This nation, which took its name from Heth the second son of Canaan, is frequently mentioned in the

Bible in connection with the Amorites. They were concentrated principally in Syria, but their settlements extended as far southward as Hebron. Carchemish on the Euphrates and Kadesh on the Orontes were the chief cities, or garrison towns, of the Hittites. Their geographical position in general was indicated, in the time of Joshua as being "From the wilderness and this Lebanon, even unto the great river the Euphrates, all the land of the Hittites." (Josh i. 4.)

A parallel statement from an inscription of Tiglath Pileser I. reads, "From the border of the distant mountains to the fords of the Euphrates, the land of the Hittites and the upper sea of the setting sun." This powerful nation of the north began to extend its conquests southward a short while before the birth of Abraham, and before the period of the conquest it was recognized as the dominant nation of Syria. So far from being a petty tribe among the scattered tribes of Syria, as some have asserted the fact has been established beyond controversy, from Egyptian and Assyrian annals, as well as from the Scriptures, that the Hittites were one of the great nations of the East. For centuries they and their allies held their ground in the northern part of Syria against the might of Egypt, Babylonia and Assyria: and from the days of Abraham until the end of the northern kingdom they were the most active and aggressive of the nations which came into close contact with Israel. Their chief cities were destroyed and their power and influence finally broken 717 years before the Christian era by Sargon the successor of Shalmanezer. So complete was this overthrow that their very name was dropped from the records of history, until the revelations of recent times restored it to its old time place and prestige. The Scripture references to the Hittites as occupants of the mountain strongholds of the land of Canaan are numerous from the days of Abraham and onward, especially in the periods connected with the history of Moses and Joshua. In the report of the spies it is distinctly stated that "the Hittites, and the Jebusites and the Amorites dwell in the mountains." (Num. xiii. 29.) In the commission given to Moses (Ex. iii. 18) the promise made to the Patriarchs was renewed to bring their children " unto the place of the Canaanites and the Hittites and the Amorites and the Perizzites, and the Hivites and the Jebusites."

This narrative, says Dr. Wright, stands in topographical order as viewed from the Egyptian standpoint. The traveller northward first reached Canaan, next the Hittite colony in the neighborhood of Hebron, and lastly the Jebusites who dwelt in Jerusalem.

There is abundant evidence that the Hittites were a literary people and had a written language, but no definite clue has yet been found to the interpretation of their writings.

3. **The Amorites.**—It seems from the Biblical statements that the Amorites preceded the Hittites in the occupation of the mountain regions of Palestine and Syria.

One of the earliest names given to this country, as we now know from the cuneiform inscriptions, was "the land of the Amorites." This is also one of the names by which it was known distinctively in the days of the Patriarchs. (Gen. xv. 16, xlviii. 22.)

It is plain from the Scripture narrative as a whole, that in the period immediately preceding the conquest the Amorites had possession of the greater part of the mountain regions east and west of the Jordan valley. On the western side they shared certain portions in common with, or alongside of other mountain tribes as confederates: but in the east they had control of the whole country from the slopes of Hermon to the river Arnon. This region was governed by Og and Sihon, who are called the two kings of the Amorites. (Deut. iii. 8; Josh. ix. 10.) With this nation Israel first of all came into conflict, in the long continued struggle for possession of the promised land.

It is said, also, that they faced "the mountain of the Amorites" when they looked over the border of the land nearly forty years before. (Deut. i. 19, 20.)

One of the Amorite strongholds in the Shephelah was the city of Lachish (Tel el Hesy), where recent excavations have shown that it was the lowest as well as the strongest in its defences of all the towns in this mound of long buried cities and civilizations.

4. **The Hivites.**—The tribe or nationality to which this name was given occupied a limited district north of Jerusalem. They had settlements also farther in the north under Hermon, and by the "entering in of Hamath." (Josh. xi. 3; Judges iii. 3.) Of the latter very little is known, but the Hivites of the southern district are frequently mentioned in the Scripture narrative. They dwelt in a group of fortified towns (fenced cities) which were leagued together for mutual support and defence. So far as known the chief cities belonging to this league were Beeroth, Gibeon, Chephirah, Kirjath-Jearim and Shechem. "Their cities were ruled by elders and they do not appear to have had kings; but, as Ewald suggests, to have adopted thus early a pure republican constitution not unlike the German free-cities." (Henderson's Geography, p. 47.)

5. **The Perizzites** dwelt in the plains of lower Galilee and in the foot hills which bordered the Sharon plain. It is impossible, says Dr. Henderson, to decide from all that is said, whether they were a different race from the Canaanites, or merely a separate class, as the peasantry of the time.[1]

6. **The Jebusites.**—This tribe is mentioned only in connection with Jerusalem and its environs. In the Tell el-Amarna tablets a correspondence is preserved between the Governor of Jerusalem and the Ruler of Egypt in which both the name and the antiquity of the City are attested beyond all question. In these tablets, which antedate the conquest of Joshua, the name appears as Uru-Salim, the city of Salim, the god of peace. It was at this early date a strongly fortified city, and its Ruler for some reason seemed to have preëminence over the districts around it. One of these Rulers, "Ebed-Tob,"

[1] Henderson's Pal., p. 47.

Early Inhabitants of the Land

declares to the Pharoah that he was not like the other governors of Canaan, that he had not inherited his royal dignity from his father or his mother, but had been appointed to it by "the mighty king." The "mighty king" is contrasted with the "great king of Egypt, and must have been an old title of the god of Jerusalem."[1] It is a significant fact that this Ruler claims the title of priest-king, a title which in Genesis is given to Melchizedek, *king of Salem*. When the lower part of the city was conquered by Joshua and burned with fire, the citadel on the higher ground remained in the hands of the Jebusites. They were not driven out of it until the time of David. (Josh. xv. 63; 1 Chron. xi. 4–7.) From Ornan, or Araunah, the Jebusite, at a later date, King David purchased the threshing floor on Mount Moriah, where he set up an altar to the Lord; and where afterward the temple was erected by Solomon.

There are incidental references in the Pentateuch to certain primitive or aboriginal tribes, such as the Avim or Geshuri, the Horites, or cave dwellers of Edom, the Rephaim or giant race of Bashan, and their kinsfolk the Anakims of the south: but aside from these brief statements, little is known concerning them. They were probably merged into the clans, or confederacies, of the later inhabitants, before the conquest.

[1] See Article by Prof. Sayce in Homiletic Review, March, 1897, p. 205.

CHAPTER IV

TRIBAL AND POLITICAL DIVISIONS

1. **THE Division of the Tribes.**—As a result of the careful surveys which have been made in Palestine, the old boundary lines between the tribes of Israel can now be followed with a degree of accuracy and precision of detail, which to say the least, is very remarkable.

This is owing mainly to the fact that the division was made to conform, as far as possible, to the natural features of the country. It implies more than a general knowledge of its configuration and adaptations. It must have been the outcome of an original survey as careful and accurate, *in its day*, as that of the Palestine Exploration Survey itself. The actual recovery of the old lines by retracing the natural features of the country, which unquestionably have remained without change; and the identification of long forgotten sites by names, which, with slight changes, have clung to them since the days of Joshua, furnish a strong incidental proof in support of the claim that the record which defines these boundaries with such painstaking fidelity, was written at the time when this allotment,—itself a matter of history,—was actually made.

It seems incredible that it should have been formulated in its present shape, or that it should have been regarded of so much value as to occupy the space of *ten* chapters of the book of Joshua, if it had been written at any period after the displacement or separation of the tribes. It is evident, also, that the confusion of lines by the events of subsequent history, and the formation of new political divisions, would make the task of preparing such a record a work of *superhuman* wisdom, as wonderful in its reach backward as the sweep of the inspired

Tribal and Political Divisions

prophets' vision forward into the future. "All these facts," says Major Conder, "serve assuredly to prove that the geography of the Book of Joshua is no idle tale, but a real division of a real country, capable of the most minute critical examination by aid of the most scientific modern research."[1] Those who desire to follow the lines of these tribal divisions in specific detail will find much valuable information in Robinson's Later Researches, Vol. II., Henderson's Palestine, pp. 72, 82; and the recent publications of the Palestine Exploration Fund. For the purpose we have in view it will be sufficient to present a brief statement of the relative position of the several tribes.

On the western side of the Jordan the first allotment of territory was made to the **Tribe of Judah**. It included the whole country south of Jerusalem from the Mediterranean to the Dead Sea. Its area as originally outlined was more than 2,000 square miles. The Wilderness, the central mountain district, the Shephelah, the plain of Philistia, and the Negeb, or south country,—were all included within its limits. The southern portion was afterward assigned to the tribe of Simeon.

The boundaries of this grant are not accurately defined, but it is evident from the list of towns belonging to Simeon that the region about Beersheba and all of the district south of it to Kadesh Barnea were included. The reason for this allotment is given in Joshua xix. 9. "For the part of the children of Judah was too much for them, therefore the children of Simeon had their inheritance within the inheritance of them."

The inheritance of Judah was curtailed, also by the failure of the people to drive the Philistines from their strongholds on the coast plain. At times it was occupied as a whole, or in part, but during the greater portion of the period of Israel's national life it was in the hands of the Philistines or other alien nationalities.

The Portion of Benjamin extended northward from the border line of Judah to Baal Hazor, a conspicuous mountain about

[1] Primer of Bible Geography, p. 97.

twelve miles from Jerusalem. The eastern boundary for five or six miles was the Jordan. Thence it extended to Beth-Horon and Kirjath-Jearim, on the western slope of the mountain ridge,—a distance of thirty miles.

Its area is estimated at about 400 miles. Except a cross section of the Jordan plain, the inheritance of Benjamin was rugged and mountainous. In the early days of the occupation it included the city of Jerusalem, but after adjustments gave to Judah a joint possession in the Holy places within its walls. The two noted passes, Michmash on the east, and Beth-Horon on the west, gave to this warlike tribe the control of the whole mountain region and made it the natural defender of Jerusalem on the north. On the heights of Benjamin some of the most stirring events in Old Testament history took place, and here may still be seen on slope and summit of every shapely hill the ruins of terraced vineyards and fenced cities.

"On the northwest border of Benjamin, Ataroth Adar (Ed Darieh), and Archi (Ain Arik) have been recovered in exact accordance with the words of the Bible (Joshua xviii. 13), which define the position of the former with the greatest minuteness."[1]

The territory of Dan adjoined Benjamin on the west. It included the foot-hills and a section of the coast plain from Ekron to the river Aujeh north of Jaffa. It was never fully occupied by this tribe and was held for a time as a fortified camp ("the Camp of Dan") rather than a permanent possession. In the period of the Judges a large part of the tribe removed from this to a new location at the head waters of the Jordan. Some of the towns abandoned by Benjamin were afterward occupied by the tribe of Judah.

The tribe of Joseph—usually designated as Ephraim and Manasseh (the half tribe of Manasseh) was given a large and exceptionally rich portion of territory north of the inheritance of Benjamin and Dan. It extended westward from the Jordan

[1] Thirty Years' Work, p. 115.

Tribal and Political Divisions

to the Sea and northward to the borders of the plains of Acre and Esdraelon. The boundary between Ephraim and Manasseh is not clearly defined except on the coast plain where it is defined as the course of the brook Kanah. This brook (Wady Kanah) flows westward from the southern slope of Mount Gerizim and its course is now for the first time correctly laid down on the map of the Palestine Exploration Survey. Shechem, and other towns in its vicinity, were included in the original allotment which fell to Ephraim, but the hill of Samaria, on which in later times the capital of the ten tribes was built, seems to have fallen within the borders of Manasseh. It should be noted, however, that the whole of the mountain region north of the border of Benjamin to the break made by the plain of Esdraelon, was designated collectively as "Mount Ephraim," or the mountains of Ephraim, in the period preceding the division of the kingdom. The portion of the range south of the north border of Benjamin was called the "Mountain" or "Hill country" of Judah.

To the tribe of Issachar was given nearly the whole of the rich plain of Esdraelon. Tabor and the hills of Galilee formed the line of its northern boundary. Its extreme southern limit was En-gannim (Jenin) on the edge of the great plain. For some reason, not explained, the strong fortress town of Bethshan, at the eastward end of the valley of Jezreel was not included in its limits, but was assigned to Manasseh. (Judges i. 27.)

The territory assigned to Zebulon was northeast of the allotment of Issachar. The line between these tribes ran along the base of the hills of Galilee, which border the Esdraelon plain on the north, to the Kishon river. Thence it followed its course along the base of Mount Carmel to the Sea. Its limit on the east seems to have been in the neighborhood of Mount Tabor, but according to Josephus it afterward extended to the lake of Galilee. Its western border or "outgoing" was on the plain of Acre. The valley of Jephtah-el, on the northwest, now known as Wady el-Kurn is mentioned as one of the landmarks between Zebulon and Ashur: and another is given at Hamathon (Kefr' Anān) on the northeast, which Henderson locates eleven miles north of Rimmon. Without entering into detail these points indicate that the line ran north of the rich plain of Buttauf through the Wady el-Kurn to a point at, or near the mouth of the Belus river, to the Sea.[1]

The inheritance of the tribes of Ashur and Naphtali extended northward of this territory side by side to the northern limit of occupation of the land of Israel.

Ashur held the portion next the sea while **Naphtali** possessed the hill country to the Jordan valley, including the western border—according to the original allotment—of the sea of Galilee. Dr. Henderson thinks it possible that the actual possessions of Ashur were extended much farther north than the Litany, inasmuch as Joab went as far as Riblah in taking the census of Israel. It is certain, also, that the allotment extended north of Sidon, which is twenty miles beyond the city of Tyre. (Joshua xix. 28–39.) Ijon, in the Merj 'Ajûn, is the farthest town northward which has yet been identified in the inheritance of Naphtali.

On this side of the Jordan *Kedesh of Naphtali*, *Shechem*, and *Hebron* were designated as **Cities of Refuge.**

The territory conquered by the Israelites on the eastern side of the Jordan was divided between **the tribes of Reuben and Gad, and the half tribe of Manasseh.** This division was made along the lines suggested by the natural divisions of the country.

To Reuben was assigned the northern portion of the land of *Moab:* **to Gad** the land of *Gilead*, extending to the river

---

[1] " From some expressions it would seem as if the territory of Ashur, as at first assigned, went south of Carmel: but if so some of the land in the first instance given to Ashur must have been ceded to Zebulon, which certainly reached the Bay of Acre, and possessed the north slope of Carmel."—Henderson's Palestine, p. 101.

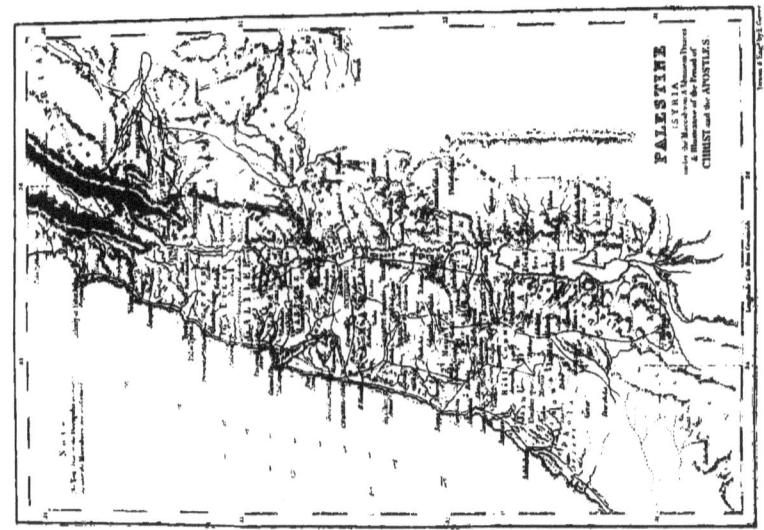

Tribal and Political Divisions 41

Jarmuk : and to the **half tribe of Manasseh** the land of *Bashan*.

The Cities of Refuge on this side of the river were *Golan* in Bashan ; *Ramoth* in Gilead, and *Bezar* or *Bosor* in Moab.

2. **Division of the Kingdoms.**—In the division of the Kingdom after the death of Solomon the line of separation between Israel and Judah was on, or very near the old division line between Benjamin and Ephraim. There were periods in the history of the rival kingdoms when slight changes were made, Bethel being at first within the northern : and in later times within the limits of the southern kingdom. Hence, as Major Conder suggests, the name of Mount Ephraim sometimes applies in the Bible to country south of the border of the tribe of Ephraim as laid down in the Book of Joshua.

All the territory east of the Jordan was included in the kingdom of Israel.

3. **Political Divisions in the time of Christ.**—In the period of Roman rule the entire country south of Lebanon was divided into three Provinces, viz : Galilee, Samaria and Judea. Galilee was north of Mount Carmel, and the southern border of the plain of Esdraelon. Samaria extended southward of this province to the boundary line which separated Ephraim from Manasseh. Conder defines its limits in general terms, as "the land of Manasseh west of Jordan." On the coast plain the brook Kanah—as we have seen—was the dividing line.

The country south of Samaria, from the Mediterranean to the Jordan valley and the Dead Sea retained the old name of Judah, or Judea. Its southern portion was sometimes regarded as a separate province under the name of **Idumea**. The Idumeans were Edomites who took possession of this region during the time of the captivity. They were conquered during the period of the Maccabees, but were permitted to remain in the land on condition of receiving the right of circumcision. The Herodian family were of Idumean descent.

In the Roman period Phœnicia included the whole of the coast plain from Tripoli to Achzib, ten miles north of Acre.

The trans-Jordanic country south of the Hieromax, or Yarmuk river was usually designated as **Perea**—the region beyond. In a narrower sense this term was sometimes limited to the land of Gilead.

After the captivity, **Bashan,** the northern province of Eastern Palestine, was divided into five districts, known as *Gaulanitis, Auranitis, Iturea, Trachonitis,* and *Batanea.*

Gaulanitis, corresponding with the modern Jaulan, covered all of the western slope of the mountains, and the more rugged part of the plateau, south of Lake Hulch.

Auranitis, the Hauran in its restricted sense, included the level plateau east of Gaulanitis.

Iturea, the modern district of Jedur, was in the northern part of the province, above the districts of Gaulanitis and Auranitis.

Trachonitis was the lava district east of the Hauran, and **Batanea** was probably a strip of border-land to the southeast, which included the cluster of mountains now called Jebel Hauran.

The region of Decapolis, mentioned in the New Testament (Matt. iv. 25 ; Mark vii. 21) was southeast of the Lake of Galilee. The ten cities, which gave the name to the district, were all east of the Jordan, except Bethshan, or Scythopolis as it was termed after the captivity. This was a convenient grouping of towns but not a geographical division of territory.

Before the advent of Christ the Jews were scattered through all the provinces of the country. Everywhere they came into close contact with Greek and Roman civilization, but they remained separate and distinct in their religious life and national characteristics. " Before the Roman occupation under Pompey all Gilead and Bashan with Moab were again Israel's and the Greek cities were Judaized."[1]

West of the Jordan the influence of the Jews was paramount also, except in Samaria, which was regarded as a heathen or semi-heathen province.

[1] Smith's Hist. Geog., p. 590.

CHAPTER V

HIGHWAYS AND CARAVAN ROUTES

THE Land of Israel was brought into communication with the outside world mainly through *four* great highways,—

1. The oldest and most notable of these international routes was the great thoroughfare along the Mediterranean coast, connecting Egypt with Phœnicia, Syria, and the empires of the East. At the northern end of the Lebanon range it passed through the natural gateway, called the entrance of Hamath, into the Orontes valley and thence to the Euphrates.

2. The caravan route from Tyre and Sidon across Lebanon to Damascus, Palmyra and the Euphrates.

3. The route from Gaza by way of Petra and Duma to the Persian Gulf.

4. A parallel to the coast road, on the eastern border of the land, from Damascus to the Ælanitic Gulf and the peninsula of Arabia. In general direction this corresponded to the modern Haj or pilgrimage route to Mecca. Over the northern part of this route, most probably, the patriarch Abraham and his grandson Jacob, journeyed from Damascus to the crossroads, or wadies, which led to the upper fords of the Jordan.

The coast road was the favorite military route between the Nile and Euphrates valleys. For about 5,000 years this has been the well-trodden " war path of the nations." [1]

On a bold promontory, which juts out almost to the sea at Dog river, ten miles north of Beirut, there are *nine* tablets covered with inscriptions deeply carved on the rocks.

---

[1] This route, which was obstructed by several spurs from the mountains, extending across the plain to the sea, was made passible for armies by the engineering skill of the Egyptians and Assyrians. " The steps or zigzags which surmounted these natural obstacles were known to the Greeks and Romans under the name of Climaces." See Rawlinson's Phœnicia, p. 7.

ASCENT OF PASS OF NAHR EL KELB
FROM NORTH, WITH ONE OF THE TABLETS

Highways and Caravan Routes

After a silence of many centuries these tablets have at last declared their secrets, and they prove to be the boastful records of some of the greatest of the leaders of the Egyptian and Assyrian hosts, who took this method of celebrating the passage of the narrow, and apparently impassible way. Three of the tablets bear the name of Rameses II. On the others are the names of Tiglath Pileser, Asur-banipul, Shalmanezer, Sennacherib and Essar Hadden.

"Among the striking features of this pass are the old road beds cut in the solid limestone rock by successive monarchs of antiquity. The foot holes of the horses and the grooves worn by the chariot wheels of armies are still distinctly traceable in the rock. Here passed Pul, Tiglath Pileser, Sesostris, Shalmanezer, Sargon, and Sennacherib; here swarmed the hosts of Alexander the Great en route for Egypt; here passed the Romans, the later Greeks, the Arabs, the Turks, and the Crusaders; and here pass constantly the traders and travellers of the East."[1]

The main arterial route of travel and commerce between the east and west for centuries has been the section of the coast road between Gaza and Mount Carmel. While for some reason, probably for greater security from attack, its continuation north of Carmel was traversed by most of the great military leaders of ancient times, there was a deflection from the main line eastward by way of the valley of Dothan, and the Esdraelon plain, which was a favorite route for those bent on commerce or ordinary travel. This led to the principal fords of the Jordan near Bethshan and thence along the uplands of Bashan to Damascus and the East. Over this great trade route the caravan of Ishmaelites, to whom Joseph was sold as a slave, "came from Gilead, with their camels, bearing spicery and balm and myrrh, going to carry it down to Egypt." (Gen. xxxvii. 25.)

The main routes of a local character within the limits of Israel's possession were:

1. From Jerusalem to Jaffa by way of Beth-Horon and Lydda.

[1] Article in Picturesque Pal., by Dr. H. W. Jessup, Vol. II., p. 31.

2. From Jerusalem to Bethlehem and Hebron; thence westward to Gaza and eastward to the desert.

3. From Jerusalem to Jericho and thence across the Jordan into Perea. This route recrossed the river at one of the upper fords into Galilee. An alternate route was up the west bank of the Jordan to Bethshan.

4. From Jerusalem to Galilee over the patriarchal highway, which for the most part led along the summit of the mountains of Benjamin and Ephraim. A continuation of this road passed on to Damascus by way of Capernaum, the Hulah basin, and the eastern slope of Mount Hermon.

5. From Acre to the trans-Jordanic country across the plain of Esdraelon and down the valley of Jezreel.

6. From Hamath in the valley of the Orontes to Baalbec and the head waters of the Jordan. In the Bible the first intimation with respect to the construction of public roadways is given in connection with the establishment of the Cities of Refuge. (Deut. xix. 3.) The rock beds of the paved roads of the Roman period may still be seen in many places, especially in some sections of Eastern Palestine.

The use of chariots in war, and for display in the time of the Kings, implies the construction of suitable roads, but these were usually constructed on the plains or in the valleys leading up to the rugged highland country. In general the roads over the mountain districts were pathways, or trails.

At suitable distances on all the roads Khans were maintained for the accommodation of the travelling caravans. When once established their location was seldom, if ever, changed. In many instances modern travellers have found a resting place for themselves and their horses, or camels in caravansaries, whose names and histories antedate the Christian era. While these rude structures have doubtless changed and given way to others many times, the sites still remain; and the names handed down from generation to generation attest the use to which they have been originally set apart.

CHAPTER VI

PRESENT CONDITION OF THE LAND

THERE is much in the general aspect of the country at the present time, suggestive of change, desolation and decay. Palestine is preëminently a land of ruins.

The terraced slopes, which were once cultivated with extreme care, have been broken down; the rich soil has been washed away, and naught remains except the bare shelving rock swept smooth with wind and rain. In many places the highways of former times have shrunken into camel paths or mountain trails. All over the land the scattered debris of towns and villages crown the heights or lie half hidden in the luxuriant overgrowth of the valleys and plains; while beneath the soil in hundreds of tells or artificial mounds, lie the ruins of superimposed cities, some of which contain the relics of former civilizations as old as the days of the Patriarchs.

A few of the towns and ancient cities are now inhabited: but over the greater part of the country nomads wander as in the time of Abraham with flocks and herds. Except where the flags of European nations extend their kindly protection, the roving bands of Bedouins make life and property insecure.

In view of all these things, it is scarcely possible to resist the impression that a series of judgments, such as were long ago foretold by the prophets of Israel, have overtaken the land and its inhabitants.

There are some things, however, that remain unchanged, amid these changes and desolations. The geographical features we have been considering have not changed in form or general characteristics since it was given to the people of Israel for a possession. The rugged framework of the land: its towering mountains and deeply grooved valleys present the same aspect to-day as when Moses looked down upon them from the summit of Mount Nebo. While the destruction of the forests and the breaking down of terraces and aqueducts have in many places turned the fruitful field into a wilderness, the country as a whole is still subject to the conditions which governed its climatic changes in the period of the Sacred writers. Now as in the past the early and latter rains come in their appointed seasons: the heavy dews give moisture to field and hillside; wonderful transformations follow the time of clear shining after the rain " and the corn and wine and oil have not ceased from the land." " The true curses of the country," says Major Conder, "are injustice and ignorance; and the decay of population has led to the shrinking of agriculture and to the spread of briars, thorns, and rough brushwood where once were wine-presses and vineyard towers."[1]

Within the last quarter of this century, and especially within the last decade, there have been important changes in the opposite direction, that point unmistakably to a restoration of long lost privileges. These consist mainly in the planting of prosperous colonies in various parts of the country; and the opening of new carriage roads and railroads to important centres both east and west of the Jordan. At the present time Jaffa and Jerusalem are connected by a railroad fifty-four miles in length, which was opened for travel and traffic August 27th, 1889.

The Damascus-Hauran rail road, running to Meserib, the starting point for the caravans to Mecca, has been completed and is said to be yielding large returns on the investment. The line over the Lebanons from Beirut to Damascus has also been opened for travel. In addition to these, railroads have been projected from Haifa to Damascus; from Tripoli to Damascus; from Beirut to Sidon, and northward to Tripoli; and from Egypt to the Euphrates over the old military route by way of Gaza, Jaffa and the Entrance of Hamath.

[1] The City and the Land, p. 34.

A little steamer, built by a Greek priest of the Monastery, "Mar Hauna," carries passengers from the Nimrim ford of the Jordan to the landing-place of Kerak on the Dead Sea, reducing the distance between Jericho and Kerak to a journey of a single day. A well graded carriage road has taken the place of the rough mountain trail which formerly led down from Jerusalem to the Jordan and the Dead Sea.

On the high ground overlooking this "silent sea" a modern "Café" has been erected; and at Jericho the traveller may now enjoy the comforts of a good "Hotel."

In all of these movements we may read the signs of a special providential oversight, never wholly withdrawn from this land, which is surely bringing out of the night of its long, gloomy past the dawning of a better day.

CHAPTER VII

HISTORY AND ASSOCIATIONS

THE Geography of the Holy Land is so closely associated with its History that the one cannot be studied intelligently without a definite knowledge of the salient points, at least, of the other. These may be briefly grouped under three periods of national or provincial occupation; viz: The Canaanite, Israelite and Gentile.

1. The Canaanite Period.—In the Scripture narrative the land of Canaan comes into view about 2,000—or as some good authorities reckon it 2,200 years before the Christian era. Under the general term Canaanite, as we have seen, the Amorites, who were probably the first settlers in the mountain district, with other associated tribes, were included. For many centuries this account of the country and its inhabitants stood alone, and there are few of its historical statements which have not been questioned or repudiated as mythical or unhistoric.

In recent years, however, a flood of light has been poured upon this region and its early inhabitants. Out of this mass of information, which has been diligently collected and carefully stored in libraries and museums, a new history of the ancient world has been constructed in which may be found confirmations, parallelisms, and illustrations of the Sacred record both numerous and striking.

(1) CANAAN AS A BABYLONIAN PROVINCE.—From the cuneiform records, which antedate the historical statements given in the Bible by several centuries, we find that this land in the earliest period of its settlement was regarded as a province or dependency of Babylon. The general name given to

History and Associations 51

the country, including Phœnicia was "mat Amuri," the land of the Amorites.

In the annals of Sargon, king of Agade, the founder of the first Chaldean Empire, mention is made of *four* expeditions to this "land of the Amorites," over which he claimed the exercise of supreme authority. His son Naram-Sin, extended this dominion to the Sinaitic peninsula and developed its famous copper mines.

If the statement on the cylinder of Nabonidus, translated by M. Pinches in 1880, can be accepted as historic, this king reigned 3,200 years before the time of Nabonidus or about 3800 B. C. Previous to the finding of this inscription the general consensus of scholars had assigned the date of Sargon's reign to a period about 2000 B. C. All the evidence, which bears upon this point confirms the view, so generally held by all the authorities, that he could not have lived *later* than this date.

On the assumption, therefore, that the date given by Nabonidus is only a boastful declaration, of doubtful authority, it is still true that this "Westland" of the old world was under the influence and control of Babylonia and Elam, as the Scripture narrative implies, before the birth of Abraham. Says Professor Sayce:

"We have learned from the cuneiform monuments of Babylonia that long before the days of Chedorlaomer campaigns were undertaken against Palestine by the Babylonian monarchs, and that in the age of Abraham the rulers of Chaldea claimed to be also kings of Syria and Canaan."

King Gudea whose date is given, about 2500 B. C.—according to the statement of Nabonidus—"ruled over the whole of Mesopotamia. He tells us how he hewed cedars in Lebanon and brought granite from Sinai to carve his statues, which have been brought recently from the Tigris to the Louvre in Paris."[1]

[1] The City and the Land, p. 36.

These and many other statements of like character show conclusively that in the earliest periods known to history, Canaan was a dependency of the empires of the East, being subject to them, at times at least, and receiving from them its literature and culture. In the first glimpses which we have of the country it appears to be sparsely settled. Outside of Phœnicia and the great plains it was an open common, where herdsmen and confederated bands of different nationalities moved about at will.

There were cities in the plains, and walled towns and fortresses on the frontiers in which the settled population dwelt and carried on the various avocations peculiar to the time and locality.

Near the close of this long period of Eastern supremacy (c. 1600 B. C.) these permanent centres of civilization had become the rallying points for numerous independent principalities and petty kingdoms, which, in case of need, were allied together for mutual support and protection. A great change had also come over the hill country. The rocky slopes in every portion of the land had been brought under cultivation by means of terraces and artificial appliances for the distribution of water; and walled cities of great strength had arisen upon commanding elevations in all the habitable districts of the several tribes. The records of the Bible and the monuments agree in their representations of the rapid growth, advanced culture and material strength of the people of the land in the period in which the Israelites dwelt in Egypt. They also agree in their classification of the three dominant races at this time, —the Amorites, the Canaanites and the Hittites.

(2) CANAAN AS AN EGYPTIAN PROVINCE.—The battle of Megiddo, which took place about 1550 B. C., gave to the Egyptians the dominant control of the southern portion of Syria for about three centuries. The contestants in this conflict were the Egyptians under Thotmes III., the Napoleon of the eighteenth Dynasty, and the Hittites with their allies. The power

History and Associations

and wealth of the latter nation, which at this time stood between Egypt and Assyria, may be inferred from the description of the spoils taken from them in this memorable campaign.

In connection with a list of 119 captured towns inscribed upon the columns of one of the temples at Karnak mention is made of precious stones of great value, vessels and ornaments of solid gold, and 924 chariots including the chariot of the Hittite king, covered with plates of gold.

The Tell el-Amarna tablets and the inscriptions on various temples of Upper Egypt have thrown much light upon the history of the country during the time of its subjection to the rulers of Egypt. They furnish us with long lists of its principal cities in the cuneiform language, including Megiddo, Kedesh, Tyre, Sidon, Gebal Gezar, Lachish, Jerusalem. These towns were either ruled by Egyptian governors or by native rulers who reported directly to the reigning Pharoah. For a short period—a half century or more—the Egyptians seem to have lost their hold upon the country, which was left without a central government, or a chief ruler, who had the power to bind the independent of the various localities together.

2. The Hebrew Period.—The time of Israel's occupation of the land, beginning with the conquest under Joshua and ending with the final destruction of Jerusalem under the Roman general Titus, covered a stretch of nearly fifteen centuries. The golden age of this period—as we have seen—was in the days of David and Solomon, when the whole land from the entrance of Hamath to the river of Egypt was held as a possession, and the nations around from the sea to the great river were subject; contributing to its resources and renown the choicest products of their labor and skill.

After the death of Solomon and the division of the kingdom, the territory of Israel was "cut short" and gradually diminished on every side. This was in accordance with the oft-repeated warnings of the prophets, in consequence of the persistent idolatry of the people and their long continued disavowal of the principles of righteousness, by which alone they held the tenure of the land. (2 Kings x. 32, 33.)

On the north the scattered tribes and nationalities from Lebanon to the Euphrates revolted from the dominion of Israel and formed the kingdom of Syria. The head of this kingdom, which soon became the leading power in all Syria, was Damascus.

Except a brief period in and after the reign of Jereboam II., (circa B. C. 800) this rival kingdom occupied and held the whole of the district of Lebanon.

For more than two centuries it wasted, at times, the northern borders of the ten tribes and menaced the safety of their seat of government at Samaria. In the reign of Hazael (c. 860) the Syrians conquered all of Israel's possessions east of the Jordan (2 Kings x. 32, 33): and at the same time reduced the allied tribes on the west, for a time, to a state of vassalage. (2 Kings xiii. 1–8.)

In the middle of the eighth century B. C. the kingdom of Syria came under the power of the Assyrian Empire, and the ten tribes abandoned of Jehovah, shared in their fate.

In the year 721 they were carried away to Halah and Habor beyond the Tigris. "And the king of Assyria brought men from Babylon and from Cuthah and from Ava, and from Hamath, and from Sepharvaim, and placed them in the cities of Samaria, instead of the children of Israel: and they possessed Samaria and dwelt in the cities thereof." (2 Kings xvii. 24.)

With the kingdom of Judah were some representatives of the ten tribes, who had cast in their lot with it, in the dark days of Israel's idolatrous defection, but this territory had also been cut short by the revolt of Edom, the falling away of Simeon on the south, and the possession by foreign powers of the cities of the Philistine plain.

From the date of the first invasion of Nebuchadnezzar (B. C. 606) the Kingdom of Judah became a province of

History and Associations

Babylon, and many of the people were carried away into captivity. The revolt of Zedekiah, the last ruler of this kingdom (B. C. 587) brought down upon him a swift retribution resulting in the utter destruction of Jerusalem and the deportation of the greater part of the population. The remnant which remained tilled the fields and dwelt in the ruined cities of Judah for seventy years. Meanwhile the Babylonian empire fell and the victorious Persian conquerors extended their dominion far beyond the original bounds of the old Assyrian empire. With the sanction, and under the protection of Cyrus and his successors, the Jews were permitted to return to their land, occupy their former possessions, and rebuild their temple and ruined cities. For 200 years they dwelt securely under the protectorate of the Persian empire, increasing rapidly in population, wealth and influence. Then followed in succession the short period of the Macedonian supremacy (332-331); the period of the Egyptian supremacy—under the Ptolemies, or Greek rulers of Egypt, lasting for 123 years (321-198); the period of the Maccabees, or independent rulers (166-64); and the period of Roman supremacy (B. C. 64-A. D. 614).

3. **The Gentile Period.**—The national life of the Hebrews ended with the destruction of Jerusalem, A. D. 70. From this time until now they have remained a distinct people, scattered among all the nations; and yet without a Ruler or a Country they could call their own. A feeble remnant, which survived the horrors of the war with Titus, made a desperate effort, under the leadership of Simon (Bar Cocheba), a pretended Messiah, some fifty years later, to throw off the yoke of Rome but miserably failed. The result was a wholesale prescription and banishment by order of the emperor Hadrian, from the land of their fathers. From this date Palestine became a Roman colony in which the Jew had neither part nor lot.

In 641 A. D. the whole of Syria was severed from the Roman empire by the Persians.

A few years later (A. D. 636) it came under the dominion

of the Moslem hordes from the desert. For more than 1,000 years following the Holy Land of the Hebrew and the Christian has been in the hands of the Arabs or their successors, and co-religionists, the Turks. The one notable interruption of Moslem rule was the period—lasting for nearly a century (1098-1187)—in which it was conquered and held by the Christian Crusaders. They have left the impress of their brief occupation in ruined monasteries and churches all over the western portion of the land.

A deeper and more abiding impression, however, has been left upon the land by the centuries of Greek and Roman occupation. The evidences of Græco-Roman civilization, literature and life are found in every part of the country, but especially in the region east of the Jordan. Here amid the ruins of great cities may be seen the remains of temples, forums, triumphal arches, gateways, bridges, aqueducts, colonnaded streets, amphitheatres, beautifully wrought columns and capitals, and many wonderful works of art, both elaborate and delicate. On this side of the Jordan not less then 500 miles of solid Roman roads have been traced. Here too in mosaic pavements, broken fragments of pottery, long lost coins of Roman emperors and free Greek cities, have been found the data for more accurate information with respect to time and place than that which has been transmitted to us by the pen of the classic historian. To the history of the early Christian Church a new and most interesting chapter has been added, also, from the numerous emblems and inscriptions unearthed here and there, which were traced on basalt slabs, rock tombs or marble tablets in the dark days of persecution and martyrdom.

Between some of these cities, in which Greek culture was protected and encouraged by the might and majesty of Rome, may still be seen, in places, the solid rock bed of the old roadways, deeply grooved by the chariot wheel; or the mile stone with its accurate record of distance from point to point. It is a

History and Associations 57

significant fact that the messengers of the gospel carried over Roman roads, from Jerusalem to the ends of the earth, a message to all nations and for all time, which was written in the beautiful, flexible, and almost universally disseminated language of the Greeks.

These monuments of the Christian age, like those of the earlier days, may now be read alongside of the records of Sacred history; and with wonderful unanimity they bear testimony to its accuracy of historical and geographical statement.

Sacred Associations.—Preëminent among all the things which abide, and more indestructible than the framework of its everlasting hills, are the sacred associations interwoven with the history of the land of Israel. It has been brought into close relations, at some time in its wonderful history, with every great nation of the Ancient or Roman world, but from none of these associations does it derive its peculiar charm or its distinguishing glory. It stands apart from all as the "Holy Land"; because here as nowhere else, the Almighty has manifested His glory and unfolded His purpose of redeeming grace. "Its hills and valleys have been transfigured by meanings and mysteries mightier than physical influences," and over it all there shines a light that fades not but grows richer and more radiant with the ages.[1]

It is the land of the Patriarchs; of the Prophets; of the Sacred Poets; of the Apostles; of David and Solomon, and a host of saintly men and women whose names are familiar to us as household words. But more than all it is the land where the Son of God was made flesh and dwelt among men.

> "Here lie those holy fields,
> O'er whose acres walked those blessed feet
> Which '1900' years ago were nailed
> For our advantage to the bitter cross."

From this land, long trodden under foot of the Gentiles, over

[1] Fairbairn's Studies of Christ.

which the gloomy shadows of the dark ages yet linger—has gone forth an influence more potent than ever came from schools of philosophers or the collected wisdom of the ancients. That influence to-day is ruling the world. There are many mountains celebrated in story and song, but there is only one Mount Zion, one Olivet, one Calvary, go where we may. There are many interesting cities of antiquity, which men have travelled weary miles to see, but there is only one Bethlehem and one Jerusalem in all the world.

These sites are sacred above all else because they have been touched by the beautiful feet of Him who brought good tidings and published peace. "It is historically incontrovertible that in Palestine appeared He whose precept, example and pierced right hand have lifted heathenism off its hinges and turned into new channels the course of human thought."[1]

[1] The Testimony of the Land to the Book, Dr. Gregg, p. 10.

CHAPTER VIII

THE TESTIMONY OF THE LAND TO THE BOOK

IN recent years the evidential value of sacred geography has been recognized and emphasized as never before.

In the "New Apologetic" of the Christian faith this study, in connection with its kindred branches of archæological science, has already risen to a place of prominence, as a supplemental evidence to the historical accuracy of the Old and New Testament narratives. The close correspondence between the locality avowedly chosen of God for the unfolding of His purpose of grace and the Book in which this revelation is made known, can only be explained on the assumption that both owe their origin to the same intelligent cause, and have been prepared and adapted for a predetermined end. "No fable, however cunningly devised, no myth or legend coming into existence at a later age, could have adapted itself so precisely to the topographical details of the scene."[1] Its framework is the setting of the Bible, and wherever tested it has been found that the one answers to the other as the die to its impress.

In such works as the "Researches" of Dr. Robinson or "The Land and the Book" by Dr. Thompson, who spent more than forty years of his active life amid the scenes he has so graphically depicted, there are proofs and illustrations of a correspondence so minute and striking that it is scarcely possible for a candid mind to resist the conclusion that both were made to fit together into one unique and grandly comprehensive plan.

Nor are we surprised, in view of these impressive facts, that Renan, a noted leader and representative of the broadest

[1] Dr. Manning "Those Holy Fields," p. 5.

school of skeptical thought, should join his testimony on this point with that of the most devout and conservative scholars of his day, after an experience of two or more years of travel and research in the heart of Palestine.

"I have traversed," he says, " in all directions the country of the Gospels. I have visited Jerusalem, Hebron and Samaria; scarcely any important locality of the history of Jesus has escaped me. All this history, which at a distance seems to float in the clouds of an unreal world, thus took a form, a solidity which astonished me. The striking agreement of the texts with the places, the marvellous harmony of the gospel ideal with the country which served it as a framework, were like a revelation to me. I had before my eyes a fifth gospel, torn, but still legible."[1]

In an admirable article on the connection of sacred history and sacred geography Dean Stanley clearly defines the value and pertinence of this testimony, in its application to the Old Testament as well as to the New.

"The question which the geographer of the Holy Land, which the historian of the chosen people has to propose to himself is, ' Can such a connection be traced between the scenery, the features, the boundaries, the situation of Sinai and of Palestine, on the one hand, and the history of the Israelites on the other?' It may be that there is much in one part of their history, and little in another; least of all in its close, more in the middle part, most of all in its early beginnings. But whatever be the true answer, it cannot be indifferent to any one who wishes—whether from the divine or human, from the theological or the historical point of view—to form a complete estimate of the character of the most remarkable nation which has appeared on the earth. If the grandeur and solitude of Sinai was a fitting preparation for the reception of the decalogue and for the second birth of an infant nation; if Palestine, by its central situation, by its separation from the great civilized powers of the eastern world, and by its contrast of scenery and resources both with the desert and with the Egyptian and Mesopotamian empires, presents a natural home for the chosen people; if its local features are such as in any way constitute it the cradle of a faith that was intended to be universal; its geography is not without interest, in this its most general aspect, both for the philosopher and theologian."[2]

[1] The life of Jesus by Renan, pp. 30, 31.
[2] Preface to Sinai and Palestine, pp. 15, 16.

Testimony of the Land to the Book

We cannot, as yet, give a full and complete answer to the question proposed by Dean Stanley: for all the evidence is not yet before us, but it is surely a significant fact that up to this hour it all points to one definite conclusion.

"There are," says Major Conder, "more than 840 places noticed in the Bible which were either in Palestine or the desert of Beersheba and Sinai, and of these nearly three-quarters have now been discovered and marked on maps." Omitting those which may in any sense be doubtful—and these for the most part are unimportant or have bare mention in the record—it cannot be said of one that remains that its local features are out of harmony with the history connected with its name.

The substance of the argument based on the foregoing facts has been tersely stated by the Rev. Dr. Gregg of New York, in a charming little book, which is commended to all who are interested in this phase of the study of sacred geography. In the development of this argument, he says:

"The Book weaves the physical features of the land into its statements. It does this fearlessly. It does this knowing that it can be refuted if its references are false or inaccurate. No book in all the literature of the world has as honest a face as the Bible. Impostors avoid details and keep to general statements, taking care to introduce no names, places, distances, which might serve to betray the fraud and publish the imposition. But the Bible in almost every chapter stands committed on all of these points. Its narratives are accompanied with all the minute circumstances of time and place and situation and distance. Thus the sacred writers commit themselves with perfect fearlessness to statements always avoided in apocryphal writings and which could be easily disproved if untrue. Yet in no single instance has geographical incorrectness been detected. Each new traveller is adding fresh confirmation to the precision and accuracy of the Book." [1]

The well known author, Walter Besant, Hon. Secretary of the Palestine Exploration Fund, has recently given a remarkable presentment of a like view, based upon the general work of this society and its adjuncts, during the twenty-five years of his official connection with the inner circle of its active management.

[1] "The Testimony of the Land to the Book," Dr. Gregg.

"I have been often asked," he says, "whether these researches actually prove the historical part of the Old Testament. It is a difficult question to answer. Suppose, however, we were to discover a papyrus two thousand or three thousand years old, containing a history, fragmentary in part, and in part full and connected, covering many hundreds of years. Suppose we were, without any prejudice against the authenticity of this history, or any presumption in its favor, to discover on examination that we could assign any single event recorded in the narrative exactly to the ground on which it was said to have taken place. Suppose further, we could prove that the event must, from the conformation of the ground, have taken place on that spot and on no other. Suppose we could prove that the writer of the history had an exact knowledge of the place he was describing; and that if there were twenty writers every one of them had also an exact knowledge of the country, would not these facts go very far indeed to make us believe in the truth of this history? Well, such is exactly what we have proved for the historical books of the Bible. Such and no more. If we are asked to argue for the inspiration of the Bible, we reply that this is another branch of inquiry altogether, and that we leave it for those who are capable of undertaking it.

"Again, to use another familiar and homely illustration, many men and women in these days practice the art of fiction. It is in that art a recognized and well understood rule that it is impossible to describe what you have not seen; so that if you are going to describe a house, a piece of scenery, a country, you must go there and describe it from personal knowledge, or, at least, from the personal knowledge of some one who will describe it for you. For instance, one of these literary persons, a few years ago, was proposing to write a novel which required an exact knowledge of the county of Northumberland. He obtained this knowledge by four journeys in the district; he walked from end to end of the county, and saw everything there is to be seen in it; until he had done this he found it impossible to begin his work. Here is a modern instance—a trivial instance—of the necessity of local knowledge for a historian.

"It shows with what care and trouble truth of detail must be acquired. To my mind *absolute truth* in *local details—a thing which cannot possibly be invented, when it is spread over a history covering many centuries—is proof almost absolute as to the truth of the thing related.*"[1]

With such testimony before us, it must be evident to every thoughtful man that we have in this study "no common lesson

[1] The City and the Land, pp. 121-3.

Testimony of the Land to the Book

of earth's geography." The conviction which has directed the feet of countless hosts toward this Holy Land for long ages; which has stirred the enlightened nations of Europe to emulous activity in keeping watch and ward over its sacred places; which to such an extraordinary degree has awakened and held the attention of the literary and scientific world in an age so practical as ours; which has made it by common assent the theme of Christian poetry and song, and the type of all that is beautiful and good in the better country beyond—does not rest upon a passing fancy or a tissue of cunningly devised fables. The marvellous adaptation of the land—as we see it to-day—to all the conditions of its marvellous history; its exceptional physical features; its typical universality, its double relation of exclusion from, and ready intercommunication with the nations; its manifest correspondence of places with the events described, and its silent witness to scores of prophetic judgments long ago uttered, but still preserved in the volume of the Book,—cannot in the nature of things, have been coincidences or accidents of geographical position.

PART II

Sectional View of the Land

In the preceding chapters a general bird's-eye view of the Holy Land has been presented. In the study of its special features, at close range, the most satisfactory outline of division and subdivision is suggested by its physical geography. It is a remarkable fact that the Biblical names and descriptions of the minor divisions of the country accord with this outline, and hence are still our best guides in the study and identification of the several sections of this wonderfully diversified land. With scarcely an exception, they are indicative of some peculiarity of position or feature which distinguishes them from contiguous sections.

In the political or provincial divisions, which have come down to us with but slight changes since the days of Roman occupation, this conformity to the natural features of the country is only found where it falls in with other considerations of policy or statecraft, which were regarded as more important. For this reason we seek in the *older* history the real boundaries of Israel's possession, and the best analysis of its characteristic features.

As the starting point of this analysis we shall take up in succession each of the four longitudinal strips or sections into which the country is naturally divided as already indicated in the general outlook. (Chapter I., p. 20.)

These are the Maritime plain, the parallel mountain ranges of Lebanon and Anti-Lebanon, and the deeply cleft valley which lies between them.

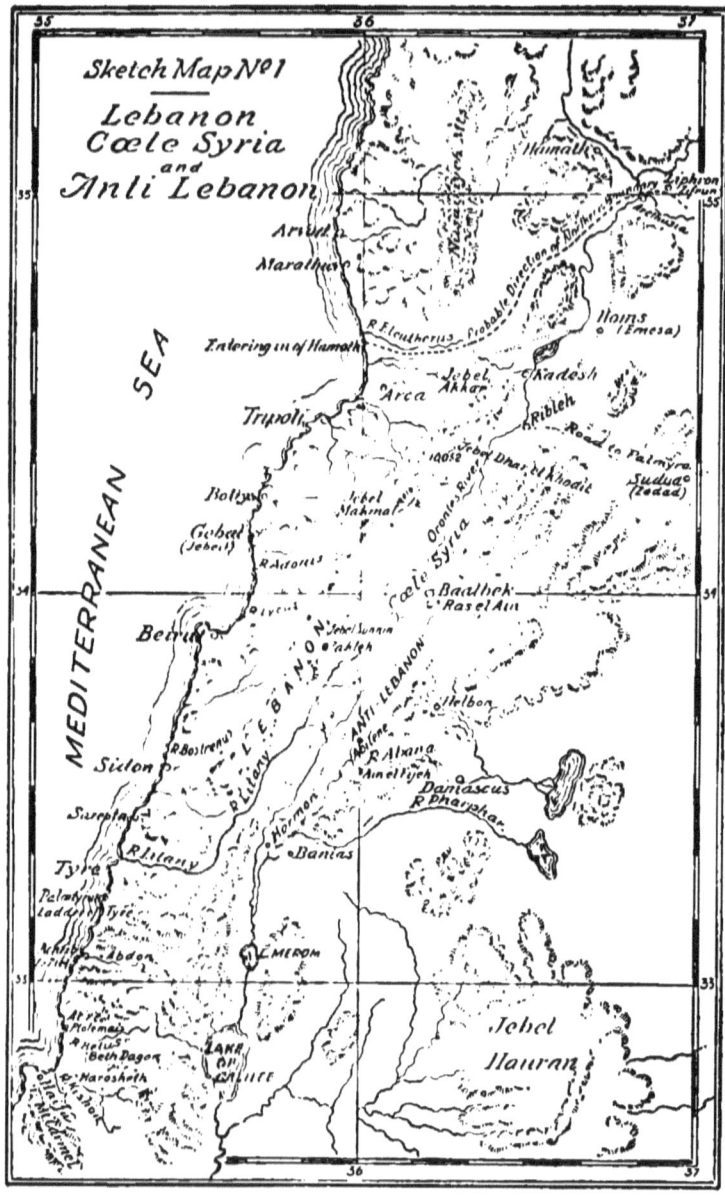

The First Longitudinal Section

CHAPTER IX

THE MARITIME PLAIN NORTH OF MOUNT CARMEL

THIS long and narrow strip of seacoast territory is separated into two portions, known as the plains of Phœnicia and Acre, by the Ladder of Tyre.

The Ladder of Tyre is a famous headland, or lateral offshoot from the mountains of Lebanon, which projects into the sea for a distance of two miles. This projection is seven miles in width and consists of three contiguous capes.

"The first is Ras el Abyad, which does not project into the sea more than a mile beyond the general line of the coast; the second is Ras en Nakurah, the real ladder or Scala Tyriorum, and the last is Ras el Musheirifeh, which is the highest of all, and shows boldest toward the sea, and hence has often been confounded with the true 'Scala.'"[1]

Two bold headlands of similar character, but of lesser proportions, interrupt the continuity of the plain northward. The one shuts in the course of the river Lycus to the south and the other blocks the way between Tripolis and Byblus. These natural obstacles were impassable to armies until surmounted by the engineering skill of the early Babylonian and Egyptian invaders.

I. THE PHŒNICIAN PLAIN

This plain extends from the northern end of Lebanon to the ladder of Tyre. It is about 120 miles in length and varies from two to fifteen in width.

[1] The Land and the Book, Vol. II. p. 266.

"The coast line of the region," says Rawlinson, "though not deeply indented, was sufficiently irregular to furnish a number of tolerable harbors; and when art was called in to assist nature, it was found fairly easy to construct ports, which, according to ancient ideas, left little to be desired."

While the abundance of the sea was the chief source of material prosperity to the Phœnicians, their scant territory was wonderfully rich in the number and variety of its productions. Close to the sea was a sandy belt, which was admirably adapted to the growth of the date-palm. So luxuriant was its growth in this region that it received from the Greeks, in ancient times, the name Phœnicia or Palm Land.

Inside the Palm belt was a fertile, well-watered strip of territory, cultivated with great care, which varied in width from one to ten miles. Along this tract may still be traced by their ruined heaps a succession of cities and villages. These, like the towns now occupied, were once surrounded by orchards and gardens.

Back of this cultivated tract was a stretch of low hills, the foot-hills of Lebanon, which were well adapted to the culture of the olive, mulberry and vine. This region belonged partly to the mountain and partly to the plain, but was occupied by the Phœnicians, and may properly be included in the lowland section.

Five noted streams cross this plain on their way to the sea. These are:

(1) **The Eleutherus** (Nahr el-Kebir) which drains the great plain of Akkar at the northern end of Lebanon, known in Scripture phraseology as the "entering in of Hamath." Strictly speaking, this river marks the northern limit of the Phœnician plain.

(2) **The Adonis**, associated with the well-known mythological fable of the classics.

(3) **The Lycus**, or Dog river at the mouth of which are the inscribed tablets of the Egyptian and Assyrian conquerors. (See page 50.)

(4) **The Bostrenas** or Awaly, which supplied the old city of Sidon and its environs with water.

(5) **The Litany**, or Kasimiyeh, the largest and most notable of all the rivers which water the plain of Phœnicia. Its source and general direction have already been indicated (page 25). It enters the sea five miles north of Tyre, and is usually regarded as the limit northward of Palestine proper.

The local subdivisions of this plain are known as the plains of *Tripoli, Berytus* (Beirut), *Sidon* and *Tyre*.

Cities and Towns.—Of these the most important only can be noted.

Tripolis or Tripoli (Tarablus) is situated on the eastern border of the small plain of the same name nearly thirty miles south of the Eleutherus river (Latitude 34° 26′). It was colonized by three cities,—Sidon, Tyre and Arvad. The colonists, it is said, originally occupied separate quarters; hence the name Tripolis or triple city. The Kadisha, or sacred river, coming down from the vicinity of the Cedars, passes through the city. It is famous for the wealth and beauty of its groves and gardens, which not only surround the city, but stretch across the plain, two miles in width, lying between it and the sea. The ancient city, which lays claim to great antiquity, was much nearer the sea. It has no associations with Biblical history unless it be, as some suppose, "the place of the Zemarites" mentioned in Genesis x. 18. Tripolis was a stronghold of the Crusaders for 180 years, and was one of the last which surrendered to the Saracens. On a neighboring hill is the well preserved ruin of the celebrated castle built by Count Raymond of Toulouse.

The present population is quoted at 25,000. In virtue of its position, spacious harbor, and natural advantages, it is already indicated on the survey chart as the *terminus* of the projected railroad to the valley of the Euphrates. If this project should be realized, it may yet rival the most prosperous of the old merchant cities of the Phœnician plain. A good carriage road connects Tripolis with Hums and Hamath, in the valley of the Orontes.

Tell Arka, about ten miles north of Tripolis, marks the probable site of a city of the Arkites. (Gen. x. 17.)

Gebal.—Jebail is the modern Arabic name for the city called Byblos by the Greeks. It is evidently the equivalent of the Hebrew word Gebal. (Ps. lxxxiii. 7 ; Ezek. xxvii. 9.)

Gebal was situated on a round hill close to the shore, thirty miles south of Tripolis. Its residents were called Giblites or "Stone-squarers," in Joshua xiii. 5 and 1 Kings v. 17, 18. They were celebrated for their skill in hewing and squaring stone, ship building, etc. They assisted in the construction of the foundation work of Solomon's temple, and it is probable that the huge stones recently uncovered in some portions of the encircling wall of the temple area were fashioned by their hands.

In the collection from Tell Amarna, there are thirteen letters from the Egyptian Governor in Gebal to the reigning Pharoah of Egypt, and the name is frequently mentioned in the Assyrian inscriptions.

Gebal was sacred to Adonis and near to it were celebrated some of the grossly immoral rites, which characterized both the earlier and later forms of the idolatrous worship of the Canaanite nations. "Mourning for Adonis," says Dr. Thompson, "is supposed to be identical with the weeping for Tammuz, referred to in Ezekiel viii. 14." [1]

From the port of Gebal, cedars were floated in rafts to Joppa, the seaport of Jerusalem, for the temple of Solomon. There is a road over the mountains from Jebail to Baalbec in the Cœle-Syria Valley.

Beirut—the Berytus of the Greeks and Romans—is delightfully situated on the northern slope of a projecting headland, twenty-three miles south of Jebail. A gracefully curved bay opens out to the sea on its front; while behind the plain,

[1] The Land and the Book—Phœnicia, p. 609.

which at this point is six or eight miles in width, rises, in a series of ascending terraces, a matchless background of pine covered ledges, beetling cliffs, and snow crowned heights.

One who has seen this rare combination of sea and plain and mountain-side from the most favorable view-points is, not likely to forget the picture while life or memory lasts. "In the 'plain of Berytus,'" says Rawlinson, "the beauty and fertility of Phœnicia culminate; and it is not surprising that of all the Phœnician cities Beirut should alone have maintained its prosperity." In the Tell Amarna tablets this city is mentioned along with other ancient cities of the coast, under the name of Beruta. This is the first distinct proof of its early origin. It did not come into prominence in later times until the age of the Maccabees, but it is now the most enterprising and enlightened of all the cities of Syria. It has macademized streets, modern methods of living and transportation, substantially built residences and an exceptionally large number of handsome churches and mosques, colleges and schools. The Syrian Protestant College founded by the friends of the American mission, is one of the finest buildings in the city and stands at the head of all the literary institutions of the country. The population of Beirut has increased from 20,000 in 1860 to over 100,000. No Biblical associations are suggested by its name; but it is the recognized educational metropolis of western Asia, and the centre of missionary agencies and operations throughout the Arabic-speaking population of the East.

A good carriage road and a recently constructed railroad connect Beirut with Damascus.

Sidon, or Saida as it is termed in modern Arabic, is situated on a low promontory, or spur of Lebanon which juts out a few hundred yards into the sea. It is twenty-seven miles south of Beirut and eighteen north of the Litany river. "Three reefs or low ridges of rock running parallel with the shore, with narrow openings between them, offered the nucleus of a harbor, which Zidonian art converted after awhile into a small but safe harbor." [1] The Auwaly or Bostrenus, enters the sea two miles above the city and from time immemorial has been utilized to irrigate the gardens and orchards which extend southward from it to the city, and form a broad belt of living green around it. These luxuriant gardens gave to it in classic times the appellation of "Flowery Sidon": and to-day, as in the past, they are the glory of the city and plain. Here the orange, lemon, apricot, pomegranate, banana and palm seem to find every condition favorable to luxuriant growth and abundant fruitage.

Sidon is the oldest of the chief cities of Phœnicia. It has maintained its hold on the site, where according to Josephus, it was located by Sidon, the grandson of Noah, and from that time until now has had, with all its reverses, a continuous history.

Isaiah speaks of it as the mother of Tyre (xxiii. 12): and as far back as the time of Joshua it was called "great Sidon." (Joshua xi. 8 and xix. 28.) It is mentioned in the Pentateuch and the songs of Homer: and at this period its residents were already famous among the nations for their skill in artistic and ornamental handiwork.

Originally a fishing port by the sea, it became in time the cradle of the world's commerce. Within the historic period it held the second place in importance among the cities of Phœnicia, but never had the advantage of a seaport like that of Tyre.

In one of the mulberry gardens near the city several copper pots containing gold coins with the stamp of Alexander and of his father Philip, were found a few years ago by native workmen. Only two were recovered by the authorities, yet these contained between two and three thousand coins of pure gold worth about five dollars each. The whole amount of this long-buried treasure—hidden in the field—was estimated at $200,-000.[2] Researches in the necropolis of Sidon have brought to light several sarcophagi, two of which are surpassingly beauti-

[1] Rawlinson's Phœnicia, p. 46.
[2] The Land and the Book, Vol. II., p. 639.

ful in design and workmanship. One has a life-like figure of Alexander the Great mounted upon a splendid charger.

> "It bears," says Dr. De Long, "the undoubted portrait of Alexander, easily recognized by every one who has ever held in his hand one of the best coins, or medallions, of the Macedonian conqueror. This magnificent tomb, worthy of him or any other monarch who ever lived, has received by general popular consent the name of the Alexander tomb."

The best authorities do not accord with this popular verdict, however, and the probabilities are on the side of those who claim that it was constructed as a memorial of one of the noted generals, or favorites of Alexander.

The Rev. Canon Curtis brings forward some strong evidence in support of the supposition that it is a memorial to Clitus who saved Alexander's life at the battle of Granicus; and that the battle scene so vividly represented on the monument has for its central figure the hero of this timely rescue.[1]

This valuable collection of sarcophagi, numbering eighteen in all, is preserved among the art treasures of the Imperial Museum at Constantinople.

In the Louvre is a royal tomb of red syenite, found near Sidon, in 1855. It has on its face an inscription of twenty-two lines, which furnishes one of the important links in the chain of evidence establishing the close connection between the Phœnician and Hebrew alphabets.

In the Old Testament there are frequent references to Sidon and its inhabitants. Some of the most suggestive are,—Gen. x. 19, xlix. 13; Josh. xix. 28; Judg. i. 31, x. 6; Isa. xxiii. 12; Ezek. xxvii. 8, xxviii. 21, 22.

On His last northward journey Jesus visited the coasts of Tyre and Sidon, and it is not unlikely that He entered this city also. Says Canon Tristram:

> "His fame had already reached Phœnicia, and probably He had many disciples in these heathen cities. (Luke vi. 17.) The negotiations of

[1] Pal. Exp. Quarterly, April, 1894.

Tyre and Sidon with Herod Agrippa I., and the visit of St. Paul to the believers there, complete the New Testament incidents connected with Sidon."[1]

Zarephath.—The city of Zarephath,—the Sarepta of the New Testament (Luke iv. 26)—was on the coast road almost midway between Sidon and Tyre. The modern village of Sarafend is usually identified with it, but the true site is nearer the sea, where broken columns and scattered fragments of ruined buildings, extending for a mile or more along the shore, attest the existence in former days of a town of more than ordinary importance. Here Elijah the prophet dwelt with the widow woman and her son, sharing with them in the unfailing supply from the barrel of meal and the cruse of oil, during the sore famine of Ahab's day. (1 Kings xvii. 9, 10.) Tradition has also associated the woman of Canaan, whom Mark designates as a Syro-Phœnician, with the city of Sarepta. (Matt. xv. 21–28; Mark vii. 24–30.)

Tyre.—Ancient Tyre was a double city, part being built on the shore and part on an island of 125 acres in extent, separated from the mainland by a strait almost a half mile in width. The city on the land, which according to tradition was the original site (Palætyrus), extended, in the height of its prosperity, over a circuit of about fifteen miles. Its location on the plain is eleven miles north of the White Cape of the ladder of Tyre (Ras-el Abyad), and five south of the Litany. Its distance from Sidon is twenty-three miles. The latitude is 33° 30'.

Tyre is first mentioned in Scripture in the list of cities assigned to the tribe of Asher. (Joshua xix. 29.) At this date it is designated as "the strong city of Tyre."

The mainland portion was destroyed by the Assyrians in their earlier campaigns in Syria; and its ruins were utilized by Alexander the Great to build a causeway to the city in the sea. Long before its fall this seagirt city had outrivalled it in power

[1] Tristram's Topography of the Holy Land, p. 293.

and magnificence. It is of this island city mainly that the Old Testament prophets speak. Against it they prophesied in the name of the Lord, because of its towering pride, and its pernicious influence over the people of Israel. These utterances are among the most striking in expression, and minute in detail within the lids of the Bible, and in the records of subsequent ages their fulfillment to the letter has been verified.

In 2 Samuel xxiv. 7 it is recorded that the census-takers of Joab, who went through all the land in the space of nine months and twenty days, came also to the stronghold of Tyre. This would seem to imply that at this period it was recognized as a city of Israel; but it is more likely that only the Israelite residents were included in this census. In the prophetic period Tyre had reached the zenith of its glory as the great commercial metropolis of the ancient world. In the book of Ezekiel (chapters xxvi. to xxviii. inclusive) its wealth and magnificence are set forth in a detailed statement which stands unrivalled amid the literature of the world for its wonderful accuracy of description and rare felicity of expression.

Near the close of the eighth century before Christ, Shalmanezer besieged the stronghold of Tyre for five years without success. One hundred and twenty years later Nebuchadnezzar destroyed the mainland portion, and then directed all his energies to the overthrow of the insular city. For thirteen years it held out against this powerful assailant, when an amicable treaty was arranged which seems to have averted its utter destruction. In 332 B. C. the restored city endured a siege of seven months, conducted by Alexander. Making a peninsula of the island by means of a laboriously constructed causeway, he at length carried it by storm, slaughtered its defenders and left it a ruined heap. Partial restorations and destructions followed under the successive dominion of Greeks, Romans, Crusaders and Saracens, but its former glory had departed. "Broken by the seas in the depth of the waters, her merchandise and all her company in the midst of her are fallen." "Swept like the top of a rock," it is now a place "for the spreading of nets in the midst of the sea." (Ezek. xxvi. 14.)

At the present time an unpretentious town has grown up amid the outlying ruins on a portion of the area once occupied by this princely city. The most interesting relic of mediæval Tyre is the "Crusader's Cathedral," a portion of which is still standing. It occupies the site of the Basilica of Paulinus, built by Constantine and consecrated by Eusebius in 323. In its vaults lie the bones of Origen and Frederick Barbarossa. With the multitude which came to see and hear Jesus, from all parts, when He was at the lake of Galilee, were representatives also from about Tyre and Sidon (Mark iii. 8): and at the time of St. Paul's last visit to Jerusalem there was a Christian community in Tyre with whom he and his company tarried seven days.

On this Tyrian shore the impressive incident took place, as they were about to depart, which the Evangelist Luke has so graphically described:—"They all brought us on our way, with wives and children till we were out of the city; and we kneeled down on the shore and prayed. And when we had taken our leave one of another, we took ship; and they returned home again." (Acts xxi. 5, 6.)

While the Phœnician plain was as clearly within the limits of Israel's heritage as the *lower reaches* of the coast plain, it was nevertheless a Gentile province in name and population. Between the lower tribes and the Philistines there was almost constant strife for centuries; each being intent upon excluding the other from the occupation of debatable territory. Between the tribe of Ashur, to whom this portion was assigned, and its Canaanite inhabitants, on the contrary, there was no strife for supremacy after the death of Joshua. To a certain extent at least there was, by mutual consent, a joint occupation of the land. In no case were the cities above described dispossessed of their original inhabitants. Fond of ease and unmindful of the oft repeated warnings of Jehovah, the Ashurites entered into sinful alliances with the people of the land, and with few exceptions abandoned their covenant engagements and privileges.

In the book of Judges we are told that Ashur did not drive out the inhabitants of Accho (Acre), nor the inhabitants of Zidon, nor of Ahlab, nor of Achzib, nor of Helbah, nor of Aphik, nor of Rehob: But the Asherites *dwelt among the Canaanites, the inhabitants of the land: for they did not drive them out.* (Judges i. 31, 32.)

II. THE PLAIN OF ACRE.

This designation is given to the section of the coast plain between the promontory called the "Ladder of Tyre" and the promontory of Mount Carmel. It is twenty miles in length. The average width is about five miles. . . . The low hills of upper Galilee bound it on the east, separating it from the great plain of Esdraelon, whose only connection with this plain is the narrow pass, or cleft, through which the Kishon river finds its way to the sea. The Acre section itself is somewhat broken by low ridges which come down from the mountains. It is fertile and well watered. The crescent shaped shore line in the southern portion forms the only natural harbor on the coast plain.

Rivers.—Two rivers, the Belus and the Kishon cross the plain and flow into the bay of Acre: the one at its northern and the other at its southern extremity.

The Belus (Nahr Naman) rises in the upland region north of Nazareth. At its mouth the shell fish (Murex brandaris and M. trunculus) abounded, from which the famous Tyrian dye was extracted. From the sand of the river, according to Greek tradition glass was first produced by the accidental combination of materials in the camp fires of the Phœnician sailors. While there is nothing improbable in the discovery of the art of glassmaking in this locality, it is certain that it was not the first discovery of this nature, for among the exhumed treasures of

Egypt, beautiful articles of glassware have been found dating back as far as the eleventh and twelfth Dynasties. *The Kishon*, which flows from the western side of the Esdraelon plain, enters the plain of Acre through a narrow pass (Wady el Kasab) between Mount Carmel and the hills of Galilee. Keeping close to the base of Carmel it follows its general direction to the sea, between steep banks of loamy soil about fifteen feet high, heavily fringed with oleanders, rushes, reeds and grasses.

Cities and Towns.—*Acre* has been from earliest times the most important city in this section of the Maritime plain. It is situated on a projecting headland which forms the northern horn of the Bay, at the mouth of the Belus river. In the book of Judges it is referred to as a well-known Canaanite town called Accho (i. 31).

In the New Testament it is mentioned but once. Here, on the occasion of his last journey to Jerusalem, St. Paul found Christian brethren, and abode with them one day.

In this passage the Evangelist Luke gives to the place its Greek name, Ptolemais. (Acts xxi. 27.) From the Crusaders it received the designation—St. Jean d'Acre. Its later history is crowded with stirring events. From the period of the crusades it has been regarded as the "Key of Palestine"; and next to Jerusalem, the coveted stronghold of contending factions and nationalities. It has been besieged and bombarded in turn by Baldwin, Saladin, Richard, Sultan Khalil, Napoleon, Ibrahim Pasha, and the united fleets of England, Austria and Turkey. The modern city is surrounded by massive walls. It covers an area of fifty acres, and is built upon the heaps of former ruins. Nowhere, perhaps, can a more perfect representation be found of a typical city of the Feudal times. Acre is the emporium of the grain trade from the Hauran. It is said that from 4,000 to 5,000 camel loads arrive daily from this district in the season. Basalt grindstones are also brought in large numbers from the Lejah, one being regarded as a load for a camel.

The present population is about 10,000.

Haifa, ten miles south of Acre, is the second town of importance on this plain. In the future it is likely to outgrow Acre as a commercial emporium. It lies on the southern horn of the crescent shaped bay directly under the ridge of Carmel.

Haifa is essentially a modern city in its structure and appointments. It is the terminus of the railroad now in process of construction to Damascus, and is connected with Nazareth by a good carriage road. It is also the port at which the Austrian Lloyd Steamers touch, once a fortnight, in each direction. Canon Tristram associates Haifa with the old Canaanite city of Achsaph, whose king was smitten by Joshua. (Josh. xi. 1, xii. 20.) "Two miles out of it are the sculptures and ruins which mark the site of the Greek and Roman city of Sycaminum, still overshadowed by the sycamine fig trees whence it derived its name."[1]

Achzib, now Es Zib, is an old Phœnician port, seven miles north of Acre. It is mentioned in Joshua xix. 29 and Judges i. 31. This town was regarded as the northern limit of the Holy Land, after the return from the Captivity.

"**Harosheth of the Gentiles**" has been identified with the village of El-Harothieh on the north side of the Kishon, about nine miles from Haifa. It is situated at the entrance to the lower end of the narrow pass through which the Kishon issues into the plain of Acre. Tell Harothieh a little lower down, on the other side of the river, is covered with ruins, and its position would indicate the existence of a garrison town from the earliest period of the country's occupation.[2] Harosheth was the camp of Sisera before his disastrous battle with Barak. From this point he advanced against Barak to a position on the Great Plain near Megiddo, eight miles distant.

The wild rush for safety in the midst of the terrible storm which suddenly burst upon the flying army was evidently in

[1] Topography of the Holy Land, p. 204.
[2] The Land and the Book, Vol. II., p. 216.

the direction of the narrow pass up which they had recently come. "There horses and men became mixed in horrible confusion jostling and treading down one another; and the river, swifter and deeper than above, runs zigzag from side to side, until, just before it reaches Tell Harothieh, it dashes against the perpendicular base of Carmel. There is no longer any possibility of avoiding it, and, rank upon rank, the flying host plunge madly in, those behind crushing those before." "The river of Kishon swept them away, that ancient river, the river Kishon."[1] (Judges iv. 14–16, v. 21.)

Several of the mud built villages which dot the eastern border of the plain rest upon the ruins of ancient towns, to which the old names current in the days of Joshua, with but slight changes, persistently cling. Among these are Kabul, southeast of Acre, the Cabul of Joshua (xix. 27); Abdeh the Abdon of Joshua (xxi. 30) on the northern limit of the plain; and Amkah the Beth-emek of Joshua.

[1] The Land and the Book, Vol. II., p. 215.

CHAPTER X

THE MARITIME PLAIN SOUTH OF MOUNT CARMEL

THERE are three recognized divisions in this portion of the seacoast plain, viz: The plains of Athlit, Sharon and Philistia.

I. THE PLAIN OF ATHLIT

Between the promontory of Mount Carmel and the Crocodile river (Nahr ez Zerka), a distance of eighteen miles, there is a narrow stretch of coast plain, which does not properly belong to the plain of Sharon. It has no distinctive name as a whole, but the upper portion is sometimes designated as the plain of Athlit and the lower as the plain of Dor, or Tanturah. This section is for the most part shut in between a low ridge of sandstone hills bordering the coast line and the western slope of the Carmel range. The ancient road, on which the deeply worn tracks of chariot wheels may yet be seen, runs within the seacoast ridge as far as the town of Athlit, eight miles from Carmel; after which it passes outside through an artificial gateway, cut through the ridge of rock, and skirts its western base. From this point the coast plain becomes a well-defined strip, varying from half a mile to a mile or more in width. **Athlit** was a strongly fortified garrison town in the period of the Crusades, and was, for a time the chief seat of the order of the Knights Templar. It was the last citadel held by the Crusaders in the Holy Land. Athlit has no Scriptural associations.

Dor.—The modern town of Tantura, six miles south of Athlit, occupies the site of the ancient city of Dor, or Dora, as it was called by the Romans. It was a royal city with several outlying towns. "The ruins," says Tristram, "are still extensive, projecting into the sea, while the old tower, broken as it is, is still a conspicuous landmark from afar." The Scripture references are Josh. xi. 2, xii. 23, xvii. 11; Judges i. 27, and 1 Kings iv. 11.

In the vicinity of Dor the hills bordering the coast recede, and the great plain opens out, widening as it extends southward, to the desert.

II. THE PLAIN OF SHARON.

The Nahr el Zerka, or Crocodile river marks the northern boundary of the plain of Sharon. Its eastern border is the rugged framework of the mountains of Ephraim.

There is no natural division between Sharon and Philistia, but the dividing line is usually drawn eastward along a low ridge from the mouth of the Nahr Rubin, seven or eight miles south of Jaffa. As thus defined, the Sharon plain is forty-four miles in length. In width it varies from six to twelve miles. In the northeast corner there is an oak forest extending over into the foot-hills, which is nearly nine miles in circumference.

At intervals small groves of oak extend southward for several miles. These are, without doubt, the survivors of a continuous forest which at one time bordered the eastern side of the plain. "It is the same," says Dr. Adam Smith, "which the Crusaders named the Forest of Assur; Tasso the Enchanted Forest; and Napoleon the Forest of Miski."[1] South of the Crocodile river for ten or twelve miles the plain is marred by marshes and drifting sand dunes. This has been described as "a district of deserted ruins, haunted by Bedouins, who occasionally cultivate some patches of land and reap scanty crops of wheat and barley."

The remaining portion is an unbroken stretch of undulating prairie or pasture land, diversified at intervals by grain fields, gardens, and thickly set groves of oranges, pomegranates and palms, which cluster around the scattered villages or spread out

[1] Hist. Geog., p. 148.

over the rich valleys, into which the numerous wadies from the mountains pour their fertilizing floods year by year. From the sea to the mountains there is a gradual ascent of nearly 200 feet. In some places, however, there are ridges or groups of hills that rise to an elevation of 250 and 300 feet above the general level. Sharon is crossed by several perennial streams, which converge near the sea into the Zerka, the Mufjir, or Dead river of the Crusaders, the Iskanderuneh, and the Aujeh. The latter drains a large section of the hill country of Samaria.

The main trunk of the Aujeh is formed by the confluence of the waters of Kanah and numerous smaller streams. It is less than ten miles in length. While the Aujeh is noted as the *shortest* river in Palestine, it is also the *largest* next to the Jordan. It rolls to the sea "between deep banks, a yellow, turbid, sandy volume of water nearly as wide as the Jordan at Jericho, unfordable in winter and nearly dry in summer."[1]

The Nahr Rubin properly belongs to the Philistine section. It touches the plain of Sharon only at its outlet by the sea, where it is barred by the inrolling sand, and spreads out to a width of more than 200 feet. The richest, and most highly cultivated, portion of the plain lies south of the Aujeh. Here also may be found the most of the ruined towns and cities. A few miles below the mouth of the Iskanderuneh is the centre of a famous melon growing district, where field joins to field for miles on every hand. In the season hundreds of camels are required to bear their luscious fruitage to the market.[2]

In Old Testament times the excellency of Sharon was proverbial; and in all ages it has been celebrated for its beauty, fertility and rich pasturage. (Isa. xxxv. 2.)

Over its wide expanse in the early springtime "a million of flowers are scattered,—poppies, pimpernells, anemones, the convolvulus and the mallow, the narcissis and blue iris-roses of Sharon and lilies of the valley." Under the charge of his

[1] Thirty years' Work, P. E. F., p. 93.
[2] Pict. Pal., Vol. II., p. 130.

chief herdsman Shitrai the Sharonite, one of the large herds of King David were fed in Sharon. (1 Chron. xxvii. 29.) The sweet scented narcissus was probably the rose of Sharon, to which allusion is made in Cant. ii. 1. With all its desolations Sharon is still a favorite resort of the herdsmen and "a fold of flocks." (Isa. lxv. 10.)

CITIES AND TOWNS

Cæsarea, the royal city of the Herods and the Roman capital of Judea, was built on a rocky ledge by the sea in the northeast corner of the plain. It lies about sixty miles northwest of Jerusalem, and twenty-five south of the promontory of Carmel. The city was planned and completed by Herod the Great, who spent twelve years in its building and adornment. He constructed an artificial harbor in its front by erecting a massive mole or breakwater far out into the sea. According to Josephus this mole was 200 feet wide and of great strength. Cæsarea was "a city of great beauty and magnificence, with a harbor looking Romeward and nothing in common with the Jewish city of the plain or mountain." It had much to do, however, with the spread of the Gospel, and numerous references are made to it in the Acts of the Apostles. It was the residence of Philip the evangelist; and in it were baptized Cornelius—the first Roman convert—and his household (viii. 40, xxi. 8 and 16; also chapters x. and xi.).

Here Herod Agrippa I. was stricken with a loathsome disease, while appropriating honors which belonged to God alone (xii. 19-23). From its famous seaport St. Paul sailed in his early ministry to Tarsus, and to it he returned on his second and third missionary journeys. (Acts ix. 30, xviii. 22, xxi. 8.) Here he made that pathetic appeal to his friends, who sought to detain him from going up to Jerusalem "What mean ye to weep and break mine heart? for I am ready not to be bound only, but also to die at Jerusalem for the name of the Lord Jesus" (xxi. 13). To the same city, after a little while

Maritime Plain South of Mount Carmel 83

he was brought back by Roman soldiers to endure an imprisonment of more than two years. In one of its magnificent palaces of state he stood in turn before Felix, Festus, and Agrippa (chapters xxiv.–xxvi.). It is a significant fact, that from this harbor "looking Romeward" St. Paul went forth at last, albeit as a manacled prisoner, to preach the gospel to them that were at Rome also (xxvii. 2). No more important event than this, in its bearing on the whole world, was ever chronicled of this great city and its overcrowded seaport. Thus it came to pass that "in seeking separation from his people, and an open door to the west, Herod had secured these benefits for a nobler cause than his own."

In the year 69 Vespasian was proclaimed Emperor in Cæsarea, and gave to it the privileges of a Roman colony. Eusebius, the historian of the early Church, was Bishop of Cæsarea in the early part of the fourth century and Origen was, for a time, a teacher in its famous school. The Crusaders found it a city in ruins, and partly rebuilt its crumbling towers and walls. In the year 1205 its walls were battered down by Sultan Bibers, and all that pertained to its former greatness was ruthlessly laid low.

Since that period it has been a desolate ruin in the midst of widespread desolations, caused by time and the neglect of man. On the north side of the harbor the waves still wash over a great number of prostrate columns which long ago were thrown down into the sea. The excavations made by the Palestine Exploration Survey have disclosed the outlines of a magnificent city with wide streets, a noble forum, a vast amphitheatre, and long rows of columns—all of which confirm the record of its former greatness and glory.

Jaffa or Yafa, was known as Japho in the Old Testament and Joppa in the New.

It is thirty-two miles south of Cæsarea, thirty-eight northwest of Jerusalem, and about midway between Carmel and the desert. The town is built upon the abrupt slope of a hill which rises 153 feet above the water. "The houses rise tier above tier from the very verge of the sea. The declivity is so precipitous that the flat roofs of the lower tier of houses form the terrace in front of those above and the ascent and descent along the narrow streets is one continual stairway." As seen from the deck of an approaching steamer this unique combination of closely compacted buildings gives the city a very picturesque appearance. On the landward side it is surrounded by luxuriant groves of oranges, olives, pomegranates, figs, apricots, and other choice fruits of Oriental lands. It is said that there are more than 350 gardens of fruit-bearing trees, which join each other in one continuous belt stretching north and south for seven miles and extending inland about one and a half.

The average yield of the orange crop alone, in this district, is estimated at 8,000,000 annually.

The port of Jaffa is regarded as the most dangerous landing place on the shores of the Levant. It is encircled by great rocks, and its narrow passage-ways are guarded by long lines of wave-washed ledges and subterranean reefs. Through these narrow channels little boats ply back and forth between the shore and the open roadstead, more than half a mile away, where seagoing vessels ride at anchor. When the surf dashes with more than ordinary violence against this rock-bound shore, the passengers and goods are landed on the backs of the Arab boatmen, who from long habit, have become wonderfully expert in this manner of delivery. This ancient seaport—one of the oldest known to history—notwithstanding its evil reputation, has been for many centuries the gateway of approach to the Holy City, for countless hosts of travellers and pilgrims from Europe and all the far-away lands of Christendom. The only recorded instance in which it was used as an outgoing port of the Israelites themselves, is given in the book of Jonah. Here the unwilling prophet took passage for Tarshish when flying from the presence of the Lord. (Jonah i. 3.) In Solomon's

Maritime Plain South of Mount Carmel

day it was the landing place for the cedar rafts sent down from the forests of Lebanon for the building of the Temple in Jerusalem. (2 Chron. ii. 16.) Here in like manner Ezra received his floats of trees for the building of the second Temple. In this rock-girt harbor was laid the scene of the classic legend of the deliverance of Andromeda from the sea monster. The first scriptural reference to the city is in Joshua xix. 46, where it is represented as fronting the border of the tribe of Dan.

Jaffa was held as a possession of Israel during the reigns of David and Solomon, and also for a time during the period of the Maccabees. After the Roman conquest, it was distinctively a Jewish city. Here Peter raised Tabitha (Dorcas) from the dead. (Acts ix. 36–42.) A few days later he had in this city the wonderful vision on the house top, overlooking the sea, which made the way plain for the evangelization of the Gentiles: and hither came the three messengers to guide him to the house of Cornelius in Cæsarea. (Acts x. 9–18 and 23.) The house accredited to Simon the tanner by tradition is still shown in Jaffa. Excavations in its front have disclosed oval cisterns which may have been used in tanning. These with other accessories give color to the supposition that the house stands on or near the original site of Simon's house. Jaffa has been frequently destroyed and rebuilt during its long history.

It has associations of thrilling interest in connection with the Maccabean struggle, the Arab invasion, the Crusades and the brief, but darkly clouded period of its occupancy by Napoleon.

The present population, as given by Baedecker, is 23,000. Jaffa is connected with Jerusalem by a carriage road and a recently constructed railroad, which carries passengers to Jerusalem in three hours. The fare is $3.00 first class and $1.00 second class.

Lydda or Ludd, is eleven miles inland from Jaffa, on one of the main roads leading to Jerusalem. It seems to have belonged to Benjamin and was known as Lod. (1 Chron. viii. 12.)

The Romans called it Diospolis, but the old name, with a slight modification (Ludd) has survived all the changes of the past. After the captivity, Lydda was reoccupied by the Jews. (Ezra ii. 33; Neh. xi. 35.) It was the home of Eneas the paralytic, who was miraculously healed by Peter. It became the central point afterward, of the Apostle's successful ministry among the residents of the plain of Sharon. (Acts ix. 33–35.) The most interesting relic of the past in the modern village is the ruined church of St. George. According to the medieval tradition St. George, the patron Saint of England, was born and buried in Lydda. "Within a few miles are Ono, Hadid and Neballat, (1 Chron. viii. 12) still bearing the names of Kef'r Auna, Hadithet, and Beit Neballat."[1]

Ramleh is pleasantly situated, amid fruitful orchards and olive groves, on a slight eminence two or three miles southwest of Lydda. It dates from the eighth century and has many associations connected with the period of the Crusades. The principal object of interest in Ramleh is a massive square tower resembling the famous Giralda of Seville, which rises from a base of ruined buildings to a height of 120 feet. It is probably a relic of the Crusading days. A circular stairway conducts to the summit of the tower from which the view is wonderfully comprehensive and distinct.

"The whole plain of Sharon from the mountains of Judea and Samaria to the sea and from the port of Carmel to the sandy deserts of Philistia, lies spread out like an illuminated map."[2] Ramleh is the first station on the railroad to Jerusalem. It is the most prosperous of all the inland towns of the plain, and at present has over 8,000 inhabitants.

Antipatris.—The true site of this Herodian stronghold has been definitely located by the Palestine Exporation Fund Survey at Ras el Ain, twenty-six miles from Cæsarea and forty-two from Jerusalem.

[1] Tristram's Topography of the Holy Land, p. 51.
[2] Land and Book, p. 113.

Maritime Plain South of Mount Carmel

There were two main routes from Jerusalem to Cæsarea, both of which passed through Antipatris. One was by way of Lydda; and the other by way of Gophna, farther to the north. It is probable that the Apostle Paul was sent, as a prisoner, to the Roman governor, by the latter route. In the vicinity of Antipatris a portion of the solid road bed has recently been uncovered. It bears the marks of centuries of travel, but is still in good condition. The abundant supply of water which gushes out from the foot of the mound of ruins that marks the site of Antipatris, is an indication of the importance of the place as a principal station on this great thoroughfare.

Gilgal.—The Gilgal of Joshua xii. 23 has been identified with Jiljulieh, fourteen miles northeast of Jaffa and five north of Antipatris; Arsuf, on the coast with Apollonia; Beth-Dagon with Beit-Dagon, five miles northwest of Lydda (1 Sam. v. 2); and Rakkon with Tell-er Rakkut, near the mouth of the Aujeh. These points cover all the places of special interest in this section.

Roadways.—Two important roads, nearly parallel in their course, traverse the plain of Sharon from south to north. One, the great coast route, already referred to—borders its western side: the other its eastern side, keeping as close to the mountain ridge as the nature of the ground permits. The inland caravan route northward, which passes through Ramleh, Lydda, Antipatris and Gilgal enters the plain of Esdraelon by the Megiddo pass at the eastern base of Mount Carmel. Another main route diverges from this road at Wady Abur Nar and passing to the northeast by way of the plain of Dothan enters Esdraelon at Jenin. This, says Dr. Adam Smith, is no doubt the historical road from Egypt to the east of the Jordan and Damascus. It was on this road near Dothan that Joseph's brethren, having cast him into a pit, lifted up their eyes, and behold, a company of Ishmaelites came from Gilead, with their camels bearing spicery and balm and myrrh, going to carry it down to Egypt. (Gen. xxxvii. 25.)

A road diverging from the coast road at Jaffa crosses the inland route at Gilgal and thence leads to Shechem or Nablous. Aside from the railroad, there are two great thoroughfares across the plain from Jaffa to Jerusalem. One, by way of Lydda and the Beth-Horon pass, enters the city from the north : the other, by way of Ramleh and Wady Ali, enters at the Jaffa gate on the west. The railroad diverges from this route southward at Ramleh and follows the Wady-es-Surar (Valley of Sorek) to Beth-shemesh, approaching Jerusalem by way of the valley of Rephaim on the southwest.

III. THE PHILISTINE PLAIN

The plain of Philistia extends from the Nahr Rubin to the Wady el-Arish, a distance of about fifty miles. Its average width is greater than the Sharon section, especially to the south. It is lower and flatter, also, but is diversified in some places by gentle elevations. The irregular mass of the low hills, or Shephelah, which belong to the plain rather than to the Central Range, encroaches upon its eastern border, contracting its limits at some points, and at others merging so closely with the rising ground of the plain itself, that it is not possible to draw a definite line of distinction between them. The portion which lies between Gaza and the Wady el-Arish is a noted pastoral region, having the general characteristics of the Negeb, to which it properly belongs. Before the period of David's conquests it was known as "the south of the Cherethites" or Philistines. (1 Sam. xxx. 14 and 16.) At times, however, it seems to have been occupied altogether, or as a joint possession of Amelek. (Num. xiii. 29, xiv. 25.) In the days of Abraham it belonged to the kingdom of Gerar, which was ruled by Philistine princes.

North of Gaza the soil is exceedingly rich and fertile. For two or three miles inland there is a continuous line of barren, drifting sand along the shore. Back of this throughout its whole extent, the plain is one vast grainfield. Without any

Maritime Plain South of Mount Carmel 89

other fertilizers than nature has provided, it has yielded enormous crops continuously for forty centuries. The streams which come down from the hill country during the rainy season, sink down into the porous soil, and find their way underground to the sea.

"You may leave the water at the commencement of the wady mouth, ride over the plain without seeing any of it, and meet it again welling out of the ground close to the seashore, forming wide lagoons there." While surface irrigation by the mountain streams is not practicable under present conditions, a good supply of water can easily be obtained by boring or sinking wells a few feet below the level of the ground.

In the vicinity of the towns and villages the orchards and gardens are as famous for their rich variety and luxuriant growth, as those which border the coast of the plain of Sharon.

Cities and Towns.—There were five chief or royal cities of ancient Philistia, included under one united government, or confederacy, viz: *Ekron, Gath, Ashdod, Askelon,* and *Gaza.* Their rulers were styled "Lords of the Philistines." With each of these chief cities were associated groups of villages, the remains of which, if they exist at all, are not distinguishable from the ruins of later towns, scattered at intervals all over the plain. All of the chief cities, except Gath, have carried up with their names, through the long ages of their existence, the unquestioned evidence of their location and identity.

(1) **Ekron**, or Akir as it is now called, was on the northern frontier of Philistia, and was within the limit of territory originally assigned to Judah. It is situated on the southern slope of a low ridge, which overlooks the Sorek valley. It is nine miles from the sea and five miles northwest of Ramleh. Ekron was the last of the Philistine cities to which the ark of God was sent: and thence it was returned, on the new cart drawn by milch kine, by way of the well worn road up the Sorek valley to Beth-shemesh in the mountains of Judah.

(1 Sam. vi. 7-13.) A collection of fifty or more mud hovels is all that represents the former glory of this royal city of the Philistines.

(2) **Ashdod** (Esdud), Azotus of the New Testament, lies on the coast road, three miles from the sea. It is nearly midway between Jaffa and Gaza. It had a seaport in former times, but its site has been swallowed up by the encroaching sands. The site of the town is marked by a Tell which was probably the Acropolis of the ancient city. Ashdod was one of the notable strongholds of the Philistine plain, and from the days of the Anakim, its original occupants and defenders, until the closing period of the Crusades, its history is mainly a record of battles and sieges. Psammeticus, King of Egypt, invested it closely for twenty-nine years before it fell into his hands. This, on the authority of Herodotus, is the longest siege recorded in history. Preceding this destruction, and within a period of less than two centuries, Ashdod had been besieged and taken in turn by Uzziah of Judah (2 Chron. xxvi. 6); by the army of Sargon (Isa. xx. 1), and by Sennacherib.

To this city, the chief seat of worship of the god Dagon, the Ark of the Covenant was removed after its capture by the Philistines. Its presence was attended with consequences so disastrous to the image of Dagon, and the residents of Ashdod, that it was hastily transferred to the neighboring city of Gath. (1 Sam. v. 8.) The only New Testament reference is the brief account of Philip's visit on his evangelistic tour among the cities of the coast. (Acts viii. 40.) The modern village of Esdud has a few substantial buildings surrounded by an unsightly collection of mud huts.

(3) **Gath** has not been identified with certainty. **Tell es Safi** at the foot of the low hills, ten miles east of Ashdod, has been suggested as a possible site.

This is the famous Blancheguarde of the Crusaders, where a castle was built to command the outlet of the valley of Elah.

Gath was the home of Goliath and his associates of the race

Maritime Plain South of Mount Carmel   91

of Giants. (1 Sam. xvii. 2; 2 Sam. xxi. 18-22.) In this city David found a refuge for a time from the persecutions of King Saul. (1 Sam. xxvii.) Some good authorities have seen in Beit Jibrin, farther south, evidences of identification with this ancient city which have more weight than those adduced in favor of Tell es Safi.

(4) **Askelon** (Askulan) is a deserted ruin ten miles southwest of Ashdod. It lies some distance west of the coast road, and is only one of the confederate towns which was built on the seashore. Its natural position is one of great strength. William of Tyre describes it as "lying within a semicircle of ramparts—partly natural and partly artificial—the diameter of which was formed by the sea on the west." The white limestone cliffs which formed this rocky amphitheatre, could be seen far out to sea and gave to the place the distinctive name of "The White City." An inscription on the walls of Karnak gives an account of the capture of Askelon by Rameses II. on his northward march into Syria; and it has been the scene of many a fierce struggle since that day.

By the Crusaders it was regarded as the key to Southwest Palestine. "Within the walls and towers, still standing, Richard of England held his court," and most of his daring adventures were in its immediate vicinity. There are numerous references to Askelon in the Old Testament, but it is not mentioned by name in the New. Two remarkable prophecies concerning it have been literally fulfilled,—viz: "Askelon shall be a desolation." (Zeph. ii. 4.) "Askelon shall not be inhabited." (Zech. ix. 5.)

(5) **Gaza** was the most important stronghold along the line of the great coast road. Its modern representative, which the Arabs call Guzzeh, stands on or near the original location. It is eight miles from Askelon and three miles from the sea. The better part of the city is built upon a rounded or oblong hill, which rises sixty or seventy feet above the plain. The walls and fortifications above ground have disappeared and in

their stead is a broad, green belt of flourishing orchards and gardens. Its present population is estimated at 18,000.

"There is a large field to the west of the town buildings," says Dr. Bliss, "which has the genuine Tell slope, and a cutting near its base has already revealed a splendid mud brick wall *in situ* with early pottery in connection. This I take to be the old city wall, and doubtless precious remains lie concealed under the barley field beyond."[1]

Gaza was the last of the important towns on the highway to the desert, and hence the outfitting station for caravans and armies moving southward, as well as the supply depot for those coming up from Egypt. Thus, in virtue of its commanding position, it was the gateway to Africa on the south and Syria on the north.

Evidences of the great antiquity and importance of Gaza are furnished by the Minnean inscriptions of Arabia;[2] the records of Thotmes III. of the eighteenth dynasty; and the Old Testament Scriptures. In each of these records the name with slight modifications, is the same. In Deut. ii. 23, it is written "Azzah."

This frontier city of Philistia was taken by Joshua and apportioned to the tribe of Judah. Not long after the death of Joshua it was retaken by the Philistines and remained in their hands until the reign of David. (Josh. x. 41, xv. 47; 1 Chron. xviii. 1.) In the period of the Judges, Samson carried off one of the double gates of the city and left it on the top of a neighboring hill. Gaza was also the place of Samson's imprisonment, and here he overwhelmed the Philistine nobles, with himself, in one common destruction, by pulling down the pillars of the great house in which a crowd of revellers were assembled to make sport of him. (Judges xvi. 29, 30.) Gaza is mentioned but once in the New Testament. The reference is in connection with the instructions given to Philip. (Acts viii. 26.) During its long history this stronghold of the border has yielded in

[1] Bib. Research in Bible Lands, p. 40.   [2] Ibid., pp. 11, 143.

Maritime Plain South of Mount Carmel 93

turn to almost all the great conquerors of the world—including Thotmes III., Rameses II., Joshua, David, Alexander the Great, Pompey, Omar, Saladin, Richard of England, and Napoleon.

Outside of this group of chief cities there are several towns of importance on the Philistine plain, which we briefly notice in order of succession, beginning at the north.

(6) **Jabneel** or Jabneh (Joshua xv. 11 ; 2 Chron. xxvi. 6), has been identified with the modern village of Yebna, on the south bank of the Nahr Rubin, three miles from the sea. Its Greek name was Jamnia. It was an important Jewish town in the time of the Maccabees and the seat of the Sanhedrin after the destruction of Jerusalem.

(7) **Libnah**, a royal city of the Canaanites, is mentioned several times in the Old Testament. The site is not definitely known. The best modern authorities have pronounced in favor of Tell es Safi, whose white cliffs may have suggested the name. Dr. Thompson thinks it may be identical with Yebna. (Joshua x. 29–39, xii. 15, xxi. 13 ; 2 Kings viii. 22, xix. 8 ; 1 Chron. vi. 57 ; 2 Chron. xxi. 10 ; Isa. xxxvii. 8 ; Jer. lii. 1.)

(8) **Makkedah.**—The village of Mughar, eight miles southeast of Ramleh, has been identified by Captain Warren with Makkedah, the hiding-place of the fugitive kings of the Amorites after the battle of Gibeon. (Joshua x. 16–26.) The name signifies the place of the caves. This identification has been confirmed by the Survey party, "who found that at this site only of all the possible sites for Makkedah in the Philistine plain do caves still exist. The position also agrees well with the identification of the towns Gederoth, Beth-Dagon and Noamah mentioned in the same group with Makkedah."[1]

(9) **Migdol** (Joshua xv. 37), is probably the modern village of Mejdel, two and one-half miles inland from Askelon.

(10) **Lachish.**—In the light of recent investigations the identification of this ancient Amorite town with Tell el Hesy is confirmed and generally accepted. It is favorably situated at

[1] Thirty Years' Work, p. 110.

the junction of two wadies, on the edge of the Shephelah, eighteen miles northeast of Gaza, or nearly half way between Gaza and Hebron.

> The Tell has been described as "one of the most imposing objects on the plain, above which it rises to a height of nearly 120 feet. Sixty feet of this consists of an artificial mound formed by the decay of the successive cities that stood upon the spot. Nature had marked it out as the site of one of the chief fortresses of Southern Palestine. Immediately under its wall is an abundant spring of fresh water, the only fresh water to be found for miles around."[1]

Excavations at this place under the direction of the Survey Fund were commenced by Professor Petrie in 1890, and continued by Dr. Bliss until one-third of the great mound was laid bare, from top to bottom, and its various levels were exposed. In the superimposed towns, eight of which were clearly distinguished from each other by the diverse collection of objects among the debris, Dr. Bliss found the remains of walls and towers, storehouses, ovens, wine-presses, a public hall, private dwellings, a smelting furnace, weapons, tools, bronze and iron implements, scarabs, flints, pottery, and—most valuable of all—a clay tablet in the cuneiform language addressed to Zimrida, Governor of Lachish, from Egypt. This is the counterpart of the letters found at Tell Amarna, in Egypt, in the year 1888, from Zimrida to the reigning Pharoah, whose servant or vassal he acknowledges himself to be. This tablet is an important link in the chain of evidence which establishes the identity of Lachish with the foundation city of this series. It is not the only evidence, however, of its great antiquity. Within its massive brick walls, twenty-eight feet, eight inches in thickness, were found Amorite pottery of a distinctive type and many other articles, such as bronze weapons and tools, having the undoubted characteristics of a Pre-Israelite age. Here, then, we may confidently affirm, has been laid bare one of the long buried cities, which was captured by Joshua: and which the

[1] Prof. Sayce, N. Y. Independent, Aug 28th, 1890.

CAPTURE OF LACHISH BY SENNACHERIB

Maritime Plain South of Mount Carmel

faint-hearted spies of a generation before described as "walled up to heaven." (Joshua x. 31, 32; Deut. i. 28.) The probable date of the original occupation of this foundation city is fixed by Drs. Petrie and Bliss at the beginning of the seventeenth century before Christ. There is evidence also that *four* distinct buildings and destructions of the series of great walls took place before the Israelite invasion. A later record of its restoration as a garrison town by Rehoboam, King of Judah, is given in 2 Chron. xi. 9. In its subsequent history Lachish appears as one of the "fenced cities of great strength" which held out against the forces of Sennacherib (2 Chron. xxxii. 9), and also against Nebuchadnezzar (Jer. xxxiv. 7). A collection of Assyrian slabs in the British Museum, which bears the name of Sennacherib, gives a vivid representation in detail of the besieged city and its defences. "The details of the situation of the city as shown there are exactly in accord with the point of view from the southern side; and the resemblance strongly suggests that the royal scribe or artist made sketches during the campaigns for the future sculptures."[1] The higher levels of the Tell furnish evidence of Greek and Roman civilization and occupation. It has been a ruined heap since the fifth century A. D.

(11) **Eglon.**—Three miles northwest of Tell el Hesy is a low mound of shapeless ruins similar in appearance, that still bears the name of Ajlan. This evidently marks the site of the ancient Eglon, another of the confederate cities of the Amorites. It fell into the hands of Joshua immediately after the capture of Lachish. (Josh. x. 34.)

(12) **Gerar.**—The site of Gerar has been found at Umm Jerar, six miles south of Gaza, in a valley running eastward from Beersheba.

"There is little to describe beyond a gigantic mound on the side of a deep, broad water course (Wady Sheba) in the midst of a rolling plain."[2]
"There are pits in the valley bed whence the Arabs obtained water even

[1] The City and the Land, p. 202. [2] Thirty Years' Work, p. 106.

in summer. If the wells which Isaac digged again (Gen. xxvi. 18) were anything like the pits now existing, it is easy to understand how the Philistines filled them up after Abraham's death."[1]

In this region Abraham sojourned for a long time, and the narrative implies that it was the birthplace of Isaac. (Gen. xx. 15, xxi. 34.)

During a period of famine in the mountain districts Isaac returned to this rich pasture land and dwelt in Gerar and its immediate vicinity. (Gen. xxvi. 1-22.) The springs called "Esek" and "Sitnah" were apparently in the same valley near Gerar, but no trace of such names has been found by recent explorers.

It should be noted that the whole of the Philistine Plain bears evidence of a thickly populated region in the past, and ruins of nameless towns are found all over its widely extended surface. The sites of several ruined towns, long without inhabitants, have also been found along the "way of the Philistines" from Wady el-Arish to Gaza.

[1] Conder's Bible Geography, p. 42.

CHAPTER XI

THE SHEPHELAH

THE term Shephelah, as used by the latest authorities in Sacred Geography, applies to the range, or rather the irregular mass, of low hills which lie between the Central Range of the Mountains of Judah and the Philistine Plain.[1] It belongs to the plain rather than to the mountains, and in some places can hardly be distinguished from its higher elevations. From the mountains, however, it is distinctly separated by a series of almost continuous breaks or depressions 500 to 1,000 feet in depth.

The Shephelah has been aptly described as a loose gathering of chalk and limestone hills, round, bare and featureless, but with an occasional bastion flung well out in front of them. . . . " Altogether it is a rough, happy land, with its glens and moors, its mingled brushwood and barley fields; frequently under cultivation, but for the most part broken and thirsty; with few wells and many hiding-places; just the home for strong border men like Samson, and just the theatre for that guerilla warfare, varied occasionally by pitched battles, which Israel and Philistia, the Maccabees and the Syrians, Saladin and Richard waged with each other."[2]

Valleys of the Shephelah.—There are six noted wadies or valleys, (wadies among the hills, and valleys in the lowlands) which begin their course in the Central Range and cut their way through the Shephelah to the plain. These are known as the *Valley of Ajalon* (Wady Selman), *Valley of Sorek* (Wady es Surar), *Valley of Elah* (Wady Sunt), *Valley*

[1] For full discussion in ref. to usage of the term in Old Test. Septuagint and Talmud see Smith's Hist. Geog., p. 209.
[2] Smith's Hist. Geog., p. 209.

of Zephathah (Wady el Afranj), *Wady el Hesy* (Wady el Jizair), and *Wady esh Sheriah.*

Each of these afford passage-ways into heart of the mountain strongholds of Judea, and each has its distinct characteristics and historical associations.

"To realize these valleys is to understand the wars that have been fought on the western watershed of Palestine from Joshua's time to Saladin's."[1]

1. **The Valley of Ajalon.**—The northern border of this valley may be regarded as the limit, in this direction, of the Shephelah. Its identity with the vale now called Merj-Ibn-Omier is established with certainty by the location of the town Ajalon (Yalo) on its southern slope, and by the recent discovery of the site of Gezer at its mouth.

It is a broad, green upland vale, which gradually opens out into the great plain with its mouth inclined slightly northward, toward Lydda. Three wadies from the height of Benjamin converge in its upper basin, and from it, by way of these narrow water courses, three ancient roadways lead up to the city of Jerusalem. The most famous of these was the route by way of the Beth-horon pass to the plateau of El Jib or Gibeon five miles north of Jerusalem. "This has always been the easiest passage from the coast to the capital of Judea. Throughout history we see hosts swarming up this avenue, or swept down it in flight."[2] Down this pass and through this valley Joshua pursued the fleeing hosts of the Amorites on that memorable day when he commanded the "sun to stand still upon Gibeon and the moon in the valley of Ajalon." (Josh. x. 10-14.)

Up the same valley on several occasions the marauding hosts of the Philistines found their way to the very heart of the territory of Israel, and on two occasions were driven down it with great slaughter—once by Saul and Jonathan and again by David, "who smote them from Gibeon until thou come to Gezer." (1 Sam. xiv. 31 ; 2 Sam. v. 25.) In the Maccabean

[1] Smith's Hist. Geog., p. 209.   [2] Ibid., p. 210.

The Shephelah

wars this valley was the route by which Jonathan led his forces down to the plain in the campaign which gave Joppa into the hands of the Jews; and anon, when the tide turned, it was the route by which the Syrians swept up to the plateau on which Jerusalem stood. In the year 66 A. D. a Roman army under Cestius Gallus was driven down this rugged defile to Ajalon by a host of avenging Jews, and, as in the past, multitudes perished in the headlong flight. Centuries afterward Godfrey d' Bouillion led the first army of the Crusaders up the same rugged passage-way to the walls of the Holy City. "Up none of the other valleys of the Shephelah," says Dr. Adam Smith, "has history surged as up and down Ajalon and past Gezer, for none are so open to the north, nor present so easy a passage-way to Jerusalem."

It has been frequently assumed by modern writers that the apostle Paul was taken under guard from Jerusalem to Cæsarea by this route, but it is more likely that the shorter and more northerly route by way of Gophna was followed to Antipatris on the plain. The sites of historic interest in the valley are:

Ajalon (Yalo)—frequently mentioned in the Old Testament, and also on the Tell Amarna tablets; *Jimzu* or Gimzo (2 Chron. xxviii. 18); *Beit Nuba*, near Yalo, the place of encampment of King Richard of England; *Amwas* or *Emmaus* (Nicopolis) a short distance west of Yalo, is mentioned in the book of Maccabees. (1 Mac. iii. 40.) The site does not correspond with the location of the town of Emmaus mentioned in Luke xxiv. 13.

Gezer or Gazar, a royal city of the Canaanites (Josh. x. 33) was situated on a commanding, oblong hill—the most northerly outpost of the Shephelah—which commanded the entrance to the vale of Ajalon. Its identity with Tell Jezer has been established by M. Ganneau, who found amid its ruins in 1874 a bilingual tablet (Greek and Hebrew) on which the Biblical name Gezer is deeply carved, "just as it is written in the Bible." Major Conder found indications of a large ancient city on this Tell. In its vicinity were a number of rock tombs and twenty-three rock-cut wine presses.

After its capture by Joshua this city was assigned to the Levites of the Kohathite family (Josh. xxi. 21), but afterward it fell into the hands of the Philistines. It was taken from the Philistines by the Egyptians at a later period and given as a dower to Solomon's Egyptian bride. (1 Kings ix. 16.) During the Maccabean wars it was captured by Judas Maccabæus and strongly fortified to guard the Jewish possessions of the plain.

"Within sight of every Egyptian and every Assyrian invasion of the land, Gezer has also seen Alexander pass by, and the legions of Rome in unusual flight, and the armies of the Cross struggle, waver and give way, and Napoleon come and go. If all could rise who have fallen around its base—Ethiopians, Hebrews, Assyrians, Arabs, Turcomans, Greeks, Romans, Celts, Saxons, Mongols,—what a rehearsal of the Judgment Day it would be! Few of the travellers who now rush across the plain realize that the first conspicuous hill they pass in Palestine is also one of the most thickly haunted—even in that narrow land into which history has so crowded itself. But upon the ridge of Gezer no sign of all this now remains, except in the name Tell Jezer, and in a sweet hollow to the north, beside a fountain, where lie the scattered Christian stones of Deir Warda, the Convent of the Rose."[1]

2. **The Valley of Sorek.**—This valley, or wady, descends to the low hills near Ain Shems (Beth-shemesh). From this point to Yebna (Jebneel) it is called Wady Surar. Thence to the sea it is Nahr Rubin. Its upper basin, which is a half mile in width, is formed by the junction of three wadies (Ghurab, Surar and Najil). This was the home of Samson and the scene of many of his famous exploits. *Zorah*, his birthplace, now called Surah, is situated on the high ridge which borders the northern side of the valley. (Josh. xix. 41.) *Eshtaol* lies to the northeast about two miles away. The ruins of *Beth-shemesh*, two and a half miles distant, lie on a knoll opposite Zorah on the southern slope. (2 Kings xiv. 13; 2 Chron.

[1] Smith's Hist. Geog., p. 217.

The Shephelah

xxviii. 18.) "'These three form a triangular group just where the stream breaks out into the Shephelah from the mountains of Judah.'"[1]

Four miles southwest of Zorah on the crest of the opposite ridge are the ruins of *Timnath*, where Samson sought a wife of the Philistines. *Timnath* is 740 feet above the sea and twenty-four miles from Askelon. The hiding-place of Samson (Judg. xv. 8) was the cleft or cave in the *rock Etam*, recently identified with Beit Atab, a few miles eastward among the Judean mountains. The *camp* or fortified place of *Dan*, was on the north side of the valley, probably between Zorah and Eshtaol.

The railroad from Jaffa to Jerusalem enters the Sorek valley about two miles south of Gezer and follows it to Beth-shemesh. Thence through the higher reaches of Wady Surar, and its connecting defiles among the mountains, it passes to the vale of Rephaim on the outskirts of the city of Jerusalem.

3. **The Valley of Elah.**—This has been identified with Wady es Sunt by the recovery of the site of Shocoh or Socoh (Shuweikeh) on its southern border. The valley is narrow and winds among the hills for the greater part of its course through the Shephelah region except in the neighborhood of Shocoh where it expands into a fertile plain one-fourth of a mile in breadth. In this plain is a large terebinth tree "fifty feet in height, with a spread of shade seventy-five feet in diameter, and a trunk seventeen feet in circumference."[2]

The valley of Elah, says Major Conder, is here a broad open vale, full of cornfields and bordered by rough hills, on which grow thick copses of lentisk. In the middle of the valley runs a deep trench, some twenty feet wide, with banks ten feet high, a water course worn by the winter torrents, its bed strewn with smooth white pebbles. This no doubt was the brook whence David took the five smooth stones when he advanced to meet Goliath. "The ridges on either side rise to a height of about

[1] Henderson's Geog., p. 90. [2] Pict. Pal., Vol. I., p. 158.

500 feet and have a steep, uniform slope, so that the armies ranged along them could see the combat in the valley." [1]

"And Saul and the men of Israel were gathered together and pitched by the valley of Elah, and set the battle in array against the Philistines. And the Philistines stood on a mountain on one side, and Israel stood on a mountain on the other side; and there was a valley between them." (1 Sam. xvii. 1-3.) [2] "From the rear of the position of Israel the narrow pass goes right up to the interior of the land near Bethlehem; so that the shepherd boy, whom the story represents as being sent by his father for news of the battle, would have almost twelve miles to cover between his father's house and the camp." [3]

The site of the "Hold of Adullam" has been recovered by M. Ganneau on a rounded hill in the upper stretch of the valley, about three miles southeast of Shocoh. This identification has been approved by the Survey party. The modern name is Aid-el-ma, in which it is possible, says Dr. Smith to hear Adullam, and its position suits all that we are told about David's Stronghold. It stands well off the Central Range and is very defensible.

Tell es Safi, at the outlet of the valley of Elah, is one of

TELL ES SAFI (GATH?)

the possible sites which have been suggested for the long-lost city of Gath (see p. 90). It is a conspicuous eminence of

[1] Bible Geog., p. 96. [2] Porter, in Alexander's Kitto.
[3] Smith's Hist. Geog., p. 228.

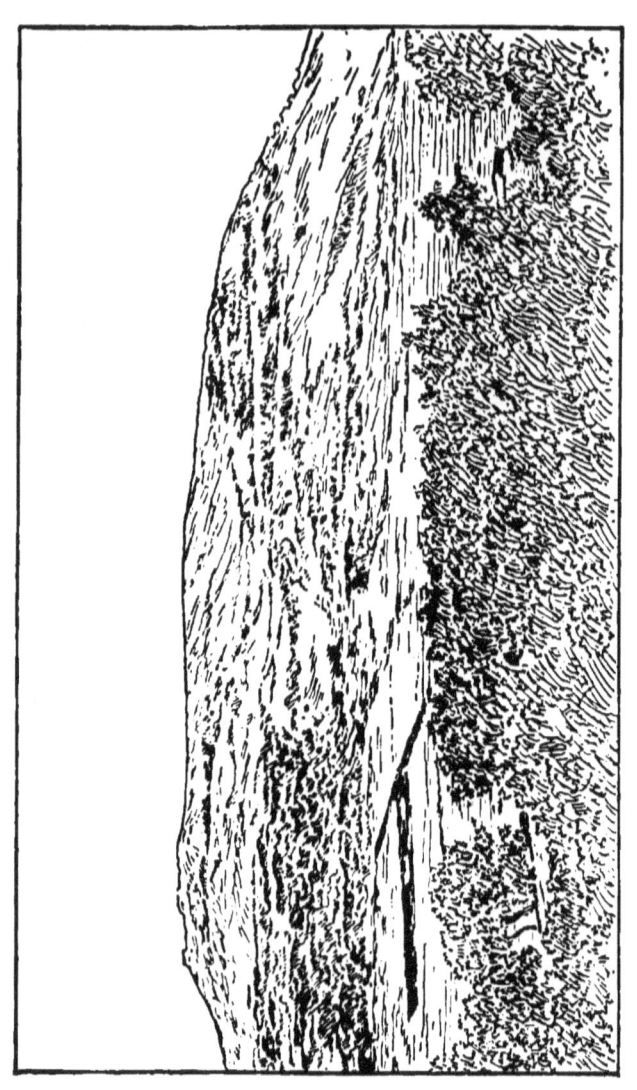

TELL ZAKARIYA

The Shephelah

white limestone formation, crowned with the ruins of a famous castle, known as Blanchgarde in the days of King Richard of England. The Palestine Exploration Fund has secured permission to excavate this Tell and the preliminary arrangements have been already made for a thorough examination of the site.

Azekah has been placed by some authorities at Tell Zakariya. It is mentioned several times in the Old Testament. See Josh. xv. 35 ; 2 Chron. xi. 9 ; Jer. xxxiv. 7, and Neh. xi. 30.

Tell Zakariya is four miles east of Tell es Safi. Recent excavations under the direction of Dr. Bliss have disclosed the remains of several buildings, one of which contains a chamber about eighty feet square. A series of small caves have also been opened up and explored. Scarabs, and pottery of Pre-Israelite types have been found amid the débris.

4. **Wady el Afranj.**—The long defile which leads into this wady begins its course near Hebron. Among the low hills it widens out into a broad, open valley apparently identical with the valley of Zephathah. On the plain it is known as Wady Simsin. It enters the sea a few miles north of Ashdod. The most interesting town in this valley is Beit Jibrin which occupies a part of the site of the famous city of Eleutheropolis of the Romans. It has been identified also with the ancient Betogabra. Dr. Thomson and other authorities regard it as the site of the city of Gath, and there seems to be good reason for this identification. The modern name Beit Jibrin signifies, or at least suggests, "the house of the giants."

Dr. Robinson, who has established the identity of this site beyond question with Eleutheropolis, describes the ruins as apparently of different ages and more extensive and massive than any he has seen in Palestine, except the substructions of the ancient temple at Jerusalem and the Haram at Hebron.[1] They consist of an irregular fortress of great strength, vaults, arches, walls, broken columns, etc., etc. In the chalk hills that enclose the valley in this vicinity there are a large number of closely connected caverns or grottoes of artificial construction. "The

[1] Rob. Res., Vol. II., p 25.

regularity and art with which these chambers have been constructed are admirable. The caverns consist of round vaulted chambers, twenty to twenty-five feet in diameter, supported by detached pillars. They are thirty to forty feet in height, each cavern is lighted from above by a well-like opening."[1]

One of these caverns was found to be nearly 120 feet in diameter and ninety feet deep.

In the days of the Roman occupation Eleutheropolis was regarded as the geographical centre of the Shephelah. From it roads radiated in all directions. "It was the half-way house between Jerusalem and Gaza, Hebron and Lydda, and the Onomasticon measures from it all distances in the Shephelah."

On the well-beaten highway through this place from Jerusalem to Gaza, in all probability, Philip crossed the path of the Ethiopian Eunuch. (Acts. x. 26-29.)

"This route," says Dr. Robinson, "lies along the north side of the meadow-like tract of Wady el Hesy and also of Wady Simsin for a short distance below the junction. In the gravelly bed of these valleys we saw water percolating through the sand and gravel and forming occasional pools. It was probably on this road Philip found the Eunuch and baptized him."[2]

Mareshah, identified with Maresh, lies less than two miles south of Beit Jibrin. At this point in the valley King Asa met the Ethiopian host under Zerah and won a signal victory, pursuing them even unto Gerar. (2 Chron. xiv. 9-14.)

"Mareshah," says Dr. Smith, "was an important and a powerful town as long as Beit Jibrin was unheard of; when Beit Jibrin comes into history it disappears. Can we doubt that we have here one of those frequent instances of the transference of a community to a new and neighboring site. If this be so, we have now full explanation of the silence of the Old Testament about Beit Jibrin; it was really presented by Mareshah."[3]

5. **Wady el Hesy** or Wady el Jizair, rises in the mountains

[1] The Land and the Book, Vol. I., p. 220.   [2] Phys. Geog., p. 119.
[3] Smith's Hist. Geog., p. 233.

a few miles southwest of Hebron and finds its way to the sea between Askelon and Gaza. The most important site in this valley is Tell el Hesy (Lachish) already described among the cities of the plain. It commanded the entrance to the valley at the point where the Shephelah pushes out one of its bastions, or advanced clusters into the plain.

6. **Wady esh Sheriah** skirts the southern base of the low hills, finding its way to the sea a few miles south of Gaza. It is joined by Wady es Seba in the plain, and the united branches are known as *Wady Guzzah*. This valley marks the southern border of the Shephelah. Below it the hills fall away gradually into the Negeb.

The region of the Shephelah is dotted over with the ruined sites of towns and villages, most of which have long been without inhabitants. As a whole it has been the theatre of many notable events in human history both sacred and secular. Its possessors held all the gateways of approach to the Holy City from the west; and yet there are but few instances on record in which the upper stretches of the mountain stronghold above it were forced in presence of a determined foe. Perhaps there is no instance of a more persistent attempt to penetrate these defiles than in the days "when all the Shephelah rang with the exploits of Richard," the Lion-hearted King of England; but with all his courage and persistency he could not drive back the forces which held the heights of Benjamin and Judah.

The Second Longitudinal Section

The Subdivisions suggested by the special features of this section are:

The Mountains of Lebanon and Galilee.—The Plain of Esdraelon.—The Mountains of Ephraim.—The Mountains of Benjamin.—Jerusalem and its Environs.—The Mountains of Judah.—The Negeb, or South Country.

CHAPTER XII

THE MOUNTAINS OF LEBANON AND GALILEE

1. **LEBANON.**—Or its equivalent expression Mount Lebanon—is a collective term applied to the high mountains of the Lebanon range. The northern boundary of this elevated tract is the valley of the Nahr el Kebir, which, as already noted, has been identified with "the entering in of Hamath." The deep gorge of the Litany river may be regarded as its boundary line on the south. Throughout its extent, a distance of nearly 100 miles, Lebanon is a continuous dorsal ridge with an average height of 7,000 feet. Its highest elevations are in the northern portion where the Dhar el Khodib, Jebel Muk-mul, and other associated peaks, rise to the height of more than 10,000 feet above the sea. It is an open question whether the word Lebanon, signifying the White Mountain, has been derived from the appearance of its snowy summits; or from its rugged masses of white limestone rock, which are even more conspicuous, as seen from below. The eastern declivity of Lebanon is steep, rugged and for the most part uncultivated:

Nº 4.
The Mountains of Galilee

the western is gradual, and presents a wonderful variety of scenery and production. From one outlook on this slope Doctor Thomson counted more than sixty towns and villages. In the Lebanon District there are 1,200 prosperous villages most of which are on the western side of the mountain at an elevation ranging from sea level to an altitude of 4,000 feet.

From time immemorial the beauty, the sublimity, the matchless fertility, the salubrious climate and the grand scenery of this goodly mountain have been celebrated in story and song. "Along its base eternal summer smiles: and along its summit 10,000 feet overhead, rests eternal snow. Between the two extremes flourish the vegetation, fruit and flowers of all climes."[1] Of this favored region Professor Rawlison says:

> The scenery is throughout most beautiful. Garden cultivation carpets the base of the mountain: above this is, for the most part, a broad fringe of olive groves; higher up the hillsides are carefully terraced, not an inch of ground being wasted: and among sharp cliffs and pointed rocks of a grey-white hue are strips of cornfields, long rows of dwarf mulberries, figs, apricots, apples, walnuts, and other fruit trees. Gorges, ravines, charming glens, deep valleys, diversify the mountain sides; here and there are tremendous chasms, with precipices that go sheer down for a thousand feet; tiny rivulets bound and leap from rock to rock and from terrace to terrace, forming chains of cascades, refreshing and fertilizing all around. In the deep gorges flow copious streams, shaded by overhanging woods of pines or cedars; and toward the summit are in several places magnificent cedar groves, remnants of the primeval forest which once clothed the greater part of the mountain.[2]

Lebanon is mentioned sixty-eight times in the Old Testament, but in every case the reference is to some of its natural features. "They speak of the head, the countenance, the sides, the roots of Lebanon: and of the snow, and the streams that run among its valleys. They sing of the glory of Lebanon and the smell of its forests—the cedar, the fir, the pine and the box together; and of its birds which sing among the

[1] Dr. J. L. Porter, Pulpit Treasury, 1884, p. 455.
[2] Story of Phœnicia, p. 18.

branches." [1] This fact together with the absence of any mention of ancient cities or towns, apart from Phœnicia, would seem to imply that Lebanon was, for the most part in its forest glory before the age of David and Solomon.

Cedars of Lebanon.—The cedar groves which crowned the higher levels of the timber belt have always been regarded as the chief glory of Lebanon. From the far-remote period of the reign of Naram Sin they were prized above all the trees of the wood, and were carried away from these rugged slopes to adorn kings' houses. In the British Museum may be seen fragments of cedar wood found by Mr. Layard, which had been built into the palaces of Nineveh more than 3,000 years ago. Of this choice timber David's palace on Mount Zion was built. Armies of skilled workmen were afterward employed, under the direction of Hebrew officers to cut and hew cedar beams on Lebanon to be used in the building of the first and second temples. These were delivered at the coast and thence were floated down in rafts to the harbor of Jaffa.

It is a common impression that the cedar has disappeared from Lebanon, except in one or two jealously guarded groves; but Dr. H. W. Jessup, an authority on this point, mentions *eleven* different groves which he has visited. These are:

1. The ancient 'Cedars of the Lord' above Bsherreh, three hundred and ninety-three in number.
2. The grove at the fountain of Ehden, fifty trees. 3. The great grove between El Hadeth and Niha, numbering tens of thousands of trees, covers an area of nearly twelve miles. 4. A small grove farther south on the summit and brink of the precipice.
5. The scattered trees above Duma. 6. The Ain Zehalteh grove of ten thousand trees, cut down by Murad Akil, and now growing up again. 7. A small grove on the cliff overhanging El Meduk. 8. A small cluster near Kulat el Bizzeh. 9. The fine grove of Masir el Fukhhar, about three hundred trees, some of great size. 10. The forest of Jird el Baruk, thousands of trees. 11. The eastern grove of Baruk, about two hundred trees.[2]

[1] The Land and Book, p. 139.   [2] Pict. Pal., Vol. II., p. 26.

The Mountains of Lebanon

In many of the public gardens and parks of Europe majestic cedars are growing from seeds of young trees, brought over by the Crusaders or later travellers from Mount Lebanon.

The principal rivers on the western slope have been mentioned in connection with the description of the Phœnician plain. All of these swiftly-flowing streams rise amid the snow fields of Lebanon and find their way down to the plain through ever deepening chasms in the mountain side. The gorges of the *Kadisha* and the *Litany* are specially notable for their depth and rugged grandeur. The latter has cut its way through one of the wildest and most romantic regions in Syria. "For thirty miles or more it flows at the bottom of a chasm so deep and so precipitous, that its course can only be traced here and there from the overhanging brow of one of the rocky eminences which close it in."[1] In some places it rushes in its impetuous course through tremendous chasms whose rocky walls rising nearly a thousand feet above the water, approach so closely together that the branches of trees from opposite sides are said to meet and interlock. At one point a mass of fallen rock has formed a natural bridge, called El Kuweh, a hundred feet above the bed of the stream. The road from Sidon to Banias passes over this bridge. The celebrated fortress known as Castle Belfort of the Crusaders (Kulat esh Shukif) rises conspicuously from the summit of a cliff within the great bend of the Litany and commands an extensive view of the surrounding country. "The lofty precipice on which it stands is exceedingly grand; the castle crowns its highest pinnacle, standing upon the very brink; so that a stone let fall from its battlements would almost drop into the stream below."[2]

The largest and most famous natural bridge in Lebanon spans the great chasm through which flows the Neba el Leben (Fountain of milk), one of the tributaries of the Dog river. It is called Jisr el Hajr—the Stone Bridge. Dr. Thomson describes it as follows:

[1] Sinai and Pal., p. 492.   [2] Robinson's Phys. Geog., p. 357.

"The height, measuring on the northern side, is 150 feet above the bed of the stream; on the southern side it is about half that height. The span is over 160 feet, and the curve is so regular and clean cut that one can scarcely believe that it is entirely natural. The thickness of the rock above the arch is thirty feet; and the breadth on top, where the road passes over it, from ninety to 150 feet. There is an excavated amphitheatre south of the bridge, about 300 feet in diameter, and enclosed by a perpendicular wall of limestone rock about 100 feet high."[1]

On the eastern side of Lebanon the water passes through underground channels, or dashes down the numerous torrent beds which furrow its declivities, to the Cœle Syria basin. Zahleh, the most prosperous town on this side of the range, lies at the southern base of Mount Sannin, 3,100 feet above the sea.

Its situation, says Dr. Thomson, is exceedingly picturesque. "There is nothing resembling it on these mountains. The town occupies both sides of the valley, which widens as it deepens, and finally opens out upon the plain to the southeast. Through the middle of the valley flows the sparkling little river of el Burduny, which descends from the southeast end of Jebel Sunnin; and after contributing to the wants of the town, its life-giving waters are distributed over a wide area of vineyards, gardens, and cultivated fields on the plain of el Buka'a below. The houses are built upon the sloping declivities on both sides of the river, and rise, tier above tier, far up the steep side of the mountain."[2]

Zahleh owes its prosperity mainly to the labors of missionaries from England and the United States, who have made it a centre of education and Christian influence.

It has churches, mission schools of higher and lower grades; and manufactures of various kinds have been successfully established. The inhabitants of Zahleh, numbering upward of 15,000, are almost wholly Christian.

The French carriage road over Lebanon, from Beirut to Damascus, is the recognized line of division between the Maronite and Druse districts of Lebanon. The former lies to the north and the latter to the south of the road.

[1] The Land and the Book, p. 228.   [2] Ibid., p. 199.

The Mountains of Galilee

2. **The Mountains of Galilee.**—This designation applies to that portion of the range which extends from the gorge of the Litany to the border of the Esdraelon plain.

On the east it is bounded by the Jordan valley: on the west by the Tyrian section of the Phœnician plain. It has many of the characteristic features of Lebanon, but is a broad, depressed region in contrast with its lofty heights. The portion which skirts the Jordan valley between the Lakes of Huleh and Galilee is called Mount Naphtali in the book of Joshua (xx. 7). This is the highest part of the Galilean range. Its dominant peak is *Jebel Jermuk*, 3,934 feet above the sea. Jebel Jermuk is twelve miles west of the Jordan on a line about midway between Huleh and Galilee. . . . North of Mount Naphtali the average elevation is about 2,800 feet: south of it the general level is less than 2,000. At a point due west of the Lake of Galilee the plateau is only 1,000 feet above the sea.

This district as a whole is noted for its beauty and fertility; its varied and picturesque scenery. It is broken by ridges and valleys in alternate succession, with here and there park-like stretches of upland, or beautiful mountain-rimmed plains.

It is well supplied with springs and water courses, and even in its present condition, justifies all that has been written about the rich portion of the inheritance of Zebulun and Naphtali. Lower Galilee included the southern portion of the highlands, as well as the plain of Esdraelon, and the low country bordering the sea of Galilee.

"Over the most of Galilee," says Dr. G. A. Smith, "there is a profusion of bush, with scattered forest trees—holly-oak, maple, sycamore, bay-tree, myrtle, arbutus, sumac and others—and in the valleys olive orchards and stretches of fat cornlands. Except for some trees like the sycamore, Upper Galilee is quite as rich. It is an undulating table-land, arable, and everywhere tilled, with swelling hills in view all round, covered with shrubs and trees."[1] "In briefer statement Renan describes it as a

[1] Hist. Geog., p. 419.

country very green, and full of shade and pleasantness, the true country of the Canticle of Canticles and of the songs of the well-beloved." [1]

Interspersed Plains.—One of the characteristic features of this highland region is the series of basins, or elongated plains which usually run in parallel strips from east to west between the ridges. The largest and most noteworthy of these are the plains of Ramah and Buttauf.

The Ramah basin lies at the foot of the southern range of Upper Galilee, a little north of the latitude of Acre. It is eight miles long and about a mile and a half wide. The road from Acre traverses the length of this plain.

The plain of Buttauf (El Buttauf), lies directly west of the Sea of Galilee. "It was properly the plain of Zebulun; the Rimmon of that tribe being still recognized in the Rummaneh of this plain. It is without doubt the great plain called Asochis by Josephus. On the south it is shut in on its southeastern part by a steep and almost isolated ridge, dividing it from the lesser plain of Turan beyond; and ending toward the west near Rummaneh." [2]

The plain of Turan is in reality a branch of Buttauf and is sometimes called the lower Buttauf. The main branch is about ten miles in length and two or three in width.

This basin is the granary of Galilee and, next to Esdraelon, it is the richest portion of the country. Its drainage is toward the river Kishon by way of the Wady Melek.

East of the low ridge which shuts in the plain of Buttauf, is a wide shelf of table-land commanding a fine view of the Lake of Galilee, lying nearly 1,000 feet below.

A conspicuous feature of the ridge which overlooks this stretch of table-land, and forms its western border, is a deeply indented mass of rock, called "Kurun Hattin"—the "Horns of Hattin." This is the traditional "Mountain of the Beatitudes" (Matt. v. 1), but the real site is probably one of the

[1] Life of Jesus, p. 96.   [2] Robinson's Phys. Geog., p. 130.

The Mountains of Galilee 113

lower slopes or ledges of the mountain in the immediate vicinity of the plain of Gennesaret. However this may be, Hattin will forever be memorable as the landmark overlooking the spot where the army of the Crusaders made its last stand, and was almost annihilated by the hosts of Saladin, July 5th, 1187. *Wady Hamam* which leads down from this elevation to the plain, terminates in a wild gorge flanked by perpendicular cliffs over 1,000 feet high. A labyrinth of caves cut into the face of the rock at dizzy heights has been for centuries in the past an impregnable stronghold of defence to the oppressed, as well as a favorite hiding-place for outlaws and robber bands.

During the reign of Herod the Great a large body of desperate men, who had hitherto defied the authority of Rome, were at length destroyed, or driven out, by soldiers let down in cages, which had been suspended from the cliffs above. "These storied caves still remain, extending for more than a mile, and many of them can only be reached by ropes."[1]

Noteworthy Places

1. **Kedesh of Naphtali.**—The modern village of Kades, five miles northwest of Lake Huleh, marks the site of this famous city of the Canaanites. It has a conspicuous position at the end of a low ridge, now covered with ruins, which borders the western side of a beautiful upland basin. Its elevation above the Jordan plain is about 1,600 feet.

"Just below the city gushed forth a copious spring. Then down a gentle slope were several hundred acres of olive groves, and beyond them a rich alluvial plain supplying abundance of corn and vegetables. Below the rugged brow of the steep ridge, it had its strip of marsh land of incomparable fertility. Thus they had every kind of produce at their very doors, like that long string of towns which studded the goodly heritage of Naphtali: 'Satisfied with favor, and full with the blessing of the Lord, (Deut. xxxiii. 23) from Chinnereth to Dan."[2]

Kedesh was one of the fenced cities in Mount Naphtali which

[1] Tristram's Holy Land, p. 244. [2] Ibid., p. 267.

"stood still in their strength" after the decisive battle between Joshua and the kings of the northern confederacy at the waters of Merom (Huleh). It was appointed as a city of refuge (Josh. xx. 7): and was allotted to the Levites of the family of Gershon. (Josh. xxi. 32.) Kedesh was the home of Barak, the warrior-judge of Israel, and from this mountain fastness he led his hastily gathered forces against Sisera on the plain of Esdraelon. (Judg. iv. 10.) It was one of the fortified cities taken by Tiglath-Pileser in the eighth century B. C. (2 Kings xv. 29.)

Hazor has been identified with Hadireh, at the foot of Jebel Hadireh, three miles southwest of Kedesh. It is directly west of Lake Huleh. A rocky hillock with a few ruins are the only evidences of the existence and former glory of the city of King Jabin, which, at one time, was the head of all the kingdoms of the northern confederates. (Josh. xi. 10, 11.) It was the only one of the captured cities of this region which was burned by command of Joshua (xi. 13). The city was subsequently rebuilt and reoccupied by another Jabin, king of Canaan, the oppressor of Israel in the period of the Judges. (Judg. iv. 2.) Hazor was selected as one of the garrison towns of the north by King Solomon and a part of the levy which he raised in Israel was devoted to the rebuilding and strengthening of its fortifications. (1 Kings ix. 15.) It was taken and destroyed by Tiglath-Pileser.

Edrei, mentioned in the list with Kedesh and Hazor, is supposed to be identical with a ruined site known as Tell Khuraibeh, about three miles southeast of Kedesh. (Josh. xix. 37.)

Safed, ten miles south of Kedesh, is situated in an upland basin 2,775 feet above the sea. It is one of the sacred cities of the Jews and the traditional site of the city set upon a hill to which Christ referred in the sermon on the Mount. Safed has no Scriptural associations apart from this supposition.

The names and probable sites of other towns which have been recently discovered may be briefly summed up as follows:

The Mountains of Galilee

Janoah (Yanu) seven miles east of Tyre (2 Kings xv. 19); *Migdal el* (Mujeidel) ten miles east of Tyre (Josh. xix. 38); *Heleph*, now Beit Lif, eight miles south of Mujeidel (Josh. xix. 33); *Horem* (Khurbet Harah) ten miles northeast of Kedesh (Josh. xix. 38); *Beth Anath* (Anitha) five miles west of Kedesh (Judg. i. 33); *Iron* (Yarun) four miles south of Beth Anath (Josh. xix. 38); *Beth-shemesh* (Kh Shema) three miles west of Safed (Josh. xix. 38; Judg. i. 33); *Ramah*, on the northern edge of the plain of Ramah (Josh. xix. 36); *En-Hazor* (Ain Hazzur) five miles north of Iron (Josh. xix. 37); *Hukkok* (Yakuk) seven miles south of Safed and six west of the north end of the Lake of Galilee (Josh. xix. 34); *Zebulun* (Neby Sebalan) at the eastern base of Jebel Jermuk (Josh. xix. 27).

Gischala, now El Jish, five miles northwest of Safed, was a prosperous city in the time of Christ. It was the last of the cities of Galilee to hold out against the Romans.

Upper Galilee was renowned for its strongholds. In the period of the conquest sixteen of the nineteen cities mentioned in Joshua (xix. 35-38) as belonging to Naphtali were strongly fortified. "In the time of Josephus the list of fortresses is a long one, and some of them will be famous while the records of the Hebrew nation are preserved."

In the hill country of Lower Galilee there are two places, unknown in Old Testament history, whose names are indissolubly joined with the name and story of Jesus—"the Man of Galilee." One was His early home, where He grew up with sinless character and winsome manners from infancy to mature manhood: the other was the place where He hallowed with His presence the cheerful festivities of a marriage; and "manifested forth His glory" in the first exercise of His miraculous power. These places,—Nazareth and Cana of Galilee—rank with Bethlehem and Jerusalem in importance, and their natural features have been studied with unusual interest and accuracy of detail.

Nazareth.—There never has been any question concerning the site of Nazareth. It nestles in a broad, green valley or upland plain, in the southern slope of the last, and lowest range of the Galilean hills. "Itself resting on a very steep slope, it is encircled by hills on all sides, leaving an undulating saucer-shaped basin, with many little valleys running into it on both sides and in front of the town. . . . The enclosing sides are, toward the south and east, well cultivated, corn fields mingle with vineyards and fig trees, and the occasional date palms, which here reach their northern limit, are marked features in the home landscape. But the encircling rim is bare, rocky, and in winter white and naked, a soft chalky limestone."[1]

Nazareth is 1,100 feet above the level of the sea. The fifteen crumpled hills which "rise around it like the edge of a shell to guard it from intrusion" are 400 or 500 feet higher. It is twenty-one miles from the Mediterranean Sea and seventeen from the lower end of the Lake of Galilee. While it is true that none of the great roads of the country led up to this sunny nook,—and, in this respect, it was secluded,—it was, nevertheless, very close to the central routes of travel which communicated with the outside world.

Just below it was the broad thoroughfare of the nations over the plain, intersected by the great trunk road running north and south. On the other side of Nazareth, four or five miles to the north was Sepphoris, the Roman capital of Galilee, where many roads centred; and through which passed the well-worn caravan and military route from Acre to the trans-Jordanic towns. The town, as the modern traveller sees it, lies on the western side of the enclosed basin and extends for some distance up its slope. "Its streets rise in terraces and the flat-roofed houses, built of the yellowish-white limestone of the neighborhood, shine in the sun with a dazzling brightness, from among gardens and fig trees, olives, cypresses, and the white and scarlet blossoms of the orange and pomegranate." Nazareth is to-day, as it has been in the past, a quiet rural town, the homestead of shepherds, craftsmen, vine dressers and tillers of the soil. The present population, as given by Baedecker, is 7,500 most of whom are of the Christian faith.

A new carriage road has been constructed from Haifa,

[1] Pict. Pal., Vol. I., p. 283.

GENERAL VIEW OF NAZARETH

twenty-three miles in length, which makes Nazareth easy of access from the coast. The so-called "holy places" shown by the representatives of the Greek and Latin Churches are clumsily-devised modern substitutions for realities which have passed away long centuries ago. The one thing, however, which makes Nazareth and all its surroundings a holy place, is the life once manifested here, the influence and blessed memory of which can never pass away.

The public fountain on the eastern edge of the village, known as the "fountain of Mary," has been from time immemorial the one unfailing source of water supply to its inhabitants.

This overflowing basin is the only thing in Nazareth which can be directly associated with the home-life of Jesus. Hither, without doubt, the Virgin-mother was wont to come nineteen centuries ago with her Divine Child,—just as the women of Nazareth come to-day, with their children by their sides or holding to their hands,—to secure a daily supply of water for their households.

"This path under the olive trees, like that from Bethany round the base of Olivet, and like Jacob's well, is one of the few where we may be perfectly sure we are treading for the moment in His earthly footsteps."[1]

The ridge which rises to the height of 500 feet, or more, directly behind Nazareth commands one of the most extensive panoramic views in Palestine. Northward it includes in its reach the mountains of Naphtali and the snowy heights of Hermon; eastward the plateaux of Gilead and Bashan; southward Tabor, Little Hermon, Gilboa, the Esdraelon plain, the long ridge of Carmel and the highlands of Samaria as far as Mount Ebal; westward to the Bay of Acre, and far beyond to the horizon line where sea and sky appear to meet. This outlook is the only place, perhaps, where—as Dean Stanley suggests—the three sacred mountains, *Tabor*, *Hermon* and *Carmel* are conjoined in one view.

[1] Tristram's Holy Land, p. 235.

"Here unchanged and unchangeable, the ancient mountains stand up before our eyes, as once long ago before the eyes of the boy Christ on the hilltop, with this difference only—that the scene is to us full of the memories of His own life, of chapels reared to consecrate some spot where He is supposed to have stood, and is thus more sacred for His sake than because of the triumphs or woes of the race from which He sprang."[1]

Above the line of houses on the slope of this ridge, there are several precipitous cliffs, hidden for the most part by a luxuriant growth of prickly-pear, either of which might mark the spot where the bigoted men of Nazareth sought to cast Jesus down headlong. The traditional site, a full half-hour distant, does not fulfill any of the conditions of the narrative. Whatever else may be affirmed of it, the so-called Mount of Precipitation is not "the hill whereon the city was built." (Luke iv. 28-30.)

Cana of Galilee.—The generally accepted site of Cana is Kefr Kenna, five miles northeast of Nazareth. It is on the direct route from the home of Jesus to the Sea of Galilee and borders the southern arm of the plain of Buttauf. Dr. Zeller, long a resident of Cana, describes it as follows:

"Its situation is particularly suitable, pretty, and healthy, for the village lies on a hill gradually sloping down toward the west, so that the houses, built in terraces up the slope, receive the cool west wind, which has through the plain of Buttauf a free and strong current over the village. On the south the village is separated by a valley from the higher mountains, separating it from Mount Tabor and the plain of Jezreel. At the south of the village is a copious fountain of excellent water. . . . The gardens at the foot of the hill are luxuriant, and the pomegranates produced there the best in Palestine."

The modern village has a population of 600, but Dr. Zeller makes the statement that there are sufficient traces that in former times it was at least thrice as large.

Cana was the home of Nathanael (John xxi. 2); the scene of the first miracle (John ii. 11); and the place where Jesus

[1] Conder's Bible Geography, p. 147.

The Mountains of Galilee 119

received the Nobleman from Capernaum whose son was healed in accordance with His word. (John iv. 46-54.)

Khurbet Kana on the northern side of the plain of Buttauf, nine miles distant from Nazareth, has been regarded by Dr. Robinson and others as the true site of Cana of Galilee, but recent researches have brought evidences to light, which seem to give additional confirmation to the arguments and the ancient tradition in favor of Kefr Kenna.

El Meshed, the probable site of Gath-hepher (Josh. xix. 13) is situated between Sepphoris and Kefr Kenna, three miles north of Nazareth. This town was the birthplace of Jonah. (2 Kings xiv. 25.) His reputed burial-place is shown on a hill near by.

Canon Tristram regards the evidence in favor of the identification of this place with Gath-hepher as very satisfactory.

Bethlehem of Zebulun, mentioned in Joshua xix. 15; and Judges xii. 8, 10, is seven miles northwest of Nazareth.

Japhia (Yafa) mentioned as a border town of Zebulun (Josh. xix. 12) is two miles south of Nazareth. It was the scene of a dreadful massacre of the Jews by the Romans during the reign of Vespasian.

CHAPTER XIII

THE PLAIN OF ESDRAELON

THE deflection of Mount Carmel breaks the continuity of the range to which it belongs, and opens up an easy passageway from the Mediterranean sea to the valley of the Jordan. This break, or intersecting plain, divides naturally into three parts.

At Tell el Kasis, nine miles from the sea, a spur, or outlying cluster, of the Galilean hills closes down toward the ridge of Carmel, confining the valley of the Kishon to a narrow pass scarcely more than one hundred yards in width.

The first division of the Great Plain is the expansion west of this pass. This properly belongs to the Maritime plain, and has been described in connection with that section.

The second, or central division, is formed by the recession of the hills on either side, eastward of Tell Kasis, to the bases of Gilboa and Little Hermon. It is a broad, undulating plain, triangular in outline, and unbroken by ridges or deeply cleft valleys.

At the present time it is distinguished from its outgoings on either hand by the name Esdraelon, a Greek form of the Hebrew word Jezreel, but in the Old Testament it is called "the Valley of Megiddo."

The third division is broken up by the parallel ridges of Gilboa and Little Hermon into three nearly equal parts: the middle portion being the famous valley of Jezreel, which leads down to the Jordan valley.

While recognizing the close connection, historically and otherwise between the central and eastern portions of this plain, it will be more convenient to study them in detail as separate divisions.

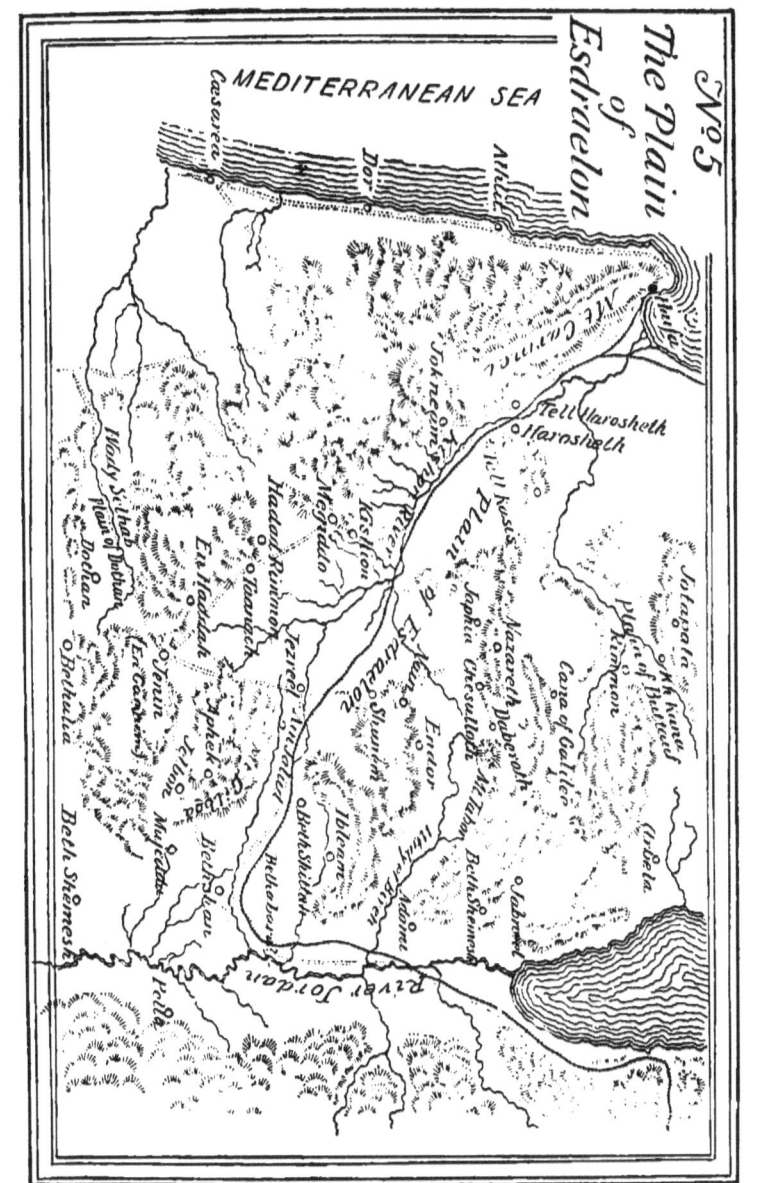

Esdraelon Proper.—As already intimated Esdraelon is a great triangle whose western apex is at Tell Kasis. Its longest side reaches to Jenin a distance of twenty miles and is bordered by the mountains of Ephraim. From Jenin to the hills of Galilee, a line skirting the eastern bases of Gilboa and Little Hermon may be regarded as its eastern side, fifteen miles in length. The remaining side extending along the hills of Galilee to the point of intersection with the eastern side does not exceed twelve or thirteen miles.

Gateways of Esdraelon.—These historic passage-ways have been happily described by George Adam Smith, as follows:

> The entrances are five in number, and are all visible from Jezreel. Three are at the corners of the triangle—the pass of the Kishon at Tell el Kasis, the glen between Tabor and the Nazareth hills, and the valley southward behind Jenin.
> The first of these is the way of advance from the plain of Acre; Harosheth of the Gentiles from which Sisera advanced, lies upon it.
> The second is the road down the plateau above Tiberias, and Northern Galilee generally; it is commanded by Tabor, on which there was always a fortress.
> The third is the passage toward that series of meadows which lead up from Esdraelon into the heart of Samaria—the Anabaseis of the Hill country.
> The other two gateways to the Great Plain were, of course, Megiddo and Jezreel. Megiddo guarded the natural approach of Philistines, Egyptians, and other enemies from the South; Jezreel that of Arabs, Midianites, Syrians of Damascus, and other enemies from the east.[1]

The fertility of the plain of Esdraelon has been one of its distinguishing features from time immemorial. Although sadly neglected it is still a prolific source of supply to the inhabitants of the land. "Checkered patches of wheat, barley, maize, millet, sesame, and even cotton, with broad, dark-brown strips of fallow land intervening, cover the surface; and along the hillsides here and there are groves of fig and olive trees,

---

[1] Hist. Geog., p. 390.

descending into the plain. The few palms at Jenin, the fruit trees, and the prickly-pear hedges surrounding most of the villages on the heights, add variety to the scene; still not a quarter of the plain is under cultivation, and the remainder is utterly desolate."[1]

It is a remarkable fact that there are no historic nor modern towns on the broad expanse of the plain. The liability to invasion from so many different quarters is the apparent cause. At the present time those who cultivate its fertile soil live in villages on the borders: and this has doubtless been the policy of all who have drawn their supplies from it in the centuries past.

The Kishon, and its numerous tributaries from the western slopes of Tabor, Gilboa and the hills about Jenin, drain the surface of the plain toward the Mediterranean.

The general direction of the Kishon (Nahr el Mukutta) is northwest. A portion of its bed is frequently dry in summer. Its close proximity to the base of the mountains of Ephraim makes it liable to sudden overflows which, as in ancient times, sweep everything of movable character before them.

Several ancient sites whose histories are connected with Esdraelon have been identified with a good degree of certainty. These we note in the order of succession beginning at the western apex of the triangle.

1. **Tell el Kasis.**—This is a green, flat-topped mound, which was probably the site of an ancient town or fortification. It is on the right bank of the river, over against the generally accepted location of the sacrifice of Elijah on Mount Carmel.

Canon Tristram regards the name ("Mound of the Priests") as an indication of the exact spot where Elijah slew the priests of Baal, when he brought them down to the "brook Kishon." It is significant, also, that the Arabic name for the Kishon is Nahr Mukutta, "the river of slaughter."

2. **Jokneam of Carmel.**—(Tell Keimum) is situated at the foot of a high bluff near the eastern end of the ridge of

[1] The Land and the Book, p. 209.

Carmel, twelve miles from the sea. It was a border city of Zebulun, and was assigned to the children of Merari of the tribe of Levi. (Josh. xii. 22, xxi. 34.)

3. **Megiddo.**—The probable site of this ancient stronghold, which before the days of Joshua had given its name to the Great Plain, is now known as *Lejjun*. It is about six miles from Tell Keimum on the border of the plain and, as already noted, guarded the approach to it from the south. "The line of hills, which beginning at Carmel thus far skirts the plain, here makes an offset toward the southwest; and then runs on again as a tract of lower hills, to Jenin or beyond. In front of this offset a low ridge extends out for some distance, leaving a nook behind it, in which are the remains of Lejjun. . . . The great road from Ramleh issues from the mouth of a valley in this nook, and immediately divides; one branch, going to Nazareth, passes down by a ruined Khan and bridge; the other, leading to Tabor and Damascus, lies about forty rods east of the Khan."[1] Dr. Robinson's identification of Lejjun with the Roman city called Legio is accepted without question. The evidence which he presents in favor of its identification with Megiddo, seems to be equally convincing and has been strengthened by recent research. Major Conder has recently suggested another location, known as Mujedda, near Bethshan as a more probable site, but the weight of evidence, as well as of authority, bears heavily against this supposition.

Dr. G. A. Smith sums up the argument in favor of Lejjun under three heads, as follows:

(1) It is close to Taanach, the location of which is not disputed.
(2) The waters of Megiddo are practically Kishon.
(3) Lejjun is as likely to give its name to the plain as Jezreel is, and did so give it in the time of Jerome.[2]

The name Megiddo appears frequently in the Egyptian records at Karnak and elsewhere, and, except in one instance,—

[1] Rob. Researches, Vol. III., p. 116.   [2] Hist. Geog., p. 387–388.

which seems to be due to ignorance of geographical details,—the descriptions of events connected with it correspond with the location of Lejjun.

Three great battles were fought in front of Megiddo in ancient times.

The first, which took place about 1600 B. C., gave Palestine into the hands of Thotmes III. and his successors. The second was in the period of the Judges. From Tabor on the opposite side of the plain the forces of Barak swept down upon the army of Sisera, and, aided by a terrific storm of rain and hail, broke their serried lines and won a signal victory. In that awful hour " the mountain torrents, rapidly swollen, poured down into the Kishon, the river overflowed, and the torrent swept them away chariots and horses in helpless confusion."[1] (Judg. v. 20-22.)

The third great battle at this place was more than six centuries later. It was a contest between Pharoah Necho of Egypt and King Josiah of Judah. It was long remembered with sorrow and lamentation in Judah; for here the good King Josiah was mortally wounded in his chariot by the Egyptian archers. (2 Chron. xxxv. 20-25.)

Another King of Judah, Ahaziah, died of his wounds in Megiddo. He was stricken by the avenging hosts of Jehu near Jezreel and fled across the plain to this city. (2 Kings ix. 27.)

There is a conspicuous mound (Tell el Mutasellim) a mile northwest of the ruins of Lejjun, which commands an extensive view of the region around, including the whole of the Great Plain. This elevation may have been within the limits of the town or its outlying defences.

4. **Taanach** (Tannuk) retains its ancient name unchanged. It is four miles east of Lejjun and seven miles southwest of Jezreel (Zerin). Some scattered ruins on a hilltop, near the modern village are all that remains of ancient Taanach. It was a noted stronghold of the Cannanites and is mentioned

[1] Tristram's Holy Land, p. 196.

The Plain of Esdraelon

five times in Scripture, in connection with Megiddo. (Josh. xii. 21, xvii. 11; Judg. i. 27, v. 19; 1 Kings iv. 12.) It is also mentioned in the Egyptian records of Thotmes III.

5. **Hadad-Rimmon**, now known as Rammaneh, is a short distance northeast of Taanach. In this place there was "great mourning for Josiah" by the people of Judah. (Zech. xii. 11.)

6. **En-gannim**, now Jenin, a town of Issachar lies at the southeast corner of the great triangle. It is twenty miles from the pass of Tell Kasis and seven miles south of Jezreel. It is the probable site of "Ginea," mentioned by Josephus, which answers to En-gannim or garden spring. "Its Hebrew name has been changed—the En for fountain was dropped, and the gannim, gardens, transformed into the present word Jenin."[1]

The spring, which long ago gave a name to the place, and which now gives life to the gardens of this prosperous village, comes from a valley to the east and is conducted into the midst of the town and out among the clustered groups of fruit trees which partially surround it. The Scripture references to En-ganim are Josh. xix. 2, xxi. 29.

7. **Jezreel.**—The modern village of Zerin, a collection of miserable hovels, occupies the site of this ancient city. It is on the eastern side of the triangle at the head of the valley of Jezreel. It has a slight elevation above the plain on a ridge or spur of the mountain of Gilboa, which juts out toward the northwest.

Jezreel was the royal residence of Ahab and Jezebel, and has been the scene of many thrilling events in the history of Israel. Its associations call up the names in turn of Gideon and Saul, Elijah and Naboth, Ahab and Jezebel, Joram and Ahaziah; and of Jehu the swift avenger of the crimes committed by the bloody house of Ahab. Rock-cut wine presses on the slope near the village suggest the vineyard of Naboth which was hard by the palace of Ahab. To secure this coveted posses-

[1] The Land and the Book, p. 172.

sion he caused its rightful owner to be put to death. In the fearful retribution that followed the dead body of his own son was cast into this plat; while from a window near by Jezebel, the chief instigator of the crime, was thrown down by her own servants to meet an ignominious death. (1 Kings xxi. 1; 2 Kings ix. 34.)

8. **Shunem**, or Sulem, as it is called by the Arabs, lies on the opposite side of the valley of Jezreel. It is three miles due north of Zerin on the southwest slope of the ridge of Little Hermon. There are some mounds in the vicinity, but no ruins above ground. In this village dwelt the Shunammite woman in whose house Elisha was always a welcome guest. As an evidence of Divine approval of this kindness her son, who had been suddenly stricken down by the heat in the harvest field, and had afterward died in her arms, was restored to life in answer to the prayer of Elisha. (2 Kings iv. 8-27.) It was also the home of Abishag (1 Kings i. 34): and of the fair maiden referred to in Canticles vi. 13.

Shunem was the place of encampment of the Philistines on the eve of the battle of Gilboa. (1 Sam. xxviii. 4.)

9. **Chisloth-Tabor** (Josh. xix. 12) has been identified with *Iksal*, a modern village, at the northeast corner of the great triangle. No historic sites have been found on its north side, unless Major Conder's supposition that Sarid (Josh. xix. 10-12) is identical with Tell Shodud, should prove to be correct.

Eastern Extension of the Great Plain.—The ridges of Gilboa and Little Hermon run side by side from Shunem and Jezreel to the border of the Jordan valley dividing this section into three divergent branches. The northern branch lies between the mountains of Galilee and the ridge of Little Hermon. Mount Tabor is included in this portion of the plain. East of Tabor it contracts to a narrow valley (Wady Bireh) which descends to the Jordan, but this can hardly be regarded as a portion of the plain. Up to the point where its expansion

The Plain of Esdraelon

ceases the trend is toward the west. The southern branch is an embayed plain or basin. It trends toward the west and its waters are tributary to the Kishon.

The central portion is the valley of Jezreel. Although greatly contracted in width this is the real continuation of the Esdraelon plain. "It is a beautiful meadow-like expanse, from two to three miles in breadth by about fifteen in length." The brook Jalud follows the course of the valley and drains the incline toward the Jordan throughout its extent. "The remarkable and distinguishing feature of these three portions of the plain is, that while both the northern and southern decline toward the west, and their waters flow off through the Kishon to the Mediterranean; the middle arm sinks down between them eastward, so that its waters, from a point within the triangle, run with a far more rapid descent to the valley of the Jordan at Beisan." (Rob. Phys. Geog., p. 132.)

The line of the watershed within the triangle, to which Dr. Robinson alludes in the above quotation, runs through or very near to the village of Fuleh, about two miles west of Shunem.

Fountain of Jezreel.—The principal source of the Jalud is the famous fountain (Ain Jalud) which issues from a cave at the base of Mount Gilboa, a mile and a half east of Jezreel. A pool fifty feet in diameter is supplied from this fountain head. This has been a favorite resort for herdsmen, and camping-place for caravans and military bands, in all ages. Its identity with the Spring of Harod has been generally admitted : and it fits in exactly with the narrative of Gideon's campaign against the Midianites. There certainly could be no more likely place for his encampment in this vicinity; nor for the testing to which his men were subjected on the eve of the battle. It is stated also in the narrative that the host of the Midianites were on the north side of them, by the hill of Moreh, in the valley. The hill of Moreh may have been some conspicuous hillock on the southern slope of Little Hermon, or the name may have been applied to the whole ridge. (Judg. vii.

1-25.) At this fountain of Jezreel King Saul encamped with his army before the disastrous battle in which he and his son Jonathan were slain on the " high places " of Gilboa. (1 Sam. xxviii. 4, xxix. 1, xxxi. 1-7.)

Beth-Shittah (Judg. vii. 22) is probably identical with Shutta, half-way between Jezreel and Bethshan.

Bethshan.—A flat-topped mound or tell in the lower stretch of the valley of Jezreel marks the site of this ancient stronghold of the Canaanites. Its modern name is Tell Beisan. It is four miles from the Jordan valley and commands the entrance to the Great Plain from the East.

> " The spur of rock on which it stands projects boldly, as if an outwork, beyond the east end of Gilboa. It rises almost perpendicularly 300 feet above the valley of the Jordan and leaves a strip of rich luxuriant plain, rather more than three miles wide, before the river is reached. But the old city was not confined to the tell on which its fortress stood. The ruins extend over a surface of three miles. The spot is not only in shape a miniature Gibraltar; it is marvellously favored by nature in other respects. No less than four perennial streams flow through the ancient city, dividing it into quarters. . . . The ruins surpass any others in Western Palestine. There are several noble Roman bridges over the Jalud, two of them tolerably perfect; a very fine amphitheatre, 180 feet in diameter, with its seats, corridors, and dens for wild beasts all entire; a large Saracenic khan, with arches and pavements, and columns of black basalt and white limestone alternating; many Roman temples, of which more than twenty tall columns are still standing erect, belonging to four or five sumptuous edifices." [1]

For a long time after the conquest this important fortress was held by the Canaanites (Judg. i. 27) and here the mutilated bodies of Saul and his sons were fastened to the city wall. From the summit of the mound under which the ruins of these walls have long been buried may still be seen the well-beaten thoroughfare to the ford of the Jordan, over which the valiant men of Jabesh Gilead came in the dead of night to take down and bear away these dismembered bodies to their own city, that

[1] Tristram's Holy Land, p. 215.

The Plain of Esdraelon

they might give to them an honorable burial. (1 Sam. xxxi. 8–13.) In the period of the Greek occupation the name of the city was changed to Scythopolis, but the old name still survives in the modern Beisan.

Scythopolis was the largest of the cities of Decapolis in the time of Christ, and the only one of that district west of the Jordan. (Matt. iv. 28; Mark v. 20.) At Jezreel the site of Bethshan can be plainly seen. Up this ascent, "the main passage between Eastern and Western Palestine," countless hosts have marched in orderly ranks, harnessed for the battle; or in loosely compacted caravan bands with camels and merchandise, on their way to Phœnicia or Egypt. Not once, but many times, the children of the East have spread along in this valley "like grasshoppers for multitude." Looking down it the watchman on the tower of Jezreel could see the clouds of dust, which the furious driving of Jehu had stirred, from the moment that his chariots had emerged from the shadowy depths of the Jordan valley. (2 Kings ix. 16–21.)

Mountains of Esdraelon.—*Three* prominent mountains lie between the broken divisions of the main range in this portion of the plain, and are separated from each other by the three branches, or arms, already described. This cluster of mountains, familiarly known as Gilboa, Little Hermon and Tabor, is an important feature in the topography, as well as in the history of the Great Plain.

1. **Gilboa.**—The general direction of the ridge of Gilboa is a little south of east. Its length is about ten miles. It rises from 500 feet above the sea at its eastern end, to an elevation of a little over 1,500 feet. On its summit, near the Eastern end, is the village of Jelbon, which seems to be identical with the appellation of the mountain. Jezreel and Bethshan, already described, stand on slight elevations or spurs at either end of the ridge. An old and well-travelled road from Jenin to Bethshan, crosses the range at Jelbon. El Mezar, a small Moslem village, rests on the western summit of the mountain about

three miles east of Jezreel. "This mountain seems still to be a stronghold of the aboriginal races. The fellahin of Mezar and Jelbon are very dark and square-built, and recall our ideal of the old Canaanites. Mohammedan in name and fanaticism, though very ignorant of the tenants of the prophet, they attach far greater importance to the worship of the new moon on the high places of this ridge, than to the ceremonial of the mosque. They seem, in fact, to be an isolated survival left overlooked by successive waves of conquerors on these barren, uninviting heights."[1]

The fatal battle in which Saul and Jonathan were slain raged along the northern slope of Gilboa. On these high places Saul and his three sons were smitten; the army was routed, and "the shield of the mighty vilely cast away." (2 Sam. i. 19-25.)

2. **Little Hermon.**—This mountain, now called Jebel Duhy by the natives, answers to the description of the hill Moreh. (Judg. vii. 1; 1 Sam. xxviii. 4.) It is a shorter ridge than Gilboa and rises more rapidly to its highest elevation (1,690 feet). "Jebel Duhy is simply the bold and abrupt end of a great upheaved basaltic dyke amidst the rolled and denuded limestone hills on all sides of it."[2]

The village of Nain, with name unchanged, stands on the northern slope of the mountain, not far from its western end. "The ruined heaps and traces of walls prove that Nain was of considerable extent and a walled town, and therefore with gates, according to the gospel narrative, though it is not mentioned in the Old Testament. A little above the present village, both on the east and west sides are many tombs hewn out of the rocks. About ten minutes' walk to the east of it is the principal burying-place, still used, and probably on this very path our Lord met the sorrowing procession."[3] (Luke

[1] Art. by Tristram in Pict. Pal. Vol. I., p. 277.
[2] Pict. Pal., Vol. I., p. 279.
[3] Tristram's Holy Land, p. 222.

vii. 11-18.) Here within a short distance of the Shunammite's home a greater than Elisha, awaked, by his own almighty power, the cold, inanimate form of the widow's only son from the sleep of death and gave him back to his mother.

Endor or Endur lies on the same side of Jebel Duhy. It is about two miles northeast of Nain. In the vicinity of its mud-built houses there are many caves which are still utilized, as they have been in the past, for human habitations.

At Endor some of the leading chieftains of the Canaanites were slain by Barak. (Ps. lxxxiii. 10.) Hither came King Saul in his extremity from his camp on the other side of the valley of Jezreel, some eight miles distant, to seek counsel from the woman who had a familiar spirit. (1 Sam. xxviii. 7-20.)

Mount Tabor is the most conspicuous landmark in Lower Galilee. It is not a ridge but a shapely mountain which carries its symmetrical proportions upward from its base to its crown. Its general contour is that of a truncated cone, but from the plain the flattened platform on its summit is not apparent.

"This strange and beautiful mountain," says Dean Stanley, "is distinguished alike in form and in character from all around it. As seen from the northwest of the plain it towers like a dome—as seen from the east like a long arched mound—over the monotonous undulations of the surrounding hills, from which it stands completely isolated, except by a narrow neck of rising ground, uniting it to the mountain-range of Galilee. It is not what Europeans would call a wooded hill, because its trees stand all apart from each other. But it is so thickly studded with them, as to rise from the plain like a mass of verdure. Its summit—a broken oblong —is an alternation of shade and greensward, that seems made for a national festivity; broad and varied, and commanding wide views of the plain from end to end."[1]

The range of vision from the summit of Tabor extends from Hermon to Ebal and Gerizim; and from Gilead to the Mediterranean. In the triad of sacred mountains—Hermon, Tabor

[1] Sinai and Palestine, p. 418.

and Carmel—so often referred to in Scripture, we have the representatives of the most conspicuous features of the mountains of Palestine, viz: majesty, grace and park-like beauty. This representative character is seen in such expressions as these: "As Tabor is among the mountains, and as Carmel by the sea," etc. (Jer. xlvi. 18.) "The north and the south Thou hast created them; Tabor and Hermon shall rejoice in Thy name." (Ps. lxxxix. 12.)

Mount Tabor was the rallying point for the hosts of Barak and Deborah (Judg. iv. 5–15): and the place where the brothers of Gideon were slain by Zebah and Zalmunna. (Judg. viii. 18, 19.) Tradition has located the Transfiguration scene on this mountain, but this does not accord with the story of the Evangelists, nor with the fact of its permanent occupation by a Roman garrison in the time of Christ.

Taken as a whole, with its outgoings toward the Jordan and the Mediterranean, there is no place, perhaps, on the surface of the earth, of similar extent, that calls up such a long train of historic associations, and stirring events of far-reaching character, as the Plain of Esdraelon. From the very beginning of human history it has been the camping-place and marching-ground and battlefield of the nations. "The ancient Canaanites, with chariots of iron, have traversed it; Midianites and Amalekites, with their vast herds have desolated it; and the Philistines, the Jews, the Egyptians, the Syrians, the Greeks, the Romans, the Crusaders, the Saracens, the French—all have passed over it, and gone on to victory or defeat. To this day it is exposed to devastating excursions from the Bedawin, those modern 'children of the East' who come up from beyond Jordan 'as grasshoppers for multitude.'"[1]

Thus in a sense more realistic than poetic, Esdraelon has been the valley of decision, where Dynasties have risen and fallen; where Kingdoms have been lost and won.

---

[1] The Land and the Book, p. 210.

The Plain of Esdraelon

Hence it is not strange that this "valley of Megiddo," with its long record of conflicts, from Thotmes III. to Napoleon, should have been selected as the typical representative of the last great field of conflict between truth and error, right and wrong. (Rev. xvi. 16.)

CHAPTER XIV

THE MOUNTAINS OF EPHRAIM

THIS division, sometimes designated collectively as Mount Ephraim, extends from the plain of Esdraelon to the northern border of the tribe of Benjamin. In the latter periods of Jewish history Bethel and its neighboring towns were included within its limits, but the term as generally used applies to the mountain tract allotted to the sons of Joseph.

Mount Ephraim differs from the highlands of Galilee in several characteristic features. Its ridges are more rugged, rocky and irregular; its plains are smaller and less frequent, but notable for their rich pasturage and abundant crops of grain; its wadies and glens are more deeply cleft, and in some localities the scenery is exceedingly wild and picturesque. This portion of the inheritance of Joseph has been happily described by Moses as "a land blessed of the Lord for the precious things of heaven, for the dew, and for the deep that coucheth beneath: for the chief things of the mountains and for the precious things of the everlasting hills." (Deut. xxxiii. 13-15.)

The mountains of this series which claim our special attention are *Carmel*, *Samaria*, the twin peaks of *Ebal* and *Gerizim* and *Baal Hazor*.

Mount Carmel.—The position of this deflected portion of the main range has been already indicated. It is a ridge about eighteen miles in length which terminates in a bold headland on the Mediterranean coast. At its eastern extremity, the starting point of the deflection, it is 1,730 feet above the sea. The elongated beak at its western extremity is 550 feet above the water. It still retains its old name, Jebul Kurmul.

"The excellency of Carmel" (Isa. xxxv. 2) has passed into a proverb, but the mountain, has no doubt, lost much of its original grace, and park-like beauty by the destruction of its trees. The few that yet remain crown the highest parts or stand in lonely isolation here and there along its sides. It is still true, however, that the "characteristic of the excellency of Carmel is the wonderful profusion of flowering and perfumed shrubs—bay, storax, linden, arbutus, and innumerable others, wafting their fragrance in volumes through the air, while the open glades, with flowers of every hue, orchis, cyclamen, tulip, lily, are like the Garden of Eden run wild. But all this 'Excellency' only lasts for a month in spring. Moreover, nothing can be more marked than the sudden contrast from the brown, bare hills of Samaria to the copse and woodland which greets us as soon as Carmel is touched."[1] "No wonder that to an Israelite it seemed the park of his country; that the tresses of the bride's head should be compared to its woods (Cant. vii. 5); that its ornaments (excellency) should be regarded as the type of national beauty; that the withering of its fruits should be considered the type of national desolation." (Amos i. 27; Isa. xxxiii. 9; Nahum i. 4.)[2] "Before him, who stands on Carmel, nature rises in a series of great stages from sea to Alp: the Mediterranean, the long coast to north and south, with its hot sands and palms; Esdraelon covered with wheat, Tabor and the lower hills of Galilee with their oaks,—then over the barer peaks of Upper Galilee, and the haze that is about them, the clear snow of Hermon, hanging like an only cloud in the sky."[3]

Carmel was a favorite resort of Elijah and of his successor Elisha. Here the name and absolute authority of Jehovah were vindicated by Elijah, in the presence of 850 priests of Baal and the assembled thousands of Israel. (1 Kings xviii. 19-40.)

The scene of this memorable conflict was at the eastern or landward end of the ridge, some twelve miles from the sea. The probable place of the sacrifice, which seems to fulfill all the conditions of the narrative, still bears the name El Mahrakah, the "burning" or "the sacrifice." It is a rock platform or terrace, 300 feet lower than the summit of the mountain and 1,400 feet above the bed of the Kishon. There

[1] Tristram's Holy Land, p. 198.   [2] Sinai and Palestine, p. 420.
[3] Smith's Hist. Geog., p. 340.

is a deep spring with a stone-built square reservoir, in the upper part of this platform, in which have been found shell-fish such as exist only in *permanent* fresh-water streams or pools. Dr. Tristram thinks this fact is sufficient of itself to establish the presumption that this deep and shaded spring, fed from the rocks of Carmel, remained throughout the three years' drought, when all the wells were dry and the Kishon itself had shrunken to a string of pools, or had been dried up at its fountain heads. He describes the site as "a glade overlooking the plain somewhat in the shape of an amphitheatre, and completely shut in on the north by the well-wooded cliffs. No place can be conceived more adapted by nature to be that wondrous battlefield of truth, where Elijah appealed to Israel, How long halt ye between two opinions? In front of the principal actors in the scene, with the king and his courtiers by their side, the thousands of Israel might have been gathered on the lower slopes, witnesses of the whole struggle to its stupendous results."[1]

Another site, about a mile north of this platform has been suggested by Mr. L. Oliphant. It is near some tanks capable of supplying water in any quantity, even at that time of drought. This spot is not far from the summit of the hill and within 100 yards of the path which leads down to Tell el Kasis, the traditional site of the slaughter of the priests of Baal. Within a radius of two and a-half miles of this spot Mr. Oliphant counted the ruins of twelve ancient towns and villages.

The after scene in the events of that memorable day, when the prophet directed the king to prepare his chariot and get down in haste lest the rain should stop him, is in keeping with all the facts of observation and experience with respect to the heavy rains, which ofttimes follow the appearance of the "little clouds which arise out of the sea"; as well those which relate to the behavior of the Kishon at this point, when there is a sudden cloud-burst over the plain. To cross this river and avoid the danger of swamping in the alluvial bed of Esdraelon,

[1] Tristram's Holy Land, p. 200, and also Hend. Geog., p. 134.

before he should reach Jezreel, eighteen miles distant, required quick work in the face of the on-coming tempest. In order that he might hasten the king's flight the stern prophet of Israel becomes, for the moment, a messenger of deliverance. "And the hand of the Lord was on Elijah; and he girded up his loins, and ran before Ahab to the entrance of Jezreel." (1 Kings xviii. 46.)

Samaria.—The Mount, or Hill of Samaria, stands in the midst of a wide green basin (Wady esh Shair), which is shut in on three sides by picturesque, fruitful hills of a higher elevation. It is twenty-three miles from the sea, six miles northwest of Shechem, and about fifteen southwest of Jenin. It is an oblong, shapely hill, wholly isolated from the mountains around it, except on the east, where a low, undulating ridge touches its base and forms a slight connection with the main range. Its elevation above the encircling plain is over 500 feet, and it is belted to the top with broad, green terraces. The outlook from the summit includes in its reach, through an opening in the hills to the west, a glimpse of the blue water of the Mediterranean Sea. The natural advantages of this watch tower among the mountains were recognized by Omri, the father of Ahab, who bought it of Shemer its owner for two talents of silver. To the royal city which he afterward built upon it he gave the name Shomeron (Samaria) "after the name of Shemer, the owner of the hill." (1 Kings xvi. 24.) For nearly 200 years this 'city on the green hill' was the capital of the ten tribes of Israel. It was central in location, beautiful for situation and rich in agricultural surroundings; but it lacked the strength of righteousness and the favor of the God of Israel, who had chosen Mount Zion for His dwelling-place. Under the lead of Ahab and Jezebel it became a famous centre of idolatrous worship in its most degrading forms: and, as the prophet had foretold, on the eve of its destruction, "its glorious beauty," which was on the "head of the fat valley," became "a fading flower and as the hasty fruit before the summer." (Isa. xxviii. 1–4.) The chief elements of the history of this northern capital of Israel are rebellions, murders, famines and sieges. (1 Kings xx. 12–29, xxii. 37, 38; 2 Kings vi., vii. and xvii. 5, 6.)

Samaria was destroyed, after a close investment of three years, by the Assyrians (B. C. 721). Its inhabitants, with their brethren of the ten tribes, were carried away beyond the Euphrates. With its fall the kingdom of Israel, which had maintained its separate existence for a period of 255 years, came to an end.

The foreign element introduced into the land by the kings of Assyria built a new city upon the ruined site of Samaria, which survived all the changes and reverses of subsequent centuries until it came under the control of Herod the Great. In his reign and under his personal direction it was rebuilt and adorned with princely munificence. Palatial buildings crowned its heights and extended down its graded slopes on every side. In honor of the Emperor Augustus' Herod changed the name of the reconstructed city to Sebaste, but the old name was retained by the people of the land: and, after the lapse of many centuries, its ruins are still designated by the name, Samaria. In the height of its prosperity Philip preached the gospel with wonderful success in Samaria: "and there was great joy in that city." (Acts viii. 5–8.) The largest of the ruined structures yet remaining on the slope of the hill is the Church of St. John the Baptist, built by the Crusaders in the twelfth century. Higher up are the remains of clustered columns and of a magnificent double colonnade, fifty feet in width, which swept around one of the upper terraces of the hill —a gleaming coronet of marble—for a distance of 3,000 feet. "In the western part," says Dr. Robinson, "about sixty of these columns are still erect, and farther east are some twenty more standing irregularly, at various intervals. Many more than these lie prostrate; and we could trace whole columns in fragments nearly or quite to the village." Near the church of St.

John is an ancient reservoir which suggests the "Pool of Samaria" where one washed the blood-stained chariot of Ahab, in which, at last, the King had met his doom. (1 Kings xxii. 38.)

After all the centuries which have intervened, no language so strikingly depicts the present condition of the cities of Ahab and Jezebel; Herod and Herodias—as the words of the prophet Micah, "I will make Samaria as an heap of the field and as plantings of a vineyard: and I will pour down the stones thereof into the valley, and I will discover the foundations thereof" (i. 16). Not more literally, says Canon Tristram, have the denunciations on Tyre or Babylon been accomplished.

Ebal and Gerizim.—The rounded summits of these celebrated mountains rise side by side on the western edge of the plain of Mukhna, in the very heart of the mountains of Ephraim. As seen from the south or west, they appear to be conical peaks, but in reality they are parallel ridges running nearly east and west, which terminate abruptly in rounded masses on the edge of the plain.

The distance between their bases at this point does not exceed 500 yards. Mount Ebal is on the north side of the vale of Shechem. Its summit (3,076) is higher than Mount Gerizim (2,848). "The contrast between Ebal and Gerizim is less real than is often supposed. The dip of the strata sinks to the north across the valley, and this causes a want of springs on the south side of Ebal, but its north side is almost as rich in them as the north slope of Gerizim." "The sides of Ebal are clad with smooth prickly-pear. Gerizim, facing north seems more bare and scarped: caves and springs diversify its face. Up the little wadies, or nullahs, which furrow its sides, rich fruit-orchards of orange, almond, pomegranate, peach, and fig trees climb, till the rocks are too bare to support them; and on the east corner, is the little Moslem chapel, which crowns the ruins of the Samaritan temple."

The survivers of the Samaritan sect, which at latest accounts numbered about 160 persons, have a synagogue in Shechem, but to this day they observe the Passover as an annual festival on the summit of Gerizim. "This mountain," to which the woman of Samaria nearly 2,000 years ago pointed as the venerated shrine where her people worshipped, is the only place on the face of the earth where this sacred festival has been celebrated continuously, in strict accordance with the law of Moses, since the fall of Jerusalem. The sacred roll of the Pentateuch, which is their warrant for this service and which they guard with jealous care, is perhaps the oldest copy of the Bible in the world.

On Gerizim the fearless Jotham, youngest son of Gideon, uttered in the hearing of the people in the valley below, the fable of the talking trees. This quaint homily embodied a fitting rebuke to the men of Shechem for their folly and sin in choosing the murderer of his brethren to be their king, as well as a presage of the calamity which was certain to overtake them in the end. (Judg. ix. 6–21.)

Along the slopes of these mountains, on opposite sides of the valley of Shechem, all the tribes of Israel were ranged on that memorable day, when the book of the Law of God, which Moses had written, was rehearsed and ratified. (Josh. viii. 30–35.) Next to the giving of the law at Sinai this was the most sublime spectacle and impressive service in the history of Israel. It is a remarkable fact that two breaks, or lateral valleys, directly opposite each other, have formed natural amphitheatres on either slope which seem to have been prepared for such an occasion. The narrative distinctly affirms that the people "stood on this side and that of the ark ; half of them in front of Mount Gerizim, and half of them over against Mount Ebal ; as Moses the servant of the Lord had commanded." (Josh. viii. 33 ; Deut. xxvii. 12, 13.) There is no intimation that either the readers or those who responded were on the top of the mountains. The objection sometimes urged on this supposition has no support in the story of this impressive service ;

The Mountains of Ephraim

nor in the topography of the site where it took place. Says Sir Charles Wilson, "It is hardly too much to say of this natural amphitheatre that there is no other place in Palestine, so suitable for the assembly of a large body of men, within the limits to which the human voice could reach, and where at the same time each individual would be able to see what was going on. The recesses in the two mountains that form the amphitheatre are exactly opposite to each other, and the limestone strata running up to the very summits in a succession of ledges present the appearance of regular benches. A grander sight can scarcely be imagined than that which the reading of the Law must have presented: the ark borne by the Levites, on the gentle elevation that separates the waters that flow westward, from those flowing toward the Jordan, and all Israel and their elders, and officers, and their judges on this side and on that, half of them over against Mount Gerizim and half of them over against Mount Ebal, covering the bare hillsides from head to foot."

In the clear, resonant air of Palestine the human voice can be distinctly heard, as many experiments have demonstrated, across these natural terraces from side to side.

The view from Mount Ebal includes a magnificent sweep of country extending from the borders of the Negeb to the snow-crown of Hermon, seventy-five miles northward, and from the plateau of the trans-Jordanic range to the shore of the Mediterranean westward.

Dr. G. A. Smith has admirably summed up the salient features of this far-reaching panoramic view, in the following description:

> All the four zones, two of the four frontiers, specimens of all the physical features and most of the famous scenes of the history, are in sight. No geography of Palestine can afford to dispense with the view from the top of Ebal. In detail it is this:
> Looking south, you have at your feet the pass through the range, with Nablus (Shechem); then over it the mass of Gerizim, with a ruin or two; and then twenty-four miles of hilltop at the back of which you dimly dis-

cern a tower. That is Neby Samwil, the ancient Mizpeh. Jerusalem is only five miles beyond, and to the west the tower overlooks the Shephelah. Turning westward, you see—nay, you almost feel—the letting down, by irregular terraces, on to the plain; the plain itself flattened by the height from which you look, but really undulating to mounds of 100 and 200 feet; beyond the plain the gleaming sand-hills of the coast and the infinite blue sea. Joppa lies south; west thirty-three miles; Cæsarea northwest twenty-nine. Turning northward, we have the long ridge of Carmel running down from its summit, perhaps thirty-five miles distant, to the low hills that separate it from our range; over the rest of this the hollow that represents Esdraelon; over that the hills of Galilee in a haze, and above the haze the glistening shoulders of Hermon. Sweeping south from Hermon, the eastern horizon is the edge of Hauran above the Lake of Galilee, continued by the edge of Mount Gilead exactly east of us, and by the edge of Moab, away to the southeast. This line of the Eastern range is maintained at a pretty equal level, nearly that on which we stand, and seems unbroken save by the incoming valleys of the Yarmuk and the Jabbok. It is only twenty-five miles away, and on the near side of it lies the Jordan valley—a great wide gulf, of which the bottom is out of sight. On this side Jordan the foreground is the hilly bulwark of Mount Ephraim, penetrated by a valley coming up from Jordan into the plain of Mukhna to meet the pass that splits the range at our feet.[1]

Baal Hazor, now called Tell Asur, is the highest peak of Mount Ephraim. Its elevation is 3,318 feet above the sea. It is nearly five miles north of Bethel; its southern base being the old border line between Ephraim and Benjamin. It is a mass of bare rock prominent in Biblical history mainly as a noted high place, or landmark. All its associations seem to have been with Baal and his worship. Dr. Henderson mentions the fact that in the "registers" (Neh. xi. 33) Hazar was counted to Benjamin, but in other descriptions it is clearly included within the portion of Ephraim. The sheep farm of Absalom was somewhere on the slope of Baal Hazor. To this place Amnon, his brother, was treacherously decoyed and put to death. (2 Sam. xiii. 23–29.)

Interspersed Plains.—These have been described as "a

[1] Hist. Geog., p. 120.

The Mountains of Ephraim

succession of level spaces, more or less connected, which spreads southward through the centre of the province to within a few miles of its southern border.

"First from Jenin is the Plain of Dothan, reached by an easy pass through the low hills; thence another easy pass leads to a series of spacious meadows lying across the country from the south end of Gilboa to the range of hills which bulwark the city of Samaria on the north; and thence another easy pass leads to a third series of plains running south past the vale of Shechem into the great Sahel Mukhna opposite Gerizim."[1]

The plains of Dothan and Mukhna are especially noteworthy because of their associations with important events in Biblical history.

Dothan.—The great caravan route, which diverges from Esdraelon at Jenin and follows the course of the Wady Selhab to the coast plain, passes through the plain of Dothan.

It lies directly south of the middle portion of the Esdraelon plain and is separated from it by a low, narrow ridge jutting out from the eastern base of Carmel.

As seen from the hills above it Dothan is a lovely crescent-shaped basin, almost encircled by hills, which converge around it from the north and south. It is still famous as a rich pasture ground to which the shepherds and herdsmen resort when the pastures of the hills and more elevated plains become dry and parched with the drought of summer.

Here Joseph found his brethren and was sold by them into slavery. The passing of a company of Midianite merchantmen afforded the opportunity of disposing of him finally, as they supposed, without imbruing their hands in his blood. (Gen. xxxvii. 17-28.)

A large mound of ruins (Tell Dothan) at the southern end of the plain still bears the name unchanged by which it was known in the days of the Patriarchs.

---

[1] Smith's Hist. Geog., p. 327.

"Here a spring yet bursts at the foot of a smooth hill. Round this spring Joseph's brethren probably sat as he drew near. They cast him into a cistern that was empty, for the season must have been advanced, and possibly had been one of drought when they took their flocks from Shechem to Dothan. The town remained till the time of the kings, when it was the scene of Elisha's deliverance."[1] (2 Kings vi. 13–17.)

Remains of the old paved road and dry cisterns or pits have been found near Tell Dothan.

Mukhna.—This upland plain lies between the eastern declivities of Ebal and Gerizim, and a broken range from two to four miles distant on the edge of the plateau.

Its length is about nine miles. The general direction is nearly north and south. The vale of Shechem enters the plain on its western side about one-third of its length from the northern end. At either extremity it is contracted by mountain spurs or ridges which close gradually around it, but in the middle portion it expands to a breadth of three or four miles. On the eastern side, directly opposite the valley of Shechem, an offshoot one-half a mile or more in width, runs up among the hills for two or three miles.

The broader expanse of the plain is noted for its fertility and is carefully cultivated. In the early months of summer it is an almost continuous grain field, from end to end. The portion of ground which Jacob bought of the children of Hamor was at the mouth of the valley of Shechem. It is doubly consecrated to the memory of the Patriarch by the well which he dug and transmitted to his posterity, and by the tomb of his noble son Joseph, who was buried here in the presence of the assembled thousands of Israel. After the conquest this "parcel of Ground" became the inheritance of the children of Joseph. (Josh. xxiv. 32.)

Wadies.—These are numerous and may be readily traced on the Relief Map.

The most prominent on the eastern side are: *Wady Farah,*

[1] Henderson's Hist. Geog., p. 66.

The Mountains of Ephraim

a notable cleft, leading down from the base of Mount Ebal to the Damieh ford and the mouth of the Jabbok; and *Wady El Aujeh*, which begins its course near Baal Hazor and enters the Jordan valley directly east of Bethel. On the western side the torrent beds are shallower with many tributaries: and hence are not so distinctly marked. Among those worthy of special mention are: *Wady Arah*, which affords a passage-way to the coast from Megiddo; *Wady Selhab*, which traverses the length of the plain of Dothan and issues in Wady Abu Nar on the coast plain; *Wady Shair* (the Barley Vale), running northwest from Shechem, via Samaria, to the coast; *Wady Kanah*, and its tributaries, beginning in the southern part of the plain of Mukhna and ending in the Aujeh river: and *Wady Deir Balut*, with its tributaries *Wady Ishar* and *Wady Nimr*.

The natural, or geographical, limit of Mount Ephraim on the south is marked by the course of "the Wady Deir Balut, the Wady Nimr, a line across the water parting to the Wady Samieh, and so down this and the Wady Aujeh to the Jordan, eight miles above Jericho."[1] The head waters of both of the lateral valleys traced in this description, are at the northern base of Baal Hazor.

TOWNS AND SACRED SITES OF MOUNT EPHRAIM

1. **Shechem.** Nablus, the modern representative of this ancient city, is in the very heart of the rich heritage of Joseph. Its position is midway between Dan and Beersheba and almost midway between the sea and the Jordan. It is thirty miles from Jerusalem; thirty miles from Cæsarea; eighteen from Jenin; thirty-three from Bethshan; and about sixteen from the nearest ford of the Jordan. The city overspreads the narrow watershed, which lies between Ebal and Gerizim, parting the rivulets which flow from their bases on either hand, to east

[1] Smith's Hist. Geog., p. 249.

and west. "The streams which burst forth copiously from springs within its walls, run from the east gate down to the Jordan; and those which dash over the pavements, at the west end of the town find their way through the plain of Sharon to the Mediterranean. A site so fair and lovely, invited by its many waters the earliest settlement of mankind. As old as Damascus and Hebron, Shechem was a city when Abram yet lived in Chaldea."[1]

There is certainly no spot in Central Palestine which rivals this narrow valley in rich verdure, luxuriant vegetation, and luscious fruitage. It calls forth the admiration of travellers from every clime, and may be regarded as a typical representative of the natural beauty and extraordinary productiveness of "the good land" when in its best estate. To the outskirts of this place Abram came, about forty centuries ago with his flocks and herds. It is probable that he crossed the Jordan at the Damieh ford near the mouth of the Jabbok, and followed the course of the Wady Farah to his camping ground, by the oak of Moreh, in front of the city. Here he erected his altar and called on the name of the Lord. (Gen. xii. 6.) Shechem has the singular honor, therefore, of being the oldest of all the sacred places in the land. It is the historical as well as the geographical centre of Palestine.

With a view to a longer sojourn than that of Abram, and doubtless for the purpose of dwelling apart from the people of the land, Jacob, on his return from Padan Aram, purchased the portion of ground which was before the city and there he pitched his tents and erected his altar. (Gen. xxxiii. 18–20.) It was under the oak which was by Shechem,—the same no doubt that had sheltered Abraham—that, before he renewed his covenant at Bethel, Jacob hid the strange gods, which some of the members of his household had brought with them from the other side of the Euphrates. (Gen. xxxvii. 12–17.)

[1] Tristram's Holy Land, p. 175.

NABLUS AND VALE OF SHECHEM

The Mountains of Ephraim 147

After the conquest Shechem was designated as the central city of refuge on the west side of the Jordan and was given to the Levites. (Josh. xx. 7, xxi. 21.)

It was the general meeting place for the tribes during the lifetime of Joshua. Here the Law was ratified and here the Covenant with Jehovah was renewed on that memorable day when Joshua addressed them for the last time. (Josh. viii. 33, xxiv. 1-25.)

In Shechem Abimelech, the usurper, established his short-lived kingdom. At a later period another usurper, Jeroboam the son of Nebat, was crowned in this place by the representatives of the ten tribes. (1 Kings xii. 16-20.) It was the first capital of the kingdom of Israel: and long afterward when the ten tribes had been carried away into captivity by the Assyrians, Shechem became the chief seat and the sacred city of the Samaritans.

The modern city (Nablus) is solidly built, but its streets are narrow, roughly paved and crooked. In some quarters they are arched over as a protection from the heat of the sun. The walls and houses are built of fine white limestone. The town is literally embowered in green, and to the traveller approaching it from either end of the valley it presents a very attractive appearance. The present population is estimated at 20,000. "When railways and other modern improvements and institutions shall have been introduced into Palestine, this city, from its natural position, abundance of water, great fertility of the surrounding country, and temperate climate, will become not only a favorite resort, but the centre of a large and productive district."[1]

Jacob's Well.—It may be confidently asserted that no spot of ground within the limits of the Holy Land has been more certainly identified than the site of this wayside well at the entrance of the valley of Shechem. The ruined chapel or crypt which has protected its mouth from the drifts of earth and dis-

[1] The Land and the Book, p. 145.

integrated rock that have been piling up around it for ages, is the successor of an older structure dating as far back as the fourth century. Its connection with the well of Jacob has been established · by the testimony of the Apostle John; by the remarkable consensus of traditions concerning it among the Jews, Samaritans, Moslems and Christians; by the testimony of Eusebius and other witnesses, from the early part of the fourth century and onward; and by the name still given it by the Samaritans (Beer Jacub), who have never lost sight of it, and in a sense have been its guardians, since the beginning of the Christian era. For many years the visible opening to Jacob's well was in the floor of the subterranean chapel, to which reference has been made; and could only be reached by a descent of eight or ten feet through a hole in its vaulted roof. Since the discovery of the real mouth of the well under the floor of the chapel by Dr. C. A. Barclay in 1881, the rubbish has been cleared away, and access to it has been made easy from the level of the ground outside. The following account of this important discovery was given by Dr. Barclay in a letter to the Palestine Exploration Fund:

> Jacob's well has again and again been described by writers on Palestine, and all have mentioned their disappointment that instead of finding any semblance to a well, or anything which would recall the interview of our Lord with the woman of Samaria, they have merely found a dark, irregular hole amid a mass of ruins in a vaulted chamber beneath the surface of the ground. I have shared this disappointment on many previous visits to Nablus, and again, as a fortnight ago I stood with my wife beside the spot, it was with great regret that we were utterly unable to picture before us the scene so graphically described by the Evangelist. We had clambered down into the vault, and were vainly attempting to peer into the dark hole amid the heaps of stones and rubbish, when we chanced to notice, a few feet from the opening, a dark crack between the stones. Fancying that possibly it might be another opening of the well, we removed some stones and earth, and soon were able to trace part of a curved aperture in a large slab of stone. Deeply interested at finding this, we cleared away more earth and stones, and soon distinguished the circular mouth of the well, though it was blocked by an immense mass

The Mountains of Ephraim

of stone. Calling to aid two men who were looking on, with considerable labor we at length managed to remove it, and the opening of the well was clear. It is impossible to describe our feelings as we gazed down the open well, and sat on that ledge on which doubtless the Saviour rested, and felt with our fingers the grooves in the stone caused by the ropes by which the water-pots were drawn up. The following day we devoted to completely excavating round the opening of the well, and laying bare the massive stones which form its mouth. This consists of the hard white limestone of the country, and is in fair preservation, though parts are broken away here and there. The annexed rude sketch gives some idea of its appearance.

The exact measurements I also give:

	ft.	in.
Length	3	9
Breadth	2	7
Thickness	1	6
Height above pavement	1	1
Breadth of aperture of well	1	5½
Depth of well	67	0
Width	7	6

We let a boy down to the bottom, but found nothing of any interest, but evidently there is a large accumulation of rubbish. I trust that a stone of such intense interest may long remain uninjured now that it has been exposed to light. [1]

[1] Thirty Years' Work, p. 198.

The accompanying sketch of a section of the well, for which the author is also indebted to the exploration fund, shows at a glance the ruined vault, as it formerly appeared; the contracted mouth; and the relative proportion of masonry and limestone-rock.

" The mouth and upper portion of the well," says Major Anderson, " is built of masonry, and the well appears to have been sunk through a mixture of alluvial soil and limestone fragments till a compact bed of mountain limestone was reached, having a horizontal strata which could be easily worked, and the interior of the well presents the appearance of being lined throughout with rough masonry. . . . Robinson states that the well in 1838 was 105 feet deep, and if his measurement is correct, débris to a depth of thirty feet has accumulated in thirty-eight years. It was undoubtedly sunk to a great depth for the purpose of securing, even in exceptionally dry seasons, a supply of water, which at great depths would always be filtering through the sides of the well and would collect at the bottom." [1]

The associations of this place carry us far back in the world's history amid pastoral scenes and patriarchal customs, but the event which the Apostle John so graphically describes, transcends all others in interest and importance. Here in the very beginning of His public ministry Jesus revealed Himself to a perplexed inquirer as the long promised Messiah, the Saviour of the world. Standing on this hallowed spot we may see to-day all the distinctive features of the landscape on which His eyes rested nearly 2,000 years ago. Here are the twin mountains which rise abruptly from the plain as if to guard the entrance to the narrow vale which lies between; the wide expanse of the vast grain field which stretches away to the north and south; the sites of Salim and Sychar and Shechem within easy reach; the place of worship on the summit of the sacred mountain of the Samaritans; the dusty road on which the lowly Redeemer travelled skirting the base of this mountain; and, stranger than all, the great stone recently brought to the

[1] Thirty Years' Work, p. 197.

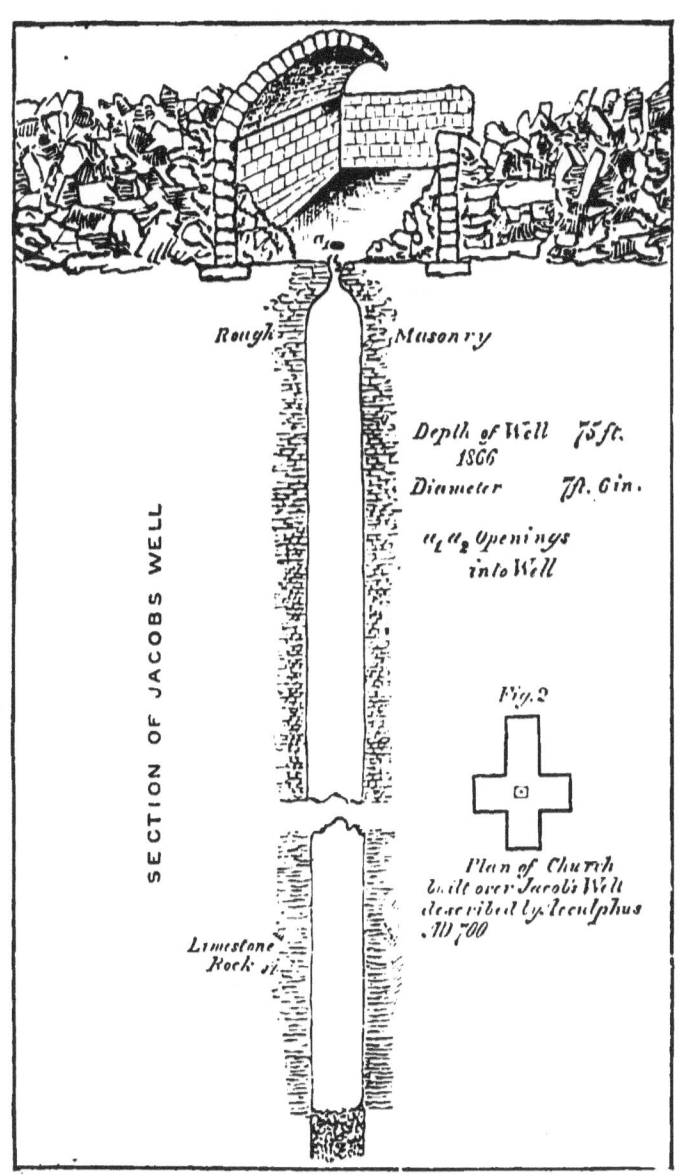

RUINED CRYPT, AND SECTION OF JACOB'S WELL

light on which for a few moments He rested His weary limbs at the midday hour.

Sychar has been identified with Askar, a small modern village on the site of an older town at the eastern base of Mount Ebal. It is about a half-mile north of Jacob's well and less than two miles northeast of Nablous. "The survey investigations have shown that the ancient Samaritan name of this village closely approached the Hebrew Sychar, and the error first made by the Crusaders, who confounded Sychar with Shechem, may now be corrected through the explorations which prove the antiquity and ancient name of the village Askar near Jacob's well."[1]

Joseph's Tomb is on a slight elevation between Jacob's well and Sychar. It is almost in the middle of the mouth of the valley. The location accords with the Biblical narrative and for many centuries it has been held in reverence by Jews, Samaritans, Moslems, and Christians, as the burial-place of Joseph.

Belata, a little village a short distance due west of the well, according to the Samaritan and early Christian traditions, marks the place of "the oak which was by Shechem." (Gen. xxxv. 4.) This is supposed to be identical with the "oak of Moreh" (Gen. xii. 6); "the oak that was by the Sanctuary of the Lord" (Judg. xxiv. 6); and "the oak of the pillar that was in Shechem." (Judg. ix. 6.)

Salim (Salem), the ancient Shalem, is situated on the eastern arm of the plain of Mukhna about two miles northeast of Jacob's well. It is mentioned in connection with the sojourn of Jacob (Gen. xxxiii. 18) and in the New Testament as a city near Ænon. (John iii. 23.)

Ænon has been identified by the Survey party with Ainun six miles north of Salim at the head of the Wady Farah. The statement of the Evangelist that there was much water, or many waters, there would seem to imply that it was not very near to the Jordan.

[1] Thirty Years' Work, p. 125.

The Mountains of Ephraim

"Ænon simply means 'springs' the plural of the oft recurring Ain or En. The situation was a central one, approachable also from the northward and from all Samaria, and by the central main road from the south. The assumption that the place where John baptized must have been in Judea, at least not in Samaria, is without show of proof." [1]

"Of the numerous sites previously proposed there is no other which unites every requisite of name and water supply. Other Ænons exist far from any Salim, and other Salims in water districts where no name Ænon is found; but in the Great Wady Farah, which, starting at Shechem, formed the north boundary of Judea, in the Jordan valley, we find a site which appears to satisfy every requirement and to agree well with the new identification of Bethabara." [2]

Doctor Thomson and others dissent from this conclusion and regard this site as one of the number not yet identified.

Tulluza at the head of the Wady Farah was formerly regarded as the probable site of *Tirzah*, but the Survey party has decided in favor of *Teiasir* a small village eleven miles northeast of Shechem. It stands on a fertile plateau close to the southern border of Issachar. "The beauty of the position," says Major Conder, "and the richness of the plain on the west, the ancient remains, and the old main road to the place from Shechem seem to agree well with the idea of its having been once a capital; and if I am right in the suggestion, then the old sepulchres are probably, some of them, those of the early kings of Israel before the royal family began to be buried in Samaria." [3] Tirzah was a royal city of the Canaanites and its king appears in the list of the rulers subdued by Joshua. (Josh. xii. 24.) It became the capital of the northern kingdom during the reign of Jeroboam. It was the residence of the successors of Jeroboam until the sixth year of the reign of Omri. Tirzah was notable among the cities of Israel for its beauty. (Cant. vi. 4.) At Tirzah Menahem organized a formidable

[1] Henderson's Hist. Geog., p. 154. [2] Thirty Years' Work, p. 125.
[3] Thirty Years' Work, p. 86.

rebellion against Shallum and thence went up to Samaria, where he slew Shallum and reigned in his stead. (2. Kings xv. 14.)

Thebez, now known as Tubas, is a prosperous village a short distance southwest of Teiasir. It lies in a little valley among the mountains and is almost surrounded by olive groves. Here Abimelech met his death at the hands of a woman, who cast a mill stone down from the wall upon his head. (Judg. ix. 50-57.)

Bezek is supposed to be identical with a ruin called Ibzik, directly north of Tubas. At Bezek Saul assembled his army before he crossed the Jordan to the rescue of the men of Jabesh Gilead. (1 Sam. xi. 8.) It is thirteen miles from Shechem on the Bethshan road, and is directly opposite the site of Jabesh Gilead.

Samaria (Sebaste) has been already described. It is five miles northwest of Shechem.

Dothan is ten miles north of Shechem. The probable site of **Bethulia** associated with the heroic exploit of Judith, is Mithilia four miles southeast of Dothan. (Judith iv. 6, xvi. 21.)

Awertah, which the Samaritans identify with Gibeah Phinehas (Josh. xxiv. 33), is situated on a little knoll, which rises in the middle of the plain of Mukhna, about three miles south of Jacob's Well. The reputed tombs of Eleazar and Phinehas, the son and grandson of Aaron are close to the village. They have been sketched and accurately described by the Survey party. Awertah was occupied as a Samaritan city until the seventh century. The supposition that these venerated structures represent the burial-places of Eleazar and his family is supported alike by Jewish, Samaritan and Christian tradition. "The Monument of Phinehas appears to be of great antiquity, but that of Eleazar has been rebuilt."[1] The traditional tomb of Ithamar is also shown below the village under a grove of olive trees.

[1] Thirty Years' Work, p. 112.

The Mountains of Ephraim

Taanath Shiloh (Josh. xvi. 6) has been identified with Ja'ana four miles southeast of Shalim.

Arumah, the residence of Abimelech, is represented by El Orma, a small village on the Mukhna plain, six miles southeast of Shechem. (Judg. ix. 41.)

Janoah (Yanum), a frontier town of Ephraim, lies on the eastern slope of the hills which trend toward the Jordan. It is three miles east of El Orma. (Judg. xvi. 6, 7.)

Timnath Serah (Timnath Heres) the possession and burial-place of Joshua has been identified by the Survey party with a village called Kefr Haris, ten miles southwest of Shechem. "A sacred shrine exists outside the village to which the name Neby Lusha (no doubt a corruption of Yehusha, or Joshua) is applied. Ancient tradition also places the tomb of Nun at this same village, and a second sacred place called Neby Nun was found close to the supposed site of the tomb of Joshua."[1] As regards these sepulchres, says Major Conder, we have an accord between four distinct lines of tradition and the existence of the name of Mount Heres in the modern form of Haris. (See Judg. ii. 9; Josh. xix. 50, xxiv. 30.)

Tiphsah the scene of a cruel outrage in the reign of King Manahem (2 Kings xv. 16), is probably represented by a village eight miles southwest of Shechem, which bears the name of Tafsah.

Shiloh, now known as Seilun, lies in a secluded upland valley, a short distance east of the great northern highway. It is twelve miles from Shechem and nine miles north of Bethel. "The proofs," says Dr. Robinson, "that Seilun is actually the site of the ancient Shiloh, lies within a small compass: and both the name and the position are sufficiently decisive. The full form of the Hebrew name was apparently Shilon, as we find it in the gentile noun Shilonite. The position of Shiloh is very definitely described in the book of Judges as on the north side of Bethel, on the east side of the highway that goeth

[1] Thirty Years' Work, p. 111.

up from Bethel to Shechem, and on the south of Lebonah." (Judg. xxi. 19.) The ruins of Shiloh are scattered over a little knoll, which rises on the north side of the valley. Except a narrow opening to the south this valley or plain is shut in on all sides by a circlet of hills. "Northward the Tell slopes down to a broad shoulder, across which a sort of level court, 77 feet wide by 412 long, has been cut. Most probably here stood the tabernacle which was, according to rabbinical tradition, a building of low stone-walls, with the tent drawn over the top. The spring (Judg. xxi.), is three-fourths of a mile northeast, up a narrow valley on the sides of which are rock-cut tombs; in some of these the old high priests of Israel may have been laid."[1] Shiloh was the resting place of the tabernacle and the religious centre of the Israelites for more than 300 years. (Josh. xviii. 1.) At Shiloh Joshua completed the division of the land according to the lot which was cast for them after the several portions had been "described by cities into seven parts in a book." (Josh. xviii. 6–10.) Here Eli ministered as high priest and Samuel grew up in the service of the Sanctuary. Shiloh was the residence of the prophet Ahijah, when the wife of Jeroboam came to inquire of him, concerning her son, who had fallen sick. (1 Kings xiv. 17.)

The site of Shiloh is utterly desolate. The rich soil has been swept from the valleys around it and the hills where once grew the olive and the vine have lost all the glory of their former covering and are now a corrugated mass of bare shelving rocks.

"Go ye now unto my place, which was in Shiloh, where I set my name at the first, and see what I did to it for the wickedness of my people." (Jer. vii. 12.)

Lebonah (Lubban) is three miles northwest of Shiloh. It is mentioned only in Judges xxi. 19, in connection with Shiloh.

[1] Henderson's Geography, p. 94.

The Mountains of Ephraim

Gilgal (Jiljilia) is four miles south of Lebonah and seven north of Bethel. It is situated on a high ridge near the western brow of the range. This is the Gilgal where Samuel established one of the schools of the Prophets. From Gilgal Elijah went to Bethel and thence to Jericho on his last visit to the "sons of the prophets." (2 Kings ii. 1, iv. 38.)

This place should be distinguished from Gilgal (Jiljulia) on the plain of Sharon, and also from the Gilgal in the Jordan valley, where Israel encamped, after the passage of the river.

CHAPTER XV

THE MOUNTAINS OF BENJAMIN

THE possession of the tribe of Benjamin, with the exception of a narrow strip of low land on the Jordan plain, was a rugged mass of mountain territory extending from the border line of Ephraim to the southern slope of Mount Zion. The habitable portion of this highland district was limited mainly to its flattened summit, or watershed, which is about twelve miles in length by two to five in breadth. It has no broad fertile valleys, nor perennial streams, nor continuous cross-ridges, as in the hill country of Ephraim. One of its characteristic features is a succession of isolated knolls which rise here and there out of the table-land "suggesting by their very appearance either the site of fortresses or high places for worship." Most, if not all, of these "little hills" mark the site of an ancient fenced city or town. While their summits were utilized for defence, the slopes were terraced and carefully cultivated. The portion of Benjamin was never an agricultural region, however. It was a mountain fastness, whose rugged surface and "munitions of rock" were accounted its chief excellence: a land, as one has described it, "more fit for the building of barriers than for the cultivation of food." While this is admitted it is evident, also, to every passing traveller that it was not always a land given over to barrenness and desolation. The thickly clustered sites of its ancient towns are the witnesses to-day, as they have been for ages, that this narrow plateau was capable of sustaining a population, at least, as large as that of the tribe of Benjamin in its most prosperous days.

Aside from the fact that it was preëminently a pastoral re-

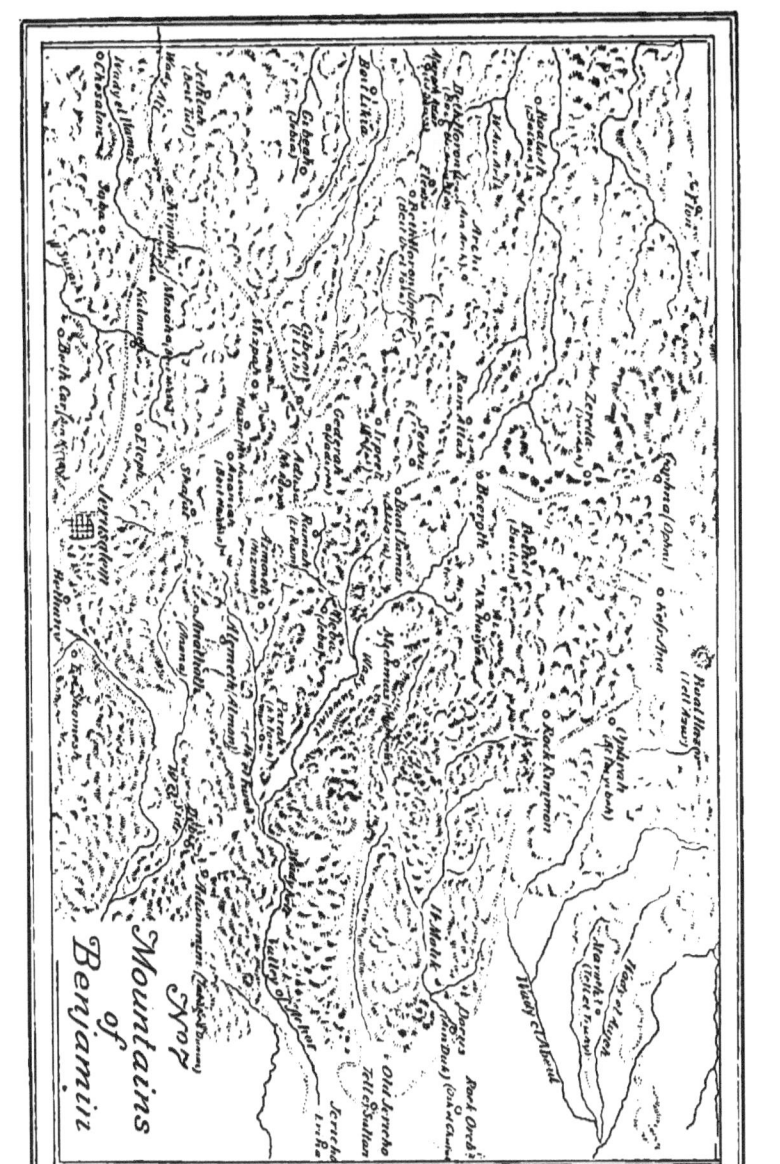

The Mountains of Benjamin

gion, it should be noted that its terraced slopes and alluvial basins, although limited in area, were capable of producing as bountiful crops and as luscious fruits as any other portion of the land. It is also true that in no other part of the country was it possible for neglect and disaster to entail such widespread destruction to field and vineyard. As we see it now it is a land *in ruins*, as well as a land *of ruins*. Its groves have been cut down; its streams have been dried up at the fountain head; its terraced walls have been destroyed or removed; the underlying rocks of vineyard and olive-yard have been washed clean and bare; and the rich soil which once covered them has been swept away by winds and winter torrents into the wadies and ravines, and thence into the great plains below.

The most conspicuous elevation, on the plateau, north of Jerusalem is Neby Samwil, the probable site of **Mizpeh**. It is five miles northwest of Jerusalem and may be regarded as one of the outer circle of mountains which environ it. Its elevation is 2,936 feet. Neby Samwil was first identified with Mizpeh, the watch tower of Benjamin, by Dr. Robinson. There are some who question this identification, and suggest Mount Scopus and other points in the vicinity, but the greater number of acknowledged authorities accept it without hesitation. It is certain, as Canon Tristram suggests, that "no other peak in Southern Palestine affords such a panorama": nor is there any other that would be so likely to suggest the name. Its modern name, Neby Samwil—the tomb of Samuel —was given it by the natives, who, on the basis of a very ancient tradition, regard this peak as the burial-place of Samuel.

To Mizpeh the people of Israel were assembled to take counsel together concerning the attitude of unjustifiable rebellion assumed by the tribe of Benjamin (Judg. xx. 1–11); to offer sacrifices and seek deliverance from the Philistines (1 Sam. vii. 5–11); and again to ratify the selection of Saul as their first king. (1 Sam. x. 17.) It was one of the three points, also, where Samuel regularly judged Israel. (1. Sam. vii. 16.)

Dr. Henderson gives the following statements concerning its relation to the tabernacle :

Mizpeh is associated with Gibeon "the great high place" in several places; and Nob is similarly conjoined with it in the Talmud (Quarterly 75, p. 37). Conder's suggestion that it is also Nob seems not improbable. It is remarkable that on Neby Samwil, a similar levelled platform to that at Shiloh has been traced. "There is a scarp of rock some five or six feet high running north and south, a narrow trench is cut between this and a sort of platform of rock, which is occupied by buildings. North of the church there is a sort of sunk court about 250 feet north and south, by 500 feet east and west, to which the narrow passage leads. On the northeast of this is a flat platform of rock reached by steps with a cave below. . . . East of the platforms are two large shallow reservoirs communicating with one another, and there are two curious shallow recesses in the scrap" (Memoirs III., p. 151). With these, at Mizpeh and Shiloh, may also be compared the platform found at Kirjath Jearim, where a place was made for the ark, similar to the tabernacle in which it should have been.[1]

During the period of the captivity Mizpeh was the scene of the massacre of Gedaliah and the remnant of Judah who had gathered around him for protection. (2 Kings xxv. 22–25 ; Jer. xli. 1–8.) It was probably the "Mountjoye" of the Crusaders, who, from this outlook gained their first view of the Holy City.

The three notable mountains, Zion, Moriah and Olivet, in and about Jerusalem can be studied to better advantage in connection with the topography of the city.

Wadies and Ravines.—The mountains of Benjamin are deeply furrowed on either side by water courses and ravines, which may readily be traced on the contour map.

On the eastern side the most prominent are the Wadies Nuweimeh and Kelt.

Wady Nuweimeh begins its course on the edge of the watershed northeast of Bethel, and, passing by the rock Rimmon descends rapidly into a deep gorge, which opens out into

[1] Henderson's Geog., p. 175.

WADY SUWEINET

The Mountains of Benjamin 161

the plain by the fountain, called Ain Duk, a little to the north of the site of ancient Jericho. An old road, marked for some distance by a Roman pavement, led up this pass to Ophra on the heights of Benjamin and thence to the great northern road.

Wady Kelt, directly behind Jericho, enters the plain on its south side passing close by the village of Riha, on or near the site of the Roman Jericho. The high mountain called Quarantina, the traditional mount of the Temptation, towers up nearly a thousand feet between the openings of these ravines. The sides of the Wady Kelt and the face of this precipitous cliff are literally honeycombed with cells and chapels, which were occupied by the Hermits of the fourth and succeeding centuries. Wady Kelt is the wildest and deepest ravine or glen on the western side of the Jordan. It is formed by the divergence of several wadies which, rising at different points, drain the greater portion of the eastern side of the plateau. The **Wady Suweinet** is the most important of these branch valleys, and the Wady Kelt, into which it passes, may be regarded as its lower basin. "It is a steep, almost impassable, valley, cleaving the land from the Jordan valley up to Bethel on the watershed, and compelling traffic to keep to the central main road." This line of natural cleavage was the probable route of Joshua's army of invasion, the objective point in the first attack being Ai at the head of the valley. The position of this city and the natural features of the defile conform to all the incidental references in the narrative. (Josh. viii. 3-23.) The celebrated Pass of Michmash is near the head of the Wady Suweinet. It is a narrow gorge, or cañon, 800 feet deep, "with a sharp rock on one side, and a sharp rock on the other." This was the scene of Jonathan's exploit. (1 Sam. xiv. 4.) He and his armor-bearer crossed over from the southern cliff called Seneh to Bozaz on the northern side.

The hiding-place of Elijah, by the brook Cherith (1 Kings xvii. 3) has long been associated with the Wady Kelt. While it must be admitted that the prophet could hardly have found a safer retreat, it seems to be too far to the south to fit in naturally with the incidents of the history. There is no positive or satisfactory proof that Elijah visited this locality at that time, and it seems more probable that he retired to some familiar resort "before Jordan" in the land of Gilead.

The old historic road from Jericho to Jerusalem crosses the Wady Kelt near its mouth and for a short distance skirts its southern brink. It then diverges obliquely to the north-west, and crossing one or two low ridges enters the valley leading up to Bethany, known as the Wady el Hod. The distance between these points is only thirteen miles in a direct line, but the ascent within that distance is 3,620 feet.

Of the twenty-six cities originally assigned to Benjamin nearly all were on the heights. The sites of several of them have been satisfactorily identified.

Gophna, represented by the modern village of Jufna, was a border town on the western side of the plateau. It was the most northerly town within the limits of Benjamin, and was called *Ophni* at the time of the conquest. (Josh. xviii. 24.) At this place the Roman road to Antipatris diverges from the great northern highway. Dr. Thomson says that traces of this road are still visible, and in some places the pavement is almost entire. Gophna was the last halting-place of Titus on his march to Jerusalem.

Ophra, mentioned in Joshua xviii. 23 and Judges vi. 11, has been identified with a village called Taiyebeh thirteen miles north of Jerusalem. It was a frontier city in the northeast corner of the plateau of Benjamin. It seems to be identical also with Ephron or Ephraim referred to in 2 Chron. xiii. 19 and John xi. 54. Its situation on a hill near to and overlooking the wilderness would make it a desirable place for the seclusion and retirement which Jesus sought, for a brief interval, between the resurrection of Lazarus and the scenes connected with the feast of the Passover.

Bethel (Beitin) is on the main highway ten miles north of

Jerusalem. The ridge on which the ruins of the ancient city are thickly strewn, is 2,890 feet above the sea.

The characteristics of the modern village, as summed up by Dr. Schaff, are "about two dozen Moslem hovels, the ruins of a Greek church, a very large cistern, and wild rocks." The cistern referred to is a vast reservoir in the valley southwest of the village. It is 314 feet long by 217 wide. It has long been a broken cistern that can hold no water, but the green pastures around it, which once attracted the eye of Abraham, indicate a good supply of water, if utilized as in the early days, for flock and herd. Some fig trees grow amid the huge boulders around the village, and bright-hued flowers abound, but with these exceptions the place, as Major Conder puts it, seems as it were turned to stone.

The first halting place of Abraham on his journey southward from Shechem was "a mountain on the east of Bethel, having Bethel on the west, and Hai on the east: and there he builded an altar unto the Lord, and called upon the name of the Lord." (Gen. xii. 8.) This was the first dedication of "the place" as it is afterward called. It was near the Canaanite city called Luz, which occupied the site of the Hebrew city of Bethel. The ruins of Berj Beitin on a little plateau half-a-mile east of Beitin mark the probable site of Abraham's camp and altar. The Jordan valley is plainly visible from this spot. Farther west it cannot be seen. "Standing just here, Lot could see the ciccar, or plain of Jordan, which allured him by its luxuriant and well-watered pasturages away from Abraham."[1] On or near the same place the exiled grandson of Abraham saw the vision of angels on the terraced ascent that reached to heaven, and heard the voice which came rolling down the awful heights, "Behold, I am with thee, and will keep thee in all places whither thou goest and will bring thee again into this land. And he was afraid, and said, How dreadful is this place ! This is none other but the house of

[1] Memoirs II., p. 307.

God, and this is the gate of heaven. . . . And he called the name of that place Beth-el." The significance of this event appears in the statement of Jacob long afterward in Egypt, "God Almighty appeared unto me at Luz in the land of Canaan and blessed me" (Gen. xlviii. 3): and still more fully in the words of Jesus: "Hereafter ye shall see heaven open and the angels of God ascending and descending upon the Son of Man." (John i. 51.) "That Bethel maintained a reputation as a sacred place, is proved by the narrative of Judges xx. 18, (where 'the house of God' should be rendered Bethel); while from verses 26-28 of the same chapter it appears that the ark of the covenant was there in those days."[1] Bethel was a school of the prophets about a hundred years after it became a high-place for the worship of false gods, "and it frequently reappears in Old Testament history, as if a lingering remnant of true Israelites always adhered to it." (2 Kings ii. 3, xvii. 28.) The prophetic utterance of the man of God, who stood by the altar of Jeroboam and cried against it in the word of the Lord, marks the turning point in its history. (1 Kings xii. 32, 33, xiii. 1-10.) Its present condition may be summed up in a single sentence, the utterance of a later prophet, "Bethel shall come to naught." (Amos v. 5.)

Beth-aven on the east side of Bethel (Josh. vii. 2) has left no trace of its former existence. The name was evidently applied to the wilderness, also, which bordered it on the edge of the plateau.

Ai, or **Hai** has been identified by the survey party with the ancient ruins of Haiyan, two miles east of Bethel. The name corresponds with Aina, which is used by Josephus as the equivalent of Ai. The surroundings of Haiyan conform very closely to the description of the natural features in the immediate vicinity of Ai. (Josh. viii. 9-12.)

A conspicuous knoll a short distance north of Haiyan has also been suggested as a possible site. Its identification with

[1] Henderson's Hist. Geog., p. 56.

The Mountains of Benjamin

Ai is based mainly on the significance of its name, **Et Tell** (the heap). On the assumption that this hillock has been the site of an ancient city, its destruction has been as complete as that which befel the city of Ai. "And Joshua burned Ai, and made it an heap forever, even a desolation unto this day." (Josh. viii. 28.)

Rock Rimmon is nearly four miles east of Bethel on the edge of the plateau. A small village, which still bears the name Rummon, clings to its rugged slopes. The cliff rises several hundred feet above the deep ravine which borders it on the north. The slopes of the wilderness below are full of caves and hiding-places. To this mountain fastness the remnant of the children of Benjamin fled after the disastrous series of battles in and about Gibeah, and here they remained for four months. (Judg. xx. 28–47.)

Michmash (Mukmas) is a small village on the north side of the pass of Michmash, four miles southeast of Bethel. There are extensive ruins in the vicinity of the modern village. At this point may be seen the upper basin and deep gorge of the Wady Suweinit; the rock up which Jonathan climbed; the place from which he started on his hazardous descent (1 Sam. xiii. 14); and portions of the deep cleft of the Jordan valley including the northern end of the Dead Sea. Michmash is mentioned in connection with several towns of Benjamin on the route of the Assyrian invader from the north to Jerusalem. (Isa. x. 28.) It was reoccupied by the children of Benjamin after the return from the captivity. (Neh. xi. 31.)

Geba or Jeba, as it is now called, was on the south side of the chasm directly opposite Michmash and is linked with it in history and association. In the reign of Josiah, Geba marked the frontier of the kingdom of Judah. (2 Kings xxiii. 8.) It was strongly fortified by Asa. (1 Kings xv. 22.) After the captivity it was also reoccupied.

Beeroth, now Bireh, was an ancient city of the Hivite confederacy. (Josh. ix. 17.) It is two miles southwest of Bethel on the northern highway. This town was the customary resting-place of the pilgrim bands on their return from the great feasts in Jerusalem. From this place, according to tradition, Joseph and Mary turned back to seek the child Jesus. (Luke ii. 44.)

Ramah of Benjamin is represented by the modern village of Er Ram. It is situated on a conical hill nearly four miles south of Bireh. Ramah was fortified by Baasha, king of Israel, in order to stop all communication with Jerusalem. (1 Kings xv. 17.) It was afterward destroyed by Asa, who took away the stones and timber to strengthen Geba and Mizpeh. (1 Kings xv. 22.) It is mentioned several times in connection with the earlier periods of Hebrew history. (Josh. xviii. 25; Judg. iv. 5, etc.) This is one of the many Ramahs, or "highplaces" mentioned in the Old Testament history. It has often been associated with the birthplace of Samuel, but this is as yet, an unknown site, within the limits, as originally defined, of Mount Ephraim. (1 Sam. i. 1.)

Gibeah of Benjamin, called also Gibeah of Saul, was formerly supposed to be identical with the ruins on the top of a conspicuous cone-shaped hill, which bears the modern name, Tell el Fûl (Hill of Beans). This location is not regarded by the Survey party as a suitable one for a city with the history connected with Gibeah. Conder is inclined to identify it with Geba, but he also recognizes the apparent use of the name to cover a district on the eastern edge of the plateau. "The similarity in the names," says Doctor Thomson, "is strongly in favor of Major Conder's theory and against Tell el Fûl, since, if the latter was Gibeah, there would then have been three cities near together, and in sight of each other, bearing radically the same names, Gibeon, Gibeah, and Geba—a conjunction without example, and one likely to prove in practice a source of confusion." Gibeah is frequently mentioned in connection with the periods of the Judges and Kings, but was specially notable as the scene of two of the most tragic events in

The Mountains of Benjamin

the history of the land. One was connected with the almost total annihilation of the tribe of Benjamin (Judg. xix. and xx.); the other was an act of retributive justice which fell upon seven of the direct descendants of king Saul. One of the most pathetic incidents in the records of the Hebrew nation was the lonely watch of Rizpah, the mother of two of the young men who were hanged at Gibeah. (2. Sam. xxi. 1–14.)

Tell el Ful seems to have been one of the signal, or beacon, stations on the heights of Benjamin. It is two miles south of Ramah, and four north of Jerusalem.

Anathoth (Anata) is situated on a broad ridge, near the road, three miles northeast of Jerusalem. It was a Levitical city (Josh. xxi. 18): the place of Abiathar's banishment (1 Kings ii. 26); and the birthplace of the prophet Jeremiah. (Jer. i. 1.)

The Beth-horons—Upper and Lower—have occupied their original locations, at the head of the famous pass of Beth-horon for nearly 4,000 years. The road from Gibeon, to the upper town while descending at some points is mainly an ascent; hence called the "going up" to Beth-horon. (Josh. x. 10, 11.) The descent to the lower is very rugged and steep and in places steps were cut in the rock. This was the "going down" to Beth-horon. The lower Beth-horon was at the northwest corner of the territory of Benjamin. Both were border towns, their assignment being with Ephraim, but their history and associations with Benjamin. They were situated on either side of the pass, but the distance between is nearly two miles. "It takes an hour to climb from the lower village to the higher, and one feels that either in ascending or descending, a hostile force would fare ill at the hands of a determined enemy, whether defending the pass, or pursuing a retreating host."

Gibeon, now El Jib, stands on an isolated, rounded hill about six miles northwest of Jerusalem. The hill is belted by horizontal strata of limestone cut into steps or terraces by the action of the winds and rains. It is nearly surrounded by a fertile plain formed by the convergence of several valleys.

"Corn fields and olive-yards surround it, and the vines run down the terraced sides of the old site, which, strengthened artificially by rock-cut scarps, presents a magnificent position for an ancient fortress. The modern village is of stone, and contains an old Crusading church, and under its houses are rock-cut tombs, perhaps as old as the time of the conquest of the Holy Land by Israel." [1]

East of the hill is a fine spring issuing from an excavation in the rock. Below it among a group of straggling olive trees is a broken reservoir, which measures 120 by 100 feet. This is the "pool of Gibeon" where the bands of Joab and Abner met in deadly conflict. (2 Sam. ii. 13.) Gibeon was the chief of the four Hivite cities which surrendered to Joshua. By a clever ruse its inhabitants beguiled the Hebrew leader and secured an alliance which saved them from the destruction that befel their former allies.

The great battle which decided the fate of the Amorite confederacy began at Gibeon and ended in the utter rout of the enemies of Israel, who were driven headlong down the Beth-horon pass. (Josh. x. 10, 11.) Amasa was treacherously slain by the Great Stone in Gibeon and near the same spot many years afterward retribution came to Joab, his murderer, by the hand of Benaiah, the chief captain of Solomon. (2 Sam. xx. 10; 1 Kings ii. 29-34.)

At Gibeon the tabernacle was set up after the slaughter of the priests by Saul. Here a brazen altar was erected in front of the tabernacle and upon that altar Solomon offered a thousand burnt-offerings. Here, also, the young King chose wisdom above the other gifts to be had for the asking. (1 Kings iii. 4-15.)

Nob, the city of the priests, was on one of the hills near to Jerusalem, but its exact site has not been determined. (1 Sam. xxi. 1, xxii. 9-19.)

[1] Conder's Bib. Geog., p. 73.

The Mountains of Benjamin

Identifications for other places of minor importance have been suggested as follows: Archi (Josh. xvi. 2) identified with Ain Arik, six miles west of Bethel; Sechu (1 Sam. xix. 22) with Khurbet Suweikeh, one and a-half miles south of Beeroth; Baal Tamar (Josh. xx. 33) with Attara; Gederah (1 Chron. xii. 14) with Jedireh, one mile northeast of Gibeon; Ananiah (Neh. xi. 32) with Beit Hanina, near Gibeon; Hazor (Neh. xi. 33) with Hazzur, near Beit Hanina; Gibeath (Josh. xviii. 28) with Jibia, northwest of Neby Samwil; Kirjath of Benjamin (Josh. xviii. 28) with Kuriet el Anab, formerly supposed to be identical with Kirjath Jearim; Mozah (Josh. xviii. 26) with Beit Mizza, five miles northwest of Jerusalem; Chesalon (Josh. xv. 10) with Kesla, west of Jerusalem; Parah (Josh. xviii. 23) with Farah, six miles northeast of Jerusalem; Alemeth or Almon (1 Chron. vi. 60) with Almit, three miles northeast of Jerusalem; Debir, in pass called Ed-Debr, near road from Jerusalem to Jericho, about midway between these cities; Eleph (Josh. xviii. 28) with Lifta, two miles northwest of Jerusalem.

CHAPTER XVI

JERUSALEM AND ITS ENVIRONS

JERUSALEM lies on a spur, or broken section, of tableland near the eastern edge of the great watershed of the country. It is thirty miles south of Shechem; thirty-two in a direct line from the sea; and eighteen from the mouth of the Jordan. Its position, as indicated by the Survey, is latitude 31° 47' north, and longtitude 35° 14' east. Its parallel of latitude touches the northern end of the Dead Sea and intersects the coast line of the Mediterranean at a point a little north of Ashdod. The elevation of Jerusalem is about 2,500 feet above the Mediterranean, and 3,800 feet above the Dead Sea.

The section of the plateau on which the city stands is almost separated from the adjoining table-land by two deep valleys, or ravines, which sweep closely around it on three sides. "These valleys, at first mere shallow depressions in the ground, take their rise within a few yards of each other, and at an altitude of 2,650 feet above the sea, in the gentle undulation which at that point parts the waters of the Mediterranean from those of the Jordan Valley. Separating at once, they soon take one of those rapid plunges downward so characteristic of the wild glens of Judea, and, after encircling the plateau, meet again at Bir Eyub (the well of Job), 672 feet below their original starting point; hence united as the Wady en Nar, 'Valley of Fire,' they pass by a deep gorge through the Wilderness of Judea to the Dead Sea."[1]

From the point where it touches the city wall the eastern, or Kedron valley, runs nearly due south. The western, or Hinnom valley runs southward along the western side of the

---

[1] Pict. Pal., Vol. I., p. 2.

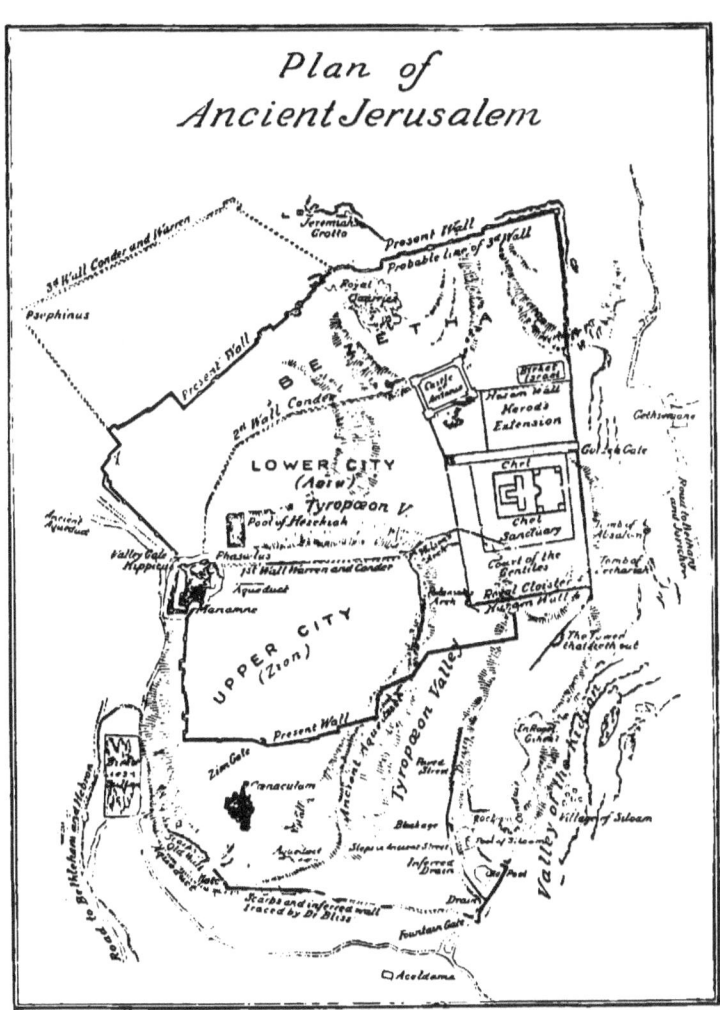

city and then turns eastward to Bir Eyub, where it joins the Kedron, or Jehoshaphat, valley. In former times these encircling ravines were much deeper, and their sides more precipitous than now. Excavations have shown that rubbish to the depth of seventy or eighty feet has accumulated in the Kedron valley, and that the original bed of the stream has been pushed eastward as much as seventy feet by avalanches of débris from the heights above it. The walls of the ancient city, as might be expected, conformed to these lines of natural defence, making the stronghold which they enclosed one of the most notable in human history. On the east, south and west it was practically unassailable. On the north there was no natural break between the shelving plateau, on which Jerusalem was built, and the table-land which adjoined it. This was the only quarter, therefore, in which there was room for expansion, but it was also the exposed portion of the line of defence; hence it was necessary to guard it with fortifications of great strength. Before the disastrous siege of the Romans under Titus, this quarter of the city was defended by three lines of massive walls, separated from each other by considerable distances. Each of these was strengthened, at intervals, by immense towers, and protected in front by deep, artificial moats or ditches. These walls, which were frequently broken down or swept away by besieging armies were not always replaced on the old foundations; and hence there is much uncertainty in regard to their relative positions. With this exception, the natural features of the place furnish the clue to the direction and sweep of the ancient walls. Where these have not been actually traced they may be inferred with a good degree of certainty.

The *recovery of Jerusalem*, as far as it has been accomplished, has dispelled the idea that it was always a small place, or that the present circlet of walls, which leaves out more than one-half of Mount Zion, is to be regarded as the counterpart of the walls which surrounded the city of David or of Herod.

" *The Mountains round about Jerusalem* " are higher than

the spur on which the city stands. The only natural or continuous break in this circuit is the valley of Rephaim on the southwest. Beginning with this break the first of the series is the Mount, or Hill, of Evil Counsel to the south; the next to the southeast of the city is the Mount of Offence, an offshoot from the Mount of Olives; directly east is the Mount of Olives, or the portion of the ridge to which the name is commonly applied; on the north the upper part of this triple crowned mountain which curves around as if to shield the city is known as Mount Scopus; to the northwest, but farther removed than any other peak of the group, is Neby Samwil or Mizpeh; to the west, an undulating ridge with occasional peaks of slightly higher elevation.

Internal Divisions.—The site included within the walls, as already defined, was divided into two unequal ridges, running north and south, by a deep ravine, called the Tyropœon valley. This depression begins on the higher level of the plateau, between the surrounding valleys, and extends southward to the Kedron, which it enters not far from its junction with the valley of Hinnom. The ridge on the eastern side of the Tyropœon is Mount Moriah, on which stood the temple and all the imposing buildings connected with it. The ridge on the western side is 120 feet higher than Moriah. It is broader in extent and has a much larger area of available space for buildings and defensive works. In the earlier period of Jewish history this ridge was probably distinguished from the other by the name Zion. The city of David, the Palace of Herod and three of the most noted towers—Hippicus, Phasaëlus and Marianne were on this side of the valley. "The researches of Captains Wilson and Warren have shown that the Tyropœon valley has been filled up to the depth of 120 feet between Zion and Moriah at the southwest angle of the Temple area: and that the rock here must have been inaccessible until a bridge was thrown across the intervening space."[1]

[1] Tristram's Holy Land, p. 129.

MODERN JERUSALEM

Jerusalem and its Environs

A lateral valley, which started very near the present Jaffa gate on the west, ran in an eastern direction to the Tyropœon valley, separating the western ridge into two parts. It has been ascertained that this valley, a depression scarcely noticeable at the present time, has been filled up with rubbish in some places to a depth of eighty feet. This was the line of separation between the Upper City of Josephus and the Lower City, which occupied the northern portion of the ridge. It is generally agreed that the name Zion properly applies to the portion south of this valley: and that the portion designated as Acra by Josephus, lies to the north of it.

On the eastern ridge (Moriah) a rubbish-filled valley has also been traced. "This ravine,—the 'Valley called Kedron,' of Josephus,—rises in the eastern half of the plateau and runs into the Kedron a short distance north of the Golden Gate; in it lies the large pool known as the Birket Israil." The portion of the ridge north of this lateral valley is called Bezetha (new Town), while that which lies directly south of it is known as Moriah. The name Ophel was applied to the southern spur of Moriah, which projected beyond the south wall of the temple area.

Summing up the foregoing in brief there are *two recognized divisions* on *the western side* of the Tyropœon valley—*Acra* and *Zion*. On *the eastern side* there are *three divisions—Bezetha*, *Moriah* and *Ophel*. While there are still differences of opinion in regard to some of these subdivisions, they are now generally accepted by the leading authorities, and are so indicated on the Ordnance map.

Modern Jerusalem.—The Jerusalem of to-day is literally builded upon its own heap. (Jer. xxx. 18.) Below its houses, courts and paved streets lie the rubbish and wreckage of not less than *eight* cities which have risen in successive periods and are now piled one above the other. The Holy City of the Prophets, Kings and Apostles is a composite, underground city, which can only be studied in a fragmentary way as the evidences of its former existence and greatness are laid bare by the pick and spade.

> "If we examine it, we have to determine at every step, among the ruins of which city we are standing. Solomon, Nehemiah, Herod, Hadrian, Constantine, Omar, Godfrey, Saladin, Suleiman—each in turn represents a city."[1]

Skillfully conducted excavations in and about Jerusalem, at various times, have not only unearthed many interesting remains of this underground city, but have given approximate measurements of the depth of the successive accumulations in the valleys and around the walls.

The rock levels and general contour lines of the entire surface throughout the city have also been ascertained by the sinking of numerous shafts.

With all its changes there is much of the Jerusalem of the past that still remains. The mighty framework of the everlasting hills on which it rested; the deep valleys which surrounded it; and the mountains which stood round about it—are the same in all their essential features as when David extolled the beauty of its situation, or when Jesus beheld its later glories and wept over it. As a necessity of its environment Jerusalem is now, and always has been, "a city compactly built together."

Its streets are narrow; its open courts few and limited in area, and its houses are massed in close juxtaposition in the several quarters. Despite all the changes and transformations of recent years it still retains the appearance of a great fortress of the Middle ages. Its massive grey walls and broad-leaved gates and flanking towers; its mosques and churches and convents; its domes and minarets, rising conspicuously above the walls and flat roofs of its houses,—present a picture of marvellous beauty and impressiveness, as outlined in the clear sunshine, from Olivet or Scopus.

The walls, which now enclose the city, were built, or rather

[1] Thirty Years' Work, p. 67.

GENERAL VIEW OF JERUSALEM
(CHURCH OF ST. ANNE IN FOREGROUND)

rebuilt, by Sultan Suleiman A. D., 1542. They rest, for the most part on the foundation of older walls. The material used was drawn from the rubbish heaps around and represents the various structures, and diverse styles of workmanship of different nationalities and widely separated centuries. "It is probable," says Dr. Thomson, "that the present west wall, from the Tower of David southward, follows the course of the first wall, since the deep valley below it would render that always the necessary line for that part. The wall which crosses Zion eastward to the Mosk of El Aksa is, of course, modern, both in its foundation and construction. The eastern wall of the Haram area is partly ancient, and I think that the part of the wall at the south end of the same area is built upon foundations as old as the time of Herod, though most of the work above ground is evidently of later date."[1] The Haram wall in places is sixty and seventy feet above the surface of the ground, but in general the height of the encircling wall ranges from twenty-five to forty feet. Its width ranges from ten to fifteen feet. Its circuit is about two and a half miles. In outline it is an irregular quadrangle. It has battlements, salient angles, and, at intervals, is strengthened by thirty-four massive square towers. The area now enclosed is 210 acres, but if we add to this the available space not included on the north and south, it would give to the city, in its period of largest extent, a circuit of over four miles and an area of nearly 1,000 acres. This would accord with the descriptions of its former extent as given by Josephus.

Gates.—There are six open gates in the wall which surrounds the city, viz: The *Jaffa Gate* on the west; the *New Gate* (Bab Abdul Hamid) in the northwest angle, opened in 1889; the *Damascus Gate* on the north; *St. Stephen's Gate* on the east; the *Gate of the Moors* (Dung Gate), and the *Zion Gate*, on the south. There are also five closed gates, viz: *Herod's Gate* on the north; the *Golden Gate* on the

[1] Land and the Book, p. 464.

east; and the *Single, Double,* and *Triple Gates* on the southern wall of the Temple area.

Quarters.—Two of the principal streets: *David Street,* running eastward from the Jaffa Gate, and *Damascus Street,* running southward from the Damascus Gate, traverse the city almost at right angles and divide it into four unequal sections or quarters.

The southwest section, as thus divided, is known as the *Armenian* quarter; the northwest as the *Christian ;* the northeast as the *Moslem ;* and the southeast (not including the Haram) as the *Jewish.* The **Haram**, or Temple area, on Mount Moriah, which contains thirty-five acres, is separated from the rest of the city by an encircling wall of great strength.

In studying the places and objects of special interest, within the city walls, it will be convenient to make use of these divisions in the order given.

1. **The Armenian Quarter.**—The most interesting monuments of the past in this section cluster around the *Citadel* (Al Kala), which occupies the northwest corner, directly opposite the Jaffa Gate.

"It consists of a group of buildings including besides soldiers' quarters, the saluting battery and four towers: three of these are evidently of modern date, though they may stand on sites of more ancient towers. Their masonry is composed of portions of arch stones, shafts of columns, etc., mixed with better dressed stones, but the fourth, known as the Tower of David is very different. It is an oblong building sixty-eight feet long by fifty-eight feet broad. Its construction is very singular. It has an escarp of masonry sloping to a ditch; round the top of this is what is known as a *berne* or *chemin des rondes;* upon this a solid mass of masonry, into which no entrance or appearance of any entrance could be found: this is twenty-nine feet high. Above this the tower is built, the actual tower, which consists of several chambers and a cistern. The lower part of the masonry is very fine, and resembles that at the well-known Wailing Place in its dressing, having, however, a large marginal draft. This tower is at the northeast angle of the citadel. The smaller one at the northwest angle also contains a cistern."[1]

[1] Our Work in Palestine, p. 24.

DAMASCUS GATE

There seems to be no doubt that these towers are the remains of the ancient structures which Titus left standing when he destroyed the city. The one at the northwest angle corresponds with the description of *Hippicus*, which Josephus took for his starting point in the description of the three walls that in his day defended the city from invasion on the north. This tower is close to the Jaffa Gate. It is somewhat smaller than the dimensions given of Hippicus by Josephus, but its location accords with the descriptions and incidental references in other respects. An additional proof of its identification with Hippicus has been furnished by the discovery of an aqueduct twelve feet below the level of the present conduit—probably that by which, according to the Jewish historian, water was brought into that building. The Tower of David has usually been associated with Hippicus, but the measurements and general descriptions do not correspond with it. The dimensions of Phasaëlus on the northeast angle agree much better with these descriptions. It is larger; has marks of greater antiquity; and this identification has now the sanction of the best authorities. This structure is the most conspicuous monument of ancient times in the city of Jerusalem. While the upper portion has evidently been restored, there seems to be no doubt that the lower base, or substruction belongs to the time of Herod. A location so important as a strategic point must always have been occupied by a defensive work of some kind in every period of the history of Jerusalem.

Miss M. E. Rogers makes the statement that thousands of skillfully fashioned arrow shafts were accidentally discovered beneath the roof of one of the upper chambers of the Tower of Hippicus, nearly fifty years ago. A leakage in the vaulted roof had damaged the ceiling, and the arrows were exposed to view. " They were piled up by hundreds of thousands in this spacious loft." but by order of the Governor they were again walled up as soon as the damage had been repaired. A few, however, were carried off by the workmen, one of which came into the possession of Mr. W. G. Rogers, the father of Miss Rogers. " Experts pronounced the form and finish of this arrow shaft to be quite perfect, but as it is neither barbed nor feathered, it is the more difficult to determine its age."[1]

Somewhere in the vicinity of the citadel stood the magnificent *Palace of Herod*, but no certain trace of its exact location has been found.

The Armenian Convent, the largest modern structure in Jerusalem, with its extensive grounds and quarters for pilgrims; the English Church; the Church of St. James, next in size, and costly adornments to the Church of the Holy Sepulchre; and some very attractive gardens cared for by the Armenian monks—are included in this quarter.

2. **The Christian Quarter.**—The objects of special interest in this division are the *Muristan*, or Hospital of the Knights of St. John, covering a large space in the southeast angle; the *Pool of Hezekiah;* the *Palace and Church of the Latin Patriarch;* the *Greek Monastery*, noted for its ancient library and manuscripts; and the *Church of the Holy Sepulchre.*

The Pool of Hezekiah is a large reservoir, 240 by 140 feet. Its estimated capacity is nearly three million gallons. The bottom of this reservoir is the natural rock, levelled and cemented. Houses rise above its enclosing walls, and the water is reached by a descent of several steps. The pool receives its water supply from the Birket Mamilla, in the upper part of the valley of Hinnom, through an underground conduit. The reservoir and its supply pipe are supposed to be identical with the " pool and conduit " constructed by Hezekiah to bring water into the city. (2 Kings xx. 20.)

The Church of the Holy Sepulchre covers the traditional site of the crucifixion and burial of Christ. It is in reality a collection of churches, chapels and shrines, grouped together under one widely-extended roof. The *Chapel of the Holy Sepulchre* is a small marble edifice of two rooms twenty-

[1] Pict. Pal., Vol. I., p. 399.

Jerusalem and its Environs 179

six feet long by eighteen wide in the centre of the rotunda beneath the dome. It is built up from the pavement of the church, and is surmounted by a small crown or dome, supported by sixteen marble columns. In the inner chamber is the so-called tomb of Christ. The only object suggestive of a burial-place, is a marble slab, raised about two feet above the floor. Here for nearly sixteen centuries, devout pilgrims, from every part of Christendom, have kneeled to kiss this cold marble slab; and yet there is no evidence, in sight at least, of even a fragment of the rock-hewn tomb which the Evangelists have described. If the real tomb where the Lord had lain had been identified beyond question in the age of Constantine it would be reasonable to infer that some of the essential features of its original form and structure would still be preserved. It is scarcely conceivable that a spot so frequently visited, and so carefully guarded, since that day should have nothing to attest its existence but an *artificial representation* of a tomb which does not accord in any respect with the scores and hundreds of tombs "hewn out in the rock" on every side of the Holy City. Until some evidence of the original tomb can be shown which was hewn out of the rock under the direction of the rich man of Arimathæa, the genuineness of the site will certainly, and with good reason, be called in question.

In another section of the church, and on a higher elevation, reached by a flight of twenty stone steps, is shown the place of the crucifixion. A large number of traditional sites, more than twenty in all, associated with scriptural incidents ranging in point of time from Adam to Christ are pointed out in various nooks and corners of the church or its crypts.

While it is admitted that the Church of the Holy Sepulchre is the successor of the church built upon this site by Constantine A. D., 325, and that it has been revered for more than fifteen centuries as the tomb of Christ, most of the leading authorities at the present time have accepted the conclusion reached by Dr. Robinson many years ago "that its genuineness is supported neither by well authenticated historical facts, nor by prior traditions, nor by archæological features." Its position in the midst of the modern city; the impossibility of placing it outside the line of the second wall, except on the theory of a reëntering angle; its close proximity to the Pool of Hezekiah, which must always have been within the walls; and the unsatisfactory, not to say damaging, evidence furnished by the number and surroundings of the traditional sites themselves —all bear heavily against the supposition that this was the place of the crucifixion and entombment of Christ. To place the Church of the Holy Sepulchre without the wall of Herod's time, with such knowledge as we now possess of its direction and bearings, would give to that portion of the city, as Dr. Thomson expresses it, "a configuration quite preposterous, and so contract the area included between the second wall and the old first wall as to make it scarcely worth while to erect it at all." To this may be added the statement of Major Conder that the recovery of the rock sections shows the improbability of so drawing the second wall as to exclude the Church.

This venerated shrine, however we may regard its traditional claims, has a history, strangely inconsistent with the character of Him who died on Calvary: and yet one of surpassing interest. No other rood of ground, not even Mecca itself, has drawn together so many pilgrim bands from afar, or has cost so much in blood and treasure. Its recovery from the hands of the Infidel was the dominant thought of Christian Europe for more than two centuries, and it is estimated that the several Crusades organized to accomplish this object, cost from six to ten million human lives.

More wonderful than all else were the errors overruled, and the transformations indirectly brought about in Christendom, by the attempt to recover this empty tomb.

3. **The Moslem Quarter.**—This is the largest division of the city. It contains the Governor's Palace; the soldiers' barracks; the consulates of several nationalities; the Church of

Jerusalem and its Environs

St. Anne; the Pool of Bethesda; and the so-called Via Dolorosa. The Church of St. Anne occupies a prominent position in this quarter. Its location is a few yards north of the street which leads to St. Stephen's Gate. This church with its extensive grounds was given to Napoleon III., by the reigning Sultan after the Crimean war.

The Pool of Bethesda.—This has been identified with an ancient reservoir, which was excavated in 1888, about one hundred feet northwest of the Church of St. Anne. It measures fifty-five by twelve and a half feet and was cut into the rock for a depth of thirty feet. A flight of twenty-four steps leads down to the east end of the basin. The pool has five supporting arches with five corresponding porches, running along the side. A twin pool was found soon after six feet away, lying end to end, and measuring sixty feet in length.

This double pool corresponds with the description of Bethesda given by Eusebius, and by the Bordeaux Pilgrim in 333 A. D.

"At a later period a church was built over the pool by the Crusaders, and they seem to have been so far impressed by the fact of five arches below that they shaped their crypt in five arches in imitation. They left an opening for getting down to the water; and further, as the crowning proof that they regarded the pool as Bethesda, they painted on the wall of the crypt a fresco representing the angel troubling the water of the pool."[1]

In the bed of the ravine or fosse, which may be traced in part along the outside of the north wall of the Haram, is a large reservoir (Birket Israil) 360 x 126 x 75 feet.

This was formerly supposed to be identical with the Pool of Bethesda, but, as Dr. Robinson suggests, it is more likely to be the remains of the deep trench referred to by Josephus, which separated the north Temple wall from Bezetha.

The traditional Via Dolorosa runs from the Governor's

[1] Buried Cities and Bible Countries, p. 327. See also Pal. Quarterly, July, 1888, and January, 1891, for plans and fuller description.

Palace, which occupies a portion of the site of the tower of Antonia, to the Church of the Holy Sepulchre. It has nothing in common with the city of Herod, and its stations and general direction through the city are merely creations of fancy.

The Royal Quarries or Cotton Grotto.—The extensive excavations designated by one or other of the foregoing names, were made underneath the rock surface of the northern portion of this quarter. From the entrance, near the Damascus Gate, the floor slopes gradually toward the south. In this direction the cavern extends for a distance of about 700 feet. In breadth it varies from sixty to 300 feet. The roof which averages about thirty feet in height, is supported by large pillars of native rock.

The material is a soft white limestone, which hardens by exposure to the air. The extent of the quarry indicates that an enormous amount of this stone was required for some purpose connected with the great structures of the city. That this was a mammoth workshop, as well as a quarry, is evident from the great blocks detached and partly-dressed blocks, and the heaps of stone chippings which everywhere litter the floor.

"In many places," says Sir Charles Wilson, "the stones have been left half cut out, and the marks of the chisel and pick are as fresh as if the quarrymen had only left their work: even the black patches made by the smoke of the lamps are still visible."

There is no improbability in the supposition that the great stones used in the substructions of the Temple of Solomon and in its surrounding walls, were obtained from this quarry and fitted for their places in this underground workshop. It was the probable source of supply also for the reconstructions of Herod.

North of this grotto are similar excavations on a smaller scale, in the hillside, which are known as Jeremiah's grotto. These excavations were probably separated from the southern portion by the cuttings made for the foundation of the present wall.

With respect to the geological formation of the plateau on which the city stands, Sir Charles Wilson says:

"The upper strata are beds of a hard reddish and grey stone called *Misseh*, the lower of a soft, easily worked stone known as *Melekeh*. The latter bed, which is some thirty-five feet thick, underlies the whole city. All the great subterranean reservoirs, nearly all the tombs, the Siloam aqueduct, and the caverns at Siloam have been hewn out of it, and the great quarries near the Damascus Gate show that it was largely used for building purposes. The *Misseh* beds have, however, yielded the best and most durable building material, and the stones from these beds can be easily recognized in the walls by their sharp edges and superior state of preservation."[1]

4. **The Jewish Quarter.**—This division contains several Synagogues, but has no imposing buildings, such as adorn the other quarters of the city. Its streets are dark, narrow and untidy; its houses are closely joined, dilapidated tenement buildings; and its inhabitants for the most part live in abject poverty. Ruins heaped upon ruins are the chief characteristics of this densely populated district.

The Wailing Place on its eastern boundary is the only part of the Holy City to which the Jews have free access. Here they assemble day after day, and especially on Fridays, to bewail their fallen estate and weep over the desolations of Zion. Here may be seen men and women standing by the wall putting their fingers into its clefts, kissing the great stones, or sitting on the ground and swaying back and forth as they intone the lamentations of the prophets of Judah. This portion of the Haram wall is 155 feet in length and fifty-five in height. Nine of the lowest courses are built of huge blocks of stone. One stone measures sixteen feet in length and another thirteen feet.

5. **The Temple Area.**—This sacred enclosure, now called the Haram esh Sherif, or "Place of the Noble Sanctuary," is an irregular quadrangle of nearly thirty-five acres in area.

[1] The City and The Land, p. 8.

"It has been formed by cutting the rock away in some places, by building supporting vaults in others, and by filling in hollows with large stones and rubbish. The dimensions are—north side 1,042 feet; east side 1,530; south side 922; and east side 1,601."[1]

Those who enter this secluded spot, in which, beyond all question, once stood the Temple of Solomon and its successors, pass in a moment from the noise and bustle of the crowded streets into a charming retreat, where no lurking intruder is found; and where eternal quiet seems to reign. Except the raised platform near the centre, which covers an area of five acres and is paved with smooth slabs of limestone, the surface of the Haram is a beautiful greensward spangled with flowers, and dotted here and there with cyprus or olive trees.

The Dome of the Rock (Kubbet es Sakhra) "next after Mecca the most sacred building in Moslem lands," and next after Cordova the most beautiful in any land,—occupies the centre of the platform. It is an octagonal building, sheathed with richly colored marbles and encaustic tiles, surmounted by an exquisitely proportioned dome. "From whatever point that graceful dome with its beautiful precinct emerges to view, it at once dignifies the whole city. And when from Olivet, or from the Governor's house, or from the northeast wall, you see the platform on which it stands, it is a scene hardly to be surpassed."[2] The interior with its wonderful variety of architectural combinations and groupings; its rich decorations in stained glass, marble and mosaic; and its lavish profusion of gilt tracery and inscriptions,—is indeed "a sumptuous building," well worthy of a visit for its own sake. But the object of special interest, which has given to it a name and world-wide fame, is the great rock, surrounded by an inner row of columns, which rises several feet above its pavement, directly under the swelling dome. This rock, known as the Sakhra, measures fifty-six feet from north to south and forty-two from east to west. Its elevation above the floor is four feet nine and one-

[1] Pict. Pal., Vol. I., p. 52.   [2] Sinai and Palestine, p. 235.

half inches at the highest point, and one foot at the lowest. If the platform were removed on which the building rests, this ledge of rock would stand fifteen feet above the level of the Temple area. It is unquestionably the summit of Mount Moriah and must have had an important place in the construction of the Holy House, which crowned this mountain and extended its courts, corridors and retaining walls adown its rugged sides. On the Sakhra itself there are chisel marks and scarping which indicate that a framework of some sort had been carefully fitted around it.

"The surface of the rock," says Colonel Wilson, of the Ordnance Survey, "bears the marks of hard treatment and rough chiselling, on the western side it is cut down to three steps, and on the north side in an irregular shape, the object of which cannot now be discovered."

Some authorities have assumed that the floor of the Temple overlaid the Sakhra, with possibly a projecting portion uprising amid the Holy of Holies, while others regard it as the foundation of the great brazen Altar.

It is generally agreed that the Dome of the Rock stands on the site of the Sanctuary or Holy House of both temples. It is scarcely possible, therefore, to conceive of any position which this huge bulk of rock could occupy except that of a central mass or core, around which the mighty structure grew. Beneath the surface of the Sakhra, at its east end, there is an artificial cave with a superficial area of nearly 600 feet, and an average height of six feet. Its floor is reached by a flight of steps which pass under an archway, but originally it was a cistern or close chamber, whose only opening was through an aperture, now utilized as a window, in the roof. In the centre of the floor is a circular slab of marble, which gives forth a hollow sound when tapped.

The underground shaft or chamber with which it evidently communicates is called by the Arabs the "Well of Spirits."

Says Canon Tristram:

"It is possible that this cave was the receptacle for the offal of the sacrifice and connected with the water supply which was so arranged as to carry off underground all the refuse of the daily sacrifices without its being seen; this we learn from the rabbinical commentaries." The same author assumes that "Araunah's threshing floor must have been close to the central Dome of the Rock, because threshing floors in the east are invariably placed on the ridges of hills and in the most exposed positions, in order that the corn and chaff may catch any breath of wind when they are thrown up into the air by the shovel."

On this supposition the cave, which may have been used as a place of storage for the grain, would be the most likely hiding-place for Araunah (Ornan) and his sons, when the Angel of the Lord suddenly appeared by the threshing floor. (1 Chron. xxi. 20; 2 Sam. xxiv. 18-20.) However this may be, it is definitely stated (2 Chron. iii. 1) that "Solomon began to build the house of the Lord at Jerusalem in Mount Moriah, where the Lord appeared unto David, his father, in the place that David had prepared in the threshing floor of Ornan the Jebusite."

On the central platform several buildings fashioned in excellent taste, but of smaller proportions, are grouped around the Dome of the Rock.

South of the platform is the Great Mosque of El Aksa and its associated buildings. This pile extends to the outer wall of the Haram and covers a space of 272 feet long by 184 wide. The original structure was probably a Christian Church built by the Emperor Justinian. "Taking it in mass and detail," says Hepworth Dixon, "this group on the Temple hill—the Mosques of Omar and El Aksa, the domes, the terraces, the colonnades, the kiosks and fountains—is perhaps the very noblest specimen of building art in Asia."

The water supply of the Temple area was provided for by a vast system of conduits and reservoirs that literally honeycombed the underlying rock. More than thirty of these reservoirs were examined, measured, and marked on the chart, by Warren and his party. One cistern of this series in front of the Mosque of El Aksa, known as the "Great Sea," has a capacity of 2,000,000 gallons. Sir Charles Wilson estimates that the total number of gallons which could be stored in these reservoirs would probably exceed 12,000,000. Solomon's Pools were the principal source of supply from without the city.

Walls of the Temple Area.—The northern boundary of the Haram for a distance of 350 feet from the northwest corner was a mass of rock thirty feet high and about 100 feet thick. It was scarped on the outside and protected in front by the ravine which separates Moriah from the hill of Bezetha. This ledge, on which the Turkish Barrack now stands, was the probable site of the great quadrangular fortress of Antonia (or Baras), the chief defence of the Temple on the side of its greatest exposure.

The towers of this stronghold rose to a great height and overlooked the courts of the Temple. It was connected with its cloisters in the time of Herod by secret passages through which soldiers might be hurried in case of need. It is probable that the chief captain, who rescued Paul from mob violence, led his band of soldiers through one of these underground passages. (Acts xxi. 31–33.) On the stairway which led up to the castle the Apostle made the noble defence recorded in the twenty-second chapter of Acts. From this citadel also, in all probability, Jesus was led away by a band of Roman soldiers to the place of crucifixion. (Matt. xxvii. 27–31.)

Farther to the east on the line of the depression between the two hills is the basin or reservoir known as Birket Israil. It is 360 feet long, 126 feet wide, and eighty feet deep. This ravine, which originally entered the Kedron valley to the south of the northeast angle, is only a shallow depression in some places at the present time, but excavations have shown that its bed, at a point near the angle, is actually 142 feet below the level of the Temple area, or 125 below the outside surface. This is the greatest accumulation of débris which has been found in or about the Holy City. No other part of the wall has been so often demolished or thrown down. As we now see it the wall which crosses the bed of this old valley is about forty-five feet high outside, but if we could clear it of these vast accumulations down to its rock foundation it would rise before us to the *amazing height of 170 feet.* On some of the great stones of this wall masons' marks in red paint have been found at a depth of 100 feet below the surface of the ground. These have been identified as Phœnician characters by the best authorities; and from the fact that the trickling of the paint is upward in some instances it is evident that the marks were put on by workmen in the quarry, or that the stones belonged to an earlier wall and were built in upside down. It is an interesting fact that these characters correspond with masons' marks found on the substructions of the harbor of Sidon. Similar marks were also found on the foundation stones at the southeast corner. "Some of these graphiti," says Mr. Deutsch, of the British Museum, "were recognizable at once as well-known Phœnician characters; others, hitherto unknown in Phœnician epigraphy, I had the rare satisfaction of being able to identify on absolutely undoubted Phœnician structures in Syria."[1]

The Golden Gate is 373 feet south of the northeast angle. It occupies the middle of a prominent projection which extends for some distance beyond the line of the wall. It has a double portal with semi-circular arches. Authorities differ with respect to the date of its construction. It is probable, however, that it belongs to the later Roman period. A shaft was sunk by the engineers of Warren's party 143 feet from the south end of the Golden Gateway, and an attempt was made to drive a tunnel from it to the wall. This was found to be impracticable, because of a massive wall intervening, which was supposed to be a retaining wall of a terrace. "It was concluded, though not with perfect certainty, from the nature of the ground and other reasons, that the Golden Gateway stands from thirty to forty

[1] Pict. Pal., Vol. I., p. 47.

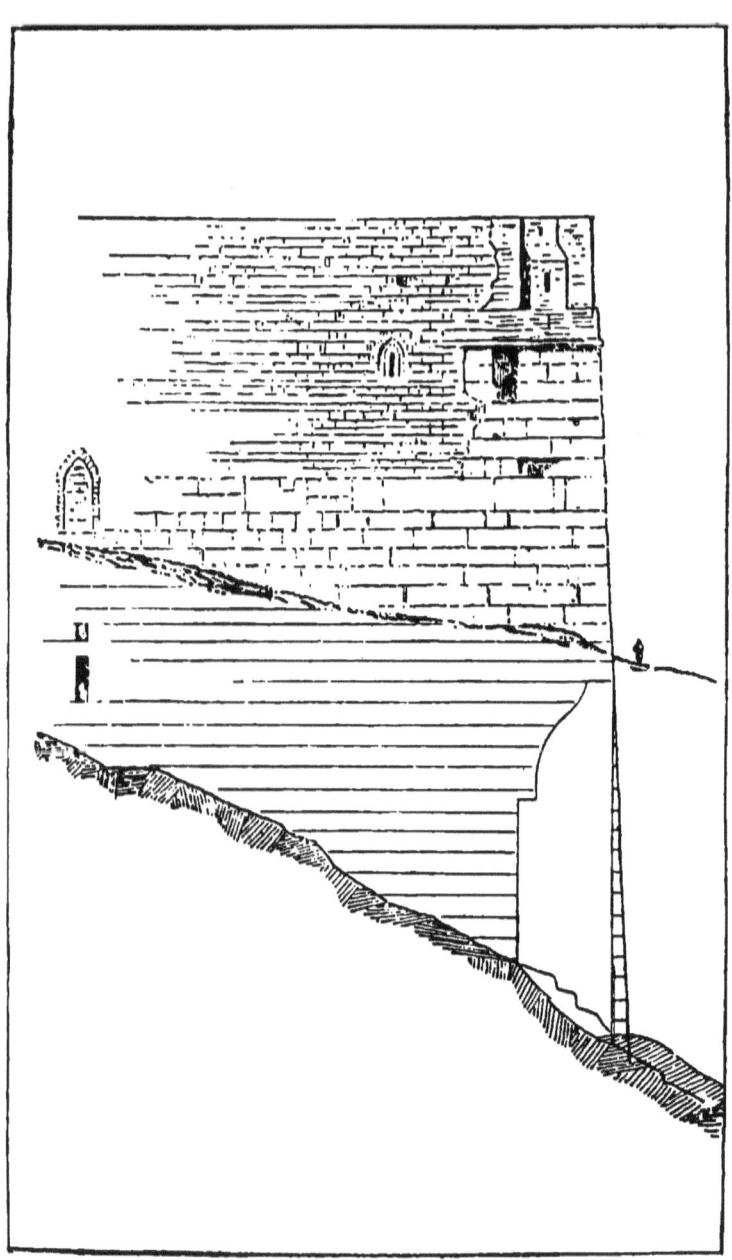

THE SOUTHEAST ANGLE OF HARAM WALL

feet above the rock. The very dangerous nature of the rubbish obliged Captain Warren to close up the shaft."[1]

The masonry from this gate to the northeast corner was found to be of a rougher sort than that to the south of it, indicating a later construction or reconstruction.

The Southeast Corner.—At this angle the wall rises to the height of seventy feet above the surface of the ground. It is the most imposing mass of solid masonry in or about the modern city: and yet the greater part of this wall lies buried beneath the surface of the ground. Its foundations have been discovered at a depth of over eighty feet, and hence the wall as it stands is not *less than 150 feet high.* "The masonry here is about the best in all the walls, and some of the stones are very great. (Mark xiii. 1.) One at the angle, a good way above the present surface is twenty-six feet long, and over six feet high by seven feet broad. It must weigh over 100 tons. It is said to be the heaviest though not the longest in the walls."[2] At the bottom of the shaft, which was sunk at this angle by Colonel Warren, an accumulation of "fat mould filled with potsherds" was found. "This was the layer of earth on the rock, and is, perhaps, the actual layer found by Solomon when he began his work of building. Close to the wall it was cut away, gradually closing into it. This, of course, was to allow the stones to be lowered into their position."[3] There were no signs of stone dressing anywhere in this vicinity. This negative proof, coupled with the evidence furnished by the quarrymen's marks, on the lower courses of the wall, make it clear that these great blocks were fashioned elsewhere and made ready to be lowered into their places without the use of "hammer or axe or tool of iron." (1 Kings vi. 7.)

Three feet east of the angle a small earthen jar was found in a recess cut out of the rock. "It was standing upright as though it had been purposely placed there." Broken pottery,

[1] Thirty years' Work, p. 127.   [2] Henderson's Hist. Geog., p. 143.
[3] Thirty Years' Work, p. 121.

a rusty nail, some charred wood, and several jar handles were also found in the red earth which had accumulated around the foundation course.

The southeast corner of the Haram is supported by a series of substructions or vaulted crypts, called Solomon's Stables. They are regarded as a comparatively modern reconstruction. The evident purpose of their original construction was the enlargement of the Temple area.

"They consist of semi-circular vaults about twenty-eight feet high, resting on a hundred square piers, chiefly composed of ancient drafted stones. In the middle ages the stables of the Frank kings and of the Templars were here, and the rings to which they attached their horses still exist. The vaults extend ninety-one yards from east to west, and sixty-six yards from south to north. There are altogether thirteen vaults of unequal length and breadth. The arches, in the shape of a rather elongated semicircle, are borne by eighty-eight columns in twelve parallel rows." [1]

There are three closed gates in the face of the south wall, which divide it into three nearly equal portions, viz: the Single, Triple and Double, or Huldah, Gates.

The following description, (somewhat condensed,) of these noted portals is given by Sir Charles Wilson:

The Single Gate, the nearest of the three to the southeast angle is a closed entrance of comparatively modern date, which at one time led directly into the vaults known as Solomon's Stables. Beneath the gate Captain Warren found the Great Passage, a narrow way from twelve to eighteen feet high and sixty-nine feet long, which lies beneath one of the aisles of Solomon's Stables.

Next in order is the *Triple Gate*, which consists of three arched portals each thirteen feet wide. The openings are closed with small masonry, but they formerly gave access to three parallel passages, which after running some distance beneath the surface of the Haram are blocked with rubbish.

The Double Gate consists of two entrances, which formerly opened into a vestibule, whence there was an ascent to the Haram area by a vaulted passage at right angles with the line of the wall. The gates are each

[1] Baedecker, p. 52.

eighteen feet wide, and they are covered with large lintels, which have been cracked by the pressure of the masonry above, and are now supported by columns. The Double Gate is undoubtedly a relic of the Temple of Herod. Close to the eastern lintel is a dedicatory inscription to Hadrian, built into the wall upside down, which some writers suppose belonged to the statue erected to that emperor in the Temple area. [1]

The vaulted passage and *vestibule* alluded to in the above description, is reached by a flight of steps from the inside of the Haram, near the entrance to the Mosque El Aksa. The vestibule is a large four domed crypt (thirty by forty feet,) the sides of which are constructed of immense blocks of stone. In the centre is a supporting column—a monolith of hard limestone—eighteen feet in girth and twenty-one feet high. Its capital has a beautiful decoration consisting of alternate leaves of the acanthus and water lily. There is good reason to believe that the Double Gate is identical with the *Huldah Gate*, mentioned in the Talmud, and, if so, it is probable that Jesus frequently entered the cloisters by the Temple of this passageway. It is possible that the double vaults beyond the vestibule have been changed in appearance or direction, but the vestibule itself is certainly as old as the gateway.

Colonel Warren found a marked difference in the structure and general appearance of the portion of the south wall which lies west of the Double Gate. He accounts for this on the supposition that Herod added this western part as a retaining wall in order that he might level up the southwest corner, and thus secure the space he desired for the enlargement of the Temple Courts. It is a noteworthy fact, in this connection, that the course of great stones, which runs continuously from the east angle, ends at the Double Gate. The longest stone above ground in the Haram wall is at the southwest angle. It measures thirty-eight feet nine inches in length.

Robinson's Arch.—On the west wall, thirty-nine feet from the southwest angle, Doctor Robinson discovered some project-

[1] Pict. Pal., Vol 1., p. 49.

ing stones measuring fifty-one feet in width which suggested the spring of an ancient arch. His inference that this was one of a series of arches supported by piers, belonging to a bridge or viaduct, which spanned the Tyropœon valley, was confirmed by the discovery of the first pier at the distance indicated by the fragment of the arch. It rested on a pavement more than thirty feet below the surface of the ground, and with it were found nearly three courses of the masonry of the arch. Below this pavement, at a distance of twenty-four feet, an ancient aqueduct was unearthed, twelve feet deep and four feet wide. Above it, and sticking fast in its vaulted roof, were two arch stones of an older bridge.

The bottom of this drain was found to be 107 feet below the level of the bridge which belonged to Robinson's Arch. In reference to this discovery Colonel Warren says:

> If we are to suppose that the roughly-faced stones at the southwest angle were never exposed to view, we must presume, also, that the two apparent voussoirs (arch stones) lying on the aqueduct under Robinson's Arch, belonged to a bridge which crossed the Tyropœon valley previous to the building of the southwest angle of the Sanctuary. This, says Dr. Thomson, would seem to imply that there was a bridge lower and more ancient than Robinson's Arch; and if the latter was constructed by Herod, the former could not have been of a later date than that of the restored Temple of Nehemiah, or even the Temple of Solomon itself.[1]

It is probable that these remains represent the bridge over the Tyropœon on which, according to Josephus, Titus stood and held parley with the Jews. (Wars 1, vii. 2.)

Barclay's Gate, or the Prophets' Gate as it is sometimes called, is a closed portal 270 feet from the southwest angle. "This gateway, which is evidently one of those that Josephus describes as leading from the western cloisters of the Temple to the suburb of the city, is partly concealed by rubbish; but excavations have shown that it was about eighteen feet ten inches wide, and twenty-eight feet nine inches high. The lintel of

---

[1] The Land and the Book, p. 515.

ROBINSON'S ARCH

the gate is one enormous stone, and its sill is no less than forty-nine feet nine inches above the rock. The gateway formerly gave access to a vaulted passage, one of the approaches to Herod's Temple, which ran for sixty-nine feet in a direction at right angles to the wall, to a domed chamber or vestibule, and then, turning at right angles to the south, gained the Temple area by a ramp or flight of steps."[1] It is an interesting fact that both of these ancient gates were discovered by American explorers.

Wilson's Arch, named after its illustrious discoverer Sir Charles Wilson, is a subterranean structure under the gate of the Chain, 600 feet from the southwest angle. Dr. Thomson describes it as follows:

> The arch springs from the foundation wall of the Haram, as does also that of Robinson's Arch, and the stones are similar to it in shape and size. It is semicircular and perfect, composed of twenty-five courses, or tiers, twelve on each side of the keystone, and is, in a word, Robinson's Arch—rather, one similar to it completed—and the perfection of the work strikes the beholder with admiration and wonder. This arch is by far the most impressive specimen of Roman architecture yet discovered about Jerusalem. Major Wilson believes that there never was more than one arch at that place, the remainder of the Tyropœon valley westward having been filled up by a solid causeway; but Warren's excavations have since shown that there was a series of arches forming a viaduct which lead up toward the palace of Herod on the western hill.[2]

The Wailing Place of the Jews, already described, lies between Wilson's Arch and Barclay's Gate.

The conclusions drawn from the study of the Temple area by Sir Charles Warren in view of all these discoveries, are "that the oldest portion of the wall is the southeast part and the south as far as the Double Gate; that Solomon's palace stood in the southeast, and that the southwest was built by Herod; and that the Temple stood in the middle; where, in fact, Jewish, Chris-

[1] Pict. Pal., p. 40, Art. by Col. Wilson.
[2] Land and Book, p. 516.

tian and Mohammedan tradition all unite in placing it."[1] In his official report Warren gives it as his conviction also, that the portions of the Haram wall from Wilson's Arch to Barclay's Gate: and from the Double Gate round by the southeast angle are Solomonic: while the wall at the northeast angle "is presumably the work of the Kings of Judah, the old wall to which Josephus tells us the wall of Agrippa was joined."

It should be noted in connection with this study of the Temple Hill that the wall we have been tracing is only the *wall of the Temple enclosure*, and not of the Sanctuary itself. Of this, as Christ had foretold, there was not left one stone upon another that was not thrown down. (Matt. xxiv. 1, 2.) In consequence of this total destruction its exact site is in controversy to-day. The entrances to which reference has been made were passage-ways to the cloisters or outer courts only. The real gates of the Temple admitted to inside enclosures on higher levels.

The general plans of the first and second Temples were the same. The principal divergence in structure, extent and appearance, was in the outer courts. Solomon's Temple, according to Warren's estimate, covered an area of 900 feet from east to west by 600 feet from north to south. The so-called Temple of Herod, which was a reconstruction and enlargement of the Temple of Zerubbabel, "appears to have consisted," says Warren, "of the old enclosure of King Solomon's Temple, the old palace, and a piece built in at the southwest angle to make the whole a square of about 900 feet a side. And besides this there was the portion on which the towers protecting the side of the Temple rested, called by Josephus the Exhedra, and connected with the main castle of Antonia by a double set of cloisters."[2]

Much confusion has arisen in the minds of Bible students from failure to distinguish between three different usages of the word "Temple" in ancient and modern times.

[1] Thirty Years' Work, p. 63. [2] Recovery of Jerusalem, p. 252.

Jerusalem and its Environs

1st. The word is used frequently to describe the Holy House with its court, which stood upon the summit of the mountain, and was double the size of the Tabernacle.

2d. It is applied to all the buildings and courts included in the Sanctuary proper, or "Mountain of the House," which was fenced off from those who were not acknowledged as "Israelites" by birth or adoption.

3d. It is sometimes used to describe all of the closely compacted structure within the limits of the retaining walls.

In the time of Christ all the space between the east and west walls, now standing, and between the Tower of Antonia and the south wall was occupied by the Sanctuary with its courts and the Court of the Gentiles.

The Court of the Gentiles was the lowest level or terrace of the Holy Mountain. It was separated from the Sanctuary or Mountain of the House by a stone wall four or five feet in height, called "the Soreg." Along this wall at intervals stone tablets were placed, warning all who were not Israelites to remain outside under penalty of death. Near the site of the Tower of Antonia, M. Ganneau found one of these tablets with a Greek inscription in large, clear-cut characters. The translation is given as follows: "No stranger is to enter within the balustrade round the temple and inclosure. Whoever is caught will be responsible to himself for his death, which will ensue." This inscription confirms the statement of Josephus and also throws additional light on the incident connected with the arrest of the apostle Paul while presenting an offering for himself and his companions in the Temple. (Acts xxi. 28, 29, xxiv. 11, xxvi. 21.)

The Outer Cloisters, which surrounded this spacious court, were known as the Northern and Western Cloisters, Solomon's Porch and the Royal Cloisters.

The Royal Cloister was the chief glory of this outer court. It extended along the entire length of the south wall and was 105 feet in breadth. It was divided by rows of stately columns into three arcades: the central one being 100 feet high and forty-five broad. Those on the sides were fifty feet high and thirty broad. "At the southeast corner the roof of the cloister was 326 feet above the bed of the Kedron. The height of the pinnacle, which is said to have risen at that corner, is unknown; whatever it was, it must be added to that giddy height of 326 feet."[1]

The Mountain of the House included the sacred space within the Soreg. According to the Mishna this enclosure was a square of 500 cubits, or about 750 feet on each side. The outer Court or Chel, as it was usually termed, was a large open space with five entrance gates. A flight of fourteen steps led up to it from the Court of the Gentiles. Within this Chel, the place of assembly for all who were recognized as Israelites, was the Temple proper, with its several courts and enclosing walls and magnificent buildings.

The Inner Court, which included the Inner Cloisters, the *Court of Israel*, and the Court of the Priests, had seven gates, —three on the north, three on the south and one on the east. *The Court of the Women* was a large, open space, surrounded by store chambers, to the east of the Inner Court. It was eight feet higher than the Outer Court and had three entrance gates. The name indicates that the women had the same privileges here as those accorded, in the other courts, to the male worshippers.

" **The Court of Israel** was ten feet above the Court of the Women; then the Court of the Priests on a level three feet higher; and lastly, the temple floor, eight feet above this and therefore twenty-nine feet above the level of the outer court of the Gentiles. It is most interesting to know that these levels correspond closely with the ascertained rock-levels round about the Sakhra or 'holy stone' now covered by the Dome of the Rock. That stone was probably of old time the resting-place of the ark of the covenant. 'The house' on the mountain was

[1] Henderson's Geography, p. 145.

seventy-nine cubits wide by 100 cubits long. The façade was 100 cubits in breadth and height, and was gilded, and over its great entrance ' was spread out a golden vine, with its branches hanging down from a great height, the largeness and fine workmanship of which was a surprising sight.' " (Ant. xv. ii. 3.)[1]

It has been suggested that the great porch in front of the Temple, whose dimensions have been regarded by some writers as an evident exaggeration, resembled the pylon of an Egyptian temple. On this supposition the difficulty in regard to the height of the porch and the great central entrance described by Josephus disappears.

Taken as a whole, with its triple walls, its grand portals and ascents, its spacious courts, its galleries and store chambers, its colonnades, porches and cloisters—the Temple on Mount Moriah was an immense structure, the like of which, for beauty and costliness, has probably never been equalled on earth. As seen from the Mount of Olives it was a terraced mountain of gleaming marble surmounted by a coronal of glittering gold.

> "The Holy City lifted high her towers;
> And higher yet the glorious temple reared,
> Her pile far off appearing like a mount
> Of alabaster tip't with golden spires."—MILTON.

No wonder the disciples, who noted how it was "adorned with goodly stones and gifts," were moved to say, as they looked down upon it from Olivet in the glowing light of the setting sun "Master, *see* what manner of stones and what buildings are here!" (Mark. xiii. 1.)

The sacred memories, the thronging events, the unuttered and unutterable longings which have been, and forever shall be associated with this holy mount, cannot be fittingly expressed by voice or pen. Crowned with the Sanctuary of Jehovah; illuminated with the brightness of His glory; trodden by the feet of Patriarchs, Prophets, Priests and Kings: and, more than

---

[1] Hend. Geog., p. 146.

all, hallowed by the presence of the Eternal Son of God, who humbled Himself to take upon Him our human nature, this place stands unchallenged among holy places as the most memorable spot on earth.

Objects and Places of Special Interest Outside the Walls.—These will be grouped together as far as possible, while making the circuit of the walls.

1. **Catacombs and Tombs.**—The so-called Tombs of the Kings and of the Judges, north of the city, a half mile and a mile respectively, are regarded as the best examples of the numerous subterranean burial-places, which have been found on every side of the city.

Both are rock-hewn tombs in a connected series, and have been excavated on the same general plan. There is nothing, however, to identify either of these tombs or catacombs with the names they bear. The former has a vestibule, or open court, ninety-three feet long by eighty-seven wide and twenty deep, sunk in the surface rock. It has been identified by Dr. Robinson—and in this later authorities concur—with the Mausoleum of Queen Helena, a Jewish proselyte, of Adiabene.

"It is remarkable," says Dr. Manning, "not only for the extent and perfect preservation of the sepulchral chambers, but for the ingenious mechanism by which the entrance was closed or opened—a huge stone being rolled to or from the mouth of the entrance. It thus affords an interesting contemporary illustration of the words of the evangelists, 'Who shall roll away the stone from the door of the sepulchre?' And when they looked they saw the stone rolled away, for it was very great."[1] (Mark. xvi. 3, 4; Luke xxiv. 2.)

The slopes and steep cliffs of the lower valleys of Hinnom and Jehoshaphat are honeycombed with burial chambers of all shapes and sizes. They are usually single or communicating chambers with a doorway in the perpendicular face of the rock. In some instances there are separate niches or recesses for the bodies. A tomb with outer court, side entrance and small

[1] Holy Fields, p. 127.

chambers was excavated a little to the west of the probable site of Golgotha, in 1881. It is nearer to the wall than any Jewish tomb yet discovered and is specially interesting because of its location and date of construction. If Major Conder is right in his suggestion it belongs to the centuries immediately preceding the Christian era.

In the valley of Jehoshaphat there is a conspicuous group of monuments and rock tombs differing in age and styles of architecture. These are known as the tombs of Absalom, Jehoshaphat, Zachariah, and St. James. "Two of these are real monuments of rock; the other two are excavated tombs with ornamented portals." The slope of the Mount of Olives in this vicinity and portions of Mount Zion, without the walls are literally paved with tombstones.

The reputed **Tomb of David** (Neby Daud) is in the crypt of a mosque on the southern slope of Zion. It is surrounded by a cluster of massive buildings one of which is called the Cœnaculum. The ancient tradition which associates this place with the upper room in which the Lord's Supper was instituted, and in which afterward was witnessed the descent of the Spirit —may be correct, but there is no reason to believe that the building which now marks the site was the one in which these memorable events took place. In 1894 a Latin inscription was found by Dr. Bliss in a wall behind one of the gates of Neby Daud, which had been blown down during a storm. It proves to be a votive tablet to Jupiter erected by the Third Legion. Canon Dalton gives the probable date of the inscription as not earlier than 115, nor later than the summer of 117, A. D.

The traditional **Aceldama** or Potter's Field (Acts i. 19; Matt. xxvii. 6–8) is a rugged plot of ground on the south side of the lower basin of the Hinnom valley. In this "field," the boundaries of which are not marked, is a cave artificially enlarged which has long been used as a charnel house. Down to a very recent period the entire plot has been used as "a field to bury strangers in." Colonel Wilson mentions the fact that clay from this neighborhood is still used by the potters of Jerusalem.

2. The Place of the Crucifixion.—A rounded knoll outside the Damascus Gate, which commands a view over the entire city, has been generally accepted as the place of the crucifixion by those who discredit the traditional site within the Church of the Holy Sepulchre. The smooth rounded summit of this elevation, especially when seen from the Mount of Olives, closely resembles a human skull in outline, and may have suggested the name Golgotha or place of a skull. On the southern side of this knoll is a precipitous cliff and at its base the opening to an artificial cavern or quarry—the so-called Grotto of Jeremiah. There seems to be no doubt that this hill was outside the second wall : and it must always have been close to that wall and also to the main road that leads to the north. Attention was called to this site by Mr. Fisher Howe of Brooklyn, in a booklet, published in 1871, and entitled "The True Site of Calvary." Major Conder of the Survey Fund, General Gordon, Sir Wm. Dawson, Canon Tristram, Dr. Henderson, Dr. Merrill, and other eminent authorities, have accepted this identification. The requirements of the Gospel narrative, as summed up by Mr. Howe, are as follows :

1. Calvary was a place outside the walls of the city. (Heb. xiii. 12; Matt. xxvii. 31, 32 ; John xix. 16, 17.)
2. It was a place nigh to the city. (John xix. 20.)
3. It was popularly known under the general designation of Kranion. (Matt. xxvii. 33; John xix. 17.)
4. It was obviously nigh to one of the leading thoroughfares to and from Jerusalem. (Matt. xxvii. 39; Mark xv. 29.)
5. It was nigh to sepulchres and gardens. (John xix. 38–42.)
6. It was very conspicuous; that is it could be seen by those at a distance. (Matt. xxvii. 55; Luke xxiii. 35; John xix. 20.)[1]

All of these conditions appear to be met and satisfied in the locations outside the Damascus Gate. More recently this view

[1] Wilson's In Scripture Lands, p. 228.

THE PROBABLE SITE OF CALVARY

has been strengthened by the discovery of the tomb already mentioned which proves the place to have been both without the gates, and nigh to rock-hewn Sepulchres; and by a Jewish tradition, which connects the knoll with the "place of stoning," or public execution ground of the Hebrews. There is also a Christian tradition as old as the fifth century which places the stoning of Stephen in the same locality. It is worthy of note in this connection that the portal now called the Damascus Gate was earlier known as St. Stephen's Gate.[1]

3. **Olivet and its Sacred Sites.**—The Mount of Olives (Jebel et Tur) is so close to Jerusalem that it has always had a place in its topography as well as in its history. It is not an isolated mountain but a ridge with three distinctly-marked, rounded summits. The southern portion runs for nearly two miles north and south, or in a line almost parallel with the ridge of Moriah. It ends toward the south in a lower ridge, the summit of which is known as the "Mount of Offence." This name has been given to it on the supposition that it was the "high place for Chemosh, the abomination of Moab, and for Molech, the abomination of the children of Ammon." These degrading forms of idolatrous worship, which Solomon encouraged in the later period of his reign, were said to be "in the hill that is before,—or eastward of—Jerusalem." (1. Kings xi. 7, 8.)

The central eminence, to which the name Olivet, or the Mount of Olives, properly applies is directly opposite the Temple area. Its elevation is 2,682 feet, or about 170 feet higher than Zion and 259 feet higher than Moriah. This summit is the traditional site of the ascension of Christ and here the so-called "Church of the Ascension" stands. The location, however, does not harmonize with any of the details of the Evangelist's story. About a mile north of this summit the ridge curves to the west, culminating in another summit, the generally accepted site of Mount Scopus, where the Roman gen-

[1] Hend. Geog., p. 164.

eral Titus drew up his legions in full view of the city, before he began its investment.

The view from the summit of Olivet is one of the most interesting and impressive within the limits of the Holy Land. It includes nearly all the sacred sites connected with the humiliation and suffering of our Lord from Bethlehem to the place of His ascension. Southward the range of vision extends to the height at Hebron; westward every object on the plateau of Jerusalem stands out with startling distinctness; while to the east is an unequalled panoramic view of the rugged Wilderness, the Jordan valley—nearly 4,000 feet below—portions of the Dead Sea and the clearly-cut outlines of the mountains of Moab and Gilead. Here the eager watchmen stood, long ages ago, to catch the first glow of the beacon light on those distant mountains, which gave notice of the appearance of the new moon by which the beginnings of the sacred feasts were regulated. The pathetic story of the passage of King David over the summit of this mountain when he fled from the face of Absalom, is the first and only important event associated with it before the time of Christ.

"And David went up by the ascent of Mount Olivet, and wept as he went up, and had his head covered, and he went barefoot: and all the people that were with him covered every man his head, and they went up, weeping as they went." (2. Sam. xv. 30.)

There were doubtless many occasions of rejoicing also, on Olivet: as when the pilgrims bands had gained its summit and looked down on the Holy City; or when the people went forth with gladness of heart over its wooded slopes "to fetch olive and pine and myrtle branches to make booths, as it is written." (Neh. viii. 15.) And yet, as Dean Stanley has said, its lasting glory belongs not to the Old Dispensation, but to the New. It is preëminent among the sacred mountains, because, more than all others, it was honored as the favorite retreat and quiet resting-place of Jesus. In the crowded city He taught and

BETHANY

ministered to the suffering and the needy, but when the shadows of evening began to fall He went out to the Mount of Olives. Here He slept through the night under the wide spreading branches of the trees, or sought retirement for meditation and prayer; or entered into the home at Bethany where He ever found the kindly sympathy and true hearted affection which His human nature craved. Here, says Dr. Thomson, the God-man chose to reveal more of His human nature than anywhere else on earth; and here also were witnessed the most affecting and stupendous scenes in the history of our Blessed Redeemer.

Four places on the slopes of Olivet are specially noteworthy in connection with the closing scenes of our Lord's earthly life and ministry. These are—*Bethany; the place where* He *wept over Jerusalem; the place of the Ascension;* and *the Garden of Gethsemane.*

Bethany is pleasantly situated amid groves of olive, fig and almond trees on the southeastern slope or shoulder of the mountain, something less than two miles from Jerusalem. "A wild mountain-hamlet screened by an intervening ridge from the view of the top of Olivet, perched on its broken plateau of rock, the last collection of human habitations before the desert-hills which reach to Jericho—this is the modern village of El Lazarieh, which derives its name from its clustering around the traditional site of the one house and grave which give it an undying interest."[1] The modern "house and grave" exhibited here are of very doubtful genuineness, but the identification of El Lazarieh with the "town of Mary and her sister Martha" and Lazarus, has never been questioned. But for this one home—the type of all that is beautiful and sacred in the Christian home on earth—it would long ago have been forgotten. Its present condition has little to commend it, but all its associations with that far-away past are tender, sacred and sublime. Here Jesus commended the choice of Mary who counted it her

[1] Sinai and Palestine, p. 256.

greatest privilege to sit at His feet and hear His word. (Luke x. 42.) Here He approved the service of Martha, so lovingly rendered, and revived her drooping faith in the hour of anguish and bereavement. Here He wept with the sisters at the grave of Lazarus, and anon with a voice which penetrated not only to the inner recesses of the tomb, but to the abode of the freed spirits, called back the dear object of their affections to life, and the further enjoyment of that sanctified home. (John, chap. xi.) In Bethany afterward the grateful Mary anointed the feet of Jesus with the costly box of ointment, and wiped His feet with her hair, while He reclined at the table, as their honored guest. And it is still true, according to the Master's word, that wheresoever His gospel has been preached in the whole world, there also has this, that this woman hath done, been told as a memorial of her. It was from Bethany that the triumphal march began toward Jerusalem on that memorable day when the rejoicing multitude took branches of palm trees, and went forth to meet Him, crying Hosanna: Blessed is the King of Israel that cometh in the name of the Lord. (John xii. 13.) Three ancient roads, or pathways, lead over the western slope of the mountain, from the bridge over the Kedron valley, to the town of Bethany. One passes around its northern shoulder; another runs southeast, and passing close to the new Greek church, ascends the steep slope to the summit; the third passes around the southern shoulder of Olivet and thence over a low bridge to the recess in which the village lies. This road has recently been made wide enough for the passage of carriages over the entire route to the Jordan. It is now, and always has been the main thoroughfare to Bethany and Jericho.

There is every reason to believe that this was the route of the triumphal procession.

The place where Jesus wept over Jerusalem was at a point where the road, slightly ascending, turns sharply around an overhanging ledge of rock. Here the whole city would come instantly into view. "It is hardly possible," says Dean Stan-

THE BRIDGE OVER THE KEDRON

ley, "to doubt that this rise and turn of the road—where His eyes beheld what is still the most impressive view which the neighborhood of Jerusalem furnishes—was the exact spot where the multitude paused, and He, when He beheld the city, wept over it."[1] The site of Bethphage which is mentioned in this connection is not definitely known.

The place of the Ascension was in the immediate vicinity of Bethany. All the circumstances of the narrative forbid its location in a public place, or in full view of the city, where an uncertain tradition has placed it. The statement of St. Luke, that He led His disciple out as far as to Bethany cannot be lightly set aside. The author has rested upon a natural platform of rock and earth overhanging the town, and shut out from view by the ridge of Olivet, where every incident recorded in the gospel narrative might have taken place. It is probable that Jesus took the direct road to Bethany as the morning was about to dawn, and at this point or somewhere in its vicinity, overlooking the place associated with so many blessed memories, "He lifted up His hands and blessed them. And it came to pass, while He blessed them, He was parted from them, and carried up into heaven." (Luke xxiv. 50–53.)

The Garden of Gethsemane.—This sacred retreat—we are told—was over the brook Kedron, and hence at the base of the Mount of Olives. The place which for many centuries has been known and revered as Gethsemane is just beyond the bridge that spans the narrow valley of the Kedron, and nearly opposite the Golden Gate. It is an enclosure of about an acre of ground, in which are eight gnarled olive trees of extraordinary girth and evidently of great age. It is scarcely possible to resist the impression that the small space which is here set apart by the Latin church, as the scene of the Saviour's mysterious agony, is in a location that does not admit of the privacy and seclusion, which the narrative of the Evangelists plainly imply. It is the meeting-place of several roads, which

[1] Sinai and Palestine, p. 260.

must always have converged in or about this spot, and it is scarcely more than 250 yards from the city wall. It is certainly a valid objection to this enclosed space that it was necessarily a public resort, and especially so at the passover season, when crowds were passing in and out the eastern gates at every hour of the day and night. It is a fact worthy of note, also, that the distinctive name, Gethsemane was given to the garden or olive-yard, which Jesus was wont to visit, because there was an oil press within it or belonging to it. Professor Rendall Harris has recently suggested a site about one fourth of a mile north of the traditional garden, where the ruins of an ancient oil press have been discovered, surrounded by olive groves, some of which are very old. This oil press, like most of its kind in Palestine, was a permanent structure with rock-hewn vats and heavy rollers for crushing the fruit. It is possible that this retired spot indicates the true location of the hallowed place where the Redeemer, on the night of His betrayal, prayed in agony of spirit while His sweat was as it were great drops of blood, falling down to the ground. (Luke xxii. 44; Matt. xxvi. 36–45; Mark xiv. 32–41; John xviii. 1.)

4. **The King's Dale** or **King's Garden**.—These designations apply to that portion of the Kedron valley which extends from the southeast angle of the Haram to the confluence of the valleys above Bir Eyub (Well of Job). It was favorably situated for irrigation and has always been noted for its extraordinary fertility. It was the place of Absalom's tomb (2 Sam. xviii. 18), and the meeting place of Abraham and Melchizedek after the rescue of Lot. (Gen. xiv. 17–24.)

5. **Tophet** (Gehenna) was the distinctive name for the lower basin of the valley of Hinnom. Its slopes are carefully terraced and fertile garden plots join each other throughout its length in almost continuous succession. The horrid rites which were practiced here by Moloch worshippers in the days of the kings: and its selection as the place of burning, where the offal of the city and the altar were consumed, have made

its name infamous throughout all succeeding generations. (2. Kings xxiii. 10 ; Isa. xxx. 33, lxvi. 24.) It is worthy of note that there is nothing in the natural features of this locality to give it the evil preëminence which now attaches to it.

6. **The Plain of Rephaim**, now known as El Bukeia, is southwest of the city of Jerusalem and extends very nearly to its walls. For a mile or more it is an open plain or basin affording a broad passage-way in the direction of Bethlehem. It then contracts into a narrow valley (Wady el Werd) which bears off toward the west. The railroad approaches the city by way of this valley and plain. Its Hebrew name associates it with some unrecorded story of the aboriginal race of giants which dwelt in the east and south. (Josh. xv. 8, xviii. 16.) It was the scene of the defeat of the Philistines in two notable battles during the reign of David. (1 Chron. xi. 15, xiv. 9-16; 2 Sam. v. 17-25.)

7. **Pools and Sources of Water Supply.**—(1) *The Fountain of the Virgin* so-called, issues from a hidden source under the eastern base of Ophel, about 950 feet south of the Triple Gate. It is the only spring of flowing water in or about modern Jerusalem.

The brook, which once flowed down the Kedron valley, has been choked by avalanches of débris from the heights above, and its streams have doubtless been diverted into subterranean channels. There are evidences, also, of a stream or fountain, with a similar history, which long ago coursed down the Tyropœon valley. Dr. Bliss thinks it probable, in view of recent discoveries along the line of the ancient southern wall, that the references of Josephus to the "Fountain of Siloam," which he places outside the city, apply to the spring-head, and not to the Pool of Siloam, as has been generally supposed. "It is quite possible," he says, "that the term Siloam might have been applied equally to the Virgin's Fountain as the source of the waters which fed the Pool of Siloam."[1] M. Ganneau's identification

[1] P. E. Quarterly, '97, p. 254.

of this well-spring with En Rogel (the spring of the Fuller), mentioned several times in the Old Testament, has been generally accepted, and it is known by this name on the Ordnance map. Directly opposite, on the other side of the Kedron valley, is a precipitous cliff, still known as Zahweileh, which without doubt is the "Stone of Zoheleth." The discovery of this ancient landmark by M. Ganneau gave the clue to the location of En Rogel. It is described in the Book of the Kings as the "Stone of Zoheleth, which is by En Rogel." At this place Adonijah prepared a great feast for his adherents, and was proclaimed King. (1 Kings i. 19.)

The straggling village of Siloam (Silwan), once mentioned in the New Testament in connection with the fall of its tower, (Luke xiii. 4) is perched on the summit of this cliff. A rugged pathway, or series of steps cut in the face of the rock, affords a direct, but somewhat perilous passage from the town to the fountain, its natural source of water supply. The suggestion that this fountain is also identical with the Upper Pool or Spring of Gihon ("the spring head"), and that the Pool of Siloam represents the Lower Gihon, has met with favor and bids fair to solve some difficulties in connection with the history of these pools. On the assumption that this proposed identification can be established it would follow that Solomon was anointed by the Pool of Siloam. Inasmuch as the hill of Ophel came between this point and the place where Adonijah was proclaimed, the party of Solomon would not be seen on their way to Gihon. "But when the anointing had taken place, and the party were going back up the Tyropœon toward David's house, the people piped their music and shouted their joy till the earth rang again."[1] It would seem from the narrative that the conspirators did not know that their plans were foiled until they *heard* the trumpet and the ominous shouts, "God save King Solomon." (1 Kings i. 38-46.)

The spring head, or visible source of En Rogel is a cave,

[1] St. Clair's Buried Cities and Bible Countries, p. 282.

Jerusalem and its Environs

artificially enlarged, which lies twenty-five feet below the present surface of the ground. It is probable that the stream from this source originally ran out at the base of Ophel and down the Kedron valley, and that the excavation was afterward made higher up, for the purpose of diverting it in another direction. The bottom of the cave in which the water rises at irregular intervals, is reached by two flights of stone steps, (thirty in all). When the flow fills the basin in the bottom of the cave it passes through a rock-hewn tunnel, 1708 feet in length, to the Pool of Siloam in the Tyropœon valley. The following description of this interesting fountain and its outgoings is given by Sir Charles Wilson:

"This spring has a constant though small flow of water, and also an intermittent one which appears to depend upon the rainfall, and which consists in a sudden increase of the ordinary flow. In winter there are from three to four flows per diem; in summer two; later on, in autumn only one; but after a dry winter the flow takes place only once in three or four days. . . . In connection with the tunnel passage Captain Warren opened out a rock hewn canal, which ran for some distance due west with a slight fall, so that the water from the spring could flow down to the west end where a shallow basin had been excavated to receive it. From this point a circular shaft more than forty feet high, led upward to a great corridor excavated in the rock, whence a flight of steps gave access to the surface at a point on Ophel, which must have been well within the ancient walls of the city. It was thus possible for the Jews on the approach of an enemy to close or seal the well with blocks of stone, and at the same time procure a supply of water for their own use by means of the shaft or well within the walls. In the corridor three glass lamps of curious construction were found placed at intervals, as if to light up the passage to the shaft. A little pile of charcoal, as if for cooking, a dish glazed inside, jars of red pottery, and other lamps, were also found, as well as an iron ring overhanging the shaft, to which a rope might have been attached for drawing water." [1]

This rock-hewn canal, sixty-seven feet long, with its shaft on Ophel, was evidently the older portion of this cutting, and was utilized as far as it extended, when the tunnel through the

[1] Pict. Pal., Vol. I., pp. 102, 104.

ridge was undertaken. This accounts in part at least, for its serpentine course.

It has been suggested by M. Ganneau that the deflection lower down was made to avoid interference with the tombs of the Kings, supposed to be on Ophel. If so they must be north of the bend, for Dr. Bliss has excavated the ground to the south of it, without finding anything of importance.

En Rogel was one of the familiar landmarks which separated the portion of Benjamin from Judah, and its identification with the Fountain of the Virgin has resolved some of the difficulties with respect to the topography of other points in or about Jerusalem. (Josh. xv. 7, xviii. 16.) We have noted already that it was close to the scene of Adonijah's feast; and it was also near to the hiding-place of Jonathan and Ahimaaz, the spies of David. (2 Sam. xvii. 17.)

The Pool of Siloam lies on the west side of Ophel near the mouth of the Tyropœon valley. It is an artificial receptacle for the overflow from the basin of En Rogel, and is wholly dependent upon it for its water supply. The Siloam inscription, accidentally discovered by an Arab boy, August, 1880, is regarded as one of the most important monumental records of Old Testament times. Its position in the tunnel was about nineteen feet from the Siloam entrance, where a space of twenty-seven inches square had been smoothed to form the face of the tablet. The letters closely resemble the Phœnician in form. It is conceded by all the leading authorities that this fragment represents the oldest specimen of the Hebrew language that has come down to us, except the writing on the Moabite Stone. Says Dr. Ward,—" This tunnel was not made later than the time of King Hezekiah, and the inscription must be of that date or earlier; and it is the only purely Jewish Palestine inscription of any length known, there being nothing else but small seals."[1] This discovery confirms, if it does not make certain, the supposition that the pool and the conduit

[1] N. Y. Indep., '94, p. 553.

Jerusalem and its Environs 211

were made by Hezekiah,—"who stopped the upper course of Gihon and brought it straight down to the west side of the city of David" (2 Chron. xxxii. 30) : or, as it is elsewhere stated, "made a pool and a conduit and brought water into the city." "The very *raison d'être* of the Siloam tunnel seems to have been to bring water within the limits of the city. It is worthy of note that while we devoted immense labor to testing the contrary theory, yet all our discoveries have tended to support this view."[1] Conder thinks that the Pool of Siloam and the lower basin or old pool below it may have existed in the time of Ahaz. (2 Chron. xxxii.; Isa. vii. 3.) The improved translation of the Siloam inscription by Professor Sayce is as follows:

1. (Behold the) excavation! Now this is the history of the excavation. While the excavators were still lifting up
2. the pick, each toward his neighbor, and while there were yet three cubits to (excavate) there was heard the voice of one man
3. calling to his neighbor, for there was an excess (?) in the rock on the right hand (and on the left). And after that on the day
4. of excavating the excavators had struck pick against pick, over against one another,
5. the waters flowed from the spring to the pool for a distance of 1,200 cubits. And (part)
6. of a cubit was the height of the rock over the head of the excavators.[2]

Recent excavations (1896–7) under the direction of the Palestine Exploration Survey Fund have brought to light much that was hitherto unknown in reference to the ancient Pool of Siloam and its surroundings. The modern pool—fifty-three feet long by eighteen wide—has been found to be a contraction within the limits of the original basin, which was almost square.

As restored, it measures seventy-five feet on its north side and seventy-one on the west. Close to its western wall, the greater

[1] Dr. Bliss in Quarterly, July, '97, p. 177.
[2] Records of the Past, second series, Vol. II.

part of which was cut out of the solid rock, Dr. Bliss uncovered an ancient stairway leading upward toward the city, which he describes as follows :

> The number of the steps is thirty-four. They vary in height from six to nine and a half inches, and are arranged in a system of wide and narrow treads alternately, the wide treads from four feet three inches, to four feet eleven inches, and the narrow ones from eleven inches to seventeen. The main part of the stairway, as seen, consists of steps built of hard, well-jointed stones laid on a bed of chips and weak mortar formed of mud and lime. But pushing along the whole breadth of the stairway to the parapet wall, we found that for ten feet nine inches from the scarp the tread consists of the natural rock, well polished by foot wear.[1]

Above this flight of steps a large mass of "blockage" was found, and beyond this to the north a paved road was traced for a considerable distance, which appears to be the continuation of the grand stairway from the Pool. The paved road and the steps were found to be of the same class of work and the general direction points to the entrance in the south wall known as the Double Gate. On the north side of the enclosing wall, near the northwest corner, a pier was found at the height of twelve feet nine inches from the pavement with the springer of an arch, which indicated the existence of an arcade at one time on that side of the pool. "We may safely assume," says Dr. Bliss, "that the arcade ran around the four sides of the pool and represents the quadriporticum, or four-sided arcade of the Bordeaux Pilgrim. . . . We have proved also that the built stairway made use of a system of rock-hewn steps, probably older, and led to a court in front of the Pool of Siloam."[2]

Directly north of the present pool a well-preserved ruin of an ancient church was found. By driving a series of tunnels the outline of the church was recovered, but the superincumbent mass of débris and earth resting upon it to the depth of twelve to thirty feet was not removed. The building with its

[1] Quarterly, '97, p. 13.   [2] Quarterly Report, Jan'y, '97, p. 16.

appendages was found to be 115 feet in length by 100 in breadth. Its south aisle was built over the north arcade of the ancient pool. Along its west wall in some places the steps of the great stairway were irregularly broken off to make room for it, while at other places they are buried beneath the level of the flooring. This clearly indicates that the steps were older than the wall of the church. There seems to be no doubt that the church belongs to the Byzantine period: and it is probable that it was built by the Empress Eudosia.

The enlarged pool, which Dr. Bliss has thus recovered piece by piece, is, without doubt, the Biblical Pool of Siloam. Its genuineness has been attested by several lines of evidence and, it is safe to say, that no site in or about Jerusalem has furnished so many interesting mementos of the past or has been more certainly identified.

The paved street and the majestic flight of stone steps, with evidences of older foot wear on the rock beneath, suggest "the stairs that go down from the city of David" (Neh. iii. 15); as well as the way of descent by which the blind man reached its healing waters in obedience to the command of Jesus. (John ix. 7.) It was from this same pool also, that water was brought in a golden pitcher on the "last, great day of the feast" (of Tabernacles), and poured out on the Altar of sacrifice amid the shouts of the rejoicing multitude. (John vii. 37.)

South of the Pool of Siloam is a large reservoir constructed by building a dam across the valley. It is known as the "Old Pool" and is connected with the upper basin by a channel cut in the rock. It seems to have been constructed mainly with the view to the irrigation of the gardens in the broad valley below. The waters which glided down this rock-hewn channel and were parted hither and thither to gladden and refresh the King's gardens, might well be described as "the waters of Shiloah that go softly." (Isa. viii. 6.) "It seems probable," says Colonel Wilson, "that the lower Pool of Siloam is the *mikvah* (ditch, R. V., reservoir) which Hezekiah made 'between the two walls for the water of the old pool.' (Isa. xxii. 11.) Thus the construction of the Siloam tunnel, and of the great dam examined by Dr. Bliss, would be due to Hezekiah. Possibly the rock-hewn steps may have been connected with 'the way of the gate between the two walls which is by the King's Garden.'" (2 Kings xxv. 4; Jer. lii. 7.)[1]

Bir Eyub, or the Well of Job, is almost directly south of the Pool of Siloam, a little below the junction of the valleys of Hinnom and Kedron. It is a shaft sunk through the limestone rock to a depth of 125 feet. It is not a natural spring head, but collects its water supply from the surface and underground streams, which descend from the higher elevations and converge at this point. Bir Eyub was formerly supposed to be identical with En Rogel, but recent investigations,—as already intimated,—have shown that this designation belongs of right to the Fountain of the Virgin.

In the valley of Hinnom there are two large reservoirs known as the *Mamilla Pool* (Birket Mamilla) and the *Sultan's Pool* (Birket es Sultan). The first lies in the upper basin of the valley, a little to the northwest of the Jaffa Gate. It is partly hewn out of the rock, its sides being walled with stone and cement. Its dimensions are 291 x 192 x 19 feet. This reservoir supplies the Pool of Hezekiah (Amygdalon) by means of a conduit which passes under the city wall.

The second or lower pool is near the southwest angle of the wall. It is the largest in the vicinity of Jerusalem, the dimensions being 600 x 250 x 35 feet. It was formed by building a dam across the valley. It is now broken and in ruins. Colonel Wilson suggests that its only use could have been the irrigation of the gardens lower down in the valley. These reservoirs have been frequently called the Upper and Lower Pools of Gihon, but the lower one is apparently of modern construction, and there is no satisfactory evidence in favor of this identification.

[1] Quarterly Statement, Oct., '97, p. 248.

Jerusalem and its Environs

Water Supply from the South.—The remains of two great conduits, which in former times furnished an abundant supply of pure mountain water to the city and its temple courts, can still be traced in almost continuous course from the hills south of Bethlehem. These have been designated as the Low-level and High-level aqueducts.

The first is connected with the Pools of Solomon near the head of Wady Urtas. These reservoirs, three in number, are supplied by surface drainage and a notable spring, flowing from an enclosed rock chamber, known as the sealed fountain. A farther source of supply was utilized by constructing a channel from Wady Arub, in which were several copious springs of water. The measurements of Solomon's Pools, as given by Doctor Robinson, are as follows: *Lower Pool*, 582 x 207 x 50 feet; *Middle*, 423 x 230 x 39; *Upper*, 380 x 226 x 25. A good supply of water is still carried to Bethlehem from these pools and arrangements are now being made by the Sultan of Turkey to repair this aqueduct along the whole line in honor of the proposed visit of Emperor William of Germany.

The total length of the Low-level aqueduct is about fourteen miles. From its starting point to the city it has a fall of thirty-two feet. It crosses the valley of Hinnom a little below the Sultan's pool on several pointed arches, and, winding around the southeast slopes of Mount Zion, terminates at length in the great reservoirs of the Temple area. "The waste overflow appears to have passed through one of the passages discovered by M. de Saulcy, beneath the Triple Gate into the main drain on the eastern hill, which discharged itself into the Kedron valley."

The High-level aqueduct is a marvel of engineering skill. It entered Jerusalem at an elevation of 100 feet above the Low-level aqueduct, and delivered its water supply to every part of the city. Its farthest source of supply was a fountain issuing from a subterranean chamber sixty or seventy feet beneath the bed of a valley, south of Solomon's Pools (Wady Byar). The following description of the course of this remarkable conduit, is given by Sir Charles Wilson:

> From this chamber a well-constructed channel cut in the rock and varying from five to twenty-five feet in height, leads up the valley for some distance until it terminates in a natural cleft of the rock. A similar channel follows the bed of the valley, downward for more than four miles, until it issues from the ground near a solid dam of masonry which extends right across the valley. This great tunnel, to facilitate the construction of which several shafts from sixty to seventy feet deep were sunk in the bed of the valley, was intended to catch the flood water of the valley, the dam being probably made to retain the water or prevent its running off before it had filtered down to the channel. . . . About 600 yards below the dam the conduit enters another tunnel 1,700 feet long, which at one point is 115 feet below the surface of the ground. Eleven shafts were sunk to aid the work of excavation, and the passage is in places fourteen feet high. After passing through the tunnel the conduit winds around the hill to the valley in which the Pools of Solomon lie. It then crosses that valley above the upper pool in an underground channel which tapped the Sealed Fountain, and formerly brought it, with its own waters to the *high level* in Jerusalem. After leaving the pools the aqueduct at first runs along the side of the valley of Urtas, but at a point not far from Bethlehem it enters a tank, and thence, when perfect, carried the water over the valley near Rachel's Tomb by means of an inverted syphon. *This syphon was about two miles long*, and consisted of perforated blocks of stone set in a mass of rubble masonry some three feet thick all round. The tube is eleven inches in diameter, and the joints, which appear to have been ground or turned, are put together with an extremely hard cement. The whole work is a remarkable specimen of ancient engineering skill, and the labor bestowed upon the details excites the admiration of all travellers. On approaching Jerusalem all trace of the conduit is lost. It has evidently been destroyed during one of the many sieges, and the point at which it entered the city is still uncertain. The most interesting feature, however, is that the supply was brought to Jerusalem at an elevation of twenty feet over the sill of the Jaffa Gate, and that the conduit would have been able to deliver water to the highest part of the city, and so provide an adequate supply for the whole population.[1]

8. The Jaffa Suburb.—This represents the largest addition to the modern city outside the walls. It lies to the west of the

[1] Pict. Pal., Vol. I., p. 115.

Jerusalem and its Environs

northwest quarter and has grown very rapidly in recent years. To the cluster of Russian buildings, which a short time ago stood alone, there have been added an imposing collection of schools, hospitals, consulates, orphanages and residences of various styles, surrounded by fruitful gardens, orchards and olive-yards. Other extensions have been made along the Bethlehem road and on the north. The terminal Station on the railroad from Jaffa is on the west side of the valley of Hinnom, near the Bethlehem road. The German Colony of the Temple, named Rephaim from the plain on which it is situated, the New Leper's Hospital and the large Jewish Hospital founded by Sir Moses Montefiore, are in the immediate vicinity of the railway station. The present population of Jerusalem, including this overflow in the suburbs, is about 60,000. It is estimated that about 40,000 of this number are Jews.

9. **Southern Wall of Ancient Jerusalem.**—One of the most interesting results of the explorations conducted by Sir Charles Warren is the recovery of a portion of the ancient wall on the eastern brow of Ophel. This wall, which had been entirely covered with débris, joined the Haram wall at the southeast angle, but was evidently of later construction and of different materials. It was traced for a distance of nearly 800 feet and was found to be fourteen feet six inches thick at its base, and from forty to sixty feet in height. The terminus reached was at a point near a rocky knoll, where the stone had probably been removed for building purposes. Several towers were unearthed along the line of the wall, one of which measured eighty feet in breadth, sixty-six in height and projected beyond it for a distance of forty feet. This accords with the position of "the tower that lieth out" to which reference is made in the book of Nehemiah (iii. 25).

The general direction of the wall, as far as traced, indicated a line of defence which included the *entire ridge of Ophel.*

On the southern slope of Mount Zion an exposed scarp, south of the present wall, suggested the existence of a lower and older wall, but its general direction and the extent of the slope that it included were not known. In 1875 Henry Maudsley, C. E., traced the scarp of this wall continuously, for over 650 feet, from the southwest angle to the eastern limit of the enclosure which contained the English School and Cemetery.

At this point, in the spring of 1894, Doctor Bliss, under direction of the Survey Fund, began his work of excavation. This work was prosecuted with slight interruptions for three years. Its results, briefly summarized, are:

1st. The tracing of the wall from the Protestant Cemetery "with more or less interruption, but always the same wall, to a point just outside and south of the lower pool of Siloam." The distance of this traced, or inferred, wall is 2,420 feet, or a little short of half a mile. The ridge along which it was found to run is, in fact, the extreme possible position southward for a line of defence. At its southwest angle it was 370 feet south of the present wall and at its southeast angle the distance was 2,010 feet.

2d. The discovery of another wall of later date, which at some points kept close to the older wall, or was built over its ruins, and at others was so distinct that it could be distinctly traced alongside of it. In a condensed report Dr. Bliss gives the results of his discoveries along these lines, as follows:

> On the upper wall were found five towers; on the lower, four, two of them very beautifully built. Two gates were found at the southwest and southeast angles of the city respectively. Both gates have superimposed door-sills, indicating three periods; the sockets, bolt-holes, and in the case of the lower gate, door-jambs are clearly seen. Under both gates large drains pass. The wall was found at greatly varying depths. At one point its ruined top was so near the surface that the fellah had often struck his plough against it, while the rock is only six feet below the surface. At another point the rock is forty-eight feet below the surface, and towering above it the wall was found still standing to a height of forty-five feet. The masonry ranged from the rudest foundation rubble to exquisitely jointed and finished work. There are good reasons to suppose that the lower wall is Jewish.

Jerusalem and its Environs

Firstly. The *débris* separating it from the upper wall indicates a time when no city wall ran along this line, and points to an interruption in the city's history like that which occurred after the destruction by Titus. The upper wall would then be Roman or Christian.

Secondly. The pottery found along the base of the lower wall is almost exclusively Jewish, while that at higher levels is Roman. The lengths of the pieces of this wall actually traced amount to a quarter of a mile. The united lengths of our shafts and trenches amount to over a mile and a quarter.[1]

3d. At the southwest corner of the old Pool of Siloam a wall was found, diverging from the main line, which ran in a northwesterly direction up the west bank of the Tyropœon valley. This was traced to a point some distance beyond the upper Pool. In the search for the continuation of this wall the great stairway, the enlarged Pool, and the ancient church were discovered. Beyond this point no trace of the wall could be found. The probability is that the material used in its construction had been carried away to rebuild other structures.

4th. In addition to the stairway, original pool, and Byzantine church, already mentioned, a broad, paved street with a drain below it was traced for a considerable distance north of the Pool. Its general direction was down the Tyropœon valley and Dr. Bliss regards it as almost certain that it had its terminus in a gate discovered by him in the ancient wall that includes the Pool within the city. "The key of the situation," he says, "is the street. This street is very plainly older than the Byzantine church, because the church is built over it. The drain we traced very much further than the street, because the latter was in a ruined condition. This drain when last seen was pointing almost directly toward Robinson's Arch, under which Sir Charles Warren discovered a Mosaic pavement, whose large polished stones correspond to the huge paving stones ten by six feet, which we discovered along our street. We appear thus to have a line of road from Robinson's Arch

[1] Quarterly P. E. F., '96, p. 234.

to our gate, which I think can be identified with the Fountain Gate of Scripture." [1]

5th. Dr. Bliss has found by a series of excavations beginning at the gate, which he identifies with the Fountain Gate, that the wall took a northeasterly direction including the Old Pool, as well as the Upper Pool, and that its terminus on the other side of the Tyropœon valley points to the wall found by Warren, which ran in a southwest direction from the corner of the Temple area. It should be added also that careful search was made for a wall north of the Pool of Siloam along the line of the paved street, but no indication of either wall or gate was found. *It follows from the accumulation of evidences furnished by this series of excavations, that all the available portions of the slopes of Zion and Ophel, including the upper and lower pools, were within the walls of the ancient city in the time of its greatest enlargement.* The Honorable Secretary of the Fund, Walter Besant, has admirably summed up the results of the excavations in and about Jerusalem, in the following statement:

"Our researches—one says it with pardonable pride—have restored the splendors of the Holy City. We have proved how the vast walls of the Temple—the grandest enclosure of the finest building in the whole world—rose from deep valleys on three sides presenting a long façade of wall crowned with pillars and porticoes, and how within them rose the gleaming white marbles of the Inner House with its courts and altars and its crowds of priests who lived by the altar. Our researches have shown the inner valley bridged by noble arches and pierced by subterranean passages. They have shown the city provided with a magnificent water supply, glorious with its palaces, its gardens, its citadel, its castle, its courts and its villas. It is a great town that we have restored; not a commercial town, but a great religious centre to which, at the Passover season, more than 2,000,000 people brought their offerings." [2]

[1] Quarterly Report, Oct., '97, p. 255.   [2] The City and the Land, p. 118.

Jerusalem and Its Environs

History and Associations.—The story of this mountain city, which for nearly forty centuries has occupied a position of commanding importance, has a large place in modern literature and is interlinked with the history of all the leading nations of ancient and modern times. Much that relates to it has been already mentioned in connection with the description of the Land as a whole, and the closer study of the several localities in and about Jerusalem, as they have come in turn before us. It will suffice for our present purpose, therefore, to indicate merely the distinguishing features of this history; and to call attention to some points of special interest which recent discoveries and investigations have enabled us to see more clearly.

There seem to have been *three distinct periods* in the history of Jerusalem before the time of Christ. The first may be designated as the *Early* Canaanite period, the second as the Jebusite and the third as the Jewish. In the first it comes into view as the royal city of Melchizedek and was known as Salem or the city of Salem ("City of Peace"). Its courtly Ruler, who met Abraham in the King's Dale, when "returning from the slaughter of the Kings, and blessed him," was a King-priest and is represented as a worshipper of the Most High God. (Gen. xiv. 18; Heb. vii. 1–3.) In this record, and again in Psalm lxxvi. 2 the city is called *Salem*. In the Egyptian records which enumerate the conquests of Rameses II. in Canaan, Professor Sayce finds the same name—Shalam—along with Gaza and other ancient towns. The strongest confirmation of the Scripture narrative, however, is found in the Tell Amarna tablets which transmit the old name Uru-Salim, in form almost identical with its familiar modern name, and give the long lost clue to its derivation. These records antedate the exodus by a period of about 120 years. It is thus made evident by three distinct lines of proof that the old name of the city was not Jebus, as has been frequently affirmed, but Salem or Uru-Salem. There is also a very remarkable parallelism between the declaration of the Ruler of Uru-Salem and the King who met Abraham. Says Professor Sayce "The description given of Melchizedek in Genesis is precisely that which Ebed-tob gives of himself, with this difference that whereas Ebed-tob was the tributary of the Egyptian monarch, Melchizedek was still an independent sovereign."

When Joshua entered the land, about 160 years after the date of the Tell Amarna inscriptions, Jerusalem was the noted stronghold of the Jebusites, and was then designated as Jebus. The old name, however does not seem to have been forgotten, for in the book of Joshua it is referred to as "Jebus which is Jerusalem." (Josh. xviii. 28.) A similar expression is found in Judges xix. 10. The men of Judah captured the lower city of the Jebusites and set it on fire, but they could not drive out the defenders from the stronghold of the upper city. (Josh. xv. 63; Judg. i. 21.) This portion remained in the hands of the Jebusites until David took it by assault and made it the capital of his kingdom. The city as a whole was frequently called Zion at a later period. From this time onward Jerusalem was the capital of the Hebrew nation and the Divinely-established centre of its religious life and worship.

In the period which elapsed between its capture by the men of Judah and its final overthrow by the Roman general Titus, Jerusalem was besieged *seventeen* times. Twice it was razed to the ground, and on other occasions the walls on the north were broken down. Its after history is a succession of desolations and restorations of a similar character up to the year 1244, when it was besieged for the last time by the Kharczmian hordes who plundered it and slaughtered its Christian inhabitants.

This is reckoned as the twenty-seventh siege of Jerusalem. There is no parallel to this record of vicissitudes in the history of any city of ancient or modern times. It has experienced all the judgments uttered against it by its own prophets to the full: and yet despite all these calamities, its spiritual associations have invested it with a peculiar sanctity and glory, even in its ruined estate, that attaches to no other city on earth. "If it had existed two thousand one hundred and seventy-seven years when overthrown by Titus, as stated by Josephus, its age at present is not less than four thousand years. More than any other city it has influenced the moral and religious character of the human race—*and the end is not yet.*"[1]

[1] Land and Book, p. 567.

CHAPTER XVII

THE MOUNTAINS OF JUDAH

THIS portion of the range increases in elevation, as it extends southward, until it culminates in the heights of Er Ramah, directly north of Hebron, 3,546 feet above the sea. From this point the elevation falls away gradually or by a series of steps, until it merges, at length, into the lower levels of the Negeb, or South Country. The border line between the Negeb and the Hill country cannot be definitely placed, but in general it was the base or southern limit of the Judean range proper, not including its lower slopes and rolling downs. Its western boundary was the irregular depression between the main range and the Shephelah: its eastern was the shore of the Dead Sea.

The characteristic features of this mountain tract correspond with those already given in the description of the Mountains of Benjamin. To this we add a very striking and life-like sketch by Dr. G. A. Smith:

> Where the plateau rolls, the shadeless slopes are for the most part divided between brown scrub and grey rock; the hollows are stony fields traversed by dry torrent-beds of dirty boulders and gashed clay. Where the plateau breaks, low ridge and shallow glen are formed, and the ridge is often crowned by a village, of which the grey stone walls and mud roofs look from the distance like a mere outcrop of the rock; yet round them, or below in the glen, there will be olive-groves, figs, and perhaps a few terraces of vines. Some of these breaks in the table-land are very rich in vegetation, as at Bethany, the Valley of Hinnom, the Gardens of Solomon and other spots round Bethlehem, and in the neighborhood of Hebron, the famous vale of Eshcol or Vine Cluster. And again between Hebron and the wilderness there are nine miles by three of plateau, where the soil is almost free from stones, and the fair, red and green

No 8
Mountains of Judah

THE WILDERNESS OF JUDEA

fields, broken by a few heathy mounds, might be a scene of upland agriculture in our own country.[1]

It is evident from this description that the Hill country of Judah is a pastoral land, and that its principal fruits are the fig, the olive and the vine. "A vineyard on 'a hill of olives,' with the 'fence,' and 'the stones gathered out,' and 'the tower in the midst of it,' is the natural figure which, both in the prophetical and evangelical records, represent the kingdom of Judah."[2] In the springtime the one ever present relief to the otherwise desolate-looking landscape is the abundance of delicate, richly-tinted wild flowers, which grow everywhere alongside the rocks, amid ruined heaps or are closely intertwined with dense tangles of undergrowth and vine.

The Jeshimon or **Wilderness of Judea** is a barren, uninhabited region which well accords with its name. It includes the whole of the eastern slope or declivity of the mountain ridge from the head to the foot of the Dead Sea. "Everywhere it is steep and sometimes precipitous and is often cleft to its base by the deep valleys or gorges that issue from the mountain. All is irregular and wild; presenting scenes of savage grandeur."[3] From several of the deep rugged chasms, which lie below the fields of Bethlehem, it would be easy to select a typical "valley of the shadow of death," such as impressed the mind of David when he kept his father's sheep. (1. Sam. xvii. 15, 28, 34; Ps. xxiii. 4.) Through all the centuries in which it has been known to history, this has been a wild, uncultivated region, save in a few spots; given over to wild beasts, to hermits, and to outlaws in hiding; or to wandering shepherds and herdsmen. Into this "land not inhabited" the scapegoat was "led by the hand of a fit man," after the iniquities of the people had been "confessed and put upon his head." (Lev. xvi. 21, 22.) In this wilderness John the Baptist sought seclusion from the world for a time while preparing

[1] Hist. Geog., p. 306.   [2] Sinai and Palestine, p. 230.
[3] Rob. Phys. Geog., p. 33.

for his mission as the Forerunner of the coming Messiah: and on its outskirts he began to preach, saying: "Prepare ye the way of the Lord, make His paths straight." (Matt. iii. 1–6; Luke iii. 2.) Somewhere, also, amid these dreary wastes the Son of man withstood the subtle temptations of the Evil One; and here, when the long trial had issued in victory, the angels found Him in His exhausted state, and ministered into Him. (Matt. iv. 1–11; Mark i. 12, 13.)

The **principal Wadies** on the east side are the Wady en Nar down which the waters of the Kedron flow to the Dead Sea and Wady el Ghar, or Areijah, running from the wilderness of Tekoa to the oasis at Engedi. . . . There are possibly a score of deep gorges besides, but they are in the flank of the mountain ridge only and do not afford continuous passage-ways to its summit. On the western side are the tributaries of the Wadies Surar, Es Sunt, and Afranj, already mentioned.

Forty-four cities, including those in the wilderness, are enumerated in the description of this mountain heritage of Judah in the book of Joshua (xv. 48–62). Many of these had outlying villages. "It is impossible," says Canon Tristram, "to wander among these hills without perceiving that the expression, 'her towns,' applied in the enumeration to many of the cities, was no mere figure of speech. The groups of ruins, 'the desolate heaps' of Judah, far outnumber any catalogue of her cities that has come down to us."[1]

The following list comprises the most important of the sites which have been identified.

1. **Kirjath Jearim.**—The site formerly proposed for this border city was Kuriet el Anab, better known as the town of Abu Ghosh, on the road to Ramleh from Jerusalem by way of Wady Ali. This place is now regarded as identical with Kirjath of Benjamin: and Kirjath Jearim has been satisfactorily identified, by the Survey party, with a ruin farther to the south called Khurbet 'Erma. It is on a ridge thickly covered with

[1] Holy Land, p. 55.

The Mountains of Judah

undergrowth on the south side of the ravine which leads down to the valley of Sorek. Its location conforms to the description of the border line of Judah; it being on the line indicated by natural features between Rachel's sepulchre and the town of Beth-shemesh. It is twelve miles from Jerusalem and four from Beth-shemesh.

"The name 'Erma corresponds to the latest form Arim, which took the place of the original Ya'rim or Jearim. (Ezra ii. 25.) This ruin is distant only three miles from the great valley toward which it looks down. It lies close to the border of the lower hills and the high Judean mountains, and shows evidence of having been an ancient site. Close to the same vicinity the Survey party fixed the situation of *Deir Aban*, 'The Convent of the Stone,' identified by St. Jerome with the site of *Ebenezer*, 'The Stone of Help,' which Samuel erected to commemorate the great victory over the Philistines. (1 Sam. vii. 12.) Its situation seems to render the traditional view not improbably correct, for the village stands at the mouth of the great valley, down which undoubtedly the Philistine hosts were driven."[1]

The Ark of the Covenant was brought from Beth-shemesh to Kirjath Jearim where it remained until it was removed to Jerusalem by David. (1 Sam. vii. 1, 2; 2 Sam. vi. 1–17; Ps. cxxxii. 6.) "After being twenty years neglected, the ark was sought for in a time of religious revival (chap. vii.), and a place, doubtless prepared for it 'on the hill.' Just such a levelled platform as remains at Shiloh has been found at Khurbet 'Erma."[2]

2. **Emmaus** has been recently identified with a ruined village, in a well-watered valley, called Khamasa, an altered form of the Hebrew word Hammath or Emmaus. It is eight miles southwest of Jerusalem. There is a cluster of springs— five or more in number—in the vicinity. An old Roman road leads past it to the coast-plain, over which in all probability our Lord journeyed with the two perplexed disciples. (Luke xxiv. 13–33.)

[1] Thirty Years' Work, p. 119.   [2] Henderson's Hist. Geog., p. 112.

3. **Bethlehem.**—The little town where Jesus was born is less than six miles from the place where He was crucified. It crowns the summit of a white chalkstone ridge or spur which projects eastward from the main range. On the north, east, and south, where the ridge stands clear of the plateau, the slopes are naturally abrupt, but have been graded somewhat, and made capable of a high state of cultivation by a series of broad terraces. These are covered with gardens, vineyards, and olive-yards. To the traveller approaching from the north the encircling walls, the terraced heights, the steep ascent to the gate, and the long line of snowy-white houses present a picture of rare beauty and attractiveness. Bethlehem, or Beit-Lahm as the natives call it, is a typical upland village of the country, with one long street, from which a few short streets or alleys diverge at irregular intervals. Its identity with the old town at first known as Ephrath and afterward Bethlehem of Judah is unquestioned. By the ridge road to the south, less than a mile from the village, is the place, still marked by a conspicuous tomb where Rachel died and was buried. (Gen. xlviii. 7.) Bethlehem was the home of Boaz; the scene of the beautiful story of Ruth and Naomi; and the birthplace of David. (Ruth, chaps. ii.-iv.) And in this city of David was born, in "the fullness of the time," a "Saviour, which is Christ the Lord." (Luke ii. 4-14.) Below the terraced slope directly east of Bethlehem there is an open valley, known as the fields of Bethlehem, where Boaz and his reapers labored, and where Ruth gleaned after them among the sheaves. Beyond this strip of corn land, in which each inhabitant of the village has his little plot of ground, indicated as of old, by the stone landmark, lies a large tract on the edge of the wilderness. This from time immemorial has been the common pasturage of the shepherds of Bethlehem. Here, and on the slopes of the wilderness below, David kept his father's flock. (1 Sam. xvi. 11, xvii. 28.) While we do not know the exact spot, it is certain that *somewhere* on this eastward stretch of open country

BETHLEHEM OF JUDAH

the shepherds were keeping watch over their flocks by night, when, suddenly, the glory of the Lord shone round about them and the angelic message was proclaimed. Between this ancient pasture ground and the stars a multitude of the heavenly hosts were revealed who thrilled the astonished watchers below, as they chanted together the praiseful refrain,—"Glory to God in the highest, and on earth peace, good will toward men." There are good grounds for the commonly accepted belief that the Church of the Nativity, at the eastern end of the village covers the site of the "inn," or Khan at Bethlehem. It was known as the "habitation," or caravansary, of Chimham, the son of Barzillai, centuries before (Jer. xli. 17), and was probably the portion of the patrimony of David, which was given to him as a reward for the kindness of his father. (2 Sam. xix. 38-40; 1 Kings ii. 7.)

Under the choir at the east end of the church a flight of steps leads down to the "grotto of the Nativity." The tradition which locates the birthplace of Christ in this grotto "seems to be credible," says Major Conder, "because throughout this part of Palestine, there are innumerable instances of stables cut in rock, resembling the Bethlehem grotto. Such stables I have planned and measured at Tekoa, Aziz, and other places south of Bethlehem, and the mangers existing in them leave no doubt as to their use and character."[1] It is an interesting fact, also, that this is the *oldest Christian tradition relating to any sacred site.* While no other can be traced back earlier than the fourth century, this concerning the birthplace of Christ goes back to the second. It rests on the authority of Justin Martyr, who described it as a cave near Bethlehem, and afterward Jerome avouched his belief in the genuineness of the site by making his abode in a grotto close beside it, where he lived and labored on his great life-work for thirty years. Here, at least, we may be sure "we are treading on ground hallowed by the footsteps of nearly fifty generations of believers." This

[1] Tent Work, p. 145.

Basilica is said to be the oldest building of its kind in the world: the date of its erection by order of Constantine being A. D. 327. The roof beams were originally of cedar brought from Lebanon, but these were replaced by beams of *English oak* during the reign of Edward IV. On Christmas Day 1101 Baldwin I. was crowned as King of Jerusalem within the walls of this Basilica.

The present population of Bethlehem is estimated at about 8,000. It is one of the most prosperous Christian villages in Palestine.

4. The fortified convent of **Mar Saba** is directly east of Bethlehem in the deep gorge of the Kedron valley. It belongs to the Greek Church and has stood in this wild, desolate region since the fifth century. This curious structure can hardly be distinguished from the precipitous cliff to which it clings: the walls being built up from ledges or rock platforms high above the level of the valley, and supported by massive buttresses from the lower levels to the summit of the cliff. From one outlook on the wall the elevation is 590 feet above the bed of the ravine.

5. **Jebel Fureidis**, or the Frank Mountain as it is sometimes called, is a little over three miles southeast of Bethlehem. It is conspicuous among the hills of Judah because of its isolation and mound-like appearance. It is probably the beacon-mountain called Beth-haccerem, on which "the sign of fire was set up" in times of invasion. (Jer. vi. 1.) It was fortified by Herod the Great and here he erected his summer palace. It is also the place of his burial.

6. The *traditional Cave of Adullam* in the contracted part of the Wady Khureitun, a short distance from the Frank Mountain, is the largest cavern which has yet been explored in this land of caverns and grottoes. It has many intricate windings and communicating chambers, the farthest of which is about 600 feet from the entrance. While capacious enough to shelter a much larger force than the band of David's men, there

is no good reason for identifying it with the Cave of Adullam. The probable site of this stronghold is, as already indicated, among the low hills, near the town of Adullam at the head of the valley of Elah.

7. **Etham** or Etam, has been identified with a mound of ruins three miles south of Bethlehem, at the head of the valley of Urtas, in the immediate vicinity of the Pools of Solomon. It is mentioned by Josephus as the source of the water supply for Solomon's gardens. It was fortified by Rehoboam. (2 Chron. xi. 6.) The *Pools of Solomon* have been already described in connection with the water supply of Jerusalem. The fountains which supply these pools are probably identical with the waters of Nephtoah. (Josh. xv. 9.)

8. **Tekoa** now Tekua, is five miles south of Bethlehem. It was the home of the prophet Amos (Amos i. 1), and also of the wise woman who came at the instance of Joab to plead the cause of Absalom. (2 Sam. xiv. 2.)

9. Bether (Cant. ii. 17) is probably represented by Bittir, in Wady Bittir, five miles west of Bethlehem; Phagor by Faghur, four miles south of Bethlehem; Soris by Saris, ten miles northwest of Bethlehem and Galem by Beita Jala, two miles west of Bethlehem.[1]

10. **Hebron** or Kirjath-Arba, as it was originally called, is nineteen miles southwest of Jerusalem. It is at the head of a fertile, well-watered valley, which extends northward for about two miles. In the Scriptures it is called the Vale of Hebron. (Gen. xxxvii. 14.) Its wider expanse north of the city is known as the Plain of Mamre, and all the indications point to this as the probable place of Abraham's encampment. It has been associated with the vale of Eshcol because of its large and flourishing vineyards, but later research indicates a location farther to the south. In his description of this rich upland valley Canon Tristram says:

Not an inch of space is lost. Terraces, where the ground is not too rocky, support the soil. Ancient vineyards cling to the lower slopes;

[1] Hend. Geog., p. 86.

olive, mulberry, fig, almond, and pomegranate trees fill every available cranny to the very crest; while the bottom of the valley is carefully tilled for corn, carrots, and cauliflowers, which in summer give place to a second crop of melons and cucumbers. Streamlets of fresh water trickle on each side of the path. . . . About two miles north of Hebron is a very interesting ruin, now called Rameh or Ramel said to be the ancient Mamre, and where Abraham's celebrated terebinth once stood, under which, after the final overthrow of the Jews at Bether, A. D., 135, thousands of captives were sold as slaves. On the hill above, Abraham could easily have seen the ascending smoke of the Cities of the Plain.[1]

Among the vineyards of Hebron, a mile or more to the northwest, is a great oak, called Abraham's Oak. It measures thirty-two feet in circumference at a height of six feet from the ground. Its leafy crown has recently been reduced in size, but the branches formerly extended over an area in one direction of fifty feet, and of ninety-three in another. It is supposed to be at least two or three centuries old.

Hebron is one of the few cities of Palestine which was located in a valley, and yet it occupies the highest ground (3,029 feet) in the whole sweep of mountain territory south of Jebel Jarmuk. It stretches across the valley from side to side, but the greater part of the modern city is on the slope of the eastern hill. The most interesting as well as the most conspicuous object in Hebron is the Great Mosque, which, without doubt, covers the site of the Cave of Machpelah. It is a massive structure 200 feet long, 115 wide and its enclosing walls are about fifty feet high. The masonry of these walls corresponds with that portion of the walls of the Temple area, which the best authorities regard as Solomonic. One stone in this structure measures thirty-eight feet in length and three and a half in height.

There are two ancient reservoirs in the valley outside the gate. The largest of these is 135 feet square and fifty feet deep. At one of these pools, probably the largest, David hanged up the murderers of Ish-bosheth. (2 Sam. iv. 12.)

[1] Holy Land, p. 64.

The Mountains of Judah

"The ancient city may have been a little more to the northwest, but the pools as well as the Haram fix the variation within narrow limits."[1]

Hebron is one of the oldest existing cities in the world. It was built seven years before Zoan or Tanis in Egypt. (Num. xiii. 22.) It was the third-halting place of Abraham on his journey southward, and afterward a favorite camping-place. It was also the abode for a time of Isaac and Jacob: and it was "out of the vale of Hebron" that Joseph was sent to deliver a message to his brethren. (Gen. xxxvii. 14.) Here in turn the Patriarchs with their wives, except Rachel, were borne to their burial in the family sepulchre, the cave of Machpelah, which Abraham bought of Ephron the Hittite. (Gen. xxxvii. 14.) For forty centuries this spot has been revered as the hallowed resting-place of the households of Abraham and Isaac and also of the embalmed body of Jacob which was brought hither from the land of Egypt. There is a tradition that the bones of Joseph which were buried at Shechem, were afterward brought to the cave of Machpelah, but there is no intimation of this in the Scriptures. "The site of this cave," says Major Conder, "may almost rank with that of Jacob's well and the Jerusalem Temple as being preserved by local tradition dating back to the times of the Jewish kingdom at least."[2]

Hebron was a Hittite city in the time of Abraham. At a later period it was a stronghold of the Anakim. After the conquest it was assigned to Caleb for an inheritance. (Josh. xiv. 10-15.) It was one of the six cities of refuge. David reigned in Hebron for seven and a half years, or until he was made the king of all Israel (2 Sam. v. 5): and here Absalom set up the standard of revolt. (2 Sam. xv. 7-12.)

Three towns in a line on the edge of the Wilderness and one in the heart of the Wilderness itself, have been made famous by their connection with the romantic history of David when he was "hunted as a partridge on the mountains" by King

[1] Pict. Pal., Vol. II., p. 183.　　　　[2] Bible Geog., p. 38.

Saul, viz: *Ziph, Carmel, Maon* and *Engedi*. All of these places have been satisfactorily identified.

11. Ziph is marked by a ruined heap which still bears the name Tell Zif. It is four miles southeast of Hebron.

Major Conder thinks that the expression "wood" (Choresh) of Ziph is the name of a place—Choresh of Ziph—and gives in support of this theory the absence of all signs of a forest in this region and the discovery of the ruins of a town called Khoreisa near Ziph. This he supposes to be the place of meeting between David and Jonathan. (1 Sam. xxiii. 16.)

12. **Carmel**, now Kurmul, is four miles south of Ziph. It was formerly a garrison town and extensive ruins of Roman days are intermingled with fragments of buildings erected by the Crusaders and Saracens. This was the place where the churlish Nabal was shearing his sheep when David sent to him for supplies for his men. It was also the native place of Abigail, who became the wife of David after the death of Nabal. (1 Sam. chap. xxv.) In Carmel, and the mountains around, Uzziah had farms and vineyards with husbandmen and vine-dressers to care for them. (2 Chron. xxvi. 10.)

13. **Maon** is represented by Tell Main. It is less than two miles south of Carmel on a higher elevation. It was the birthplace of Nabal, a direct descendant of Caleb, to whom this mountain district had been originally assigned. (Josh. xiv. 12.)

14. **Engedi** (Ain Jidy). This name applies to a celebrated fountain (Fountain of the Kid) and also to a town below it near the shore of the Dead Sea. An older name was Hazezon-tamar. (Gen. xiv. 7; 2 Chron. xx. 2.) The fountain issues from the base of a rock, which is nearly 500 feet above the level of the Dead Sea and 1,500 feet below the top of the cliff that towers above it. It is represented as "bursting forth amidst an oasis of tropical vegetation and then kid-like skipping from rock to rock, until it reaches the plain below."[1] The whole of this district, says Doctor Robinson, was apparently

---
[1] Prof. Palmer in Pict. Pal., Vol. II., p. 193.

The Mountains of Judah

once terraced for tillage and gardens.[1] The beauty of this "sub-tropical oasis" is the more notable because of the wild desolation and savage grandeur all around it. Solomon makes mention of the camphire in the vineyards of Engedi; Josephus of its balsams; and Pliny of its palms, but these have given way to native plants of a different class.[2]

In this vicinity "among the rocks of the wild goats" David had no difficulty in finding hiding-places for himself and his men. From one of these he issued forth and cut off the skirt of Saul's robe while he was sleeping in a cave. (1 Sam. xxiv. 3-8.)

The rugged pass, which leads down to Engedi from the plateau near Tekoa, has been identified with the cliff or ascent of Ziz by which the hosts of Moab and Ammon came, from the Dead Sea, to the plateau near Tekoa. (2 Chron. xx. 16-20.) The valley of Berachah, Jehoshaphat's "valley of blessing," is supposed to be an open vale between Tekoa and the Hebron road, in which is a ruined site which the natives called Khurbet Bereikuh. (2 Chron. xx. 26.) Engedi has given its name to a portion of the wilderness region around and above it. The invading army from the East under Chedorlaomer came around the southern end of the Dead Sea to Engedi where they smote the Amorites. (Gen. xiv. 7.) From thence to the northern end of the Sea the only practicable route would be by the ascent of Ziz. "This pass and cliff," says Professor Palmer, "have been from the days of Chedorlaomer and Abraham, the one ascent by which invaders from the south and east entered the hill country of Judea. As far as Engedi they could march by the shore without any obstacle; north of it the shore line is impracticable, even for footmen, and there are no paths by

[1] Rob. Res., Vol. I., p. 506.
[2] Canon Tristram says that on breaking through the limestone incrustation of the recesses of the rocks there, he found great masses of perfect palm leaves, and even whole trees, petrified where they had stood.—Nat. Hist. of the Bible, p. 380.

which beasts could be led up. Had they taken any of the openings south of Engedi this must have entailed a long march across a rough and almost waterless desert."[1]

Masada, the last refuge of the Jews after the destruction of Jerusalem by Titus, is about half way between Engedi and the south end of the Dead Sea. Tristram describes it as "a bold isolated rock—a very island Gibraltar—crowned by certainly the most remarkable ruin in Palestine."

15. **Hareth**, the city to which David went from Adullam, before he came to Ziph, (1 Sam. xxii. 5), is identical with a ruin called Kharas, five or six miles northwest of Hebron.

16. **Keilah** is west of Kharas about two miles. (1 Sam. xxiii. 1–13.)

17. The following towns have been identified, for the most part, by the names which they still retain. The distances given are from Hebron:

Bethzur, four miles north, with Beit Sur (Josh. xv. 58); *Gedor*, seven miles north, with Jedar (1 Chron. iv. 39); *Beth Tappuach*, a short distance northwest, with Tuffuh (Josh. xv. 53); *Adoraim* in Wady Afranj, six miles west, with Dura (2 Chron. xi. 9); *Arab*, seven miles southwest with Er-Rabiyeh (Josh. xv. 52); *Juttah*, the traditional residence of Zacharias, five miles south, with Yuttah (Josh. xxi. 16; Luke i. 39); *Socoh*, ten miles southwest, with Shuweikeh (Josh. xv. 48); *Jattir*, the lowest town on the border of the Hill Country proper, thirteen miles southwest, with Attir. (Josh. xv. 48.)

Debir has been identified with El Dhoheriyeh, twelve miles southwest of Hebron. This was the famous "book-town" of the Anakim (Kirjath-Sepher) Josh. xv. 15. Conder notes the fact that Debir stood in a "dry land" and locates the "upper and lower springs" given to Caleb's daughter at Dilbeh seven miles north of Debir. These seem to be the springs to which reference is made; for there are no other of like character in this entire region." They number fourteen in all and are divided into three groups. From these fountain heads a brook flows through the small gardens for four or five miles." (Judg. i. 15; Josh. xv. 9.)[2]

[1] Pict. Pal., Vol. II., p. 191.   [2] Faussett's Bib. Cyclopedia, p. 165.

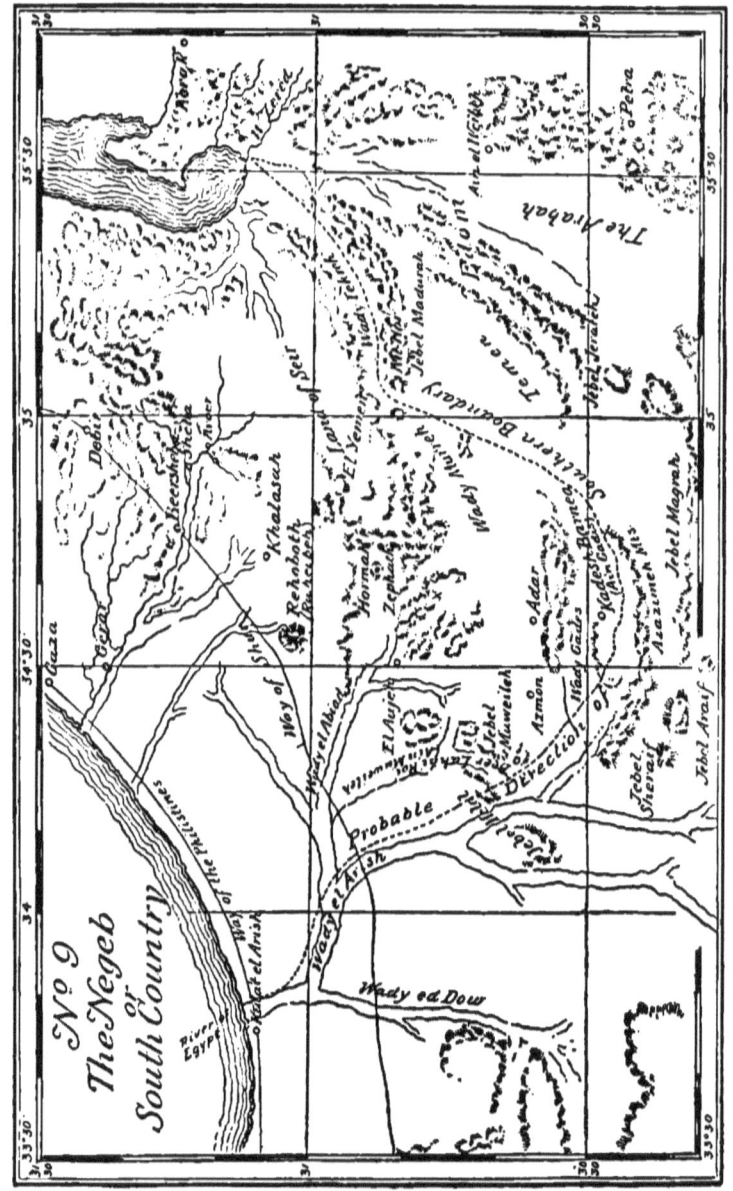

CHAPTER XVIII

THE NEGEB OR SOUTH COUNTRY

THIS district lies between the lower levels of the mountains and the desert of Paran, or Tih. Its southern limit is about sixty-five miles south of Hebron. Several of the towns described in the preceding chapter have sometimes been classed with the Negeb, but the line of division, as therein indicated, may be assumed as approximately correct.

In the Scriptures several subdivisions indicating special localities are mentioned, such as the Negeb of the Cherethites; of Judah; of the Kenites; of Caleb, etc.

The descent to the south throughout this section is by a series of steps or slightly inclined slopes. On the surface, with a few exceptions here and there, it has the appearance of a dry and thirsty land "bare and desolate as the desert itself." It is still a pasture land, however, and in most of the deeper valleys a good supply of water may be obtained by sinking wells. In many localities grass and flowers appear in the early spring, but soon wither away or become as brown and dry as the soil and rock around them. Before the conquest the greater part of the Southland was held by the Amalekites. (Num. xiii. 29.) In the southwestern part David wandered for a time when hiding from the face of Saul. (1 Sam. xxvii. 7, 8.) The northern portion was a favorite pasture range of Abraham and Isaac, but in every place of their sojourn it was necessary to dig wells. Except where groves were planted in the neighborhood of these wells the entire country was probably as treeless then as it is now. Canon Tristram, to whom this region is more familiar than most explorers of modern times, gives the following account of its characteristics and ancient habitations:

The south differs from the hill country to the north of it, not merely so much in being pastoral instead of cultivated, for its whole extent yields proof of very extensive though not universal cultivation in former times; nor in its being less hilly, for it has but few plains of any extent; but in its deep ravines, torn and rent by winter torrents (aphikim), "the streams in the south" of Psalm cxxvi. 4. These torrents, quite dry in summer, cut down steep cliffs into narrow gullies by their violence in winter. On the west side they drain toward the Arish and Philistia, on the east toward the Dead Sea, none running south into Paran or the wilderness.

The wide central expanse is now a sort of upland wilderness, a series of rolling hills, with scanty herbage more abundant on their northern slopes, but without a tree or a bush more than three feet high. Occasionally, by a well, the rich soil, scratched for barley or wheat, shows that with care, as in the days of Isaac, it might still yield a hundredfold. Probably every one of the twenty-nine cities, with their villages, in the south, assigned by Joshua to Judah and Simeon, survive. They cover many acres with ruins which might, with very slight labor, be again rendered habitable: with oil-presses and wine-presses lying at their gates; containing cisterns, reservoirs, and conduits still perfect and beautifully cemented, with a rich soil in the lower grounds; in short everything that might be supposed to attract a settled population. Nearly all of these cities have been identified, with more or less probability.

Yet throughout the whole extent of the south country, thickly strewn as it is with traces of its former occupants and peopled with hardy tribes who pay a nominal allegiance to the Turkish government, *there is not so much as a single inhabited village.*

Not until the traveller has fairly crossed its northern border and entered the hill country, does this strange spectacle of deserted towns and a houseless population cease to arrest his attention. . . . The words of Dr. Robinson, about Zephath or Hormah, may be applied to every city of the Negeb: "Once, as we judged upon the spot, this must have been a city of not less than 10,000 or 20,000 inhabitants. Now it is a perfect field of ruins, a scene of unutterable desolation, across which the passing stranger can with difficulty find his way." A mighty spell seems to rest upon the cities of the south. We turn to the word of prophecy, and we read, The cities of the south (Negeb) shall be shut up, and none shall open them: Judah shall be carried away captive, all of it: it shall be wholly carried away captive. (Jer. xiii. 19.)[1]

[1] Holy Land, pp. 14, 15.

The Negeb or South Country

SITES OF SPECIAL INTEREST

1. **Beersheba.**—This famous camping-ground of the patriarchs is situated on the northern side of the wide watercourse, known as Wady es Seba (Lat. 31° 4'; Long. 34° 47'). It is forty-six miles from Jerusalem and twenty-seven miles southwest of Hebron. The Hebrew name signifies "Well of the Oath," and it is probable that it was first known as a

ABRAHAM'S WELL, BEERSHEBA.

camping-place and afterward as a town or city. (Gen. xxi. 31.) Two of the seven wells, which were originally sunk by the servants of the Patriarchs in this valley, are still used by the shepherds who gather their flocks, as of old around them and drawing from the wells with bucket and rope, pour the water into rude troughs of hewn stone, placed at convenient distances around the mouths of the wells. Dr. Robinson says that the water in both is pure and sweet, and in great abundance; the finest indeed which he 'had found since leaving Sinai.

The larger well measures twelve and one-half feet in diameter, and is over forty-five feet in depth. In the vicinity may be seen traces of the other wells, one of which is twenty-three feet deep and nine feet two inches in diameter. They are all lined above the native rock with finely-squared blocks of limestone, which are deeply furrowed by the ropes of the water-drawers. The ruins of the ancient town are scattered over an area of a half a mile or more in extent.

The southern bank of the valley is banked up with a strong wall of solid masonry, extending for a few hundred yards along the part opposite the wells, which are thus protected from the earth falling in and filling them up. The hillside behind them is covered with ruins, though, from the confused state into which they have fallen, it is impossible now to make out with any certainty the original ground-plan of the town. Higher up in the valley are the foundations of a Greek church.

The country around Beersheba consists of a rolling plain, intersected by the wady beds of Seba and Khulil. In spring, when the rains have fallen, it is often covered for miles around with grass, flowers and herbage; at other times it is nothing but a dry, parched land. Strange and solemn are the thoughts which such a place inspires.

Here are the very wells, in all human probability, which the Father of the Faithful dug. The name he gave it still clings to the spot; the Bedawin, to whom the Scriptures are unknown, still point with pride to the great work which their father Ibrahim achieved, and as they draw water from it for their flocks and herds, the ropes that let the buckets down still glide along the same deep furrows in the masonry which, mayhap, the ropes of the patriarch's servants first began.[1]

Beersheba, more than any other place in the Land, was the centre of Patriarchal life and history. Here Abraham dwelt for about seventy-five years after the destruction of Sodom. Around the place of his tent and altar he planted a grove and called there on the name of the Lord, the everlasting God: thus establishing the first *permanent* sanctuary in the Holy Land. (Gen. xxi. 33.) Most of the 180 years of Isaac's life were spent in or about Beersheba; and Jacob was about seventy years old when he went out from this place to go to his mother's home in Padan Aram. (Gen. xxviii. 10.) To this sanctuary he came once more, when an old man, on his way

[1] Prof. Palmer's Pict. Pal., Vol. II., p. 207.

The Negeb or South Country

to Egypt, and there "God spake to him in the visions of the night" and dispelled all his fears, promising to bring him up again to the land after that his son Joseph "should have put his hands upon his eyes." (Gen. xlvi. 1–5.) Here Abraham received the strange command to sacrifice his son Isaac, and thence he journeyed to the land of Moriah in unquestioning obedience to the Divine direction. (Gen. xxii. 3, 19.) To Beersheba Rebekah came as the bride of Isaac and there her children were born. Here Esau forfeited his birthright and Jacob obtained by fraud the coveted blessing. (Gen. xxv. 34, xxvii. 23–29.)

Beersheba was originally assigned to Judah, but was afterward given to Simeon. (Josh. xix. 2.) Near the close of the period of the Judges it was the recognized limit of Israel's possession in the south, and hence the familiar expression "from Dan to Beersheba." (Judg. xx. 1; 1 Sam. iii. 20.) It does not follow, however, that this applies to the land in all periods of its history, or that it is to be regarded as its Biblical limitation in modern times. Over the district represented by this city Samuel appointed his two sons, Joel and Abiah, to be Judges. (1 Sam. viii. 2.) To this place Elijah fled from the fierce anger of Jezebel on his way to the desert solitudes of the south. (1 Kings xix. 3.) Beersheba was one of the seats of idolatrous worship in the kingdom of Judah and was denounced by the prophets in connection with Bethel, Gilgal and Dan. (Amos v. 5, viii. 14. See also 2 Kings xxiii. 8.)

Arad, the city of "king Arad who dwelt in the south," (Num. xxi. 1), lies eighteen miles east of Beersheba and seventeen south of Hebron. Its modern designation is *Tell Arad*. (Judg. i. 16.) "Tell Arad and its adjacent plains form the Negeb of the Kenites, probably extending to the southwestern end of the Dead Sea."[1]

2. **Sheba** (Josh. xix. 2) is probably identical with Tell es Seba, two and one-half miles east of Beersheba.

[1] Thirty Years' Work, p. 75.

3. **Aroer,** one of the haunts of David, is in the Wady Ararah twelve miles southeast of Beersheba. (1 Sam. xxx. 28.)

4. **Rehoboth.**—The probable site of the well to which Isaac gave this name (Gen. xxvi. 22) is in the Wady Ruhaibeh, twenty miles southwest of Beersheba. . . . "On the left of the wady is a small valley called Shatneh er Ruhaibeh, in which we see the word Sitnah, so that two of the three words (Gen. xxvi. 20–22) are preserved."[1]

5. **Zephath,** afterward called Hormah (Judg. i. 17), has been identified with the ruins of Sebaita, thirty miles south of Beersheba.

"All round the city lie the gardens which once were covered with orchards of apples and pomegranates, and terraces of clustering vines. The city itself is marked by an expanse of ruins 500 yards long by 300 wide; containing three churches, a tower, and two reservoirs of water. No timber is used in the building of the houses, the absence of wood being supplied by thick beams of stone. Nearly every house had its well, about two feet in diameter, and covered with square stone blocks having holes cut in them. The streets can still be traced, and the outer buildings are either walled in or strengthened with additional masonry, presenting a series of angles, like a fortification. Three miles to the northwest stands a ruined fortress on an isolated hill, called El Meshrifeh—the watch-tower. It commands the only pass by which the plain where Sebaita, or Hormah, stands can be approached and answers to the description in the Bible. The distance of Sebaita from Ain Gadis (Kadesh Barnea) is only twenty miles. The names Dheiget el Amerın (ravine of the Amorites), Ras Amir (a chain of low mountains fifteen miles southwest of El Meshrifeh), and Sheikh el Amir (a place in the immediate neighborhood of El Meshrifeh), all point to the identification of this region with the hill country of the Amorites.

"Thus the name, Sebaita, is etymologically identical with the Zephath of the Bible. Zephath means watch-tower, and it exactly corresponds both in situation and in name. Mr. Palmer suggests here that the city, though three miles distant from the fortress which protected it, might yet well be called the city of the Watch-Tower; so that in El

[1] Our Work in Pal., p. 300.

The Negeb or South Country

Meshrifeh we should have the Zephath itself, and in Sebaita the city of the Zephath.

"This is one of the most remarkable examples of the tenacity of the ancient names. It is 3,500 years since Judah, with Simeon his brother, changed the name from Zephath to Hormah. The country has been successively Jewish, Roman, Christian, Mohammedan, Christian again, and Mohammedan again. Yet here is the original name surviving still." [1]

This identification throws light upon the long lost site of Kadesh Barnea. It is specially interesting because of its association with the battle and defeat of the Israelites, "when they presumed to go up unto the hilltop"—of the Amorites—in disobedience to the Divine command (Num. xiv. 40-45,) and also of a later battle in which the Israelites were the victors. (Num. xxi. 1-3.) The *plain Es Seer*, which stretches northward almost to Beersheba from Hormah, has been identified with Seir, or the region of Seir, to which Moses refers in his account of the battle: "And the Amorites, which dwelt in that mountain, came out against you, and chased you, as bees do, and destroyed you in Seir, even unto Hormah." (Deut. i. 44.) The "Mount Halak (Bald Mountain) that goeth up to Seir" (Josh. xii. 7) was without doubt the rugged barrier which stretches along the northern border of the Wady Feqreh (Fekreh). "This wady ascends southwesterly from the Arabah, from a point not far south of the Dead Sea, and separates Palestine proper from the Azazimeh mountain tract, or Jebel Muqrah group. The northern wall of this wady is a bare and bold rampart of rock, forming a natural boundary as it 'goeth up to Seir'; a landmark both impressive and unique, and which corresponds with all the Bible mentions of the Mount Halak." [2] The identity of the plain Es Seer with "the land of Seir in the country or field of Edom," where Esau dwelt when Jacob returned from Padan Aram (Gen. xxxii. 3), has also been satisfactorily established. This tract—which lies close to the

---

[1] Our Work in Pal., pp. 296, 298.
[2] Trumbull's Kadesh Barnea, p. 95.

southern limit of the land of Canaan—is to be distinguished from *Mount Seir* on the eastern side of the Arabah.

6. **Kadesh Barnea.**—This important site has been definitely located, after many years of uncertainty and controversy, at Ain Gadis or, as it is sometimes written, Ain Quadis. The name in either form is the equivalent of the Hebrew word Kadesh. The wady at the head of which Ain Gadis is situated, expands into a fertile plain about ten miles long by six broad.

KADESH BARNEA.—P. E. F.

"At the northeast of the plain is a bold and bare rock, a promontory of the northern mountain rampart, from the foot of which issues a copious spring, which begins by falling in cascades into the bed of a torrent, and ends by losing itself in the sands. The plain of Gadis is strictly within the limits of that southern desert now called et-Tih, and yet it is quite close to the Wady Murreh, which with its sandy expansions toward the east may well have been the Wilderness of Zin."[1]

Ain Gadis is forty-eight miles from Beersheba and nearly the same distance from the base of the Mount Seir range (Lat. 30° 28'; Long. 34° 36').

This long hidden site was discovered by the Rev. J. Rowlands, an English explorer, in 1842, but all traces of it were again lost for nearly forty years. The honor of its re-discovery belongs to Dr. H. Clay Trumbull of Philadelphia, who has

[1] Butler's Bible Work, p. 557.

fully described and identified it in his well-known work entitled Kadesh Barnea.

Near the middle of the Wady Dr. Trumbull found "rich fields of wheat and barley," artificial ridges for retaining and utilizing the rainfall and a large magazine for grain "dug into the ground, with a mound heaped upon it, somewhat after the fashion of the Egyptian granaries shown in the tomb picture-galleries of the Pharoahs." In the quotation which follows, Dr. Trumbull gives his first impression of Ain Quadis and its surroundings :

> It was a marvellous sight! Out from the barren and desolate stretch of the burning desert-waste, we had come with magical suddenness into an oasis of verdure and beauty, unlooked for and hardly conceivable in such a region. A carpet of grass covered the ground. Fig trees laden with fruit nearly ripe enough for eating, were along the shelter of the southern hillside. Shrubs and flowers showed themselves in variety and profusion. Running water gurgled under the waving grass. We had seen nothing like it since leaving Wady Fayran ; nor was it equalled in loveliness of scene by any single bit of landscape, of like extent, even there.
>
> Standing out from the earth-covered limestone hills at the northeastern sweep of this picturesque recess, was to be seen the "large single mass, or a small hill of solid rock," which Rowlands looked at as the cliff (Sel'a) smitten by Moses, to cause it to "give forth his water," when its flowing stream had been exhausted. From underneath this rugged spur of the northeasterly mountain range issued the now abundant stream.
>
> A circular well, stoned-up from the bottom with time-worn limestone blocks, was the first receptacle for the water. A marble watering trough was near this well. Down the slope, a little distance was a second, much like the first, but of greater diameter; and here again was a marble trough. . . . A basin or pool of water larger than either of the wells, but not stoned up like them, was seemingly the principal watering place. . . . Around the margin of this pool, as also around the stoned-wells, camel and goat dung—as if of flocks and herds for centuries—was trodden down and commingled with the limestone dust so as to form a solid plaster-bed. Another and yet larger pool, lower down the slope, was supplied with water by a stream which rippled and cascaded along its narrow bed from the upper pool ; and yet beyond this, westward, the water gurgled away under the grass, as we had met it when we came in,

and finally lost itself in the parching wady from which this oasis opened. The water itself was remarkably pure and sweet; unequalled by any we had found after leaving the Nile. There was a New England look to this oasis, especially in the flowers and grass and weeds; quite unlike anything we had seen in the peninsula of Sinai. Bees were humming there, and birds were flitting from tree to tree. . . . It was, in fact, hard to realize that we were in the desert, or even near it.[1]

Elsewhere Dr. Trumbull says.

All the conditions of the Bible-text are met in Quadis (Gadis), as in no other suggested site. A Wady Quadis, a Jebel Quadis, and an Ain Quadis are there. Wady Quadis is an extensive hill-encircled region of sufficient extent to encamp and guard a host like Israel's. Large portions of it are arable. Extensive primitive ruins are about it. Springs of rare abundance and sweetness flow from under a high cliff. By name and by tradition it is the site of Kadesh. Just north of it is a lofty mountain, over which is a camel-pass toward Hebron. It lies just off the only feasible route for an invading army from the direction of Sinai, or from east of Akabah, and is well adapted for a protected strategic point of rendezvous prior to an immediate move northward. It is at that central position of the southern boundary line of Canaan which is given to Kadesh in its later mentions in the Bible-text. Its relations to the probable limits of Edom and to all the well-identified sites of Southern Canaan, and its distance from Mount Sinai, conform to the Bible record.[2]

The Biblical associations, of which hints are given in the foregoing statements, are numerous and important. In the account of Chedorlaomer's aggressive campaign Kadesh is mentioned for the first time. (Gen. xiv. 7.) It comes into view also in connection with the story of Abraham's sojourn in the South country. (Gen. xx. 1.)

A succession of important historic events took place during the sojourn of Israel at Kadesh Barnea. Here the order was issued to go up and possess the land, and spies were sent out to search it from the wilderness of Zin unto Rehob, as men come to Hamah. (Deut. i. 19, 20; Num. xiii. 17–21.) Here afterward the report was made; the rebellion took place follow-

[1] Kadesh Barnea, pp. 271–274.
[2] Schaff-Herzog Encyclopedia, p. 1222.

ing that report; and the sentence of the rejection of all the men of that generation, except Joshua and Caleb, was pronounced. (Num. xiii. 26-29, xiv. 1-10.) It was the place where Miriam died and was buried (Num. xx. 1); and the place where the rock was smitten from which the water came out abundantly. (Num. xx. 2, 13.) From several hints in the Scripture narrative the inference has been drawn that Kadesh Barnea was the rallying place of the tribes of Israel during all the years of the wandering in the wilderness.

Here, at least, they abode many days after their defeat at Hormah (Deut i. 46), and here also we find the entire camp of Israel again after the rebellion of Korah. From this encampment, after vainly endeavoring to secure a passage-way through the border of Edom they started, at length, on their circuitous journey around the confines of Edom and Moab toward the Jordan. (Num. xxi. 4; Deut. ii. 1-18.) In Numbers xx. 16, Kadesh is mentioned as a city. After the conquest it is frequently mentioned as the lowest city on the southern border line of the heritage of Israel. (Num. xxxiv. 4; Josh. xv. 3; Ezek. xlvii. 19, xlviii. 28, etc.) "Its location is admitted to be a key both to the wanderings of the Israelites and the bounding of their domain."

7. **Mount Hor.**—A short distance westward of Hormah (Zephath), and some twenty-five miles northeast of Kadesh Barnea, an isolated mountain rises from a barren plain over which it towers as a conspicuous landmark from all sides, but especially from the south. Its modern name is *Jebel Madurah*. Every indication in the Scripture narrative points to this mountain as the true site of Mount Hor. Dr. Trumbull has summed up the arguments which support this location, and, at the same time, has shown the impossibility of reconciling the traditional site, within the limits of Mount Seir, with the requirements of the Bible text. (See Kadesh Barnea, pp. 127-135.)

"In its location, Jebel Madurah stands at a triangular site, where the boundaries of Edom, of Canaan, and of the Wilderness of Zin, or in a larger sense of the Wilderness of Paran, approach each other so as to pass along this mountain without touching it. It is at the extremest northwestern boundary of the land of Edom, yet it is not within that boundary line. It is on the very verge of the Land of Promise, yet it is not within the outer limits of that land. The border wadies—Feqreh, Madurah, Murreh, and Hanjoorat—which separated Canaan from Edom, and both Canaan and Edom from the unclaimed wilderness, so run as to form the surrounding plain, above which is upreared this remarkable mountain-tower, this lofty, solitary mountain-citadel. . . . Jebel Madurah is in the line from Kadesh of the route which the Israelites seem to have had in mind, when they proposed to pass along Edom's royal road from the east of the Arabah, and eastward of the Dead Sea; possibly through the broad Wady el Ghuwayr which offers an easy passage. The Israelites would not unnaturally move thitherward as they planned for that route, and such a move on their part would not unnaturally be looked upon by the kings of Edom and Arad as a threatening move, to be met and resisted vigorously." (Num. xx. 20, 21, xxi. 1-3.) [1]

One of the records which relates to the death of Aaron (Deut. x. 6), conveys the impression that the Israelites were encamped in the Wady Madurah, or Moserah, when Moses and Aaron and Eleazar "went up into Mount Hor in the sight of all the congregation."

On this lone summit the garments of Aaron were transferred to his son Eleazar; "and Aaron died there in the top of the Mount." (Num. xx. 22-28.)

8. **Eshcol.**—The location of the valley of Eshcol, whence the spies brought the cluster of grapes, which was "borne upon a staff between two" (Num. xiii. 23, 24), is not definitely known. It may have been in the Negeb, a long way south of Hebron, its supposed site.

In this southland region, now given over to barrenness, except in favored spots, Professor Palmer found miles of country —hillsides and valleys—covered with small stone heaps, swept in regular swathes, and called by the Arabs to this day "*teleilat el anab,*" or grape mounds.

9. **Hagar's Well**—Beer-lahai-roi—has been identified with a

[1] Kadesh Barnea, p. 133.

The Negeb or South Country

spring in the Wady Muweileh, about fifteen miles northwest of Kadesh. (Gen. xxi. 19.)

It follows from the hints and partial descriptions, already given, that the southern boundary of the Land of Israel, which conformed to the physical divisions of the country, was irregular, or wedge-shaped in outline, Kadesh Barnea being its lowest point.

Roughly speaking the line ran southward from the end of the Dead Sea about twelve miles to the mouth of the Wady Feqreh. Thence by way of this Wady to the Akrabbim or steep pass, represented by Es Suffah or El Yemen near Mount Hor. Thence hinging on this mountain the line turned southward so as to include Kadesh Barnea, the extent of its southern limit. From Kadesh the general direction of the border line was northwest along the Wady el Arish (River of Egypt) to its mouth. This Wady has several branches, but the principal one runs northwest about 150 miles before it enters the Mediterranean. In the rainy season it is often a rushing torrent, but at other times it is a dry, stony watercourse.

A short distance north of the mouth of Wady el Arish are two pillars erected by Mehemet Ali to mark the boundary line between Africa and Asia.

The Third Longitudinal Section

CHAPTER XIX

THE VALLEY OF LEBANON

THE Buka'a, or valley of Lebanon (Josh. xi. 17), lies between the great parallel ranges north of the head-waters of the Jordan. This valley or plain—the Cœle-Syria (Hollow Syria) of the classic writers—is about seventy-five miles in length. In breadth it varies from four to nine miles. The lower portion of the Lebanon valley is separated from the upper portion of the Jordan valley by a low or secondary ridge which follows the general direction of the great ranges for several miles. This ridge, which at first is hardly distinguishable from the mass of the eastern mountains, becomes more sharply defined as it extends southward. At the base of Mount Hermon it trends toward the west, gradually contracting the valley, until it ends at the point where the Litany is abruptly deflected westward through a deep gorge in the Lebanon mountains.

The highest ground in the Lebanon basin is in the immediate vicinity of Baalbek, some fifty miles from its southern limit. From this watershed the streams, which flow abundantly from springs in the plain or on the mountain-sides, part to north and south to join, by longer or shorter routes, the waters of the Orontes or Litany.

Dr. Robinson describes this great plain as "superbly rich and beautiful; a gem lying deep in its setting of mountains, and fringed with the brilliant snows of Lebanon." [1]

"Looking down upon the Buka'a," says Dr. Thomson

[1] Rob. Res. Vol., III. p. 504.

The Valley of Lebanon

"From any one of the hundred standpoints on Lebanon and Hermon, the beholder is charmed with the checkered and endlessly-varied expanse of blending wheatfields, green or golden, recently ploughed land, black or reddish-brown, and broad belts of dun-covered fallow ground, reaching to the foot-hills, and losing themselves amongst the vineyards that cling to the mountain-sides."[1]

The modern villages of the plain are numerous along the lines of its principal roadways, but there are very few of its ancient sites which have been recovered. Among those which have been identified satisfactorily, the most noteworthy are *Baalbek* and *Ribleh*.

Baalbek, or Heliopolis as it was called by the Greeks, lies on the eastern side of the valley. A beautiful fountain near by, whose bright sparkling waters overflow the basin provided for them, and irrigate a portion of the adjacent plain, was doubtless one of the determining features in the selection of the site.

The majestic structures and vast heaps of massive ruins which cover the acropolis of Baalbek have been for centuries the wonder of the world. The bulk of these remains belongs to two great temples which Dr. Robinson describes as follows:

> The larger, with its magnificent peristyle and vast courts and portico, *extended a thousand feet in length* from east to west. It stands upon an artificial vaulted platform, elevated from twenty to thirty feet above the adjacent country. Besides the dilapidated ruins of the courts and portico, there now remains only the six southwestern columns of the lofty peristyle; and these are still the crowning glory of the place.[2]
>
> The lesser temple stands likewise upon its own similar, though less elevated platform. It is on the south of the greater temple; is parallel with it; and its front is a few feet east of the eastern line of the great

---

[1] The Land and the Book, Vol. III., p. 338.

[2] "These columns are seven and a half feet thick and sixty-two feet high. The top of the entablature which they supported must have been eighty feet above the ground and 130 feet above the level of the plain."
—(Land and Book, p. 325.)

peristyle. It had no court; and its length is less than one-fourth part of that of the greater temple with its courts.

It was finished, and that most elaborately, and the larger portion of it still remains; while not improbably the larger temple was never completed. . . .

Not less wonderful than the other parts of the great temple are the *immense external Substructions*, by which the walls supporting the peristyle are enclosed and covered; if indeed that term can be properly applied to huge masses of masonry, on which nothing rests. . . . The most imposing of these substructions is the western wall, as viewed from the outside. It rises to the level of the bottom of the columns, some fifty feet above the ground; and in it is seen the layer of *three immense stones* celebrated by all travellers. Of these stones, the length of one is sixty-four feet; of another sixty-three feet eight inches; of the third sixty-three feet; in all 198 feet eight inches. Their height is about thirteen feet; and the thickness apparently the same, perhaps greater. They are laid about twenty-three feet above the ground; and below them are seven others of like thickness, and extending somewhat beyond the upper ones at each end.[1]

These temples have been the wonder of past generations; and will continue to be the wonder of future generations, until barbarism and earthquakes shall have done their last work. In vastness of plan, combined with elaborateness and delicacy of execution, they seem to surpass all others in western Asia, in Africa, and in Europe. They are like those of Athens in lightness, but surpass them far in vastness; they are vast and massive like those of Thebes, but far excel them in airiness and grace.[2]

It is probable that these great buildings are constructions or reconstructions of the Roman period, but the immense platform upon which they stand has doubtless been from time immemorial the seat of Baal or Sun worship.

There is no positive evidence upon which to base its connection with Baal-Gad, but the brief description of the location of this ancient gathering place of the worshippers of Baal—" in the

---

[1] A great stone in the quarry nearly a mile distant, measures sixty-eight feet four inches in length, seventeen feet in width and fourteen feet seven inches in height. Its estimated weight is 1,100 tons.

[2] Rob. Res., Vol. III., p. 507.

The Valley of Lebanon

valley of Lebanon under Mount Hermon" (Josh. xi. 17), exactly accords with the location of Baalbek.

The identification of the "plain of Aven," mentioned by the prophet Amos (i. 5), with the plain of Baalbek is generally admitted. "Aven is given in the Septuagint as On, the domestic name of the Egyptian Heliopolis. The allusion is clearly to the Buka'a of Baalbek, and the Eden mentioned in the same verse is supposed to be the Paradisus of Ptolemy, about forty miles north of Baalbek." [1]

Riblah.—The identity of this ancient border town of the land of Israel (Num. xxxiv. 11) with the modern village of Ribleh is unquestioned. It lies on the right bank of the Orontes at the northern end of the Lebanon valley. The surrounding country is open, easily accessible from every side, and is noted for its fertility.

Riblah was within the limits of the land, or kingdom, of Hamath (2 Kings xxiii. 33); and was one of the famous camping grounds of the armies of Egypt and Assyria. The old caravan route from the coast which leads through the "Entrance of Hamath" to Sudad, Palmyra, and the east, intersects the main thoroughfare down the valley of the Orontes at Riblah, making it a centre of four great routes—eastward, westward, northward, and southward. Here, while resting for a time with his army, Pharaoh-Necho deposed Jehoahaz of Judah and put him "in bands." (2 Kings xxiii. 33.) At a later period Zedekiah was brought up to Riblah, "where Nebuchadnezzar gave judgment upon him." "Then the king of Babylon slew the sons of Zedekiah in Riblah before his eyes: also the king of Babylon slew all the nobles of Judah. Moreover he put out Zedekiah's eyes, and bound him with chains to carry him to Babylon." (Jer. xxxix. 5–7.)

[1] Dr. Merrill—Pict. Pal., p. 468.

CHAPTER XX

THE VALLEY OF THE JORDAN

THE connecting link between the basins of the Lebanon and the Jordan is a long, narrow valley, known as **Wady et Teim**. This valley is bordered on the east by the foot-hills of the Anti-Lebanon; on the west by the secondary ridge, already described, which runs parallel to the Anti-Lebanon range. A low watershed, not far from the upper end of the Wady, diverts a few streamlets northward into the Buka'a, but in general the drainage from the slopes on either side flows southward into the Jordan valley. The largest and longest tributary, coming from the northern slope of Hermon, is reinforced by a swiftly-flowing stream from a perennial fountain near Hasbeiya, and is known as the Hasbany branch of the Jordan.

West of the lower stretch of Wady et Teim, and separated from it by a wooded ridge, is a beautiful upland plain called Merj Ayun (the "Meadow of Springs"). Robinson describes this plain as oval in outline, level as a floor, and about three miles in length by two in breadth. It is nearly 1,800 feet above sea level and drains toward the south. The westmost tributary of the Jordan—the Derdarah branch—rises in this plain. It is frequently dry in summer and hence is not reckoned with the main sources of the river.

Tell Dibbin, near the upper end of Merj Ayun, is the generally accepted site of the ancient city of Ijon. The Hebrew name Iyon is still preserved in the Arabic name (Ayun) of the plain. Ijon was one of the cities of Naphtali. It was taken and destroyed by Benhadad of Syria (1 Kings xv. 20; 2 Chron. xvi. 4); and, at a later period, by Tiglath-Pileser. (2 Kings xv. 29.) The town of Abel-beth-Maachah, or Abel-Maim (2 Chron. xvi. 4), which on each of the above-men-

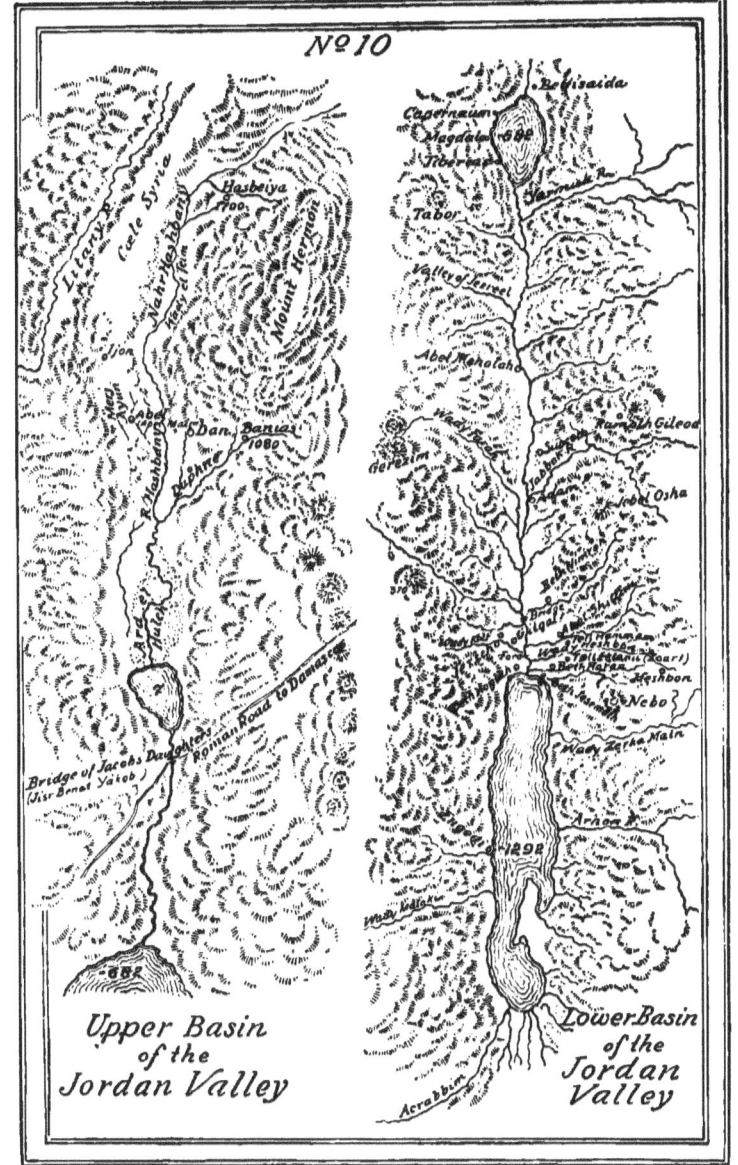

The Valley of the Jordan

tioned invasions was involved in a like destruction, has been identified with the little town of Abil, seven miles south of Tell Dibbin. "The Derdarah, from Merj Ayun, glides swiftly along the western declivity of the Tell, and from the neighboring mountains gushes out the powerful stream of er Ruahineh. Such rivulets would convert any part of this country, under skillful cultivation, into a paradise of fruits and flowers, and entitle it to be called 'Abel on the waters,' 'a mother in Israel.'"[1]

When besieged by Joab's army this city was saved from destruction by the timely interference of a wise woman, who, calling out to the chief captain from the wall, obtained a respite until she could persuade her townsmen to deliver up the head of the traitor Sheba, whose cause they had rashly espoused. (2 Sam. xx. 14-22.)

The Jordan valley proper begins at the base of Mount Hermon and extends to the southern limit of the Dead Sea basin. This is marked by a line of white cliffs which cross the Valley (Arabah) obliquely eight miles south of the lower end of the Dead Sea. The general direction of the valley is almost due south. Its total length is about 158 miles.

There are *three distinct levels or basins* in the Jordan valley, each of which contains a lake famous in history, and unique in its setting. The river passes through two of these lakes in its course and discharges the full volume of its accumulated waters into the third. The first, Lake Huleh,—known as the waters of Merom in the days of Joshua—touches the level of the Mediterranean Sea; the second—the Lake of Galilee—lies 682 feet below; the third—the Dead Sea—lies 1,300 feet below sea level.

The connection between the upper lakes is a contracted valley down which the river flows in a series of rapids. The connection between the lake of Galilee and the Dead Sea is a broad valley, shut in by high hills, called El Ghor.

[1] The Land and the Book, Vol. p. 545.

These natural features suggest five subdivisions of the valley, viz:

The Upper Basin of the Jordan, the Descent between the Upper Lakes, the Galilee Basin, the Ghor, and the Dead Sea Basin.

1. **The Upper Basin of the Jordan.**—This, as Dr. Robinson suggests, may properly be called the Basin or Plain of the *Huleh*. It connects with the narrower plain at the mouth of the Wady et Teim on a line with the southern base of Mount Hermon, and extends to the lower extremity of the Huleh Lake. The Huleh basin is about five miles in breadth and eighteen miles in length. Its northern portion is a green, meadow-like tract, varied with occasional thickets of undergrowth and patches of reedy marsh-lands. Here the numerous rivulets from the mountains unite with streams of greater volume, bubbling up from the ground or bursting forth from the crevices of the rocks, to form the Jordan—a river almost full grown from the beginning of its course. The real source of all these tributaries, and hence of the river itself, is the vast reservoir of snow and ice on the summit of Mount Hermon. The volume of the flood which the Jordan carries down to the basin of the Dead Sea is regulated by the periodic melting of this never-failing supply of frozen moisture.

Three large streams sometimes called rivers,—known as the Leddan, the Banias, and the Hasbany—find their way to the plain from the base of Hermon, and unite to form the Upper Jordan. The copious fountains from which they issue are the main sources of the Jordan.

(1.) **The Fountain of the Hasbany** flows out from the base of a cliff near the village of Hasbeiya on the western side of Mount Hermon. This is the *most remote* source of the Jordan. It is 1,700 feet above the sea level and about 115 miles from the northern end of the Dead Sea. The descent of the river, in other words, from its farthest perennial source to its mouth is 3,000 feet or nearly twenty-eight feet to the mile of its direct distance. The Hasbany begins its course, as al-

The Valley of the Jordan

ready noted, in the watershed of the Wady et Teim, far beyond this noted fountain, but this northern portion is not a perennial stream.

(2.) **The Fountain of the Leddan** rises under the western shoulder of Tell el Kady, the generally accepted site of the ancient city of Dan. Here a deep, clear pool is formed which sends a broad stream down the plain. This is the largest of all the fountains of the land of Israel, and is said to be the largest single fountain in the world. Its location at the head of the valley, and its immense volume of water entitle it to be named as the *chief source of the Jordan*. Its elevation is a little over 500 feet.

The Tell rises about forty feet above the plain. It is oblong in outline and somewhat depressed in the centre. The ruins of the ancient city cover a considerable extent of ground and the region around, when under careful cultivation, must have been singularly beautiful and productive: "a place where there was no want of anything that is in the earth." (Judg. xviii. 10.) There is a famous oak on a gently inclined slope of this mound, not far from the fountain, which is almost as large and stately in appearance as the oak at Mamre. Other trees of vigorous growth occupy the higher ground in the immediate vicinity: while along the beds of the rushing streams below, dense thickets, and jungles of rank vegetation almost hide the water from view.

The story of the conquest of this old Phœnician city—originally called Laish—by the Danites, is recorded in Judges xviii. Here after the conquest the children of Dan departed from the faith of their fathers by setting up a graven image before which worship was offered "all the time that the house of God was in Shiloh." (Judg. xviii. 29–31.)

At a later period the worship of the golden calf was instituted at Dan, and until the ten tribes were carried away it continued to be a noted shrine of idolatrous worship. (1 Kings xii. 28, 29; Amos. viii. 14.)

At this place, long before any of these events occurred, Abraham, at the head of his band of armed retainers, overtook the marauding hosts of Chedorlaomer, and smote them by night, pursuing them unto Hobah, which is on the left hand of Damascus. (Gen. xiv. 14, 15.)

(3.) **The Fountain of Banias** springs directly from the southern base of Mount Hermon. It is four miles northeast of Tell el Kady and the way to it leads through a long stretch of green glades and meadow-land, dotted here and there with clumps of oaks and olives. The name Banias, which is applied to the site of the ruined city as well as to the fountain, is the Arabic equivalent of the old Greek name Paneas—the abode or shrine of the god Pan. The prominent features of the place are a broad terrace clothed with luxuriant vegetation "all alive with streams of water and cascades"; a precipitous cliff at the mountain's foot something more than 100 feet high; the remains of ruined temples; and, at the bottom of the cliff, a cave whose mouth is partly closed with loose stones which have fallen from the roof, or from the summit of the cliff. Out of this mass of boulders and débris, and apparently from crevices between the strata of the rock alongside, a foam-crested stream bursts forth, "along a line of thirty feet, a full-born river." A short distance from its source this flood of seething waters is collected together in a large pool and thence becomes a swift torrent, roaring and dashing over the rocks, and gliding amid dense thickets of oleander, hawthorn and cane, until it is lost to view in the depths of a .dark ravine. About four miles south of Tell el Kady the Banias joins the Leddan. A mile or more below, the Hasbany flows into the bed of this united stream and here the Jordan proper begins its course. The elevation of the spring-head at Banias is 1,080 feet, or nearly 600 feet higher than the source of the Leddan. The Leddan is more than twice the size of the Banias : and the Banias is more than twice the size of the Hasbany. The stream from the fountain at Banias is the clearest of all and its site is the most picturesque. There is no place in Palestine, and there are but few places perhaps in the world, where so many elements of grandeur and beauty are combined. Dean Stanley describes it as "almost a Syrian Tivoli"; Dr. Robinson, as "a noble fountain unique" in its setting; Dr. Smith as a "very sanctuary of waters"; Dr. Thomson, as "one of Nature's grandest temples, whose oak glades and joyous brooks, happy birds and frisking flocks, all bear part in her services"; and Dr. Schaff, as "the most charming landscape in all Palestine, adorned with tropical vegetation of flowers and trees, and musical with the murmur of rivulets and cascades."

The site of the ancient city which grew up around this "sanctuary of waters" can still be traced by its ruins, most of which belong to the Roman period.

Herod the Great built a temple of white marble near the fountain in honor of Augustus. At a later period the city was rebuilt and "adorned with temples, villas and palaces" by Philip the Tetrarch, who named it Cæsarea Philippi. The Castle of Shubeiah which overlooks the town from a high hill to the east, is by far the most extensive ruin in this region, and there is good reason to believe that it occupies the site of one of the most ancient fortresses in the land. It is the "Heidelberg of Syria," and the views which it commands over the gorges of the Hermons and the upper valley of the Jordan are unsurpassed.

Near the close of His public ministry our Lord entered the coasts of Cæsarea Philippi, and, in some retired nook in this restful region, dwelt for several days with His disciples. Here, apart from the crowds which thronged Him in Galilee, He unfolded to them the nature of His redemptive work and spake of "the decease which He should accomplish at Jerusalem." This was the place of Peter's confession; of the prophetic announcement concerning the Church; and of the healing of the demoniac child. Every circumstance and detail of the story of the Evangelists points to the "high mountain" which towers above this plain as the place where Jesus took His disciples apart, and was transfigured before them. (Matt. xvi. 13–28, xvii. 1–21 ; Mark. ix. 2 ; Luke ix. 28 ; 2 Peter i. 17.)

Lake Huleh occupies the lower portion of the Huleh basin. The Jordan enters this broader expanse of its channel twelve miles below the site of Dan. The lake is triangular in outline and is about four and a half miles in length by three in breadth. The base of the triangle is the northern end of the lake, the exit of the river being at its apex. Between the junction of the three tributaries of the Jordan and the head of the lake there is a great marsh larger than the body of the lake itself; this march is so closely shut in by dense masses of tall canes and papyrus reeds that it is impossible, as the Arabs declare, for even a wild boar to make its way to the water. John Macgregor, of Rob Roy fame, is the only man, in all probability, who has ever explored the interior of this great swamp: and in order to do this, he was obliged to enter the channel from the open country above. The canoe in which he made this memorable journey, was launched at first on the Hasbany at its source. Floating down this stream until he reached the plain, Mr. Macgregor transferred his little boat to the pool at Dan, and thence, by skillful paddling and shooting of rapids with occasional lifts over the shallows, he traversed the entire length of the river to its terminus in the Dead Sea.

West of the lake is a rich farming region which extends to the foot of the mountains. On this plain by the Waters of Merom the decisive battle was fought between Joshua and the confederate kings of the north. (Josh. xi. 5–8.) The surface of Lake Huleh is only seven feet above the level of the Mediterranean. In round numbers the descent from the upper source of the Jordan to this lake a distance of twenty-four miles is 1,700 feet ; from the source at Banias—one half the distance—it is 1,100 feet. The semi-tropical climate and luxuriant vegetation of this upper stretch of the Jordan valley present a strong contrast to the almost perpetual line of snow, within easy range of vision, on the summit of Mount Hermon.

The following description of this region, viewed as a whole, is given by Dr. Thomson :

> The Huleh—lake, and marsh, and plain, and fruitful field—is unrivalled in beauty in this land, no matter when or from what point beheld —from the heights of Hermon, the hills of Naphtali, the plain of Ijon, or the groves of Banias, in midwinter or midsummer, in the evening or in the morning. It lies like a vast carpet, with patterns of every shade, and shape and size, and laced all over with countless silver threads: those laughing brooks of the Huleh, now revealed, now concealed; here weaving silver tissue into cunning complications with graceful curves, and there expanding into broad and gleaming patterns, like full-faced mirrors. The plain is clothed with flocks, and the solemn stork is there, and herds of black buffalo bathe in the pools. The lake is alive with fowls, the trees with birds, and the air with bees. At all times fair, but fairest of all in early spring and at eventide when the golden sunlight pervading the ethereal amber fades into the fathomless blue of heaven.[1]

The darker side to this picture, in which "every prospect pleases," may be seen in the wretched and homeless condition of the nominal possessors of this bountiful region. Owing partly to the insecurity of life and property, and partly to the deadly malarial exhalations from earth and water, the plain does not have a single permanent habitation throughout its extent, except in the border village of Banias.

There are said to be forty Arab villages in this lowland district, but their inhabitants are tenants at will and the houses are flimsy constructions of papyrus reeds and mud.

2. **The Descent between the Lakes.**—The distance in a direct line between the lake of Huleh and the lake of Galilee is eleven miles. About two miles below Lake Huleh the river is crossed by an ancient bridge, called by the Arabs, Jisr Benat Yacub (the Bridge of Jacob's Daughters). This bridge is a substantial structure with three pointed arches. A ruined Khan at its eastern end, and the remains of an old road beyond it,

[1] The Land and the Book, p. 478.

paved with basaltic blocks, indicate that this has been the crossing place of one of the main routes from Galilee to the East for centuries. The bridge itself may not be older than the fifteenth century, but it unquestionably marks the site of one of the oldest and most notable fords of the Jordan. Here, in all probability Saul of Tarsus, breathing out threatening and slaughter against the disciples of the Lord, crossed the Jordan as he journeyed to Damascus.

It is an interesting fact that the river at this point is on a level with the Mediterranean Sea. Above it lies the upper basin of the Jordan whose elevation ranges from sea level to 1,100 feet; below it the Great Rift of the Lower Jordan begins its descent to the extraordinary depth of 1,300 feet. Here the hills of Naphtali close in toward the east obstructing the continuity of the channel and contracting the river-bed to a narrow depression or gorge, on its eastward side. Down this gorge the Jordan plunges in a succession of rapids, or cascades for a distance of six or seven miles to the level of the lower basin, some two miles north of the Sea of Galilee. The descent for this distance is more than ninety feet to the mile. On a ledge, at one point on this line of descent, we caught a glimpse of the Lake of Galilee and the deep trench below it, before the waters of Merom and the valley of the Upper Jordan had passed out of view.

The banks of the river in this part of its course are "fringed with an extraordinary growth of oleander, which at times completely conceals it from view; and the scenery is among the wildest as well as the most beautiful in the Holy Land."

3. **The Galilean Basin.**—The length of this trough-like depression does not exceed fifteen miles, and its greatest breadth is less than nine miles. Its maximum depth below sea-level is 838 feet. The lake, which lies deep down in this secluded basin (682 feet), is twelve and a half miles long, and not over seven miles at its widest point. It is lyre-shaped in outline "with the bulge to the northwest,"

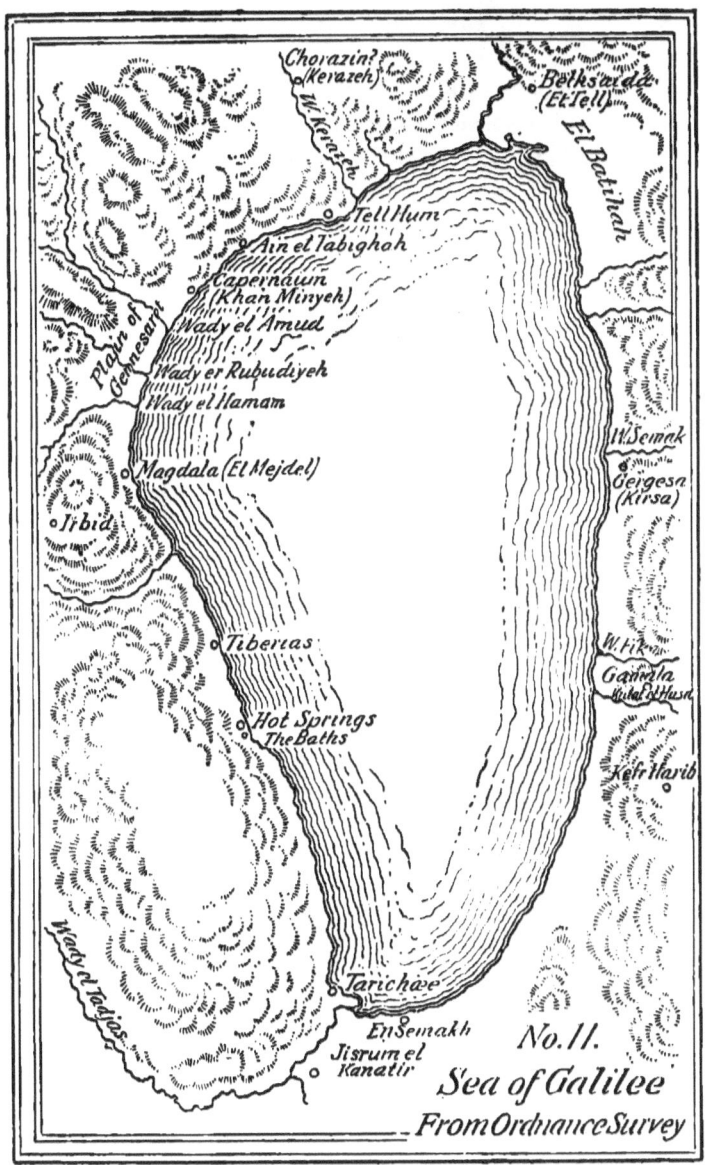

The mountains on the eastern and western sides have different characteristics which are apparent at a glance. On the east they rise to the height of nearly 2,000 feet, and the general impression is that of a bare rugged wall of rock, cleft here and there by deeply-gashed torrent beds. In these there are occasional patches of green, but the prevailing colors are the red and brown of the vast masses of bare basaltic rock. On the western side the range trends gradually toward the lake. It is broken into rounded hills and grass-covered slopes, which, in some places, terminate abruptly, as they approach the margin of the sea. The hills on this side, for nearly two-thirds of the length of the water-basin, come down close to the beach, leaving only a narrow "ribbon of coast." To the northwest there is a notable recession in which lies the crescent-shaped plain of Gennesaret. It is nearly four miles long and a mile or more in breadth at its widest point. It is watered by several streams now running to waste, which in former days were so utilized as to irrigate every portion of the plain. In the period of the Romans, Gennesaret was one of the garden spots of the world. Its climate was a "harmonious blending of the seasons"; its orchards and gardens yielded their luscious fruits in tropical profusion; its grapes and figs ripened "during ten months in the year"; and its cultivated fields produced the finest of the wheat.

Over most of its extent, at the present time, Gennesaret has reverted to its primitive condition. Back of its silvery strand—made up of myriads of tiny shells—an almost continuous hedge of oleanders holds back a wild tangle of luxuriant vegetation, which gives evidence, not to be disputed, of the wonderful fertility of the soil and its adaptation to the growth of plants from widely differing climes.

On this side of the lake, in the Saviour's day, towns and villages were thickly clustered on plain and hillside, and every foot of land was carefully cultivated. On the "other side" the towns were few: the only suitable locations for them being at

The Valley of the Jordan

the mouths of the wadies which came down from the plateau above. It was a region of "desert places" where our Lord often sought retirement and rest when wearied with His arduous labors amid the crowds that thronged Him on the western side. (Mark iv. 35, 36, v. 21 ; Matt. xiv. 13-15, etc.)

It is a common impression that the hills on the eastern side press down closely to the margin of the lake, but this is not the case. Except at the ruined site of Gergesa (Khersa) the hills recede for fully one half of a mile; and, at the upper end is the broad plain, known as the Batihah, which is nearly as large and as fertile as the plain of Gennesaret. The passage-way along the northern shore of the Lake from Gennesaret is interrupted by cliffs which push into the water, and also by swamps at the upper end of the numerous bays on this portion of the coast. It is necessary, therefore, as in former times to "take shipping" for this part of the journey, going or returning. (John vi. 24.) The water of the lake is a deep rich blue, and still, as of old, it is noted for the abundance and variety of its fish.

The Old Testament name of the Lake of Galilee was the Sea of Chinnereth. (Num. xxxiv. 11 ; Josh. xi. 2 ; 1 Kings xv. 20.) In the Roman period it was also called the Sea of Tiberias, (John vi. 1), and the Lake of Gennesaret. (Luke v. 1.)

This inland lake and the region around it have been made blessedly familiar by the story of the Evangelists. It was the home of many of the disciples as well as the favorite dwelling-place of Jesus. No other spot on earth awakens so many hallowed recollections of His lowly, unselfish life and beneficent ministry. Here by mountain side and lake side, and in the crowded synagogue, He preached the Gospel of the Kingdom, speaking in parables for the most part, and drawing His illustrations of spiritual truths from familiar objects around Him on land and sea.

Here He healed the sick; cleansed the lepers; opened the eyes of the blind ; cast out demons ; calmed the raging of the winds and waves by a word; walked upon the sea to rescue His imperilled disciples; comforted the sorrowing; gave rest to the weary and heavy laden; and awaked from the sleep of death the little daughter of the ruler of the synagogue. The story of Galilee, in a word, is the story of the larger part of the public ministry of Jesus. (Matt. chaps. iv.-xviii.; Mark i.-ix.; Luke iv.-ix.; John vi. and xxi.) It has been said with truth that there is nothing amid these surroundings "to distract our thoughts from that Divine Presence which here abode in human form. One great memory lingers undisturbed amongst these hills and valleys. The bustle of modern life and the squalid misery and degradation of the eastern peasantry would equally clash with the sacred, tender associations of the spot where 'most of His mighty works were done,' most of His 'gracious words' were spoken. The stage is empty, and there is nothing to prevent our peopling it with hallowed memories of Him who spake as 'never man spake,' who was Himself 'the way, the truth, and the life.'"[1]

Here the words of McCheyne most fitly express the Christian pilgrim's thought:

> "How pleasant to me thy deep blue wave,
>   O Sea of Galilee;
> For the glorious One who came to save,
>   Hath often stood by thee.
>
> "Graceful around thee the mountains meet,
>   Thou calm reposing sea,
> But, oh, far more! the beautiful feet
>   Of Jesus walked o'er thee."

Towns on the Coasts of Galilee.—Only two of the towns or cities mentioned by the Evangelists are now inhabited. These are Tiberias and Magdala, both of which are sadly changed since the prosperous days of the Roman period.

Tiberias is situated in a recession of the hills on the west-

---

[1] Holy Fields—Doctor Manning, p. 196.

ern shore of the lake, a little less than half way from its southern end. A mile or more below the present village are the celebrated Hot Springs, which made this portion of the coast so attractive to the Romans. The city, which once extended to the immediate vicinity of the springs, was built, or possibly rebuilt, by Herod Antipas and named by him for the Emperor Tiberius. The ruins of this Herodian city cover acres of ground along the shore, and recent researches have shown that the enclosing wall was nearly three miles in length. This wall included a citadel, 580 feet above the lake, on a declivity behind the city. In the time of Christ it was "a pile of noble buildings rising from the level of the lake behind a low, strong sea wall. Theatres, amphitheatres, Forum, prætorium, temples, synagogues, baths, rich houses—all crowned by the lofty fortress looking down upon the city."[1] There is no mention of any visit made to this city by our Lord or His disciples, but He must often have been near it, and its massive buildings running up the slope of the hill were frequently before Him as a picture of worldly magnificence when He sailed back and forth upon the lake.

Magdala is represented by the modern village of Mejdel (Migdol or watch-tower) at the lower end of the Plain of Gennesaret. The name is mentioned in Matt. xv. 39, but the place is best known as the home of Mary, the devoted friend of Jesus, to whom He first showed Himself after His resurrection. (John xx. 16–18.)

Capernaum.—The site of this city, so highly favored in point of privilege during the period of the Galilean ministry, has long been in dispute. The most probable location, in view of all the evidence at present attainable, is at the northern end of the Gennesaret plain on a little swell of ground directly south of Khan Minyeh.

Another location, whose claims have been earnestly advocated by eminent authorities is *Tell Hum* at the end of the

[1] The City and the Land, p. 112.

lake, some two and a-half miles northeast of Khan Minyeh. At this place there are extensive ruins, the most conspicuous of which has been found to be a Jewish synagogue of white limestone. On one of the large blocks near by there is a beautifully engraved representation of the "pot of manna," which for centuries had been preserved as a memorial in the ark of the covenant. (Heb. ix. 4.)

Aside from these ruins, which without doubt indicate the existence of a prosperous city of the Roman period, there are no special features of the place or its surroundings which directly suggest its identification with Capernaum.

The main points of the argument in favor of Khan Minyeh have been briefly summed up by Dr. Merrill as follows:

> At Capernaum there was (1) *a garrison*. For this there would naturally be some fort or castle, of which there should be remains. There was (2) *a customhouse;* and this would be on the road leading northward past the Lake to Damascus. There are no traces of there ever having been a road leading past Tell Hum, or existing anywhere in the angle formed by the river and the north end of the Lake. At Khan Minyeh there are traces of a Roman road, and it is still in use. Tell Hum is fully two miles distant from this road. This road coming from the north would first touch the lake at Khan Minyeh, and the customs stations being there, it would accommodate both the lake and the road. The garrison would be at the same place as the customhouse. No remains of a fort of any kind exist at Tell Hum, while the hill overhanging Khan Minyeh between the old Roman road just referred to and the present road which follows the trench in the brow of the bluff, has been shaped artificially, and gives every appearance of having been occupied by an ancient castle. I attach no importance to the ruins at Khan Minyeh that are still visible above ground; but I have seen enough to convince me that a town of considerable size is buried there.[1]

The principal argument advanced by Magregor in favor of Khan Minyeh is its open, safe harbor to which storm-tossed vessels would naturally be directed; while at Tell Hum there is no secure harborage and not even a safe landing-place in rough weather.

[1] Butler's Bible Work, p. 673.

The Valley of the Jordan

To these may be added the argument emphasized by Dr. Robinson that Tell Hum lies outside the definite and well-known district, known as Gennesaret, or the plain of Gennesaret, in which, according to the Evangelists, Capernaum was situated. (Matt. xiv. 34; Mark vi. 53; John vi. 17–25.)

For Khan Minyeh, says Keim, the whole situation vouches in a high degree. Here is the plain of Gennesar, and here too it leaves off, for directly north of it stretches the mountain-chain which had retired in a half-circle to make room for that fair district, and abuts again upon the lake; so much so, that it is only by a narrow and difficult pathway that the rocks are artificially penetrated, and the great road to Damascus on leaving the Khan strikes straight up hill and inland. Here there is water and vegetation. Close at hand are several springs. Along the lake-side is a strip of luxuriant green, consisting of grass and clover, an emerald meadow-carpet; "no other in Palestine so green"; the shore is adorned with a tall growth of sedge. Numerous herds and flocks graze on this part of the plain; indeed it is just the pastures of Minyeh which, according to Burckhardt, have become proverbial for their richness among the dwellers in the neighboring districts. Finally, the district of Minyeh served as a harborage; a half-circle seems to mark the harbor, which has become choked up in the lapse of time, sheltered by the mountain promontory from all the northern winds; here the wood from the east shore is still landed for Acco (Acre).[1]

Capernaum was exalted in point of privilege above all the cities of Galilee. It was the home of Jesus, and of His inner circle of disciples, for nearly three years. Matthew speaks of it as "His own city." It was the scene of many of the miracles of healing; "the central pulpit of our Lord's teaching"; and the birthplace of the Christian Church. Two at least of the Apostles, Peter and Matthew, occupied houses in Capernaum which were always open to the Master, and at some period in His earlier ministry Mary, the mother of Jesus, transferred her residence from Nazareth to Capernaum. (Mark i. 29, ii. 14, 15; Matt. xii. 46; John ii. 12.) Three of the Evangelists have given us a record of the blessed ministries

[1] Butler's Bible Work, p. 672.

which filled one Sabbath day at Capernaum, and so deeply were the people impressed with His gracious words and miracles of healing that at even all the city was gathered at the door of Simon's house; and "all they that had any sick with divers diseases brought them unto Him; and He laid His hands on every one of them, and healed them." (Mark i. 21–34; Luke iv. 33–41.)

Bethsaida of Galilee, which was evidently near to Capernaum, (Mark vi. 45; John vi. 17), was probably situated on the other side of the headland which cuts off Gennesaret from the northern shore of the Lake.

Some ruined buildings and an octagonal fountain about a mile north of Khan Minyeh mark the site of the old town. The modern village, known as Et Tabiga, is inhabited by fishermen and the little bay in its front is still the favorite fishing-ground of the lake. This city was the birthplace of Peter, Andrew and Philip.

Bethsaida Julias was on the plain of Batihah east of the Jordan and not far from the upper end of the lake. It was also originally a fishing village, but was raised to the rank of a city by Philip the Tetrarch who enlarged it and gave to it the name of the Emperor's daughter—Julias. On a grassy slope near this place Christ fed the five thousand (Luke ix. 10–17); and on one of the mountains near by He was alone praying when the storm arose which delayed the progress and imperilled the lives of the disciples who were heading toward Bethsaida of Galilee. (Mark vi. 45, 46; John vi. 15–17.)

Chorazin.—The only clue to the location of this city is given in the prophetic announcement of its doom. (Matt. xi. 20–24; Luke x. 20–24.) In this sentence of condemnation Bethsaida and Capernaum are included. Hence the inference that the three cities were near the sea, and so closely grouped together as to have practically the same advantages in connection with the beneficent ministry of Christ. On the assumption that the other cities of this group have been correctly

The Valley of the Jordan

located, Chorazin would fall naturally into place at Tell Hum. This identification was suggested by Dr. Robinson and has been approved by Merrill and other eminent explorers. The discovery of a ruined heap about two and a-half miles north of Tell Hum called Kerazeh has suggested another probable site, which has found favor with some of the leading authorities. While the name is practically the same, the location is objectionable because of its isolation from the main lines of travel and from the prosperous cities by the lake-side. It is possible also that the name was transferred to this inland town after the destruction of the old city by the Lake.

Gergesa.—The ruins of a town called Gersa or Khersa on the eastern shore, at the mouth of the Wady Semakh, have been identified by Dr. Thomson with the ancient city of Gergesa, which gave its name to a limited district around it. (Matt. viii. 28.) This was included in a larger district of which Gadara, an important city eight miles away, was the capital; hence it was said to be "in the country of the Gadarenes, *which is over against Galilee.*" (Luke viii. 26.) Gersa is four or five miles from the upper end of the lake and almost opposite Magdala. In the immediate vicinity of this town and landing-place was the scene of the healing of the fierce demoniacs and the destruction of the herd of swine. (Matt. viii. 28-34.)

Dr. Thomson describes the characteristic feature of the place as follows:

> In Gersa we have a position which fulfills the requirements of the narratives, and with a name so near that in Matthew as to be in itself a strong corroboration of the identification. The site is within a few rods of the shore, and a mountain rises directly above it, in which are ancient tombs; out of some one of them the man possessed of the devils may have issued to meet Jesus. The lake is so near the base of the mountain that a herd of swine feeding above it, seized with a sudden panic, would rush madly down the declivity, those behind tumbling over and thrusting forward those before, and, as there is no space to recover on the narrow plain between the base of the mountain and the lake, they

would crowd headlong into the water and perish. . . . Farther south the plain becomes so broad that the herd might have stopped and recoiled from the lake, whose domain they would not willingly invade.

To this description Dr. Thomson adds the fact that wild hogs abound at this place, and in a state as wild and fierce as though they were still "possessed."[1]

The deepest furrow in the hills on this side of the lake is the **Wady Fik**, which enters the lake three miles below Gersa. On the precipitous heights above are the ruins of **Gamala** (Kulat-el Husn), a well-nigh impregnable stronghold, famous for the desperate resistance its defenders made to the Romans. The mouth of the Wady is almost directly opposite the city of Tiberias. The road from Bethshan to Damascus passes up through this cleft to the plateau above. The projected railroad from Haifa to Damascus follows the same route.

The village of *Semakh* on the southeastern shore of the lake was formerly supposed to occupy the site of *Hippos*, one of the cities of Decapolis, but later research has recovered it at a site known as Susiyeh, the Arabic equivalent of Hippos. *Tarichœa*, famous for its fisheries and for ship-building, is probably identical with a ruined site now called Kera on the southwestern shore near the outgo of the Jordan. This city is not mentioned in Scripture, but is fully described by Josephus who fortified it to meet an attack of the Romans.

4. **The Ghor.**—The Arabs use this term to designate the lower valley of the Jordan, or that portion which extends from the Sea of Galilee to the line of cliffs beyond the southern border of the Dead Sea. In its popular usage by writers who have adopted the term, it applies only to the deep trench or sunken valley between the lakes. This section is sixty-five miles in length. In breadth it varies from four to fourteen miles. Its contractions and expansions have been briefly described by Dr. Smith as follows:

[1] The Land and the Book, p. 355.

The Valley of the Jordan

For thirteen miles south of the lake the breadth is hardly more than four miles, then it expands to six or seven in the Plain of Bethshan, which rises by terraces toward the level of Esdraelon. Ten miles south of Bethshan the Samarian hills press eastward, and for the *next thirteen* the river runs closely by their feet, and the valley is three miles wide. Again the Samarian hills withdraw, and the valley widens first to eight miles and then gradually to fourteen, which is the breadth at Jericho. What we have therefore between Galilee and the Dead Sea is a long, narrow vale twice expanding—at Bethshan and Jericho—to the dimensions of a plain.[1]

Through the last named expansion the river runs almost in the middle, separating it into the Plain of Jordan on the one side, and its counterpart, the plain of Shittim on the other, which the Arabs now call Ghor-es Seisaban. Above this expansion,—designated by the Old Testament writers as the Ciccar or Circuit (Gen. xiii. 10–12)—except for a short distance in the vicinity of Bethshan, the strip of plain on the eastern side of the Jordan is much wider than that on the western side.

Climate and Products of the Ghor.—This portion of the Jordan valley has been aptly described as an enormous hothouse. It is a region of never-ending summer. Cold winds sweep over the mountain ridges which border it and snow rests at times on their summits, but in this sheltered groove far below the level of the sea, frost and snow are alike unknown. The products of its lower levels, especially on the eastern side, correspond with those in the equatorial belts and rank vegetation may be seen wherever water reaches its fruitful soil. The only exception to this tropical luxuriance is the portion touched by the salt marshes in the neighborhood of the Dead Sea.

Tributaries of the Jordan.—The two principal affluents of the Jordan which enter the valley from the east are the Yarmuk (Jarmuk) or Hieromax and the Jabbok. The Yarmuk joins the Jordan four miles below its outgo from the lake; and

[1] Hist. Geog., p. 482.

the Jabbok about twenty miles from the upper end of the Dead Sea. On the west there are two principal affluents also,—the Wady Farah and the Wady Kelt. The former coming from the plateau near Shechem runs for several miles nearly parallel with the Jordan, joining it some six or seven miles below the mouth of the Jabbok. The latter crosses the plain of Jericho and enters the Jordan a few miles above its mouth.

Places of special interest.

(1) **Abel Meholah** (Meadow of the Dance) has been placed by Conder at Ain Helweh, ten miles south of Bethshan. It was one of the places to which the Midianites fled (Judg. vii. 22), and the place of Elisha's residence before he was called to the prophetic office. (1 Kings xix. 16.)

(2) **Kurn Sartaba.**—The most conspicuous landmark in the Jordan valley is a lofty conical peak called the Kurn or "Horn" of Sartaba. Its position is on the west side of the valley near the junction of the Wady Farah with the Jordan. "Its summit, 2,400 feet above the bed of the valley, is capped by a cone 270 feet high, with steep smooth sides like those of the so-called Frank mountain near Bethlehem."[1] A mass of ruins on the summit indicated that this apparently inaccessible height had at one time been fortified as a stronghold. It was also used, according to the Talmud, as an observatory along the line of selected mountains between Jerusalem and the plateau east of the Jordan, on which beacon-fires were kindled to announce the appearance of the new moon.

(3) **Adam.**—The site of this city was probably at or near the Damieh crossing close to the mouth of the Jabbok. When Israel passed over Jordan it is said "that the waters which came down from above stood and rose up upon an heap very far from the city Adam, that is beside Zaretan." (Josh. iii. 16.) The site of Zaretan has not been definitely located, but the district of Zaretan extended from Abel Meholah to Succoth.

(4) **Succoth** (place of booths) has been identified with

[1] Tent Life, p. 224.

The Valley of the Jordan

Tell Dar'ala about a mile north of the Damieh ford on the east side of the Jordan. This identification rests mainly upon a statement of the Talmud that Succoth, in the later periods of Jewish history was called Tarala, the equivalent of the present name Dar'ala. At this place Jacob dwelt for a time on his homeward journey from the east, and constructed booths for his cattle. (Gen. xxxiii. 16, 17.) The brass foundries of Solomon were in "the clay ground of the plain of Jordan between Succoth and Zarthan" (Zaretan). (1 Kings vii. 46.)

(5) **Jericho.**—The site of ancient Jericho—the city of palm-trees—is indicated by a large mound (Tell es Sultan) on the western border of the plain, about six miles from the Jordan. The waters of the Wady Kelt flow out from the mountains a short distance to the south of the tell. A famous fountain (Ain es Sultan) issues from the eastern base of the mound, and was doubtless used for irrigation of the plain as well as for the supply of the city. An early, and a generally accepted tradition, has identified this with the fountain whose waters were miraculously healed by Elisha at the intercession of the people of Jericho. (2 Kings ii. 19–22.) Dr. Bliss made a brief visit to this mound in 1894, and found fragments of pre-Israelite pottery, similar to some of the types found at Tell el Hesy, and traces of a mud-brick wall *in situ*. "I confess," he says, "that this wall sent a thrill through me. If Tell es Sultan is a mass of *débris* caused by the ruin of several mud-brick towns over the first Jericho, then there is good reason to suppose that this wall, uncovered near the base of the mound, at its edge, is the very wall which fell before the eyes of the Captain Joshua. Tell es Sultan is a long mound, over 1,200 feet in length from north to south, about fifty feet high, with four superimposed mounds, the highest being some ninety feet above the fountain, which is at the east, but not more than sixty or seventy feet above the ground at the west, as the mound occurs where the land slopes down to the plain."[1] In the

[1] Quarterly, P. E. F., July, '94, p. 176.

earlier history of the country the plain in the immediate vicinity of Jericho was famous for its fertility and tropical luxuriance. Aqueducts, the ruins of which may still be seen in several places, carried abundant supplies of water from the mountains and distributed it over the plain, making it a rich garden spot, or as Josephus describes it—"a divine region." It was especially noted in the days of the Roman occupation for its almost priceless balsams; its choice varieties of palm trees and fragrant spices. The princely revenues derived from this region were given over by Mark Antony to Cleopatra, and were afterward recovered for himself by Herod the Great. The revenues of this plain in the time of its occupation by the Crusaders were valued at $25,000 per annum. These were derived from the cultivation of sugar cane.

Jericho was a noted stronghold of the Canaanites. It was the first place invested by the Israelites after the passage of the Jordan. (Josh. chap. vi.) Its first mention in the book of Joshua is in connection with the visit of the spies (Josh. chap. ii.): and when the city fell Rahab, who had hidden the spies, and all her household were saved. (Josh vi. 22–25.) Jericho was assigned to Benjamin, but, because of the curse pronounced upon the man who should rebuild it (Josh. vi. 26) the actual site remained for a long time a desolation. In the reign of Ahab, Hiel, the Bethelite, incurred the curse by rebuilding its walls. (1 Kings xvi. 34.) One of the schools of the prophets was established at Jericho, and it was frequently honored by the visits of the prophets Elijah and Elisha. To this school Elijah came on his last round of visitation just before his translation. (2 Kings ii. 4–7.) On the return of Elisha he healed the bitter waters of the fountain. (2 Kings ii. 19–22.)

It should be noted that there were *three* Jerichos, in the long history of this region, which occupied *three different sites*. The site of the first, or the Old Testament Jericho has been already described. The site of the Roman Jericho was farther to the south along the line of the Wady Kelt. It was enlarged

The Valley of the Jordan

and adorned with magnificent buildings by Herod the Great, and his successor Archelaus. It was the favorite winter residence of Herod and the place of his death. The position of this city, at the opening of the pass leading up to Jerusalem, made it a place of general rendezvous for the pilgrim bands going to and returning from the great festivals at Jerusalem. On his last journey to Jerusalem our Lord tarried for a short time in this Roman city. Here He healed the two blind men and called Zacchæus the publican. (Matt. xx. 29–34; Mark x. 46–52; Luke xix. 5.)

"'The distinction between the new and the old towns may solve the seeming discrepancy between Matthew (xx. 30), who makes the miracle on the blind to be when Jesus was leaving Jericho, and Luke, who says it was when Jesus was come nigh unto Jericho (xviii. 35).'" [1]

Modern Jericho, known as Eriha or Riha, occupies a site nearly two miles from Tell es Sultan on the north bank of the Wady Kelt. It is a small Arab village of rudely constructed houses. A square tower dating from the period of the Crusades is the only relic of antiquity within its limits. Quite recently the appearance of the place has been improved by the erection of a hotel and a Russian Hospice for the accommodation of the pilgrims who swarm past it year by year to the fords of the Jordan. The town itself is probably not older than the twelfth century.

(6) **Gilgal.**—The site of Gilgal has been discovered on a slight elevation about a mile east of the village of Riha, which still bears the name Jiljulieh. The only remains apparent on the surface of the ground, are a large ruined reservoir by the side of a wide-spreading tamarisk tree, and several rounded hillocks of artificial construction. In some of these mounds hewn stone pottery and flint knives have been found. [2]

Gilgal was the first camping-place of the Israelites after the passage of the Jordan, and hither the twelve stones taken from

[1] Fausset's Bib. Cyclopedia Art. Jericho.   [2] Ibid., p. 399.

the bed of the river were brought and set up as a memorial. (Josh. iv. 19–24.) Here also the covenant of circumcision was renewed and "the reproach of Egypt rolled off." (Josh. v. 2–9.) At Gilgal by Divine direction the Passover was celebrated and from this date the manna ceased. (Josh. v. 11, 12.)

From this place Joshua went up by night to the help of the Gibeonites (Josh. x. 6–9), and the narrative of the conquest seems to imply that the camp at Gilgal continued to be the rallying-point of the tribes, and the abode of the ark of the covenant, until the removal of the tabernacle to Shiloh.

(7) **Beth-Hogla**, a frontier city of Benjamin (Josh. xviii. 19-22), has been identified with Ain Hajlah, five miles southeast of Jericho. There are numerous tells on the plain which have not as yet been identified.

(8) "**The Cities of the Plain.**"—There is no evidence in the Scriptures on which to base the supposition that the five Canaanite cities of the plain—Sodom, Gomorrah, Admah, Zeboim, and Zoar—were situated at the southern end of the Dead Sea; nor is there any intimation that the four cities which were destroyed, were submerged in its waters.

On the contrary it is implied, if not directly stated, that they were in the plain at the northern end of the Sea. The proofs which bear upon this point may be summed up as follows:

1. It is said (Gen. xiii. 10–12) that Lot beheld all the plain of Jordan —in which these cities were located—from a ridge east of Bethel. From this ridge modern explorers have been able to see the lower valley of the Jordan river and the upper end of the Dead Sea, but they are unanimous in their testimony that the depression at the lower end of the Sea is completely cut off from view by the mountain wall in the vicinity of Engedi.

2. Abram's outlook near Hebron was "toward Sodom and Gomorrah, and toward all the land of the plain." It is not said that he beheld the cities of the plain, but he saw the "smoke of the country, which went up as the smoke of a furnace." This description exactly accords with the northward view, as described by modern travellers, but not with the limited outlook southward.

3. The word translated "plain" in the passages cited is Ciccar (cir-

The Valley of the Jordan

cuit) in the original. Without limitation it might be applied to the depression at the lower end of the lake, but here and elsewhere it is called the plain (Ciccar) of the Jordan. It is evident that this expression would be inapplicable to a valley which is removed more than forty miles from the mouth of the Jordan.

4. The route taken by Chadorlaomer on his marauding expedition furnishes a confirmatory proof in support of the northern location which can hardly be questioned. Coming from the east by way of the southern end of Mount Seir he turned northward to Kadesh Barnea and thence to the Vale of Siddim by way of Engedi. (Gen. xiv. 1-16.) On the supposition that the confederated cities were at the south end of the Sea, the four kings would certainly have met the invader long before he reached Engedi, or, at least they would have attacked him at a great disadvantage on his return journey to the south. Of such a doubling on his track, however, there is no hint in the narrative. The direction of march was evidently continuous from Kadesh Barnea to Dan and, hence "there is a topographical sequence in the whole story."

5. The fact that Zoar, which was not destroyed, is mentioned by some of the prophetic writers in connection with contiguous sites on the plain of Moab (Abel Shittim) is worthy of note, as indicative of the general location of the entire group. (Isa. xv. 5, 6; Jer. xlviii. 34.) This harmonizes also with the statement that Moses, from the top of Pisgah, beheld the south (Negeb) and the plain of the valley of Jericho, the city of palm trees, unto Zoar. (Deut. xxxiv. 3.) This could not have been the traditional Zoar, at the southeast end of the Dead Sea; for that portion of the valley is completely hidden by the high mountains intervening from every outlook on, or in the vicinity of, Nebo.

The exact sites of the cities which were destroyed will probably never be known. They were overthrown and consumed by fire; the ground on which they stood was made a desolation "and their names were blotted out of the later topography of the time of Joshua." Concerning these sites Major Conder says:

Although no ruins were found by the Survey party, and were not to be expected, yet there are names in the district, applying to portions of the ground, which seem to me to have a possible connection with those of Gomorrah, Admah and Zeboim.

The great spring of Ain Feshkah is a probable site for one of the Cities of the Plain and the great bluff not far south of it is called Tubk Amriyeh, and the neighboring valley Wady Amriyeh. This word is radically identical with the Hebrew Gomorrah, or Amorah as it is spelled in one passage. (Gen. x. 19.) It is possible then that the name of Gomorrah is preserved in this modern district title.[1]

The Plain of Abel Shittim.—This beautiful expanse—the meadow of the Acacias—or, as it is most frequently designated in the Pentateuch, "the Plains of Moab" extends from the Nimrim ford or ferry of the Jordan—nearly opposite Jericho —to the limit of the Jordan plain at the head of the Dead Sea. Its dimensions, according to Dr. Thomson's estimate, are fifteen miles in length by eight in breadth, including the mouths of the wadies, and adjacent hillsides. The plain is broken in places by torrent beds, little knolls, and rocky spurs which push down from the main range. Near the river it is exceedingly fertile but farther back it is an undulating pasture land. " The old and gnarled acacias, scattered here and there upon this Shittim plain, testify in the strongest degree to the appropriateness of its Biblical name, and they are no doubt the descendants of the shittah-trees which covered this plain in the time of Moses." [2]

This was the last camping-place of Israel east of the Jordan. (Num. xxii. 1; Josh. iii. 1.) The rows of tents extended from "Abel Shittim"—the town which gave its name to the plain—on the north, to "Beth-Jeshimoth" on the south. (Num. xxxiii. 49.)

"Neither pencil nor picture," says Dr. Thomson, "can adequately describe the wonderful scene, nor can imagination reproduce it. History records nothing with which to compare it in this or in any land, and no wonder that Balaam, when he looked upon the scene from the mountains of Nebo, and 'saw Israel abiding in his tents, according to their tribes,' exclaimed, 'How goodly are thy tents, O Jacob, and thy tabernacles, O Israel! As the valleys are they spread forth, as gardens by the river's side, as the trees of lign-aloes which the Lord hath planted, and as cedar trees beside the waters, and blessed is he that blesseth thee.'"[3]

[1] Tent Work, p. 207.   [2] The Land and the Book, p. 672.
[3] The Land and the Book, p. 672.

There are a number of tells on this plain whose names or locations have suggested identifications with the cities of Reuben and Gad. Of these the most important are: *Tell Nimrim*, opposite Jericho which, with name scarcely changed, marks the site of *Beth-nimrah* ("House of the Leopard") one of the fortified cities of Gad (Num. xxxii. 36); *Tell Kefrein* identified with *Abel Shittim*, the city from which the plain derived its name (Num. xxxiii. 49); *Tell er Ramah*, near Wady Heshbon, with *Beth-haran*, a fenced city of Gad (Num. xxxii. 36); *Tell Ektanu*, a little farther east, with *Zoar* the city of the plain to which Lot fled (Gen. xix. 23); and *Tell es Suweimeh* at the southern limit of the plain, with *Beth-jeshimoth*, a city of Reuben. (Josh. xiii. 20.)

"At *Tell Kefrein*, according to Josephus, Moses completed the book of Deuteronomy, and amid the palm trees of the place delivered his last address to the children of Israel." (Ant. iv. 8, 1, 2.) In the Septuagint the name *Beth-nimrah* is translated Bethabara and hence the ford of the Jordan near by has been regarded by many as the place of John's baptisms, to which reference is made by the Evangelist. (John i. 28.)

It is an interesting and suggestive fact that the name,— "Plains of Moab,"—which is used nine times in connection with this camping ground of Israel, is not found outside of the Pentateuch, "except in one quotation from it in the book of Joshua." "The district had been conquered by the Amorites just before the coming of Israel, and in later days was always known as Amorite territory. Accordingly it was only at a time when the memory of its former ownership was still fresh that it could thus be called by its ancient designation." [1]

The Jordan River in its progress through the Ghor makes a descent of about 600 feet. It is a swift, turbid, swirling stream, with numerous rapids, islands, bends and loups, and frequently for miles its course is completely hidden from view by dense masses of trees and undergrowth. The width of

[1] Pres. and Ref. Review, Vol. II., p. 632.

the river, except in its flood-time, is seldom more than 100 feet.

It has two channels with two sets of banks. The lower channel is the narrow bed in which the river ordinarily flows. The upper is a mile or more in width, in some places, and is covered with an almost impenetrable jungle of tamarisks, oleanders, willows, and reedy vegetation of mammoth growth. This high-level channel is called the Zor.

In March and April—the harvest season of this part of the valley—the Jordan overflows its banks and spreads out over the surface of this wider basin, driving the wild beasts from their lairs in the jungle and making the river for the time an impassable barrier. During this season the Jordan in the vicinity of Jericho is nearly a mile wide; at its close it sinks down within its natural borders.

Fords of the Jordan.—The Survey party tabulated a list of not less than forty crossing-places in the Ghor, most of which are available for passage only in summer.

The principal fords in ancient times are the following:

(1) The crossing place of the great highway from Galilee to Bashan, just below the point where the Jordan leaves the lake of Galilee. This is marked by the ruins of an ancient bridge of ten arches, known as the bridge of Um el Kanater.

(2) The crossing of the caravan road from Galilee to Gadara and the East by way of the gorge of the Yarmuk (Hieromax). This ford is six miles below the lake and one mile below the junction of the Yarmuk with the Jordan. The bridge (Jisr el Mejamia) which spans the river at this point, is the only one now available for travel south of the lake of Galilee. Here the proposed railroad to Damascus will cross the Jordan.

(3) The crossing at the opening of the valley of Jezreel by the road leading to Pella, Jabesh, Gilead and eastward. There are three fording places in reality at this point very near each other. One of them, a mile north of the mouth of the Jalud, still bears the name Arabah, meaning "passage," or "ferry,"

THE NEW JORDAN BRIDGE AT MOUTH OF WADY SHAIB

and is radically the same word found in the name "Bethabara."[1] Major Conder's suggestion that this ford marks the probable site of the baptism of Jesus (John i. 28) has been favorably received by some leading authorities, but a serious objection to this location is the fact that it was *within the limits* of the district of Galilee. This position does not accord with the statement of Matthew, that "Jesus came *from* Galilee to Jordan unto John, to be baptized of him"; nor with other contemporary events which evidently belong to John's ministry in Judea. (Matt. iii. 13; Luke iv. 14; John i. 29.) At one of these fords the men of Jabesh Gilead crossed over by night and brought away from the wall of Bethshan the bodies of Saul and his sons. (1 Sam. xxxi. 12.)

(4) **The Damieh ford**, just below the junction of the Jabbok, was the well-known crossing-place of the road from Mount Gilead to Shechem. This was evidently the place of Jacob's passage over the Jordan on his return from Padan Aram, and not improbably of Abraham's, also, at an earlier day. (Gen. xii. 6, xxxiii. 18.) It is supposed to be the place where the Ephraimites who could not say "Shibboleth" were slain by the men of Gilead. (Judg. xii. 5, 6.)

(5) **The Nimrim or Nuwaimeh ford**, near Beth-nimrah, to which reference has been already made, is the most interesting of all the passages of the Jordan. It is nearly opposite Jericho, at the mouth of the Wady Shaib. It is sometimes called the "upper ford" to distinguish it from a lower crossing a short distance below the Pilgrims' bathing-place. The main thoroughfare from Jericho to Gilead has always been by way of this upper ford. By this route to the Jordan's brink, in all probability, the ark of the covenant was borne by the priests when the waters stood on heap far up the Ghor, and rolled away to the Sea from all the valley below. (Josh. iii. 15, 16.) Hither Elijah came with his faithful friend and associate, Elisha, from Jericho, and "the river that had drawn back at a nation's feet, parted at

[1] Thirty Years' Work, p. 99.

the stroke of one man and they two, went over dry-shod." And it came to pass, as they still went on and talked, that, behold there appeared a chariot of fire, and parted them both asunder; and Elijah went up by a whirlwind into heaven. It is a notable fact that one of the two men who communed with Jesus on the transfiguration mount passed from earth on the top of Mount Nebo, and the other from the plain which lies at its foot. All the circumstances of the gospel narratives, as well as the name, which the Septuagint supplies, point to this spot beyond Jordan as the preaching place where Jesus was baptized. (John i. 28.) "There is surely a deep significance in the fact," says Dr. Tristram, "if this be so, of him who came in the spirit and power of Elias, thus exercising his function of herald of the kingdom, and completing his mission by the baptism of Christ, at the very spot where his prototype had ceased from his mission and been carried unto heaven. As suddenly as the first Elijah disappeared, so suddenly did the second Elias appear to prepare the way of the Redeemer. Where the first dropped his mantle, in that very spot did the second take it up."[1] By this ford Christ and His disciples crossed the Jordan when coming from Perea to Jerusalem. Here, also, He remained two days when He heard that Lazarus was sick. (John x. 40, xi. 6.)

(6) **The lower ford**, known as the Pilgrims' Bathing-place, is five or six miles south of the Nimrim ford. It was used almost exclusively for the passage to Moab. This was one of the "fords toward Moab" which Ehud took when he delivered Israel from the oppression of the Moabites. (Judg. iii. 28.) This ford was the probable crossing-place of Naomi and Ruth on their journey to Bethlehem. (Ruth, chap. i.)

It is evident from this brief study that the Jordan as a whole has several remarkable features, some of which are absolutely unique.

Its time-honored name—"the Descender"—is indicative of

[1] Sunday Mag., 1868, p. 256.

The Valley of the Jordan

one of these features, viz:—its unparalleled descent—not only a down-going of 3,000 feet in its course of 115 miles, but its descent to a *lower point* than is reached by any other water basin of its class on the surface of the earth. Other features hardly less noteworthy than this are: the rapidity of its flow; the almost countless windings of its channel, especially in the lower valley where there is "no reach of half a mile in a straight line"; its three picturesque sources, which are but reservoirs for the down-rushing floods of Mount Hermon's melting snows; its three lake-basins, unlike each other in almost every physical feature; its double channel; its dense borderings of undergrowth hiding the flow of its waters; the periodic overflow of its banks in the *harvest* season; and the wonderful variety of soil and scenery, climate and vegetation through which it passes on its way to the deep, lifeless basin, which swallows up its continuous flood and yet is never full.

The history of the Jordan has been inwoven with the story of Redemption from the memorable day that Abram passed over it into the Land of Promise. It is more frequently named in poetry and song, more attractive to pilgrim bands from every land, "more spoken about by mankind," than the Nile, the Euphrates, the Abana or any other stream, because of the Divine manifestations of power, healing, and grace displayed from age to age all along its course from the fountain of Banias to the fords of Jericho.

"The Jordan marks the termination of the wanderings of the children of Israel from the banks of the Nile, and the beginning of their history as an independent nation in their own home. It blends the memories of the Old and New Covenants, as the culmination of John's testimony and the inauguration of Christ's kingdom."[1] "Surely," says Magregor, "the Jordan is by far the most wonderful stream on the face of the earth, and the memories of its history will not be forgotten in heaven."[2]

[1] Schaff's Bible Lands, p. 299.   [2] Rob Roy on Jordan, p. 406.

The Dead Sea Basin.—The Dead Sea—or Salt Sea as it is usually termed in the Scriptures—occupies the upper portion of this basin almost exclusively. On the northern half of its west side there is a narrow strip of coast-land, interrupted at two places by towering cliffs which push down to the water's edge. South of Engedi the beach is wider, admitting a broad uninterrupted passage-way to the lower end of the lake. An ancient roadway from the south followed the coast to Engedi where it diverged westward, passing up by way of the cliff of Ziz to the summit of the plateau. This was the route taken by the army of Chadorlaomer from Kadesh Barnea to the cities of the plain (Gen. xiv.), and it is still used by the camel trains, which carry salt from Jebel Usdum to Jerusalem.

Jebel Usdum is a narrow, isolated ridge of crystallized rock-salt, six or seven miles in length, near the southern extremity of the western coast. This salt mountain has a slight covering of chalky limestone and gypsum which protects it from rapid disintegration. Beneath this, however, portions of the ridge frequently split off in great masses and lie in heaps at its base. In some places it is pierced with long, narrow caverns. Its height varies fron 200 to 300 feet.

The portion of the basin south of the water-line of the Dead Sea is a marshy, salt-covered region given over to barrenness and desolation—except on its eastern side near the southeast corner of the lake. This favored district is called the Ghor-es-Safieh. Here there is an abundance of fresh water and the soil is wonderfully fertile. In no other spot perhaps in the whole valley of the Jordan can such a collection of plants and trees peculiar to tropical climes, be found.

The width of the whole valley south of the lake varies from five to six miles. Its length is a little over eight miles. The basin ends at the line of high cliffs which cross the valley at this distance from the Sea. Here begins the Arabah which extends due south 112 miles to the Gulf of Akabah. This long valley for more than one-half its distance drains toward the

The Valley of the Jordan

Dead Sea. "There are also many springs on the shores of the lake, and within its shallower waters, some hot, some salt, some sulphurous, and others fresh, which contribute to its bulk."[1] The most prominent feature on the eastern shore is the peninsula near the lower end called El Lisan—the tongue—which pushes its huge bulk more than half-way across the lake. It is about twelve miles in length by six in breadth. Lieutenant Lynch describes it as "A bold, broad promontory, from forty to sixty feet high, incrusted with salt and bitumen, the perpendicular face extending all round, and presenting the coarse and chalky appearance of recent carbonate of lime."[2]

Above the Lisan, excepting a slight recession at the mouth of the Arnon river, there is a narrow continuous beach overshadowed by the towering mountains of Moab.

Driftwood stripped of its bark, bleached, and salt covered, marks the high-water line of the coast on either side. Lumps of bitumen or asphalt so pure that they will ignite when held in the flame of a lamp, may be picked up at almost any point on the shore.

The Dead Sea is forty-six miles long and nearly ten wide, at its widest part. Its maximum depth is 1,308 feet. The point where this depth was found is about one-third of the length of the lake from its north end, on the eastward side of the channel. This portion of the valley or cleft is 4,300 feet below the level of the Hashbany source of the Jordan, and about the same distance below the summit of the mountains of Moab, which rise directly above it. If a plummet were dropped from a level corresponding with the summit of the Mount of Olives to this depth, it would require the paying out of a line 5,260 feet long: and yet the distance between these points in a direct line is less than twenty miles. The water of the lake is famous for its *density*, its *bitterness* and its *buoyancy*. It holds in solution more than five times as much salt as the water of the ocean, mingled with chlorides of magnesium, calcium, potas-

[1] The Holy Land, p. 76. [2] Narrative of Lieutenant Lynch, p. 297.

sium and other mineral salts, which impart to it an extremely bitter and nauseous taste. To float on this briny deep requires no effort; to make progress in swimming is not so easy, because of the difficulty experienced in keeping the feet and lower limbs beneath the surface. Contrary to the impression which generally prevails, the water is clear, delicately tinted and so transparent that pebbles may be seen at a depth of twenty and thirty feet. The reflections of the mountains on the surface of this deeply-set, heavily-framed mirror are surpassingly beautiful, and the mists which rise from it as from a steaming chaldron, impart to every object lying beyond it, that rare purplish tint which Holman Hunt has sought to reproduce in his famous picture of the Scape-goat. In all Judea, says Doctor Smith, there is no view like that one bounded by the range of Moab, as you see it across the wilderness from the Mount of Olives.

While there is nothing in the atmosphere of the lake or its shores, or in the appearance of its waters, to suggest the ominous name which it now bears, it is nevertheless true that it is a sea of death. "No fish can live in it; no tree grows on its banks, and its air is like the blast of a furnace." Few of those who have tarried by its shores to sound its depths or explore its coasts, have escaped the effects of its blighting malaria or deadly fevers.

The narrative of the carefully conducted explorations of the Jordan valley under the direction of Lieutenant Lynch of the United States Navy, gives the fullest and most accurate information concerning the characteristic features of the Dead Sea and its surroundings. See also Bible Researches of Doctor Robinson, The Land and the Book—Doctor Thomson, Tristram's Topography of Holy Land, Conder's Tent Work, etc.

The Fourth Longitudinal Section

CHAPTER XXI

THE ANTI-LEBANON MOUNTAINS

(Consult Sketch Map No. 1.)

THE Eastern or Anti-Lebanon range is lower in elevation and more irregular in outline than Lebanon. While pursuing the same general direction southward, Anti-Lebanon is, for the most part, a series of broken, parallel ridges. In the Scripture it is designated as "Lebanon toward the sun rising." (Josh. xiii. 5.)

There is a marked depression or break in the range, a little north of the latitude of Damascus, which has been utilized in the construction of the carriage and railroad routes from Beirut to Damascus. This break separates Anti-Lebanon Proper, known as the East Mountain (Jebel esh Shurky), from Mount Hermon (Jebel esh Sheikh).

Mount Hermon trends farther to the west than the main ridge and is properly an outlier of Anti-Lebanon.

The East Mountain for more than two-thirds of its length northward is a treeless, verdureless waste. Here there are no perennial streams and but few valleys or patches of level ground amid the chalky ridges, that are capable of cultivation. The southern end of the range is broken up by the deep valley of the Barada, the Abana of ancient times (2 Kings v. 12) which brings life and fertility all along its zigzag course from the plain of Zebedany, near the summit of Anti-Lebanon, to the plain of Damascus, at its foot. "Along the river on both sides, in the deep narrow valley, every inch of land that can be reached by irrigation is cultivated, and the rows of tall poplars extend for miles, marking the course of the river as with a fringe of green, running back and forth among the chalky hills." [1]

The chief tributary of the Abana is the celebrated fountain called Ain el Fijeh. The crystal waters of this fountain burst forth from a double cavern in front of which are the ruins of an ancient temple. This spot is an ideal resting-place which the wayfarer over the Lebanons is not likely to forget while life and memory last. Here at Ain el Fijeh, says Doctor Thomson, one is at a loss which most to admire—the great quantity of water that bursts from beneath this ruined platform, cold and beautifully clear, or the rushing, roaring cataract, foaming and tumbling over the rocks as it plunges down its narrow channel; or the thick forests of tall trees, willows and walnuts, sycamores, planes and poplars, that overshadow the banks, or the magnificent cliffs that rise a thousand feet or more and shut in this happy vale on every side.

A modern village (Suk Wady Barada) in a bend of the river, three miles above the Fijeh fountain, occupies the site of the ancient city of Abila, the capital of Abilene. This district is mentioned by Luke in connection with the tetrarchy of Lysanias (iii. 1). The place has been identified by Latin inscriptions on the face of a cliff above the road dating from the middle of the second century.

The **Zebedany plain**, seven miles long by one to three wide, is noted for its rich verdure and luscious fruits. Its apples, pears, quinces, apricots, plums, and grapes are in great demand in Beirut and the towns of northern Syria. The elevation of the plain is over 3,500 feet.

The **Jebel esh Shurky** has no Scriptural associations except the casual references to sites already named.

The ancient city of **Zedad**, a landmark on the northern border line of Israel, lies out on the open plain along the road

[1] Doctor Merrill—Pict. Pal., p. 444.

The Anti-Lebanon Mountains

leading from Ribleh to Palmyra. It is about twenty miles east of the northern end of the main ridge of Anti-Lebanon, and seventy miles northeast of Damascus. The site of Zedad has been recovered after the lapse of more than thirty centuries mainly by the identification of its name with the name of the modern village of Sudad. The outgoings of the border line from this point were at Hazar-enan, and thence the line passed westward to Riblah, and southward to Baal-Gad and the eastern shore of the Sea of Galilee. (Num. xxxiv. 9–11. See also Ezek. xlvii. 16–18.) The site of Hazar-enan is not definitely known, but if Zephron is identical with the modern village of Zifrun, three miles east of Arethusa, the border line must have been drawn northeast from the " entrance of Hamath " toward the city of Hamath; then southeast by Ziphron, Zedad and Hazar-enan; and thence westward to Riblah.[1] (See Sketch Map No. 1.)

Damascus.—The city of Damascus lies on the edge of a sandy desert which stretches eastward from Anti-Lebanon to the valley of the Euphrates. It is two miles from the base of the mountain; seventy miles from Beirut by way of the carriage road; fifty-five miles east of the Mediterranean coast, and 133 miles in a direct line from Jerusalem.

The plain of Damascus known as the Ghutah is a dark island-like mass of green covering an area of more than thirty miles in circumference. It is an oasis of marvellous beauty and fertility shaped and nourished by the life-giving waters of the Barada, the Abana of Scripture. Close to the place of its outgo from the mountains this swiftly descending stream is parted into several branches and these into smaller streams with lateral water courses which irrigate every foot of ground within their reach. According to the estimate of the natives there are 365 canals in the Ghutah which distribute water to more than 30,000 gardens. The main branches of the river flow over the plain in a southeasterly direction for

[1] Porter's Holy Places of Syria, p. 316.

sixteen or eighteen miles, where they unite in a lower basin to form two marshy lakes.

To this river the city of Damascus owes its origin, its long existence and its distinctive charms. Everywhere amid groves and gardens, in public resorts and in quiet, retired nooks, the flash of its swiftly moving currents or the murmur of its unseen rivulets may be seen or heard. Every mosque and khan, every house and court has its fountain or fountains, and there are no restrictions on their constant flow. This paradise of the Arab world has been briefly described as "a 150 square miles of green, thronging and billowy as the sea, with the white compact city rising from it like an island. There is apparently all the lavishness of a virgin forest, but when you get down among it you find neither rankness nor jungle."[1] Here every shade of green is visible, from the dark of the orange to the silver-grey of the olive; every tinge of color from the rich bloom of the oleander and the damask rose to the snowy white of the almond and the apricot. On every side of Damascus, except the west there are numerous villages surrounded by gardens and orchards. On the right bank of the river, beyond the Ghutah proper, there is a notable expanse of greensward called the Merj. This is the favorite outdoor resort of the citizens of Damascus and the usual starting point for the caravans and pilgrim bands. There is not another city in Syria, says Dr. Thomson, which can boast of such a verdant meadow.

The Awaj river, supposed to be identical with the Pharpar, rises among the rugged clefts of Mount Hermon and flows eastward across the plain to a lake a few miles south of the twin lakes of the Barada. This stream borders the southern portion of the Ghutah, and contributes its share to the irrigation of the greater plain which lies beyond it. "Next to the Barada, this is the most important stream in all the region around Damascus; and is therefore most probably to be regarded as the Pharpar of Scripture."[2] These rivers of Damascus—the

[1] Smith's Hist. Geog., p. 644. [2] Rob. Phys. Geog., p. 365.

Abana and Pharpar—fresh from the mountains and capable of such wonderful transforming power, were regarded by Naaman the Syrian as "better than all the waters of Israel" (2 Kings v. 12), until he found in the Jordan the evidence of a Divinely-imparted efficacy far transcending the natural agencies of his own highly-favored land.

Damascus has more of the characteristic features of a city of the Caliphs than any other city of the East. The spirit of the Arabian Nights yet lingers in its streets and courts imparting to it a charm peculiarly its own. It is also true that "Damascus furnishes, in many respects, the best living illustrations of the Holy Book that are now to be found in any part of the Promised Land."[1] Its crowning glory is its undisputed antiquity. It holds the first place among all the great cities of the past ages because it is the only one which has retained its name and individuality unchanged. It has suffered from reverses, from sieges and frequent invasions; its streets have ofttimes been stained with the blood of its defenders and its defences have been reduced at times to a ruinous heap, but it has never become an utter desolation. It has never wholly lost its place of power and influence. With a present population of 250,000, it still holds its ancient place as the "head of Syria." In this sense it may be appropriately styled the "mother-city of the world."

Damascus was included in the *dominion* over which David and Solomon had rule, but it is not mentioned in the lists of the cities belonging to the inheritance of Israel.

In the second book of Kings we are told that "Jeroboam (II.) recovered Damascus and Hamath which belonged to Judah, for Israel" (xiv. 28), but this evidently means that he regained a portion of the empire over which Solomon had ruled. It does not necessarily imply that Damascus was a recovered part of Israel's possession. In this sense there could be no propriety in saying that it formerly belonged to Judah.

[1] The Land and the Book, p. 371.

In the book of Joshua we find that the inheritance of the two and one half tribes beyond Jordan included "all Mount Hermon, and all Bashan unto Salcah, and all the kingdom of Og in Bashan" (xiii. 11). Elsewhere it is recorded that "the children of the half tribe of Manasseh increased from Bashan unto Baal-Hermon and Senir, and unto Mount Hermon." (1 Chron. v. 23.) This extension was close to the border of the plain of Damascus if it did not include it, but at most it was only a temporary possession.

The situation of Damascus accounts for its close relationship to the people of Israel. Its unbroken history of more than four thousand years is interwoven with many of the prominent events in both the Old and the New Testament dispensations.

Josephus asserts that Damascus was founded by Uz, the great-grandson of Noah. There can be no doubt that it was on the line of Abram's journey to Canaan, and the tradition that he tarried for a time in or about this city is strengthened by the fact that the chief steward of the household, in his old days, was Eliezer of Damascus. This faithful servant was born in his house. (Gen. xv. 2, 3.) The city is mentioned for the first time in Scripture in connection with the story of Abram's pursuit of the army of Chadorlaomer. (Gen. xiv. 15.) When David extended his conquests northward to the Euphrates all of the country covered by the name "Aram of Damascus" fell into his hands. "Then David put garrisons in Syria of Damascus; and the Syrians became servants to David and brought gifts." (2 Sam. viii. 6.) This captured territory belonged to the empire of Solomon also, but in the latter part of his reign was held as a nominal rather than a real possession. (1 Chron. xviii. 6.) After the division of the kingdom of Israel the several tribes of Syria united their strength under one government the head of which was at Damascus. Between this aggressive power and the northern kingdom there was almost constant strife, until both came under the dominion of the Assyrians. At this time the inhabitants of Damascus were

The Anti-Lebanon Mountains

carried away into captivity unto Kir, as the prophet Amos had foretold (i. 5).

The home of Naaman, the famous captain of the hosts of the king of Syria, who was healed of his leprosy by the prophet Elisha, was in Damascus, and here dwelt the "little captive maid, brought away from the land of Israel," at whose earnest solicitation he undertook the journey to Samaria. From this city, Naaman went forth with horses and chariot and a retinue of servants, expecting to be healed in a manner comporting with his great rank and dignity, but ere he returned that way he had learned that there was "no God in all the earth, but in Israel." (2 Kings, chap. v.) During one of the brief intervals of peace between Israel and Syria, Elisha came to Damascus with a message from God to Hazael. Well knowing that his advancement to the throne of Syria was with a view to the execution of long-threatened judgments upon his own people, the prophet wept as he delivered his message. When Hazael knew the meaning of this uncontrollable emotion, he indignantly exclaimed, "Is thy servant a dog, that he should do this great thing." Notwithstanding this disclaimer Hazael, during his long and infamous reign, was guilty of all the atrocities that the prophet had foreseen and foretold. (2 Kings viii. 7–15.)

The most important and far-reaching event in the long history of Damascus was the conversion of Saul of Tarsus. Hither he came from Jerusalem, "breathing out threatenings and slaughter against the disciples of the Lord," but, ere he reached the confines of the city, a light above the brightness of the sun shone round about, and as he fell prostrate to the earth, he heard a voice saying unto him, Saul, Saul why persecutest thou me? In that supreme moment of his life the bigoted persecutor saw the glorified Saviour and recognized in Him the long-promised Messiah. From that moment he yielded himself without reserve to Him and to His service. Within the city, where his sight was restored after three days, Saul was baptized by Ananias. "And straightway he preached Jesus in the synagogues, that He is the Son of God." (Acts ix. 1-26.) Here as one has well said, in view of his baptism, "the rivers of Damascus," became more to him than "all the waters of Judah" had been. Driven from the city by the violence of the Jews, Paul went into Arabia. Some time afterward he returned again unto Damascus (Gal. i. 17) where he preached boldly and with great success in the name of Jesus. When at length it was known that the Jews were lying in wait to kill him "the disciples took him by night, and let him down by the wall in a basket." (Acts ix. 24, 25.) Over one of the portals of "the Great Mosque," which was once a Christian Cathedral, may still be seen the significant, prophetic words: "Thy kingdom, O Christ, is an everlasting kingdom, and Thy dominion endureth for all generations."

Helbon, a city noted for its wine and wool in the olden time (Ezek. xxvii. 18) has been identified with a village still bearing the same name, about nineteen miles north of Damascus. "It lies on the eastern slope of Anti-Lebanon in a deep and wild glen, the sides of which are covered with vineyards; and the vintners of Damascus regard the grapes of Helbon as the best in this part of Syria."[1]

Mount Hermon.—This majestic mountain stands out distinctly from the main range of Anti-Lebanon, and towers high above it. Its elevation above the sea is 9,383 feet. It is buttressed by ridges of lesser elevation, so compactly grouped around it that it seems to rise as one gigantic mass, almost directly from the plains that skirt it on the south and east. The noble contour of its glittering dome may be seen from the lowest reaches of the Jordan valley; from the shores of the Sea of Galilee; from the Huleh basin; and from almost every elevated plain, and mountain in Eastern and Western Palestine. As seen from the south it stands, with snowy summit reaching to the clouds, apparently at the very head of the great cleft between the great mountain ranges. From the east no better con-

[1] Barrow's Sacred Geog., p. 290.

ception of its appearance can be given than the poetic description of it in the book of Canticles,—"the tower which looketh toward Damascus" (vii. 4).

The crest of Hermon terminates in three peaks about one fourth of a mile apart. The lowest lies to the west; the two which lie to the north and south respectively, are about equal in height. The plural of the Hebrew name, "the Hermons"—incorrectly translated "the Hermonites"—is used in Psalm xlii. 6 with evident reference to the triple peaks of the mountain. Baal-Hermon seems to have been the designation of one of these peaks, or possibly, as Dr. Robinson suggests, of that part which was adjacent to the city Baal-Hermon. (Judg. iii. 3; 1 Chron. v. 23.) By the Phœnicians Hermon was called Sirion; by the Amorites, Shenir. (Deut. iii. 9.) It was also called Sion, "the lofty or elevated." Its modern name is Jebel esh Sheikh, the Chief Mountain or Mountain of the Chief. Hermon was the sacred mountain of the ancient worshippers of Baal. The remains of a temple have been excavated on its summit near the southern peak, and the whole of the mountain, as Dr. Robinson puts it, "was girdled with temples. They are found in all situations crowning hills and mountain-tops, or secluded in deep valleys and gorges."[1]

The view from the summit of this mountain, when it is free from clouds, is said to be unequalled in its sweep, especially toward the east, where the dim outlines of Jebel Hauran, seventy miles away, may be seen; and toward the south, where the whole of the depressed line of the Jordan can be traced. In midsummer the snow melts away from the smooth faces of the upper slopes of Hermon, but it remains in the deep furrows and clefts throughout the entire year. As ordinarily seen by travellers to the East its lofty heights are covered with a glittering mantle of ice and snow. On the twentieth of March we found snowdrifts so deep as to be almost impassable, on the road to Damascus over the shoulder of Hermon, at an elevation of less

[1] Bib. Res., p. 409.

than 5,000 feet. The crystal streams which issue from this mass of slowly-melting snow pour out from the base of the mountain to the south and west, going down by the valleys, and through each successive level of the descending course of the Jordan to the deep basin of the Dead Sea. Here the imprisoned waters, obeying the impulse of another great law of nature, begin to ascend in the form of vapor, steaming up as from a heated chaldron, to the summit of the hills. Thence, by the subtile movements of other forces and currents, it hastens by an irresistible attraction to the " place of the gathering of the clouds " directly over the lofty summit of Hermon. The descent of the rain, the copious dews or the feathery flakes of snow—from the clouds, which thus collect over the mountain, complete this circuit of never-ending movements and transformations. Here where cloud and snow can hardly be distinguished the phenomenon which the wise man of Israel noted many centuries ago is evermore repeated; and in a circuit so contracted that its farthest limit comes within the range of ordinary vision. " Unto the place from whence the rivers come, thither they return to go again." (Eccl. i. 7.)

The Place of the Transfiguration was probably on one of the elevated platforms on the southern slope of Hermon, in the vicinity of Cæsarea Philippi. There is no intimation that our Lord returned to Galilee in the six days that intervened between the first announcement of His approaching death, and the scene of the Transfiguration.

Evidently this was a period of retirement from the world for a definite purpose and this wonderful manifestation of the glory of the incarnate Saviour was the closing event in this sacred preparation period. On that memorable evening Jesus took three of the inner circle of His disciples to some point on this "high mountain apart by themselves" for a season of uninterrupted communion and prayer. "It is natural to suppose," says Dean Farrar, "that our Lord, anxious to traverse the Holy Land of His birth to its northern limit, journeyed slowly forward till he reached the lower slopes of that splendid snow-clad mountain, whose glittering mass, visible even as far south as the Dead Sea, magnificently closes the northern frontier of Palestine—the Mount Hermon of Jewish poetry. Its very name means 'the mountain' (Luke ix. 28), and the scene which it witnessed would well suffice to procure for it the distinction of being the only mountain to which in Scripture is attached the epithet 'holy.' On these dewy pasturages, cool and fresh with the breath of the snow-clad heights above them, and offering that noble solitude among the grandest scenes of nature, which He desired as the refreshment of His soul for the mighty struggle which was now so soon to come, Jesus would find many a spot where He could kneel with His disciples absorbed in silent prayer."[1] "There, as He prayed He was transfigured before them : and His face did shine as the sun, and His raiment was white as the light. And behold there appeared unto them Moses and Elias talking with Him." "And there was a cloud that overshadowed them : and a voice came out of the cloud, saying, This is my beloved Son : hear Him." (Matt. xvii. 1-8; Mark ix. 1-9; Luke vii. 28.) "There was a deep significance in the time and place at which this manifestation of Divine glory was made. It was the northern limit of His earthly ministry. It was also at the close of His last missionary journey. Henceforward His face was 'steadfastly set to go up to Jerusalem,' for 'the time was come that He should be received up.' He now commenced the pilgrimage southward of which the cross was the foreseen goal. Step by step along the return road He pressed onward, each step bringing Him nearer to the decease which He should accomplish at Jerusalem, of which 'Moses and Elias spake with Him' as they appeared in glory."[2]

While by common consent Mount Hermon is accorded a place among the Sacred Mountains, it is generally regarded as a border land-mark *outside* the inheritance of Israel. In other

[1] Life of Christ, p. 242.   [2] Dr. Manning's Holy Fields, p. 219.

words the boundaries of the land on the west, south and east, as usually defined, extend only to the base or outskirts of Mount Hermon. This virtual exclusion of the "Holy Mount" from the "Holy Land" does not seem to be warranted by the Bibical definition of the trans-Jordanic territory. In the book of Joshua the statement is made that Og king of the race of giants "*reigned in Mount Hermon* and in Salcah and in all Bashan." (Josh. xii. 4, 5.) Following this is the record that the northern portion of the inheritance which Moses gave to Israel beyond Jordan, eastward, included "*all Mount Hermon*, and all Bashan unto Salcah." (Josh. xiii. 11.) It is true that the extent of this possession as a whole, is elsewhere indicated by the brief formula—"from the river of Arnon unto Mount Hermon" (Deut. iii. 8, iv. 48, etc.), but this phraseology does not necessarily *exclude* the mountain, or any part of it. Its equivalent is the more familiar phrase—"from Dan even to Beersheba." In this case Beersheba is as certainly included as Dan. A similar expression occurs in the description of the boundary eastward, viz:—"all Bashan *unto* Salcah and Edrei, *cities of the kingdom of Og.*" These border towns were noted cities of the Amorite king, and afterward became a part of the possession of the half tribe of Manasseh. (Deut iii. 13; Josh. xii. 6.) The statement above quoted—"all Mount Hermon, and all Bashan unto Salcah"—is given in connection with the account of the actual distribution of the land in accordance with the original assignment by Moses, and it is as definite as language can make it. It is possible that Hermon was the "high hill of Bashan" to which reference is made in Psalm lxviii. 14, 15, but it is usually named with Bashan as though it were regarded as distinct from it. It is certain, however, as Dr. Smith intimates, that the reference to Bashan in Deut. xxxiii. 22—"*Dan is a lion's whelp; he leapeth from Bashan*" carries the name to the very foot of Hermon. "Whether Hermon itself was known as the *mount or mountains of Bashan*, or whether the latter name designates the whole of that eastern range is uncertain—the poet says, *mountains of bold heights are the mount of Bashan.* This epithet, not applicable to the long, level edge of the table-land, might refer either to the lofty triple summit of Hermon, or to the many broken cones that are scattered across Bashan, and so greatly differ in their volcanic form from the softer, less imposing heights of Western Palestine."

[1] Hist. Geog., p. 550.

CHAPTER XXII

THE TRANS-JORDANIC HIGHLANDS

THE inheritance given by Moses to the two and one half tribes on "the side of Jordan toward the sun rising," included all the territory taken out of the hands of the two Amorite kings Sihon and Og. (Deut. iii. 1-16; Josh. xii. 1-6, xiii. 8-15.) Its boundary on the north was on or near the southern limit of Aram of Damascus. On the east it was bordered by the irregular line of the desert; on the south by the river Arnon.

The territory thus defined is not less than 130 miles in length. In breadth it varies from twenty-five to seventy or eighty miles. The widest part is at the upper or northern end. It is a broad expanse of table-land throughout the greater part of its extent. Its average elevation is nearly 2,000 feet above sea level or 2,800 above the level of the Jordan valley. The elevated region between the river Arnon and the lower end of the Dead Sea was the possession of the Moabites when Israel reached the Jordan, and was secured from invasion by the command of Jehovah. (Deut. ii. 9.) Moab was tributary to Israel during the reign of David and Solomon, and after the separation of Israel from Judah continued under Israel until after the death of Ahab. This territory is so closely related to the adjoining possession of the Israelites north of the Arnon, and so closely associated with its people and its history that it is usually grouped with it under the name of Moab.

The Old Testament divisions of the land, east of the Jordan, now known as Eastern Palestine, were Bashan, Gilead and Moab. We shall follow these divisions in their order in the study of this section.

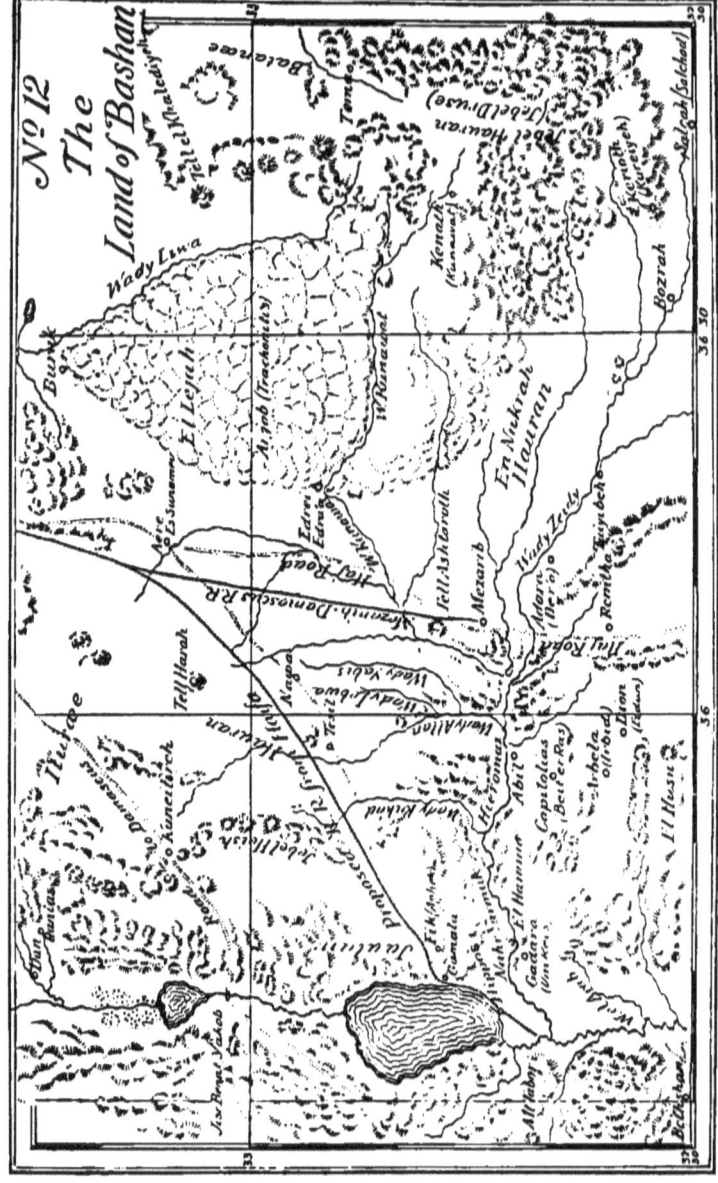

The Trans-Jordanic Highlands

I. BASHAN.

The land of Bashan extends from the border of the highland region south of the Awaj or Pharpar river to the river Yarmuk or Hieromax. The line of division between Bashan and Gilead inclines to the southeast and terminates at Salcah, on the edge of the desert, at the lower end of the Jebel Hauran.

The district of Jedur, which was called Iturea in the days of the Roman occupation (Luke iii. 1), occupies the northmost portion of this territory. The southern boundary of Iturea is not definitely given, but it probably extended in a southeast direction as far down as the latitude of the northern end of Lake Huleh. This district was occupied in the period of the Judges, and possibly from an earlier date, by a strong force of Hagarites, or Ishmaelites, who gave their names to its towns. The district itself took its name from Jetur, a son of Ishmael. (Gen. xxv. 15.) Jedur is a rich pastoral region to which the descendants of Ishmael still come from the edge of the desert in the early spring to find pastures for their flocks and herds. In the days of King Saul, the Hagarite occupants of this portion of the country were conquered by the Israelites beyond Jordan and the children of Manasseh took possession of their cities "and dwelt in their stead until the captivity. The spoils taken at this time included 50,000 camels, 250,000 sheep and 2,000 asses." (1 Chron. v. 18–23.)

Canon Tristram describes Jedur as "a table-land with many conical hills: the southern portion consisting of fine pasture plains, but the northern, nearer Hermon, very different, looking like a stormy sea of black molten rock suddenly arrested and petrified, which indeed it is, being a rugged surface of lava, with deep fissures in all directions." Dr. Porter collected the names of thirty-eight ruined sites in this district, but none of them have any Scripture associations.

South of Jedur Bashan divides naturally into three longitudinal sections, known as the Jaulan (Gaulanitis), the Hauran, and the Lejah or Trachonitis.

The Jaulan takes its name from Golan one of its chief cities, which Moses designated as the northern city of refuge. (Deut. iv. 43; Josh. xx. 8, xxi. 27.) This district includes the western slope of the mountains with a broad strip of the plateau on the summit, from the basin of the Huleh under Hermon to the Yarmuk.

"The Roman province of Gaulanites," says Dr. Smith, "must have been practically the same as the present Jaulan, or all the country between the Yarmuk (Hieromax) and Hermon, with an uncertain eastern border along perhaps the river Allan." Its width in this case at the widest part would be about fifteen miles. Schumacher, who has surveyed and described the Jaulan, estimates its extent to be about 560 square miles. Like the Jedur this district abounds in rich pastures. It rises by a series of steps or terraces to the breezy heights which stretch far beyond its limits, and its ruined sites indicate that it once sustained a large settled population. Oak forests cover some of the conical hills and are occasionally found along the slopes of the mountains. Golan, the city which gave this district its name, has not been satisfactorily identified. A possible site, suggested by Dr. Merrill, is Nawa near the source of Wady Allan.

Tell Ashtarah a few miles south of Nawa is supposed to be the site of the city of Ashtaroth, of the Rephaim. (Gen. xiv. 5; Deut. i. 4; Josh. xii. 4.)

Aphek, now Fik, is situated at the head of Wady Fik on the high road to Damascus. This place was the scene of two battles with the Syrians which resulted in victory to the Israelites. (1 Kings xx. 26–30; 2 Kings xiii. 17.)

Gamala (Kulat-el Husn) has been mentioned in connection with the sites on the eastern shore of Galilee.

The Hauran, strictly speaking, extends eastward of the Jaulan to the desert. In its narrower sense it applies to the level treeless plain between the Jaulan and the Lejah and southeastward to the Jebel Hauran range. This central plain is nearly fifty miles in length and fifteen or twenty in width. The portion of the plain which inclines to the southeast and is directly south of the lava district (El Lejah) is called En Nukra (Hollow Hearth) by the Arabs. Some authorities apply the name Hauran to this portion exclusively and extend the limits of the Jaulan so as to include all of the plateau west of the Lejah.

The great Hajj road traverses the length of the Hauran and the Damascus road which enters the Jaulan by way of Wady Fik enters it in the vicinity of Nawa and continues northward in close proximity to the Hajj. The proposed railroad to Damascus takes the same route. The Damascus-Hauran railroad runs directly south to Mezarib very near the lower end of the great plain. This road is now carrying grain and produce of various kinds to Damascus and is reported to be a profitable investment.

The loose volcanic soil of the Hauran produces the finest wheat in all Syria. The grain is hard and semi-transparent and the yield is enormous. "The natural wealth of the soil here," says Dr. Merrill, "is a constant surprise. I have seen men on this plain turning furrows which were nearly one mile in length and as straight as one could draw a line." This description of the southern portion of the plain is applicable to it throughout its whole extent. Dr. Smith gives the following description of its harvests and threshing floors:

The surface of the plain is broken only by a mound or two, by a few shallow water-courses, by some short outcrops of basalt, and by villages of the same stone, the level black line of their roofs cut by a tower or the jagged gable of an old temple.

All else is a rolling prairie of rich, red soil, under wheat, or lying for the year fallow in pasture. It is a land of harvest, and if you traverse it in summer fills you with the wonder of its wealth. Through the early day the camels, piled high with sheaves, five or seven swaying corn stacks on a string, draw in from the fields to the threshing-floors. These lie along the village walls, each of them some fifty square yards of the plain, trodden hard and fenced by a low, dry dyke. The sheaves are strewn to the depth of two or three feet, and the threshing sledges, curved slabs of wood, studded with basalt teeth, are dragged up and down by horses, driven by boys who stand on the sledges and sing as they plunge over the billows of straw. Poor men have their smaller crops trodden out by donkeys driven in a narrow circle three abreast, exactly in the fashion depicted on the old Egyptian monuments.

When the whole mass is cut and bruised enough, it is tossed with great forks against the afternoon wind, the chopped straw is stored for fodder in some ancient vault that has kept the rain out since the days of Agrippa or the Antonines; but the winnowed grain is packed in bags and carried on camels to the markets of Damascus and Acre.[1]

The Lejah.—The Hauran plain is bordered on the east by a lava district absolutely unique in its physical characteristics. It is called El Lejah "the refuge" by the Arabs. Its identification with Trachonitis "the rough region" of the Greeks, (Luke iii. 1) and with Argob "the stony" of the Hebrews (Deut. iii. 4) has been satisfactorily established.

The Lejah is a vast uplifted mass of congealed lava, sixty miles in circumference and 350 square miles in extent. It is an irregular oval in outline, about twenty-five miles in length from north to south by fifteen in breadth. This rugged mass, which rises to an elevation of twenty to thirty feet above the plain, is encircled by a rampart "as clearly defined as a rocky shore line."

The Lejah has been described as a "tempest in stone"; as a "black motionless sea, with waves of petrified lava"; as "an impregnable mountain fortress"; and a "labyrinth" whose intricacies, and cavernous depths and winding paths can only be traced by a native guide. "Although barren and incapable of cultivation, and almost entirely destitute of fountains and streams, yet there are several "pasturing places" in and about the Lejah; and it is dotted with the remains of old towns, some of which were places of considerable size and importance. Thither the people restorted in ancient times from all sides, and in this Lejah or asylum they dwelt secure from the raids of law-

[1] Hist. Geog., p. 612.

less tribes, and bade defiance to the attacks of even regular and well-disciplined troops."[1] "The bed in its outline or edge," says Dr. Merrill, "is far from being regular, but sends out at a multitude of points black promontories of rock into the surrounding plain. Through this rugged shore there are a few openings into the interior, but for the most part it is impassable, and roads had to be excavated to the towns situated within it."[2]

The Lejah or Argob was the stronghold of the kingdom of Og. In this region, at the time of the conquest, were "threescore cities, all fenced with high walls, gates and bars; beside unwalled towns a great many." (Deut. iii. 4, 5.) It is also recorded that "Jair the son of Manasseh took all the country of Argob unto the coasts of Geshuri and Maachathi; and called them after his own name, Bashan-havoth-jair." (Deut. iii. 14.) In Solomon's time it had lost none of its distinctive features, for it is reported in the list of tribute paying districts as a region containing "threescore great cities with walls and brazen bars." (1 Kings iv. 13.) It is interesting to note in this connection that more than seventy-five villages and cities of ancient towns have been found by explorers within and immediately around the Lejah. Many of these are deserted cities or dead towns, and "are still in such a condition that but few repairs are necessary to render them habitable. The explanation is, that all the dwellings and larger edifices in this region were constructed entirely of stone gateways, walls, doors, windows, stairs, and roofs were all made of the imperishable doleritic lava, hard as adamant."[3]

Of the sixty great cities of the Argob only two are mentioned by name—Edrei and Kenath—and these have been identified with two of the ancient cities which encircle the rocky rampart of the Lejah.

[1] Porter's Five years in Damascus, p. 282.
[2] Merrill's East of Jordan, p. 11.
[3] The Land and The Book, p. 470.

Edrei, now known as Edhra, stands on a rocky promontory forty or fifty feet above the plain on the southwest border of the Lejah. It is almost due east of Nawa, and about sixty miles from the north end of the Sea of Galilee. On the maps of eastern Palestine Edhra is frequently designated by its Roman name Zora or Zorava.

> "This ancient city is in a locality which meets the requirements of the Biblical narrative, and still bears a name which may be regarded as identical with that mentioned by Moses. (Deut. iii. 1.) The existing ruins are nearly four miles in circumference, and although many of the houses and other edifices in their present condition are of an age comparatively modern, yet they were erected on foundations and out of materials far more ancient. Most of the present inhabitants reside in the vaults of old structures which may fairly be said to be under ground, so great is the accumulation above them of the débris of ruined buildings. To reach them one has to descend into subterranean courts and caverns."[1]
>
> "The most interesting remains," says Tristram, "are the small houses of remote antiquity, known familiarly as those of the giant cities, with their walls of great blocks of basalt, closely fitted, but not in regular courses, their stone roofs and their solid stone doors and windows still moving in the same sockets or cup and ball joints on which they have turned for thousands of years."[2]

Edrei was the capital of the giant King Og, and the battlefield where he lost his life and kingdom was in the immediate vicinity. (Num. xxi. 33–35 ; Josh. xii. 4, xiii. 12.)

The ruins of an ancient city called Dera or Dra'a, sixteen miles southwest of Edhra have been suggested as a possible site of Edrei, but the northern city appears to have the weight of argument and authority in its favor. It is possible that there were two places with the same name in Bashan, as some writers have suggested, and that Dra'a or Dera was the place mentioned in Deut. i. 4, and Josh. xii. 4, in connection with Ashtaroth.

Kenath, (Kanatha of the Greeks) has been identified with a ruined city of large proportions at the lower or southeast extremity of the Lejah, called Kunawat. "The city overlooks a

---
[1] The Land and the Book, p. 461.   [2] Holy Land, p. 305.

vast region, and is surrounded by a cluster of cities or towns, all within a distance of half an hour or two hours from it. There could not be a more appropriate phrase than 'Kenath with her daughter towns,' (Num. xxii. 42; 1 Chron. ii. 23), which is applied to this ancient city in the midst of a large group of smaller, but still important places."[1] The following description of the present appearance of Kunawat is given by Dr. Porter:

> The wall, still in many places almost perfect, follows the top of the cliffs for nearly a mile, and then sweeps round in a zigzag course, enclosing a space about half a mile wide. The general aspect of the city is very striking—temples, palaces, churches, theatres, and massive buildings whose original use we cannot tell, are grouped together in picturesque confusion; while beyond the walls, in the glen, on the summits and sides of wooded peaks, away in the midst of oak forests, are clusters of columns and massive towers, and lofty tombs. The leading streets are wide and regular, and the roads radiating from the city gates are unusually numerous and spacious. . . . Many of the ruins of Kenath are beautiful and interesting. The highest part of the site was the aristocratic quarter. Here is a noble palace, no less than three temples and a hippodrome once profusely adorned with statues. In no other part of Palestine did I see so many statues as there are here. Unfortunately they are all mutilated; but fragments of them—heads, legs, arms, torsos, with equestrian figures, lions, leopards, and dogs—meet one on every side. A colossal head of Ashtaroth, sadly broken, lies before a little temple, of which probably it was once the chief idol. The crescent moon which gave the name Carnaim ("two horned") to the goddess is on her brow.
>
> About a quarter of a mile west of the city is a beautiful peripteral temple of the Corinthian order, built on an artificial platform. Many of the columns have fallen, and the walls are much shattered; but enough remains to make this one of the most picturesque ruins in the whole country.[2]

It is recorded in the book of Numbers that "Nobah went and took Kenath and the villages thereof, and called it Nobah, after his own name" (xxxii. 42). It was known by this name

[1] Merrill's East of the Jordan, p. 37.
[2] Giant Cities of Bashan, p. 42, 43.

in the period of the Judges, for we are told that Gideon, when pursuing the two kings of Midian, "went up by the way of them that dwell in tents on the east of Nobah, and smote the host." (Judg. viii. 4-11.) In later times the old name was restored. Afterward it took the form of Kanatha. Kenath was one of the cities of the Decapolis and the farthest to the east, in this group.

Jebel Hauran.—The range of mountains which borders the east side of En Nukra—the lower basin of the great plain—is usually designated as Jebel Hauran. It is sometimes called the Druse mountain or Jebel ed Druze. The length of the range is about forty miles. It has several conspicuous peaks and divergent spurs. The highest point, El Kuleib, is 5,730 feet above the sea. These mountains have been described as "picturesque and occasionally even grand." The ridges are clothed with forests of evergreen oak and the slopes give evidence of careful terrace-cultivation in former times. The best specimens of the famous "oaks of Bashan" grow on these rocky heights, and the richest portion of the Hauran, "the granary of Syria" lies at their base. Farther to the north and west were the great cattle ranges, to which reference has been already made, where "rams of the breed of Bashan" and "bulls of Bashan" found nourishing pasturages long centuries ago; and where flocks and herds still roam in almost countless numbers. Says Dr. Smith:

"One afternoon which we spent at Edrei, the Aneezeh tribe, that roams from Euphrates to Jordan, drove their camels upon the plain to the north of the town till we counted nearly a thousand feeding, and there was a multitude more behind. Next day we passed their foes, the Beni Sahr, one of whose camel-herds numbered 400, and another 200. We looked southeast from the hills above Amman, and there were hundreds more of the Sherarat Arabs from Ma'an. '*Profusion of camels shall cover thee, camels of Midian and Ephah, all of them from Sheba shall come.*' The Bedouin had also many sheep and goats. The herds of the settled inhabitants were still more numerous." [1]

[1] Hist. Geog., p. 523.

The Trans-Jordanic Highlands

The exact limits of the district of Batanæa cannot be defined, but it is generally agreed that it included the Jebel Hauran range and a portion of the territory directly north of it which is still known as "Ard el Bathanyeh, the land of Bathanyeh."

Salcah, the eastern frontier city of the kingdom of Og and of the possession of Israel, has been identified with the ruins of a city at the southern end of Jebel Hauran, which still bears the name of Sulkhad. This frontier town, beyond which to the east lies the great desert, was defended by a fortress on a conical hill 300 feet above the level of the surrounding country. Its great castle—the Gibraltar of the desert—is a prominent landmark from the "plain country" on every side. It is built in the mouth of an extinct crater, on a conical swell or rise composed of porous lava-rock. The walls of the castle are from eighty to 100 feet high. As the crater is bowl-shaped, there is a deep natural moat entirely around the castle, and the fortress is approached by a bridge over the moat. The interior of this castle is a perfect labyrinth of halls, galleries, chambers, and vaults, which are now in a very confused and ruined state."[1] Dr. Porter estimates the circumference of the town and castle together to be about three miles. Some 500 of the houses of Salcah are still standing and "from 300 to 400 families might settle in it at any moment without laying a stone, or expending an hour's labor on repairs.[2] From the castle Dr. Porter counted upward of thirty deserted towns.

The expression "all Bashan unto Salcah" is used in two passages in describing the territory of King Og. (Deut. iii. 10; Josh. xiii. 11.) At a later period it is said that the children of Gad dwelt in the land of Bashan unto Salcah." (1 Chron. v. 11.) It may be inferred from these references, but especially from the last, which indicates the dividing line at that time between Gad and Manasseh, that Salkah was the farthest town on the eastern border of Bashan.

[1] East of the Jordan, p. 50.   [2] Giant Cities of Bashan, p. 76.

Another ancient stronghold of this region, whose ruins are said to be as extensive as those of Salcah, lies in a broad valley at the south-western base of Jebel Hauran. It is called Kureieh by the Arabs and is supposed to be the representative of the city of Kerioth to which reference is made in Jer. xlviii. 21 and Amos ii. 2. Several towns in this vicinity are mentioned in connection with prophetic denunciations against Moab. The explanation is found in the fact that the Moabites had recovered for a time their old pasture-lands on these upland plains as far north probably as the edge of the Hauran. (See Isa. chaps. xv. and xvi; Jer. xlviii. 3; Ezek. xxv. 8-11, etc.)

Bosrah, now Busrah, was the chief city of this region in the period of the Roman occupation, and was then known as Bostra. It is twelve miles west of Salcah on the line of the great Military and caravan route which crossed the Jordan below the Sea of Galilee and thence extended eastward to the desert in the direction of the Persian Gulf.

Bozrah of Bashan is probably the city to which reference is made in Jer. xlviii. 24, and should be distinguished from Bozrah of Edom. (Isa. lxiii. 1.)

"The ruins of Bozrah," says Dr. Porter, "are nearly five miles in circuit; its walls are lofty and massive; and its castle is one of the largest and strongest fortresses in Syria. Among the ruins I saw two theatres, six temples, and ten or twelve churches and mosques; besides palaces, baths, fountains, aqueducts, triumphal arches, and other structures almost without number. The old Bozrites must have been men of great taste and enterprise as well as wealth. Some of the buildings I saw there would grace the proudest capital of modern Europe. . . . Bozrah had once a population of 100,000 souls and more; when I was there its whole inhabitants comprised just twenty families! These lived huddled together in the lower stories of some very ancient houses near the castle. The rest of the city is completely desolate."[1]

The ruined cities of the Hauran furnish abundant evidence on every hand of the characteristic features of Greek and Ro-

[1] Giant Cites of Bashan, p. 64.

man civilizations. Everywhere Greek architecture inscriptions and statuary are found side by side with Roman fortresses, temples, theatres, and Roman roads. With these also are found the remains of Christian basilicas and unquestionable evidences on tablets of imperishable basalt of the existence of active Christian communities throughout this province in the days of persecution and martyrdom for the Gospel's sake. " The Christians of this region must have suffered, like those of the rest of Syria, in the persecutions under Decius and Diocletian, and it is perhaps owing to the latter Emperor's order for the destruction of all Christian buildings that we have so very few Christian remains earlier than his day. Traces of these great persecutions are still eloquent in Hauran. Here is 'the cryptogram for Christ, the Ichthus of the Catacombs. Here as in the Catacombs the dead are spoken of as "they that sleep," and many bits of basalt have been found with the words, or syllables of the words, Martyr and Martyr's Monument. These latter meet you in almost every village, rendering its very dust dear to your Christian heart. Even the nomads raised monuments to the martyrs. One longer inscription runs: For the repose of the Martyrs who have fallen asleep; it reminds of Stephen. The erection of such memorials proves a day in which Christianity was able to show itself in public, and there are others that record its gradual triumph over paganism. In several places have been found the words 'Help O Christ.' On the lintel of a house at Tuffas: 'Jesus Christ be the shelter and defence of all the family of the house, and bless their incoming and their outgoing.' On another tablet is the quotation, similarly adapted to Christ : ' If the Lord watch not the city, in vain doth the watchman keep awake.' Other notable expressions of faith and feeling are : ' O Christ, our God ' ; ' the Peace of Christ be to all ' ; ' Peace be to all men,' etc."[1]

Explorers and archæologists differ in opinion with respect to the age of the massive basaltic structures which characterize the

[1] Smith's Hist. Geog., p. 632-4.

cities in and around the Lejah. They belong unquestionably to a type peculiar to the region itself, and are found for the most part upright and unbroken, amid the magnificent ruins of Greek and Roman architecture which once overshadowed them.

One class of explorers represented by Waddington, De Vogüé and Smith assert with positive emphasis that these structures were built in the period of the Roman occupation, and present in evidence of their assertions the Greek and Roman inscriptions, and the Christian symbols, found upon them or scattered about in their immediate vicinity. These Cyclopean walls and cities of stone are designated as "the shells of the Roman peace." They are, in other words, the kind of cities which Rome would be likely to build out of the materials at hand, on this frontier province so often overswept by marauding bands from the desert. "In some primeval tranquillity of man," says Dr. Smith, "'giant cities of Bashan' may have risen, as is alleged, on this margin of the desert: but if so, these are not their ruins."[1] De Vogüé, who has given his views of Hauran architecture in a costly and beautifully illustrated volume, asserts that he had not met with structures of a more ancient date than the first to the seventh centuries of our era. These views are based upon the assumption, buttressed, as its supporters claim, by evidences drawn from the region itself, that the Hauran, prior to the period of the Roman occupation, was held by a succession of nomadic tribes, who were incapable of erecting such elaborate and carefully planned structures.

Another class of explorers, represented by Ritter, Porter and Tristram, have been convinced, as the result of careful study of this type of Hauran architecture and its comparison with the Biblical descriptions of this region in the time of Moses, that the wonderful cities now found in and around the Lejah, with their gates and bars, and habitations of imperishable basalt, are the actual remains of the ancient giant cities of Bashan. In support of this view, it is argued that the number and positions

[1] Smith's Hist. Geog., p. 624.

of these stone cities correspond with the Argob cities of the Biblical record; that the names of some of them have come down to us with locations which correspond with the sacred narrative; that in some cases these basaltic structures have been overlaid by easily distinguished structures of Greek and Roman architecture;[1] and that the assumption of a continuous reign of barbarism in the Hauran prior to the Roman occupation is not in accord with the historical descriptions given of this country and the inducements its conquest offered to invaders from eastern lands. The following quotations from the works of Porter and Tristram give the main arguments in support of this view:

 The simplicity of the style of these buildings, their low roofs, the ponderous blocks of roughly hewn stone with which they are built, the great thickness of the walls, and the heavy slabs which form the ceilings,—all point to a period far earlier than the Roman age, and probably even antecedent to the conquest of the country by the Israelites. Moses makes special mention of the strong cities of Bashan, and speaks of their high walls and gates. He tells us, too, in the same connection, that Bashan was called *the land of the giants* (or Rephaim, Deut. iii. 13); leaving us to conclude that the cities were built by giants. Now the houses of Kerioth and other towns in Bashan appear to be just such dwellings as a race of giants would build. The walls, the roofs, but especially the ponderous gates, doors, and bars, are in every way characteristic of a period when architecture was in its infancy, when giants were masons, and when strength and security were the grand requisites. I measured a door in Kerioth: it was nine feet high, four and a half feet wide, and ten inches thick,—one solid slab of stone. I saw the folding gates of another town in the mountains still larger and heavier. Time produces little effect on such buildings as these. The heavy stone slabs of the roofs resting on the massive walls make the structure as firm as if built of solid masonry; and the black basalt used is almost as hard as iron. There can scarcely be a doubt, therefore, that these are the very cities erected and inhabited by the Rephaim, the original occupants of Bashan; and the language of Ritter appears to be true: "These buildings remain as eternal witnesses of the conquest of Bashan by Jehovah."[2]

 The evidence of the sixty cities of Argob, says Tristram, is patent. The cities are there, and more than sixty, all attesting their antiquity by

[1] The Land and the Book, p. 475.   [2] Giant Cities, p. 84.

their antique Cyclopean architecture, with the basalt slabs for roofs and doors. We read of their gates and bars. The huge doors and gates of stone eighteen inches thick, and the places for the bars, which can still be seen, take us back to the very time of Moses; perhaps even earlier—for, in the first campaign recorded in history, Chedorlaomer smote the *Rephaims in Ashteroth Karnaim.* (Gen. xiv. 5.) . . . The buildings, like their names, may have come down from the days of Abraham. Chedorlaomer also smote the *Emims* in the plain of *Kiriathaim*, and the houses of Kureiyeh, or *Kerioth*, are probably the very work of the Emims. In the days of the Romans these places were held to be the work of the ancient inhabitants (M. Marcellin). This could not have been said of any Greek or Græco-Syrian building; and we may be quite sure that the tent-loving children of Manasseh were not a building race. Besides cities of some sort were there when they took the land; and it is more reasonable to suppose that not the Amorite, whom they dispossessed, but even *their* predecessors, the *Rephaim*, were the constructors, than to bring them down to a later date.[1]

Among those who accept without hesitation the Biblical testimony that Bashan had fortified cities and a settled population long before the Roman period, there are many who do not regard these habitations *in their present condition* as necessarily the work of the aborigines of the country. There can scarcely be a doubt that they for the most part occupy the sites of these ancient cities, and also represent a type of architecture which has prevailed in this region from the earliest ages, but it is scarcely conceivable that several successive nationalites should occupy these structures without making changes or modifications, even if time and the destructive forces of nature had left them unharmed. "The fact should be considered," says Dr. Merrill, "that in this country the eligible sites for cities would be selected when men first began to build, and such would remain the eligible sites as long as the country was inhabited by civilized races. It is therefore impossible to say how many layers of civilization may exist beneath any one of these important Hauran towns."[2] On this point rather than upon the actual

[1] Holy Land, p. 306. [2] East of the Jordan, p. 74.

No 13
Gilead and Moab

identification of the habitations which remain with the giant builders of the kingdom of Og, the stress should be laid.

There is certainly as good evidence for the identification of some of these places—apart from their associations with the Rephaim—with the cities occupied by the Israelites from Moses to Solomon, and presumably much longer, as for the identification of many of the cities whose sites are accepted without hesitation on the western side of the Jordan.

Job's country—the land of Uz—according to an ancient tradition of the Arabs, was situated in Southern Bashan. M. Waddington found an inscription in honor of Job at Bosrah (Busrah), and several localities in this region have been associated with his name and trials. The history of this tradition, and the arguments in favor of it, are summed up in Oliphant's Land of Gilead, pp. 83-91. While it is generally agreed that some portion of the "land of the East" *i. e.*, east of the Jordan valley or Arabah—on the border of the desert, is clearly indicated in the Book of Job, the weight of authority, at the present time, is in favor of the country bordering the desert near Petra in the land of Edom.

II. GILEAD.

The land of Gilead, as usually defined, is bounded on the north by the Yarmuk; on the south by the Wady Heshbon, which enters the Ghor near the upper end of the Dead Sea. Its extent from north to south is sixty miles.

The Yarmuk river receives a number of tributary streams which flow across the great plain from Jebel Hauran, but its perennial sources are in the vicinity of Mezarib. Here the Yarmuk proper begins. One of its principal southern tributaries, the Wady Zeideh, coming from the mountains near Salcah, may be regarded as the dividing line between Bashan and Gilead east of Mezarib. The Yarmuk flows a little north of east for nearly half its length, and thence southwest to the Jordan valley. For most of its course it passes through wild ravines and narrow, deeply-cleft chasms. "The river in the mountains runs with great swiftness along its rocky chasm; in the Ghor it has its own lower valley, like the Jordan; and is everywhere thickly skirted with oleanders. The stream is here about forty yards wide; and in the spring of the year is four or five feet deep. It enters the Jordan five miles below the lake of Tiberias; and has there nearly as much water as the Jordan."

The Jabbok (Nahr ez-Zerka) enters the Ghor a little more than half-way between the Yarmuk and the Wady Heshbon. The district north of it, sometimes designated as Northern Gilead, is a rugged, undulating ridge corresponding in its natural features to the range on the western side of the Jordan. It differs from it, however, in its exuberant fertility, and its picturesque combinations of densely-wooded heights, open glades, grass-covered knolls, and gently-rolling stretches of corn and pasture lands. The modern name of this mountain tract is Jebel Ajlun. In Southern Gilead the mountains adjacent to the line of the Jabbok rise to the highest elevation of the series, but farther to the south the summit of the range broadens out into a wide expanse of table-land, corresponding to the great upland plains of Bashan and Moab. The Arabs call the whole of Gilead south of the Jabbok the Belka. It was held by Sihon the Amorite king at the time of the conquest, but had formerly been a portion of the possession of Moab. (Num. xxi. 24–26.)

"From first to last, the valley of the Jabbok is of great fertility. The head-waters of the river rise on the edge of Moab, only some eighteen miles from the Jordan, yet to the east of the water-parting. So the river flows at first desertwards, under the name of Amman, past Rabbath-Ammon to the great Hajj road. There it turns north, fetches a wide compass northwest, cuts in two the range of Gilead, and by a very winding bed flows west-southwest to the Jordan. The whole course, not counting the windings, is over sixty miles. The water is shallow, always fordable, except where it breaks between steep rocks, mostly brawling over a stony bed, muddy, and, at a distance, of a grey-blue color, which brings it its present name of the Zerka. The best fields are upon the upper reaches, where much wheat is grown, but almost nowhere on the banks are you out of sight of sheep, or cattle, or tillage. A great road from Jordan follows the valley all the way to the desert, another runs from the desert by Amman to the west. The river has always been a frontier and a line of traffic."[1]

The "half of the land of the children of Ammon" which Sihon had taken from the Ammonites, and which afterward became the portion of Israel by conquest (Josh. xiii. 25; Judg. xi. 21, 22) was a fertile strip along the line of the head-waters of the Jabbok whose principal source still retains its old name Amman.

The volcanic deposits, which cover the limestone beds north of the Yarmuk, disappear in Gilead except in a few locations, and, as on the western side, the limestone comes to the surface. The distinguishing feature of the northern section of Gilead is the almost unbroken succession of noble forests of pine and oak which clothe the high ridges and frequently extend far down the slopes of the mountains. "Jebel Ajlun," says Dr. Eli Smith, "presents the most charming rural scenery that I have seen in Syria: a continued forest of noble trees, chiefly the evergreen oak, sindian, covers a large part of it, while the ground beneath is clothed with luxriant grass, a foot or more in height, and decked with a rich variety of wild flowers."[2] Dr. Thomson thinks it probable that the famous "wood of Ephraim" in which the battle between the armies of David and Absalom was fought was in the neighborhood of the village of Ajlun, at the head of the Wady Ajlun about ten miles north of the river Jabbok. Here, he says, may be seen "many a 'great oak' and terebinth with 'thick boughs,' and low, wide-spreading branches, large enough to have caused that fatal accident to Absalom, and which proved so disastrous to his cause."[3] (2 Sam. xviii. 6-14.) The precious balsam or "balm in Gilead" has been diligently sought among the "trees of the wood" in this region, but without success.

[1] Smith's Hist. Geog., p. 584.   [2] The Land and the Book, p. 575.
[3] The Land and the Book, p. 578.

The highest point, and the most prominent topographical feature of the Gilead range is **Jebel Osha** (3,597 feet), an isolated peak on the southern side of the Jabbok.

Dr. Merrill gives the following description of the outlook from this mountain-peak:

> Jebel Osha is perhaps the most sightly place in Palestine after Mount Hermon. Mount Hermon, Safed, the hills behind Tiberias, and the plateau which slopes toward Hattin, Tabor, the hills about Nazareth, those of Naphtali, Ephraim, and Manasseh, Little Hermon, Ebal and Gerizim, Neby Samwil, and Massada are in sight, and in fact nearly every prominent point in the unbroken range of mountains from Jebel esh Sheikh (Hermon) clear around to the south end of the Dead Sea. All the Jordan valley, more than 4,000 feet below us, is at our feet; the plain of Beisan, the tells at the mouth of Wady Ajlun and Wady ez-Zerka, all the Nimrin and the Shittim plains and the tells upon them, the mouth of the Jordan, the entire Dead Sea, including the extreme south end and el Lisan, the rolling country of Moab, or the Mishor of the Bible, the hills about Amman, the Hauran, and the mountains of Gilead are in full view.
>
> In this wide and comprehensive prospect the eye sweeps over the country to the north, the west, the south and the east—a sweep of eighty to 100 miles in extent. If one utterly ignorant of the Bible records should go east of the Jordan to find the point commanding the most extensive view on all sides, he would select Jebel Osha. It is 800 to 1,000 feet higher than Mount Nebo itself. "The hill over against Jericho" (Deut. xxxiv. 1) could just as well be this place as Jebel Neba, and this would meet the conditions of the thirty-fourth chapter of Deuteronomy better than any other point. These are claims or facts which belong to this mountain, independent of any claim of Jebel Neba to be the spot where Moses stood.[1]

It is probable that Abraham journeyed with his flocks and herds from Damascus to the land of Canaan by way of the great Bashan plain and the rich pasture lands of Mount Gilead to the valley of the Jabbok, over against the natural passageway to the plain (Wady Farah) "before the city of Shechem," where he pitched his tent and erected his altar for the first

---

[1] East of Jordan, p. 279.

The Trans-Jordanic Highlands

time in the land. It is certain that this was *Jacob's route* from the east, and it led him directly to the same place.

Gilead was the home of Jephthah, the warrior-judge of the tribe of Manasseh, and of Elijah the great prophet and courageous reformer of Israel. On the border of its coasts Jesus was baptized, and in that portion of it then known as Peræa some of the most interesting events connected with His public ministry took place. (See Matt. xix. 1, 13; Mark x. 1; Luke xiii. 22; John x. 40, etc.)

There are but few sites in the uplands of Gilead with Scriptural associations, which can be definitely located, but there are several cities of the Roman period whose ruins are extensive and exceptionally well preserved. Among these we note the following:

Gadara.—This city, which was once the capital of a Roman province including Gergesa and other places of note, is three miles south of the Yarmuk and five miles east of the Jordan. Its modern name is Um-Keis. As already noted, the "country of the Gadarenes" was the scene of the healing of the Demoniac, recorded by three of the Evangelists. (Matt. viii. 28;•Mark v. 1; Luke viii. 26.) The ruins of Gadara are over two miles in circuit, and the rich ornamental work in marble, basalt and granite lying in confused heaps or scattered everywhere over the ground indicate the existence of a wealthy and magnificent city. "The most remarkable feature in the remains of Gadara," says Tristram, "is a perfect paved Roman street, more than half a mile long, with the ruts worn by the chariot-wheels; colonnades on either side, of which the columns are lying prostrate, though many bases are standing; and massive crypt-like cells in a long row, apparently a market or bazaar. There is, of course, a fine amphitheatre, and a very perfect theatre also, partially scooped in the side of the rock, and the remains of a Christian cathedral. To the east several acres are strewn with stone coffins and lids, most of them fairly sculptured with all sorts of designs, dragged out of the caves with which the whole district is perforated. At every step there is either a cavern or an artificial cave."[1]

El Hamma, the place of the famous hot springs, known as Amatha in the Roman period, is situated in the Yarmuk valley nearly three miles from the ruins of Gadara. The remains of vaulted bath-houses and other buildings may be traced near the principal group of springs. In one the temperature of the water is 115°: in another 103°. The basin of the largest spring is 180 feet long by ninety wide. Dr. Merrill found another hot spring three miles up the valley to the east whose overflow made the little plain in which it was situated "a tropical paradise." "I counted," he says, "eighteen tropical trees growing there, while of the different shrubs, flowers, and plants I do not know the number; nor do I know that I observed all the trees. The most striking feature, however, is a grove of 200 fine palms, lifting their graceful heads above the plain and jungle below. Such a sight is not to be seen elsewhere in Syria."[2]

The land of Tob, in which Jephthah found a refuge (Judg. xi. 3), according to the Talmud, was a district southeast of the Sea of Galilee. "Its old title," says Conder, "survives in the modern name Taiyibeh, which applies to a village in this direction, and which is radically the same with the Hebrew signifying 'goodly' or fruitful."[3]

East of this district are several Roman cities of importance, as their ruins indicate.

Abila, now Tell Abil, is on the highway to Damascus, some twelve miles east of Gadara.

Capitolias, eight or ten miles south of Tell Abil, is probably identical with Beit-er Ras.

Arbela has been identified with a ruined site called Irbid, four miles south of the site of Capitolias.

Ramoth-Mizpeh (Josh. xiii. 26; Judg. xi. 34) has not

[1] Holy Land, p. 315. [2] East of Jordan, p. 146.
[3] Heth and Moab, p. 181.

been definitely located. Conder thinks the most probable site is Remtheh, or Rimthe, on the east side of the Hajj road, about fifteen miles south of Mezarib. Tristram suggests Tibneh, midway between Gadara and Jerash, while Merrill favors Kulat er Rubad.

Kulat er Rubad—"the watch tower of Gilead"—is the most prominent peak of Jebel Ajlun. Its position corresponds with that of Jebel Osha south of the Jabbok, and the view from the ramparts of the ruined castle, which crowns its summit and which has given to it its modern name, is probably as comprehensive in its sweep as from that famous outlook over the Jabbok. Dean Stanley describes it as the finest view he ever saw in this part of the world. Says Dr. Thomson: "The outlook from this fortress is, indeed, magnificent and impressive beyond anything we have seen 'on this side Jordan toward the sunrising,' and one never to be forgotten." . . . "In reality this prospect includes more points of Biblical and historical interest than any other on the face of the earth."[1]

"The view," says Merrill, "is more than a picture. It is a panorama of great variety, beauty, and magnificence. . . . As we look down from Kulat et Rubad upon this river (Jordan) and valley, the sea and the lake, our eyes rest upon the scene of a multitude of famous historical events in which many of the great men of antiquity bore a part; Chedorlaomer, Abraham and Lot, Joshua, Jacob, David and Solomon, Gideon and Jephthah, Absalom, Joab, and Judas Maccabeus, Pompey, Vespasian, and Herod the Great, John the Baptist, and Christ, the Redeemer of the world."[2]

Mahanaim.—The site of Mahanaim has not been satisfactorily identified. Several places have been suggested, including Jerash, Khurbet Suleikhat in Wady Ajlun, and Mahneh. The latter is favored by Robinson, Tristram, and Oliphant. Mahneh is on the edge of Wady Mahneh, three or four miles northeast of Kulat er Rubad. The incidental

[1] The Land and the Book, pp. 578-9.   [2] East of Jordan, p. 365.

notices of Mahanaim in the Old Testament point to a place north of the Jabbok, near the border of Manasseh and yet within the territory of Gad. (Gen. xxxii. 2 ; Josh. xiii. 30, xxi. 38.)

At this place the angels of God met Jacob, and from this event it received its name. Here Ishbosheth was crowned, and after two years was treacherously put to death. (2 Sam. ii. 8–10, iv. 5, 6.) It was the refuge of David, also, when he fled from the face of Absalom. In the gate of this city David waited for tidings of the battle between his army and the forces of Absalom, and to the chamber over the gate he went up with the bitter cry: "O, my son Absalom, my son, my son Absalom! would God I had died for thee." (2 Sam. xvii. 24, xviii. 24–33.)

Jabesh-Gilead.—A clue to the identification of this place is furnished by a wady nearly opposite Bethshan, which still bears the name Yabis, the equivalent of the Hebrew word Jabesh. Dr Robinson has identified the city with a ruined site on the south side of Wady Yabis, called Ed Deir, and this identification has been generally accepted. Jabesh-Gilead is mentioned for the first time in connection with the story of the defection and restoration of the tribe of Benjamin. (Judg. xxi. 8–14.) In the beginning of his reign Saul went to the rescue of the inhabitants of Jabesh who were in sore straits by reason of the cruel and insolent demands made upon them by a superior force of Ammonites, who "came up and encamped against Jabesh-Gilead." Gathering his army at Bezek on the opposite side of the river the King of Israel made a rapid night march, and, in the morning watch attacked and utterly routed the hosts of Ammon. (1 Sam. xi. 1–11.) This opportune deliverance was gratefully remembered by the men of Jabesh-Gilead, who afterward rescued the dead bodies of Saul and his sons from the dishonor to which they were subjected at Bethshan, by making a perilous foray into the midst of their victorious foes under cover of the night. In their own city they gave to these rescued bodies an honorable burial, and for this brave deed were publicly commended and blessed by David. (1 Sam. xxxi. 11–13 ; 2 Sam. ii. 5.)

Pella has been identified with a deserted site, called Tabakat Fahil, six miles northwest of Jabesh-Gilead. It was one of the cities of the Decapolis. It was the place to which the Christians fled from Jerusalem, in obedience to the prophetic warning of Christ, just before the siege of Titus.

Peniel, or Penuel, the place where Jacob wrestled with "the Angel and prevailed," was on the bank of the Jabbok at, or near, one of the fording-places, but its exact location has not been determined. It is said that the Patriarch " passed over Penuel " after he had received the blessing : hence the natural inference that Penuel was a ridge or summit by the side of the river. (Gen. xxxii.) Afterward we read of a city in this locality called Penuel. Conder suggests Jebel Osha on the south side as a probable location. Merrill, after a careful examination of the whole region, and its approaches, places Penuel at Tellul edh-Dhahab. Here the road from the east crosses to the south bank of the Jabbok.

"As to the site of Penuel," he says, "there is but one suitable point on the Jabbok, and that is at Tellul edh-Dhahab, or Hills of Gold. These mounds are about four miles east of Canaan's ford, a crossing which is not far from Tell Deir Alla (the probable site of Succoth). They rise from the middle of the valley to a height of about 250 feet. They are conical in shape, with abrupt sides. The line of the hills is east and west, the same as that of the valley; but the stream winds so that one hill is on one side of it, and the other on the other side. Whether approached from the east or west, or looked down upon from the mountains above them, they form very striking objects. Further they are covered with ruins, and on the eastern of the two are the remains of an ancient castle. The road from the west follows up the north side of the river, and crosses it a little to the east of the eastern mound. It immediately rises to a small plateau, where are the ruins called El Khiuf. The Midianites, who troubled the Hebrews, were desert people, and, in making their great raids to the west, would avoid the hills and follow the most feasible route. Even after reaching Western Palestine, they kept to the lowlands. The only route open to them was that along the valley of the Jabbok. Here they would be sure of a good road and an abundance of grass and water. A castle and garrison on this route would be very necessary, if the western kingdom (as Jeroboam's) was to be protected from invasions from the eastern plains."[1]

When Gideon passed from Succoth to Penuel in his pursuit of the Midianites, he was mocked by the residents of the place, as at Succoth, and, on his return "he beat down the tower of Penuel, and slew the men of the city." (Judg. viii. 17.) Penuel was rebuilt and fortified by Jeroboam as an outpost of defence. (1 Kings xii. 25.)

Jerash or **Gerasa,** one of the chief cities of the Decapolis, was situated about twenty miles east of the Jordan on one of the northern tributaries of the Jabbok. Its site is ten miles north of the river and its elevation is 1,900 feet above sea level. Tristram describes it as "probably *the most perfect Roman city left above ground.*" "It is difficult," says Merrill, "to decide which is the most attractive feature of Gerash, its forest of columns, its ruined buildings, or its beautiful situation. It lies on both sides of a stream which flows through the city from north to south, and which is lined with a thick growth of oleanders. These bushes grow tall and rank, and, when in bloom, they present a blaze of beauty such as is seldom beheld, in Syria at least. The main street, which is paved, runs along the west bank of the stream, and, at a point near the middle of the city, is crossed by another, running east and west. The first is a mile or more in length, and was originally lined on both sides with columns. It came from the south, and on it, about half a mile before reaching the city, stood a triumphal arch, about forty feet high, with a small passage on each side of the main entrance, and niches for statues."[2]

The forum, the temples, theatres, baths, massive walls, gateways, and clustered columns, more than 200 of which are yet standing,—represent a great and magnificent city of the

[1] East of the Jordan, pp. 391, 392.   [2] Ibid., p. 287.

later Roman period. Aside from the evidence furnished by its remains, but little is known of the history of Jerash.

Ramoth Gilead.—There has been much controversy over the various sites suggested for this ancient city. Robinson, Tristram, Gesenius, Porter and others have sought to establish its identity with the modern town of Es Salt, about two miles southeast of Jebel Osha. A serious objection to this site is its rugged environment which does not accord with the story of the conflicts around it in which chariots were extensively used. Says Major Conder:—"To reach Es Salt, where Ramoth Gilead is generally shown, in a chariot, would have been a feat which no ancient charioteer is likely to have attempted, and still less any general commanding a force of chariots." Jelad, four or five miles north of Es Salt, Reimun or Remun, five miles west of Jerash, and Jerash, have also been suggested as probable sites. The latter seems to fulfill all the conditions of the Biblical narratives, and the arguments brought forward in its favor by Dr. Merrill are deserving of careful consideration.

We suggest, he says, that Ramoth Gilead was *not* identical with any place bearing the name of Mizpeh in that region; and further, that it *was* identical with the present Gerash (Jerash). 1. This place would be three days' journey from Samaria (if Josephus' statement is to be accepted. Antiq. viii. 15, 4). 2. It would be suitable for a city of refuge, because it was on one of the main routes which would be kept open (according to the command in Deut. xix. 3). 3. For the same reason it would be an appropriate point at which to command Eastern Gilead and Bashan. 4. Here chariots could be used, as we learn they were very extensively, in two notable campaigns. (1 Kings xxii. 31-35; 2 Kings ix. 16.) 5. This would verify the ancient Jewish testimony respecting the cities of refuge, that Ramoth Gilead was opposite Shechem. 6. It would also confirm the Jewish tradition that Gerash is identical with Gilead.[1]

The most notable events in the Biblical history of this place were the death of Ahab, who had joined forces with Jehoshaphat to recover the city from the King of Syria (1 Kings xxii.

[1] East of Jordan, p. 290.

34–37); the battle between Hazael and the combined forces of Ahaziah of Judah and Joram in which the city was taken, but Joram was severely wounded (2 Kings viii. 28, 29, ix. 14); and the anointing and proclaiming of Jehu as king of Israel. (2 Kings ix. 4–16.) From Ramoth Gilead Jehu rode forth in a chariot, to execute his dread commission concerning the house of Ahab, and came to Jezreel.

Suf, a village three miles northwest of Jerash, has been suggested by Major Conder as a probable site for the Mizpeh in Gilead where Jacob and Laban entered into covenant and erected the "heap of witness." (Gen. xxxi. 44–52.) The home of Jephthah was probably at the same place. (Judg. xi. 34.) "It is very remarkable that a fine group of rude stone monuments exists near Suf, showing in all probability that there was once a sacred centre here."

Debir (Josh. xiii. 26) may be identical with a village called Dibbin a few miles southwest of Jerash.

Beth-Gamul (Jer. xlviii. 23) is supposed to be identical with Um el Jemal, a deserted site with extensive ruins east of the Hajj road, and some twenty miles northeast of Jerash.

Es Salt, at the southern base of Jebel Osha (2,700 feet) has a population of over 6,000. Until recently it was the only centre of a settled population east of the Jordan. It is the capital of the Belka district, extending from the Jabbok to the Arnon. The hillsides around are covered with vineyards, which yield enormous crops of choice grapes. Baedeker notes the fact that the raisins of Es Salt are famous.

Rabbath Ammon.—This ancient capital of the Ammonites is represented by a ruined city of later date which still bears the name Amman. The ruins which now remain above ground are for the most part the remains of the magnificent Græco-Roman city of Philadelphia, but this name only survived the period of the Roman occupation.

Amman lies at the head of a ravine in which the Jabbok takes its rise. Its elevation above the sea is 2,770 feet. Its position is about eighteen miles southeast of Jebel Osha near the border of the desert. It has been described as "a strong position, shut in by high mountains, and shut in by deep valleys; an abundance of good water flowing through a narrow vale from the southwest to the northeast, with a sufficient space on the left bank of the stream for edifices of all kinds, public and private; while a large isolated hill, some 300 feet high, overhangs it on the northwest and north, affording on its summit a broad platform for a large and almost unassailable citadel." The ruins of Amman cover a larger space than those of Jerash but they are not so well preserved. Traces of the ancient city of Ammon may be seen in the lower courses of the walls and in the substructures of the citadel. Ewald advances the theory that Ammon was one of the first cities built after the flood, but it is more likely that it was built by the sons of Ammon who gave to it the name of their father. In the first reference to it in the Old Testament (Deut. iii. 11) it is called Rabbath of the children of Ammon. It was besieged by Joab two years before the lower city—" the city of waters" —was taken, and in front of its walls Uriah the Hittite was slain. (2 Sam. xi. 16, 17.) The citadel was afterward taken by David. "And he took their king's crown from off his head, the weight whereof was a talent of gold with the precious stones: and it was set on David's head. And he brought forth the spoil of the city in great abundance." (2 Sam. xii. 30.) The prophetic denunciations against this city and its inhabitants have been strikingly and most literally fulfilled. (Jer. xlix. 1, 2 ; Ezek. xxi. 20, xxv. 5 ; Amos. i. 14.)

Jogbehah (Num. xxxii. 35) has been identified with the ruins of a place called Jubeihah, seven miles northwest of Amman. This place is mentioned in connection with Gideon's pursuit of the Midianites. (Judg. viii. 11.)

Kulat Zerka, a caravan station on the Hajj road about fifteen miles northeast of Amman, is supposed to be the site of the Roman town of Gadda. It is on the edge of the desert.

Traces of a solid roadway have been discovered between Ammon and Kulat Zerka. "There can be little doubt," says Oliphant, "that the force sent by Moses to conquer Bashan must have passed by this spot after the battle of Jahaz." (Num. xxi. 23.)

Jazer has been identified by Dr. Merrill and others with Khurbet Sar or Seir, one mile west of Amman. If this identification is correct the "land of Jazer," famous for its cattle ranges is the plateau region west of Rabbath Ammon. (Num. xxi. 32; Josh. xiii. 25; 2 Sam. xxiv. 5, etc.)

The castle of Hyrcanus, a prince of the Maccabean line, now called Arak el Emir stands on an elevated platform or "natural amphitheatre" some eight or ten miles southwest of Khurbet Sar. The remains of this stronghold are said to be "the most remarkable *purely* Jewish ruins existing, and have never been altered or retouched by Roman or Saracen. . . . Half a mile above the castle is a vast series of rock dwellings, impregnable by ancient warfare, with chambers, halls, stables for one hundred horses, with rock-hewn mangers still perfect, and inscriptions in the old Hebrew character over the rock-hewn portals."

III. MOAB.

The land of Moab, as already indicated, is a broad, almost treeless, plateau elevated 3,000 feet above the Mediterranean, and 4,300 feet above the Dead Sea. This is the "Mishor" or table-land of Moab in distinction from the lowlands or "plains of Moab" in the Jordan valley. From the crest or ridge above the Dead Sea there is a gradual, almost imperceptible slope to the eastern desert. The Abarim or mountain-wall, which towers above the Dead Sea, is cleft almost to its base by the two deep ravines of the Callirhoe and the Arnon.

The Callirhoe (Cal-lir'-ho-e), now called Zerka Main, was known in ancient times as "the valley of God." (Nahaliel— Num. xxi. 19.) This awful chasm, or cañon, is bordered by

The Trans-Jordanic Highlands

cliffs at one point 1,700 feet in height. On the south side of the stream a series of basaltic columns rise several hundred feet and almost block the gorge, while far below the hot springs are indicated by the thin cloud of vapor which rises to the skies.

In giving his impressions of this dark valley Major Conder says:

> It took a full hour to reach the bottom of the gorge, and the scene was wonderful beyond description. On the south, black basalt, brown limestone, gleaming marl. On the north, sandstone cliffs of all colors, from pale yellow to pinkish purple. In the valley itself the brilliant green of palm clumps, rejoicing in the heat and in the sandy soil. The streams, bursting from the cliffs, poured down in rivulets between banks of crusted orange sulphur deposits. The brooks (which run from ten springs in all) vary from 110° to 140° F. in temperature, and fall in little cascades amid abundant foliage, to join the main course of the stream. At one point the stream has bored through the sulphurus breccia, and runs in a tunnel of its own making, issuing from this hot shaft about 100 feet lower, in the gorge itself. Of all scenes in Syria, even after standing on Hermon, or among the groves of Banias, or at Engedi, or among the crags of the Anti-Lebanon, there is none which so dwells on my memory as does this awful gorge, the Valley of God, by Beth-peor, where, perhaps, the body of Moses was hid—the fair-flowing stream which Herod sought below the gloomy prison of John the Baptist at Machaerus—the dread chasm where the Bedawin still offer sacrifices to the desert spirits, and still bathe with full faith in the healing powers of the spring.[1]

The valley of the Arnon, (Wady Mojib), twelve miles below the Callirhoe, is the deepest furrow on this side of the Dead Sea. While the channel of the river is not over 100 feet in width the breadth of the valley from crest to crest is more than two miles. Its maximum depth is not less than 2,000 feet. The sides of this great trench, except where they fall away in precipitous cliffs, are clothed with rich verdure. The Arnon is the largest stream that enters the Dead Sea on this side and its mouth is just half-way down the shore.

At **Aroer,** about twelve miles from its mouth, the Arnon

[1] Heth and Moab, pp. 150, 151.

proper is formed by the junction of three wadies, one coming from the east called Saideh, and two from the south; "these two latter first join together and then unite with the eastern branch." The name Lejjun or Makherus applies to the central, and Balus to the smaller branch.[1]

The itinerary of the Israelites indicates that they came up from the wilderness on the eastern side of the territory of Moab, and hence must have crossed the Arnon near its head-waters.

The highest mountain of the range of Moab is **Jebel Attarus** on the south side of the Callirhoe. The outlook from this mountain rivals that from Jebel Osha. A heap of ruins on its summit probably represents the remains of an ancient sanctuary of Baal or Chemosh. An ancient town, whose ruins cover a considerable space, called Kureiyat, a short distance south of Jebel Attarus, is supposed to be identical with the place called Kirjath-huzoth, to which Balak brought Balaam on his arrival in the land of Moab. (Num. xxii. 39.)

Bamoth Baal, the high place on which the seven altars were erected the next day, seems to have been some elevation on the north side of the ravine in the direction of the camp of Israel. Its position has not been definitely located.

Mount Pisgah, or the "top of Pisgah," over against Jericho, was the next station to which Balaam was taken, and here, as before, seven altars were erected. (Num. xxiii. 14.)

"The summit of Jebel Neba, which has been generally accepted as the mountain of Nebo, is not 300 feet higher than the plain of the Belka, yet its position near the edge of the tremendous descent to the plain of Abel Shittim adds 1,300 feet more to its height, and thus, in reality, it presents a noble standpoint 4,000 feet above the Dead Sea from which to survey the Promised Land beyond Jordan westward."[2] A projecting head-land, a half-mile or more to the west, known as Siaghah or Jebel Siaghah offers another view-point, which some explorers regarded as the top of Pisgah, but the outlook, except

[1] Quarterly P. E. F., '95, p. 215.   [2] The Land and the Book, p. 651.

the downward look into the Jordan valley, is not more comprehensive than that from the top of Jebel Neba.

With respect to the different names used in connection with this view-point of Balaam and of Moses, Dr. Thomson concludes, as the result of a careful study of the Bedawin designations and identifications, "that Nebo is 'the mountain' of which Pisgah is 'the top,' ras, or headland; and Siaghah is probably only another and an Arabic equivalent for the Hebrew and the English Pisgah."[1]

"After testing repeatedly every view in the neighborhood," says Dr. Tristram, "I am perfectly satisfied that there is none which equals in extent that from Nebo—*i. e.*, from the flat ridge which rises slightly about half a mile behind the ruined city (Nebbeh), and which I take to be the true field of Zophim, the top of Pisgah. On these brows overlooking the mouth of the Jordan, over against Jericho, every condition is met for the Pisgah both of Balaam and of Moses." Here "the Lord showed Moses all the land of Gilead unto Dan, and all Naphtali and the land of Ephraim, and Manasseh, and all the land of Judah, unto the utmost sea, and the south, and the plain of the valley of Jericho, the city of palm-trees unto Zoar." (Deut. xxxiv. 1–3.) "In this account," says Dr. Henderson, "if we only read *toward* instead of *unto* as applied to Dan and the Western Sea, the accuracy of the description is perfect."[2]

Beth-peor, the third station of Balaam, has been located by the Survey party at the western edge of a ridge on the north side of the Callirhoe. Here the plain of Moab (Abel Shittim) on which Israel was encamped, can be seen throughout its extent. (Num. xxiv. 2.) The burial-place of Moses was "in a valley in the land of Moab, over against Beth-peor, but no man knoweth of his sepulchre unto this day." (Deut. xxxiv. 6.) Menhirs, dolmens, stone circles, and the remains of ancient shrines supposed to be connected with the worship of Baal and Chemosh, have been found on many of the high places of Moab.

The sites of several of the towns belonging to the inheritance

[1] The Land and the Book, p. 654.   [2] Hist. Geog., p. 72.

of Reuben have been identified by the names which they bore in the time of Moses.

Heshbon, now Hesban, was built on a commanding eminence some 200 feet above the plain. Its position is about fifteen miles east of the northern end of the Dead Sea. Jewish, Roman, and Saracenic ruins are mingled together on the crest of the hill, and eastward of the city are the remains of a large reservoir suggestive of "the fish pools in Heshbon, by the gate of Bath-rabbim." (Cant. vii. 4.)

Heshbon was the capital of the Amorite king, Sihon, who had taken it out of the hands of the Moabites. (Num. xxi. 26.) It was rebuilt by the tribe of Reuben, but afterward became a city of Gad and was assigned to the Levites. (Num. xxxii. 37; Josh. xxi. 39.) At a later period it came into the possession of the Moabites and was included in the denunciations of the prophets against Moab. (Isa. xv. 4; Jer. xlviii. 34, 45.) In the Maccabean period Heshbon and all the cities in its vicinity were recovered from the Moabites.

Elealah, frequently mentioned in connection with Heshbon, is now known as El 'Al. Its ruins are scattered over the surface of a mound whose elevation is nearly 3,000 feet above sea level. This site is less than two miles from Heshbon in a northeast direction.

Sibmah, renowned for its choice vineyards, has been identified with Sumieh, which lies about the same distance to the northwest. The remains of wine-presses hewn out of the rock have been found at the base of this mound. (See Isa. xvi. 9, 10.)

Medeba is represented by the modern village of Madeba, which lies about six miles south of Heshbon, along the line of the old highway to southern Moab. "The name has remained identically the same," says Dr. Thomson, "since the age of Moses, a period of about 3,500 years, and the first mention of it, in Numbers xxi. 30, implies that it was a well-known place before the time of the Hebrew Lawgiver."[1] The ruins

[1] The Land and the Book, p. 638.

of ancient walls, temples, a handsome gateway, churches, basilicas, Mosaics; and three large pools, one of which measures 135 yards in length by 103 yards in width, attest the importance of the place in Roman and early Christian times. A great battle between the army of Joab and the combined forces of Syria and Ammon, resulting in victory to the Israelites, was fought in the plain before Medeba. (1 Chron. xix. 6-15.) Medeba is included among the cities of Moab in the time of Isaiah (xv. 2).

The discovery of a large Mosaic map of Palestine and Egypt, presumably of the fifth century, on the floor or pavement of an old church in December, 1896, has brought Medeba into a place of special prominence. Photographs of the complete map on ten separate sheets have been secured, and it will soon be published as a whole in reduced form. "Upon this map the tribes of Israel are marked, each tribe with its boundary and its chief towns; Biblical or Gospel events are alluded to by a word—the greater part of Jacob's prophecy is noted thereon, with some variations from the received text. (Gen. xlix. 25; Deut. xxxiii.) The administrative districts into which the country was divided in the fifth century are there also, and some hitherto unknown names of towns. Each town or holy place is represented by a building of some kind: Jerusalem, Nablus and Gaza are encircled by walls; one can recognize the chief gates, and the public buildings show the outward appearance of these cities."[1]

The full topographical value of this mosaic has not yet been ascertained, but it will doubtless aid in determining some points of uncertain identity.

At **Mashetta** on the eastward side of the Hajj road, some fifteen miles northeast of Medeba, there is a wonderful structure which has puzzled the antiquarians and excited the admiration of all travellers in this desert region. It is an unfinished building 500 feet square flanked by twenty-five towers. Its

[1] Quarterly P. E. F. '97, p. 215.

walls and towers which rise to the height of fifteen or twenty feet, are covered with sculptures, zigzag moulding, stone-tracery, "large bosses in the centre of triangular segments" and "fret-work within and about these sections of great beauty and variety of design—vines, fruit, birds, animals, and even men." It can be truly said of the façade, says Dr. Thomson, that it is "adorned with a richness and magnificence unparalleled, and scarcely exceeded in the architecture of any age or nation."[1] This palatial building is one of the mysteries of the desert. Its origin, history and purpose are alike unknown. For fuller descriptions and a discussion of the suppositions concerning it see Tristram's "Land of Moab," Merrill's "East of the Jordan" and Thomson's "Land and Book."

Baal-Meon, or **Beth-Meon** is represented by Tell Ma'in, four miles southwest of Madeba. It is mentioned among the cities of Reuben. (Num. xxxii. 38; 1 Chron. v. 8.)

Dibon, now known as Dhiban, is on the highway to the south about three miles north of the Arnon. Its ruins are extensive, covering the slopes of two adjacent hills. Taken from Sihon it was rebuilt by Gad, and, at a later period, was held by the Moabites. (Num. xxi. 30, xxxiii. 34; Isa. xv. 2.)

Here the famous *Moabite Stone* was found by Dr. Klein in 1868. This monument, now in the Louvre at Paris, is one of the most interesting and valuable which modern research has brought to light. It is a slab of basalt three and one-half feet in length by two feet in breadth. It was shattered into fragments while in the hands of the Arabs, but has been so carefully restored that only one-seventh part of the inscription, originally of thirty-four lines, is lacking. The first part of the inscription gives an account of the oppression of Moab by Omri, king of Israel, and of the subsequent deliverance accomplished by the author of the tablet, Mesha, king of Moab during the reign of Omri's son or successor. The date of this inscription is about 900 B. C. "The characters," says Dr. Neubaur, "in

[1] The Land and the Book, p. 631.

which the inscription is written are Phœnician, and form a link between those of the Baal Lebanon inscription (of the tenth century B. C.) and those of the Siloam text." On this tablet twenty-two letters corresponding to the letters of the early Hebrew alphabet have been found. We have in this monument the same names that are given in the Old Testament, the evidence of the same relationship between Moab and Israel, and a striking confirmation of the historical statement concerning Mesha in the second Book of the Kings (iii. 4, 5). "And Mesha, king of Moab was a sheepmaster, and rendered unto the king of Israel 100,000 lambs, and 100,000 rams, with the wool. But it came to pass, when Ahab was dead, that the king of Moab rebelled against the king of Israel."

Aroer, the border town of the heritage of Reuben, and "the Beersheba of the East," lies on the northern brink of the great trench of the Arnon. (Deut. ii. 36.) Its modern name is Ar'air. Aroer shared in the changes and vicissitudes of the adjacent towns of Reuben until Moab ceased to exist as a separate nationality.

The ruins of a bridge and traces of an old road across the ravine can still be seen at this point.

There are scores of ruined sites on the plateau south of the Arnon, but there are very few of them that have been satisfactorily identified.

The ancient capital of the land, " Kir of Moab," or Rabbath Moab, lies about eight miles south of the Arnon. (Num. xxi. 28.)

Kir of Moab, now Kerak (Isa. xv. 1), is perched on an isolated hill which is almost cut off from the plateau by deep ravines, one of which is Wady Kerak. It was regarded as one of the impregnable strongholds of the land of Moab.

When besieged at this place by the confederated forces of Israel and Edom, King Mesha vainly attempted to break through the opposing lines of the Edomites. "Then he took his eldest son that should have reigned in his stead, and offered him for a burnt-offering upon the wall." (2 Kings iii. 26, 27.) This deed of horror ended the siege, and the Israelites returned to their own land. Kerak is said to be the only one of the ancient cities of Moab which is inhabited. Its population has been recently estimated at 10,000.

The brook or valley of Zered is probably represented by the Wady El Ahsy—a part of which is called Wady Siddeh—the boundary between Moab and Edom. "This wady," says Dr. Robinson, "forms a natural division between the country on the north and south. Taking its rise near the castle El Ahsy on the route of the Syrian Hajj, upon the high eastern desert, it breaks down through the whole chain of mountains to near the southeast corner of the Dead Sea, forming, for a part of the way, a deep chasm."

In the narrative of the Journeyings of Israel toward the Jordan it is plainly intimated that the route was along the border or coasts of Edom and Moab. Hence the place of crossing on this memorable occasion must have been at the upper end of the valley or in the neighborhood of the Hajj road. Here while resting in camp (Num. xxi. 12) the Israelites received the stirring command:—" Rise up and get you over the brook of Zered." (Deut. ii. 13.) This passage, more significant in its results for the world than Cæsar's crossing of the Rubicon, marked the limit of the thirty-eight years of wilderness journeyings, and the beginning of a new era for the disciplined hosts which followed Moses and Joshua. (Deut. ii. 14.) From this hour their faces were set steadfastly "unto the land of their possession, which the Lord gave unto them."

Equivalents of Arabic Words

Ain=Fountain (Pl Ayun).
Arak=Cliff.
Ballut=Oak.
Beit (Heb. Beth)=House.
Bir (Heb. Beer)=Well.
Birket=Pool.
Buka'a=Valley.
Burj=Tower.
Deir=Convent.
Haram=Sacred Inclosure.
Jebel=Mountain.
Jisr=Bridge.
Kefr=Village.
Khan=Inn or Caravansary.
Kulat=Castle.

Kurn=Horn.
Kusr=Tower.
Mar=Saint.
Mejdel=Watchtower.
Merj=Meadow or Plain.
Mugharah=Cave.
Nahr=River.
Neby=Prophet.
Ras=Head, Promontory.
Sahel=Plain.
Sheikh=Chief.
Tell=Mound.
Tor=Isolated Mountain.
Wady=Valley or Watercourse.
Wely=Tomb of a noted Saint.

Index

Abana (Barada), 289, 291-292.
Abarim, 330.
Abdon (Abdeh), 78.
Abel-beth Maachah (Abel Maim), 254.
Abel Meholah (Ain el Helweh), 274.
Abel Shittim (Tell Kefrein)— Plain of Moab, 280.
Abila (Suk Wady Barada), 290.
Abila (Tell Abil), 322.
Abilene, 290.
Abraham, Oak of, 232.
Abraham, Well of, Beersheba, 239.
Absalom, Tomb of, 199.
Abu Ghosh. See Kirjath, 226.
Accho (Akka). See Acre.
Aceldama (Potter's Field), 199.
Achor, Valley of (Wady Kelt), 161.
Achsaph (El Yasif), 77.
Achzib (Es Zib), 77.
Acra, Division of Jerusalem, 173.
Acre (Accho), 76.
Acre, Plain of, 75.
Adam, Town in Jordan Valley, 274.
Admah, 278.
Adonis River, 66.
Adoraim (Dura), 236.
Adullum (Aid-el-ma), 102.
Adullum, Traditional site of, 230.
Ænon (Ainun), 152.
Afranj Wady, 103.

Ai-Hai (Haiyan), 164.
Aijalon-Ajalon.
Ain Duk, 161.
Ain Feshkhah (Spring of Pisgah), 279.
Ain el Fijeh, 290.
Ain Gadis-Ain Kadeis. See Kadish Barnea.
Ain Hajla. See Beth Hogla.
Ain Helweh. See Abel Meholah.
Ain Jalud (Well of Harod), 127.
Ain Muweileh. See Beer-lahai-roi.
Ain Shems. See Bethshemesh.
Ain Tabighah (Fountain of Capernaum), 269.
Ain Zehaltah, 108.
Ajalon (Yalo), 99.
Ajalon Valley (Merj-Ibn-Omier), 98.
Ajlun, 319.
Ajlun, Mount, 318.
Ajlun Wady, 319.
Akabah, Gulf of, 286.
Aksa El, Mosque of, 186.
Alemeth (Almit), 169.
Amalek, Territory of, 237.
Amatha (El Hamma), 322.
Amman. See Rabbath Ammon.
Ammonites, Country of, 319.
Amorites, 33.
Amorites, Mountain of the, 33.
Amwas (Emmaus), Nicopolis, 99.
Anathoth ('Anata), 167.

Index 341

Ananiah (Beit Hanina), 169.
Anti-Lebanon, Mountains of, 17, 289.
Antipatris (Ras el Ain), 86.
Antonia, Tower of, 187.
Aphek (Fik), 304.
Apollonia (Arsuf), 87.
Aqueducts of Jerusalem, 215.
Ar, of Moab=Rabbath Moab.
Arab (Er Rabiyeh), 236.
Arab Wady, 215.
Arabah Wady, 9, 286.
Arad (Tell Arad), 241.
Arah Wady, 145.
Arak-el Emir, 330.
Aram=Syria.
Arbela (Irbid), 322.
Archi (Ain Arik), 38, 169.
Arethusa, 291.
Argob. See Lejah.
Arish Wady El, 9, 249.
Armenian Quarter—Jerusalem, 176.
Armenian Convent — Jerusalem, 178.
Arnon River (Wady Mojib), 331.
Aroer of Judah (Ar'air), 242.
Arumah (El Orma), 155.
Arsuf-Apollonia.
Arka Tell, 68.
Arkites, 31.
Ascension, Church of, 205.
Ascension, Place of, 205.
Ashdod (Eshdud), Azotus, 90.
Ashtaroth (Tell Ashtereh), 304.
Ashur, Territory of, 40, 75.
Ashy El, Castle of, 338.
Ashy Wady (Zered), 338.
Askelon (Askulan), 91.
Ataroth Adar (El Darieh), 38.
Athlit, Plain of, 79.
Athlit, Town of, 79.

Aujeh River (Majarkon), 81.
Auranitis, 42.
Awaj (Pharpar), 292.
Awertah. See Gibeah Phinehas.
Aven, Plain of, 253.
Avim, 35.
Azekah (Tell Zakariya?), 103.
Azur Tell=Baal Hazor.
Azzeh. See Gaza.

Baalbek (Heliopolis), 250–251.
Baal Gad, 252.
Baal Hazor (Tell Azur), 16, 142.
Baal Hermon, 7, 297.
Baal Meon (Ma'ain), 336.
Baal Peor. See Beth Peor.
Baal Tamar ('Attara), 169.
Bamoth Baal, 332.
Banias (Cæsarea Philippi), 258–259.
Banias, Fountain of, 258.
Barada. See Abana.
Bashan, 42, 303.
Bashan, Cattle of, 310.
Bashan, Oaks of, 310.
Bashan, Giant Cities of, 314.
Batanæa, 42, 311.
Bathaniyeh, 311.
Batihah, Plain of, 265, 270.
Beer-lahai-roi (Hagar's Well), 248.
Beeroth (Bireh), 165.
Beersheba, 239.
Beirut, 68.
Beit Nuba, 99.
Beit Jibrin (Eleutheropolis), 103.
Belata, 152.
Belfort, Castle of, 109.
Belka, 318.
Belus River (Nahr Naman), 75.
Beniah, Feat of, 25.
Benjamin, Territory of, 37.

342   Index

Benjamin, Mountains of, 158.
Berj Beitin, 163.
Beth Anath (Anita), 115.
Bethabara, 283.
Bethany (El Azeriyeh), 203.
Beth Dagon (Beit Degan), 87.
Bethel (Beitin), 231.
Beth Emek (Amkah), 78.
Bether (Bittir), 231.
Bethesda, Pool of, 181.
Beth Gamul (Um el Jemal), 328.
Beth-Haccerem, 230.
Beth-Haran (Tell er Ramah), 281.
Beth Hogla (Ain Hajlah), 278.
Beth Horon, Upper, 167.
Beth Horon, Lower, 167.
Beth-Jesimoth, 280, 281.
Bethlehem of Judah (Beit Lahm), 228.
Bethlehem of Zebulun, 119.
Beth Meon. See Baal Meon.
Beth-Nimrah (Tell Nimrim), 281.
Beth Peor, 331, 333.
Bethphage, 205.
Bethsaida of Galilee (Ain Tabighah), 270.
Bethsaida Julias, 270.
Bethshan (Beisan)-Scythopolis, 128.
Bethshan, Plain of, 273.
Beth Shemesh (Ain Shems), 100.
Beth Shemesh (K'h Shema), 115.
Beth Shittah (Shutta), 128.
Beth Tappuach (Tuffuh), 236.
Beth Zur (Beit Sur), 236.
Betogabra. See Beit Jibrin.
Bezek (Ibsik), 154, 324.
Bezetha—Division of Jerusalem, 173.
Bible, Lands of the, 1.
Bir Eyub, 214.
Birket Israil, 181.

Birket Mamilla, 214.
Birket es Sultan, 214.
Blanchegarde, 103.
Bostrenus River (Awaly), 67, 70.
Bozrah (Buzrah), 312.
Bridge of Jacob's Daughters, 260.
Bsherreh, 108.
Buka'a (Lebanon Valley), 19, 250.
Buttauf, Plain of (El Buttauf), 112.
Byar Wady, 215.

Cabul (Kabul), 78.
Cæsarea, 82.
Cæsarea Philippi. See Banias.
Callirhoe (Zerka Main), 330.
Calvary, Place of, 178, 200.
Cana (Kefr Kenna), 118.
Cana (Kh Kana), 119.
Canaan, 30.
Canaan, Early history of, 50.
Canaan—As a Babylonian Province, 50.
Canaan—As an Egyptian Province, 52.
Canaanites, 28.
Capernaum (Khan Minyeh), 267-270.
Capernaum, Ministries of Christ in, 269.
Capitolias (Beit er Ras), 322.
Caravan Routes, 44.
Caravansary. See Khan.
Carmel, Mount, 134.
Carmel (Kurmul), 234.
Cedron=Kedron.
Cedars of Lebanon, 51, 108.
Chariots in Palestine, 46.
Chedorlaomer, Route of, 235, 279.
Chesalon (Kesla), 169.
Chinnereth=Sea of Galilee, 265.
Chisloth Tabor (Iksal), 126.

Index

Ciccar (Circuit) of the Jordan, 279.
Citadel, Jerusalem (Al Kala), 176.
Climate, Variations in, 23.
Cœle Syria (Lebanon Valley), 19.
Coast Route, 44.
Crocodile River (Nahr ez Zerka), 80.
Crusades, Period of, 56.
Crusades, Monuments of, 56.

Damascus, 291.
" Plain of (Ghutah), 291.
" Merj of, 292.
" Gate (Jerusalem), 175.
Dan, Territory of, 38.
Dan, Camp of, 101.
Dan (Tell el Kady), 257.
Dan, Oak at, 257.
Data for study of Sacred Geography, 2.
Damieh Ford, 283.
David, Dominion of, 11.
" Kingdom of, 11.
" City of, 172.
" Tomb of, 199.
" Tower of, 177.
Dead River (Nahr Mufjir), 81.
Dead Sea (Salt Sea), 286-288.
" " Basin, 286.
Debir (El Dhoheriyeh), 236.
Debir (Dibbin), 328.
Debir (Ed Dehr), 169.
Decapolis, District of, 42.
Deir Aban (Ebenezer), 227.
Deir Ballut, Wady, 145.
Deir Warda, 100.
Derdarah, tributary of the Jordan, 255.
Dibon (Dhiban), 336.
" Moabite Stone of, 336.
Dera (Dra'a), 308.

Dilbeh, 236.
Dome of the Rock, 184.
Dog River (Lycus), 44, 66.
Dolmens, 333.
Dor or Dora (Tanturah), 79.
Dothan (Tell Dothan), 143, 154.
" Plain of, 143.
Double Gate—Huldah—Jerusalem, 190-191.
Druze Jebel et, 310.
East Mountain (Jebel esh Shurky), 289.
Ebal, Mount, 139.
Ebenezer (Deir Aban), 227.
Ed-Debr, 169.
Edrei (Tell Khuraibeh), 114.
Edrei (Edhra), Zora, 308.
Ehden, Fountain of, 108.
Eglon (Ajlan), 95.
Ekron (Akir), 89.
El Aksa, Mosque of, 187.
Elah, Valley of, (Wady es Sunt), 101.
Elealeh (El'Al), 334.
Eleazar, Tomb of, 154.
Eleph (Lifta), 169.
Eleutheris River (Nahr el Kebir), 66.
Eleutheropolis (Beit Jibrin), 103.
El Hamma (Amatha), 322.
Elijah, Place of Translation of, 283.
El Kuleib, 310.
El Lisan, 287.
El Mahrakah, 135.
El Meshed. See Gath Hepher.
El Meshrifeh, 242.
El Mezar, 129.
Emmaus (Amwas), Nicopolis, 99.
Emmaus (Khamasa), 227.
Engammin (Jenin), 125.

Engedi (Hazezon-tamar)—Ain Jidy, 234.
En Hazor (Ain Hazzur), 115.
En Mishphat=Kadesh Barnea.
En Nukra (Hollow Hearth), 305.
En Rogel (Fountain of the Virgin), 207.
Ephraim, Mount, 16, 134.
" Wood of, 319.
" City of (Ophrah), 162.
" Territory of, 38.
Ephratah or Ephrath=Bethlehem.
Er Ramah, 16.
Eschol, Valley of, 248.
Esdraelon, Plain of, 120.
" Gateways of, 121.
Esek, Springs of, 96.
Eshtaol (Eshua), 100.
Es Seer, Plain of, 243.
Etam, Rock of (Beit Atab), 101.
Etham, or Etam in Valley of Urtas, 231.
Et Tell (Hai?), 165.
Exploration Societies, 2.

Farah Wady, 144, 274, 320.
Fauna of Palestine, 25.
Ferata=Ophrah.
Fekreh (Feqreh) Wady, 243.
Fik (Aphek), 304.
Fik Wady, 272, 305.
Flora of Palestine, 24, 26.
Fountain Gate (Jerusalem), 220.
Frank Mountain, 230.
Fuleh, 127.

Gad, Territory of, 40.
Gadara (Um Keis), 321.
Gadarenes, Country of, 271.
Gadda. See Kulat Zerka.
Gadis Ain. See Kadesh Barnea.

Gadis Wady, 244-245.
Galem (Beit Jala), 231.
Galeed=Gilead.
Galilee, Province of, 41, 111.
" Upper, 115.
" Lower, 115.
" Sea of, 262-273.
" Basin of, 262.
" Mountains of, 111.
Gamala (Kulat en Husn), 272.
Gath (Tell es Safi?), 90, 102.
Gath Hepher (El Meshed), 119.
Gaulanitis (Jaulan), 42.
Gaza (Guzzeh), 91.
Geba (Jeba), 165.
Gebal (Jebail), 68.
Gederah (Jedireh), 169.
Gehenna (Tophet), 206.
Gennesaret, Lake of. See Galilee.
" Plain of, 264.
Geology of Palestine, 20, 27.
Gerar (Um el Jerar), 95.
Gerar, Kingdom of, 29.
Gerasa (Jerash), 326.
Gergesa (Khersa), 265, 271.
Gerizim, Mount, 139.
Gethsemane, Garden of, 205.
Gezer (Tell Jezer), 99.
Ghor El, 18, 272.
Ghor-es Seisaban, 273.
Ghor es Safieh, 286.
Ghurab Wady, 100.
Gibeah (Geba or Jeba), 166.
Gibeah, District of, 166.
Gibeah Phinehas (Awertah), 154.
Gibeath (Jibia), 169.
Gibeon (El Gib), 160, 167.
" Pool of, 168.
Giblites, 10, 68.
Gihon, Pools of, 208, 214.
Gilboa, Mount, 126, 129.

Index

Gilboa (Jelbon), 129.
Gilead, Land of, 30.
" District of, 317.
" Mountains of, 318.
" Forests of, 319.
" Balsam (Balm) of, 319.
Gilead Jabesh, 324.
Gilead Ramoth, 327.
Gilgal (Jiljulieh), 87.
Gilgal (Jiljilia), 157.
Gilgal (Tell Jiljulieh) 277–278.
Gimzo (Jimzu), 99.
Gergashites, 28.
Gischala (El Jish), 115.
Glass, Discovery of, 75.
Golan, 304.
Golden Gate (Jerusalem), 175, 188.
Golgotha. See Calvary.
Gomorrah, 278, 280.
Gophna (Jufna), 162.
Greek period, 55.
Græco-Roman Civilization, 56.
" " Architecture, 309, 312–314.
Guzzeh Wady, 105.

Hadad Rimmon (Rummaneh), 125.
Hadeth El, 108.
Hagar's Well (Beer-lahai-roi), 248.
Haifa, 77.
Hajj Road, 305.
Halak Mount, 243.
Hamam Wady, 113.
Hamathites, 31.
Hamath, City of, 9.
" Kingdom of, 9.
" Entrance to, 8.
Haram esh Sherif, 183.
Hareth (Kharas), 236.
Harod, Spring of (Ain Jalud), 127.
Harosheth (El Harathiyeh), 77.

Harvest Periods, 23.
Hasbany River, 256.
Hattin, Horns of, 112.
Hauran, 304–305.
Hauran Jebel, 310.
" Architecture, 313.
" Threshing-floors of the 305.
Havoth Jair, 307.
Hazor-enan, 8, 291.
Hazerim (Enclosures of Avim).
Hazezon Tamar. See Engedi.
Hazor (Hadireh), 114.
Hazor (Hazzur), 169.
Hebron (Kirjath Arba), 231.
" Vale of, 231.
" Pools of, 232.
Helbon, 296.
Heleph (Beit Lif), 115.
Hermon Mount (Jebel esh Sheikh), 296–301.
Hermon, Little, (Jebel Duhy), 126.
Hermonites, Land of, 297.
Herod, Palace of, 172.
" Gate of (Jerusalem), 175.
Herodium. See Jebel Fureidis, 230.
Heshbon (Heshban), 334.
" Wady, 317.
Hezekiah, Pool of, 178.
Hieromax=Yarmuk or Jarmuk, 317.
Highways of Palestine, 44.
Hinnom, Valley of, 170.
Hippos (Susiyeh), 272.
Hippicus, Tower of, 172, 177.
Hittites, 31.
" Land of the, 32.
Holy Sepulchre, Church of, 178.
Horem (Kh Harah), 115.
Hor Mount (Jebel Madurah), 247.

Index

Hor Mount of tradition, 17.
" " (Hor-ha-har), 8.
Hormah or Sebaita (Zephath), 238, 243.
Hukkok (Yakuk), 115.
Hulda Gate. See Double Gate.
Huleh Lake (Waters of Merom), 260.
Huleh Basin, 256, 261.
Hyrcanus, Castle of (Karak el Emir), 330.

Idumea, 41.
Ijon (Tell Dibban), 254.
Iron (Yarun), 115.
Iskanderunch River, 87.
Israel, Land of, 2.
" Allotment of tribes of, 36.
Issachar, Territory of, 39.
Iturea (Jedur), 42, 303.

Jabbok River (Nahr ez Zerka), 273, 318.
Jabesh Gilead (Ed Deir), 324.
Jabneel (Yebneh), Jamnia, 93.
Jacob's Well, 147.
Jaffa, Joppa (Yafa), 83.
" Gate (Jerusalem), 175.
" Suburb (Jerusalem), 216.
Jalud, Brook, 127.
Janoah (Yanim), 115, 155.
Japhia (Yafa), 119.
Jarmuk=Yarmuk.
Jattir (Attir), 236.
Jaulan, 42, 304.
Jazer (Kh Sar), 330.
" Land of, 330.
Jebail (Gebal), 68.
Jebel Ajlun, 318.
" Atterus, 332.

Jebel Dhar el Khodib, 15, 106.
" Duhy (Little Hermon), 126.
" esh Sheikh, 296–301.
" es Shurky, 289–290.
" et Tur (Olivet), 201.
" Fureidis (Frank Mountain), 230.
Jebel, Hauran, 310.
" Hedireh, 114.
" Jarmuk, 111.
" Mukhmal, 16.
" Neba (Nebo), 332.
" Osha, 320.
" Siaghah, 332.
" Sunnin, 15.
" Usdum, 286.
Jebusites, 34.
Jedur, District of (Iturea), 303.
Jehoshaphat, Valley of. See Kedron.
Jehoshaphat, Tomb of, 199.
Jelad, 327.
Jelbon (Gilboa), 129.
Jerash (Gerasa), 326.
Jericho (Tell es Sultan), 275.
" (New Testament Site), 276.
" (Modern) Eriha, 277.
Jerusalem, 34, 170–223.
" Environs of, 170.
" Walls of, 171, 174.
" Gates of, 175.
" Mountains round about, 171.
Jerusalem, Modern, 173.
" Quarters, 176.
" Temple area, 183.
" Royal Quarries of, 182.
" Catacombs and Tombs of, 198.
Jerusalem, Pools and Fountains, 207.

Index 347

Jerusalem, Recent Excavations in, 217.
Jerusalem, South Wall of, 217.
" Byzantine Church of 219.
Jerusalem, History and Associations of, 221.
Jeshimon. See Wilderness of Judea.
Jezreel (Zerin), 125.
" Fountain of (Ain Jalud), 127.
Jezreel, Valley of, 127.
Jird el Baruk, 108.
Jisr Benat Yacub, 261.
Jisr el Mejamia, 282.
Jisr Um-el Kanater, 282.
Job, Well of (Bir Eyub), 214.
Job's Country, 317.
Jogbehah (Jubeihah), 329.
Jokneam (Tell Keimum), 122.
Joppa=Jaffa.
Jordan River, 18.
" Valley, 19, 255.
" Sources of the, 256.
" History of the, 284.
" Fords of the, 282.
" Plain of, 278.
" Swellings of, 282.
" Cities of the Plain of, 278.
Joseph, Tomb of, 152.
Joshua, Tomb of (Neby Lusha), 155.
Jotopata. See Map No. 4.
Judah, Territory of, 37.
" Mountains of, 224.
" Wilderness of, 225.
Judea, Province of, 41.
Juttah (Yuttah), 236.

Kabul=Cabul.

Kadesh Barnea (Ain Gadis), 9, 244.
Kadisha River, 67, 109.
Kades of Galilee. See Map No. 4.
Kana Khurbet, 119.
Kanah Wady (Brook Kanah), 145.
Kasimiyeh River (Litany R.) 67.
Kedesh (Kades) of Naphtali, 113.
Kedron, Valley of, 170, 205.
Kedron Brook, 207.
Kefr Kenna. See Cana of Galilee.
Keilah (Kilah), 236.
Kelt Wady, 161, 274.
Kenath (Kunawat), 308.
Kerak=Kir of Moab.
Kerak=Tarichæa, 272.
Kerioth (Kureieh), 312, 316.
Kerioth=Ar of Moab.
Khan Minyeh (Capernaum), 267-270.
Khan of Chimham, 228.
Khans, 46.
Khurbet Suleiket, 323.
King's Dale (Shaveh), 206.
" Garden, 206, 214.
Kir of Moab (Kerak), 337.
Kirjath (Kuriet el Anab), 169.
Kirjath-huzoth (Kureiyet), 332.
Kirjath Jearim (Kh 'Erma), 226.
Kirjath-Sepher=Debir.
Kishon River (Nahr el Mukutta), 76, 78, 122.
Kulat el Bizzeh, 108.
Kulat el Husn=Gamala.
Kulat er Rubad, 323.
Kulat Zerka (Gadda), 329.
Kurn Sartaba, 274.
Kurn Wady. See Map No. 4.
Kuweh El (Natural Bridge), 109.

Lachish (Tell el Hesy), 93.

Ladder of Tyre, 65.
Lebanon, Mount, 14, 106.
" District of, 14, 106.
" Valley of (Buka'a), 19, 250.
Lebanon, Cedars of, 51, 108.
Lebonah (Lubban), 156.
Leddan, Fountain of, 257.
Legio (Lejjun), Megiddo, 123.
Lejah (Argob, Trachonitis), 306.
Lisan. See El Lisan.
Litany (Leontes), Kasimiyeh, 19, 67, 109.
Lod (Ludd), Lydda, 85.
Luz-Bethel.
Lydda (Ludd), 85.
Lycus (Dog River), 44, 66.

Machærus, Fortress of (M'Kaur), 331.
Machpelah, Cave of, 232-233.
Madurah Jebel. See M't Hor.
Mahanaim (Mahneh?), 323.
Majarkon R. (Aujeh), 81.
Makkedah,Cave of (El Mughar),93.
Mamilla, Pools of, 214.
Mamre, Plain of, 231.
Manasseh, Territory of, 38.
Maon (Main), 234.
Maps of Palestine, 3.
Mareshah (Maresh), 104.
Mariamne, Tower of (Jerusalem), 172.
Maritime Plain, 18, 65.
Mar Saba, 230.
Mary, Fountain of, 117.
Masada, 236.
Mashetta, 335.
Masir el Fukhhar, 108.
Medeba (Madeba), 334.
" Mosaic Map of, 335.

Meduk, 31, 108.
Megiddo (El Lejjun), 123.
" Valley of, 120.
Melek Wady, 112.
Menhirs, 333.
Merj Ayun, 254.
Merom, Waters of. See Huleh Lake.
Mezar El, 129.
Mezarib, 305.
" Railroad to, 305.
Michmash (Mukmas), 165.
" Pass of, 161, 165.
Migdal El (Mujeidel), 115.
Migdal Gad (Mejdel), 93.
Mishor, 330.
Mizpah in Gilead, 328.
Mizpah (Neby Samwil), 16, 159.
" Plain of, 159.
Moab, 330.
" Plains of-Plain of Shittim, 280-281.
Moabite Stone, 336.
Moreh, Oak of, 146, 152.
Moreh, Hill of. See Jebel Duhy.
Mount Abarim, 330.
" of the Amalekites, 237.
" of Corruption, 172.
" of Evil Counsel, 172.
" Ephraim, 134.
" of Olives, 172.
" of Precipitation, 118.
" Samaria (Hill Shomer), 137.
" Tabor, 131.
" Zion, 173.
Moor's Gate (Jerusalem), 175.
Mozah (Beit Mizza), 169.
Mufjir (Dead River), 81.
Mugrah Jebel, 242.
Muristan, 178.
Murreh Wady, 248.

Index

Mujedda, 123.
Mukhna, Plain of (Sahel Mukhna), 144.

Nablus (Shechem), 145.
Naboth, Vineyard of, 125.
Nahaliel (Valley of God), 330.
Nahr Hasbany, 256.
Nahr Rubin, 81.
Nain, 130.
Naphtali Mount, 111, 262.
    " Territory of, 40.
Nar Wady en, 226.
Nativity, Church of, 229.
    " Grotto of the, 229.
Natural Bridges of Lebanon, 109.
Nazareth, 115.
Neballet (Beit Nebala), 86.
Nebo Mount (Jebel Neba), 332–333.
Neby Samwil (Mizpah), 16, 159.
Negeb (South Country), 237.
Niha El, 108.
Nimrah (Beth Nimrah), 281.
Nimrim Ford of Jordan, 280, 283.
Nob, 168.
Nun, Tomb of (Neby Nun), 155.
Nusairiyeh Mountains, 9.
Nuweimeh Wady, 160.

Oak Forests of Palestine, 80, 304, 319.
Olives, Mount of, 172, 201, 204.
Ono (Kefr Ana), 86.
Ophel Mount, 173.
Ophni (Jufna). See Gophna.
Ophra-Ephron (Taiyebeh), 162.
Orontes, 20.
Osha Jebel, 320.

Palestine, 1–57.

Papyrus, 25.
Paneas-Banias.
Parah (Farah), 169.
Paran, Wilderness of, 237.
Patriarchal Highway, 16.
Pella (Tabakat-Fahil), 325.
Peniel-Penuel (Tellul Edh Dhahab), 325.
Perea, 42.
Perrizites, 34.
Phagor (Faghur), 231.
Pharpar, (Awaj), 292.
Phasælus, Tower of, 172, 177.
Philadelphia (Rabbath Ammon), 328.
Philistines, 28.
Philistia, Plain of, 88.
Phinehas, Tomb of, 154.
Phœnicia, Plain of, 18, 65.
Phœnicians, 29.
Pisgah Mount (Jebel Neba), 332.
Pool of Siloam. See Siloam.
Ptolemais-Acre.

Quarantina Mount, 161.
Quarries Royal. See Cotton Grotto, 182.

Rabbath Ammon (Amman), 328.
Railroads, 48.
Rains. Early and latter, 22.
Rakkon (Tell er Rakkut), 87.
Ramah (Er Ram), 166.
    " (Rameh) of Naphtali, 115.
    " Plain of, 112.
Ramleh, 86.
Ramoth Gilead (Jerash), 327.
    " Mizpah (Rimthe?), 322.
Ras el Abiad, 65.
Ras en Nakura (Ladder of Tyre), 65.

Ras Sherifa, 16.
Refuge, Cities of, 40-41, 46.
Rehoboth (Ruheibeh), 242.
Reimun or Remun, 327.
Renan, Testimony of, 60.
Reuben, Territory of, 40.
Rephaim, Plain of, 207.
Riblah (Ribleh), 9, 253.
Rimmon of Zebulun (Rummaneh), 112.
Rimmon Rock, 165.
Roadways, 44, 56, 87.
Robinson's Arch, 191.
Roman Roads, 56.
Saideh Wady, 332.
Safed, 114.
Salcah (Sulkhad), 311.
Salem-Jerusalem.
Salim (Shalem), 152.
Salt, City of (Tell el Milh). See Map No. 8.
Salt Es, 327.
Samaria (Sebaste), 137, 154.
" Hill of, 137.
" Pool of, 139.
" District of, 41.
Sarepta (Zarephath), 72.
Sarid (Tell Shodud), 126.
Sechu (Kh Suweikeh), 169.
Scopus Mount, 159.
Seir Mount in Edom, 243.
Seir, Region of, 243.
Selhab Wady, 145.
Semakh, 272.
Semakh Wady, 271.
Senir-Hermon.
Sepphoris (Suffurieh), 116.
Shaib Wady, 283.
Shair Wady, 145.
Sharon-Saron, Plain of, 80.
" Roadways of, 87.

Sharon, Rose of, 82.
Sheba (Tell es Seba), 241.
Shechem (Nablus), 145.
" Plain of, 144-146.
" Vale of, 144.
Shephelah, 18, 88, 97.
" Valleys of the, 97.
Shepherd's Fields, 228.
Sheriah Wady, 105.
Shiloah, Waters of, 213.
Shiloh (Seilum), 155.
Shittim, Plain of (Abel Shittim), 273.
Shunem (Sulem), 126.
Shur (Wall), Way of. See Map No. 9.
Sibmah (Sumieh), 334.
Sinai Mount, 16.
Siddeh Wady, 338.
Siddim, Vale of, 279.
Sidon (Zidon), 69.
" Recent discoveries near Sidon, 70.
Siloam (Silwan), 208.
" Pool of, 210.
" Tunnel, 209.
" Church over Pool, 212.
" Stairway, 210.
" Old Pool of, 213.
Simeon, Territory of, 37.
Simsin Wady, 103.
Sisera, Battlefield of, 77.
Sitnah (Shutnah), 96, 242.
Socoh (Shuweikeh), 236.
Soris (Saris), 231.
Sodom, 278.
Solomon, Dominion of, 6.
" Temple of, 184, 194.
" Porch of, 195.
" Stables of, 190.
" Pools of, 215.

Index 351

Springs Hot, 267.
St. James, Tomb of, 199.
St. Stephen's Gate (Jerusalem), 175.
Sorek Valley (Wady), 100.
Succoth (Tell Dar'ala), 274, 325.
Sudad. See Zedad.
Suf, 327.
Sultan's Pool, 214.
Suweinet, 161.
Sycar (Askar), 152.
Sychem-Shechem.
Syria, 1.
" Kingdom of, 54.

Taanach (Tannuk), 124.
Taanath Shiloh (Ta'ana), 155.
Tabernacle, Platforms of, 160.
Tabiga Et, 270.
Taiyibeh, 322.
Tappuach Beth, 236.
Tarablus-Tripolis.
Tarichæa-Kerak, 272.
Teim Wady et, 254.
Tekoa (Tekua), 231.
Tell Amarna tablets, 53.
" Arka, 68.
" Ashtarah (Ashtaroth), 304.
" Azur (Baal Hazor), 16.
" Dibbin, 254.
" el Ful, 166–167.
" el Hesy, 93.
" el Kady, 257.
" el Kasis, 120, 122, 136.
" el Mutasellim, 124.
" es Safi, 90, 102, 105.
" Hum, 267–268.
Terebinth in Valley of Elah, 101.
Terraces of Palestine, 47.
Testimony of the Land to the Book, 59.
Thebez (Tubas), 154.

Thotmes III., Conquests of, 52.
Tiberias, Sea of, 262–273.
" City of, 266.
" Hot springs of, 267.
Tibneh, 323.
Tih, Desert of, 237.
Timnath (Tibnah), 101.
Timnath Heres-Timnath Serah (Kefr Haris), 155.
Tiphsah (Tafsah), 155.
Tirzah (Teiasir), 153.
Tob, Land of, 322.
Tomb of Absalom, 199.
" of David, 199.
" of Jehoshaphat, 199.
" Rachel, 228.
" St. James, 198.
" Zachariah, 199.
Tombs of the Kings, 198.
" " " Judges, 198.
Tophet-Gehenna.
Trachonitis (Lejah), 42, 306.
Trans-Jordanic Country, 56, 302.
Triple Gate (Jerusalem), 190.
Tripoli (Tarablus), 67.
Tribal Divisions, 36.
Turan, Plain of, 112.
Tulluza, 153.
Tyre, 72.
" Ladder of, 65.
Tyropœon Valley, 172.

Um el Jemal (Beth Gamul), 328.
Um-Keis (Gadara), 321.
Urtas, Valley of, 215.
Unicorn of Syria, 26.

Valley gate, 220.
Virgin, Fountain of, (En Rogel), 207.
Volcanic Formations, 21.

Wailing Place of the Jews, 183.
Wady Abu Nar, 145.
" Afranj, 103.
" Amriyeh, 280.
" Arah, 145.
" Bittir, 231.
" Bireh, 126.
" Deir Balut, 145.
" El Arish, 9, 249.
" el Ashy (Zered), 338.
" el Aujeh, 145.
" el Ghar, 226.
" el Hesy, 104.
" el Hod, 162.
" en Nar, 226.
" et Teim, 254.
" esh Shair, 137, 145.
" esh Sheriah, 105.
" Farah, 144.
" Ghurab, 100.
" Hamam, 113.
" Ishar, 145.
" Kanah, 145.
" Kelt, 161.
" Khureitun, 230.
" Melek, 112.
" Najil, 100.
" Nimr, 145.
" Nuweimeh, 160.
" Selhab, 145.
" Surar, 100.
" Urtas, 231.
" Zeidah, 317.
Wilderness of Judea, 225.
Wilson's Arch, 193.

Yarmuk River (Jarmuk), Hieromax, 273, 317.
Yazer=Jazer.
Yabis Wady, 324.

Zachariah, Tomb of, 199.
Zahleh, 110.
Zakariya (Azekah), 103.
" Tell, 103.
Zarephath (Sarepta), 72.
Zaretan, 274.
Zebedany, Plain of, 289, 290.
Zeboim, 278.
Zebulun (Neby Sebalan), 115.
Zebulun, Territory of, 39.
" Plain of. See Buttauf.
Zedad (Sudad), 9, 253, 290.
Zemarites, 67.
Zephath (Hormah), 238, 242.
Zephathah, Valley of, 103.
Zephron (Zifrun), 291.
Zered (Zarad), Brook, 338.
Zerin=Jezreel.
Zerka Nahr ez, 318.
Zidon=Sidon.
Zidonians, 31.
Zion Gate (Jerusalem), 175.
Zion=Sion, 172.
Ziph (Tell Zif), 234.
Ziph, Wood of, 234.
Ziz, Cliff of, 235.
Zoar (Tell Ektanu), 278–279, 281.
Zoheleth, Stone of (Zahweileh), 208.
Zor, 282.
Zorah (Surah), 100.

www.ingramcontent.com/pod-product-compliance
Lightning Source LLC
Chambersburg PA
CBHW032138010526
44111CB00035B/615